Physics
FOR OCR

1

Gurinder Chadha
David Sang

CAMBRIDGE
UNIVERSITY PRESS

CAMBRIDGE UNIVERSITY PRESS
Cambridge, New York, Melbourne, Madrid, Cape Town, Singapore,
São Paulo, Delhi, Dubai, Tokyo

Cambridge University Press
The Edinburgh Building, Cambridge CB2 8RU, UK

www.cambridge.org
Information on this title: www.cambridge.org/9780521724555

© Cambridge University Press 2000, 2008

First published 2000
Second edition 2008
Reprinted 2010

Printed in Dubai by Oriental Press

A catalogue record for this publication is available from the British Library

ISBN 978-0-521-72455-5 Paperback

ACKNOWLEDGEMENTS
Project management: Sue Kearsey
Picture research: Vanessa Miles

Contents

Contents

Introduction

Cambridge OCR Advanced Sciences

The new *Cambridge OCR Advanced Sciences* course provides complete coverage of the revised OCR AS and A Level science specifications (Biology, Chemistry A and Physics A) for teaching from September 2008. There are two books for each subject – one covering AS and one covering A2. Some material has been drawn from the existing *Cambridge Advanced Sciences* books; however the majority is new.

The course has been developed in an innovative format, featuring Cambridge's new interactive PDFs on CD-ROM in the back of the books, and free access to a dedicated website. The CD-ROM provides additional material, including detailed objectives, hints on answering questions, and extension material. It also provides access to web-based e-learning activities (A Level and background revision from GCSE) to help students visualise abstract concepts, understand calculations and simulate scientific processes.

The books contain all the material required for teaching the specifications, and can be used either on their own or in conjunction with the interactive PDFs and the website.

In addition, *Teacher Resource CD-ROMs* with book PDFs plus extra material such as worksheets, practical activities and tests, are available for each book. These CD-ROMs also provide access to the new *Cambridge OCR Advanced Sciences* Planner website with a week-by-week adaptable teaching schedule.

Introduction to Physics 1 for OCR – the physics AS text

This book covers the entire OCR AS Physics A specification for first examination in 2009. Chapters 1 to 8 correspond to Unit G481, Mechanics. Chapters 9 to 20 correspond to Unit G482, Electrons, Waves and Photons. The content of the chapters closely matches the sequence of modules and sections as laid out in the specification. Each chapter ends with a summary. The summary includes all the definitions, principles and concepts required by the specification.

The book is designed to be accessible to students who have studied Double Award Science at GCSE, or who have a separate qualification in physics. The language is kept simple, to improve accessibility for all students, while still maintaining scientific rigour throughout. Care is taken to introduce and use all the specialist terms that students need for the specification. In the text, key terms are highlighted in bold. The glossary at the end of the book carefully defines these terms so that they match with the expectation of the OCR examiners.

The depth and breadth of treatment of each topic is pitched at the appropriate level for OCR AS students. The accompanying CD-ROM also contains some extension material that goes a little beyond the requirements of the specification, which should engage and stretch more able students.

Some of the text and illustrations are based on material from the endorsed text *Physics 1*, which covered the earlier OCR specification, while some is completely new. All of it has been scrutinised and revised, to match the specification and examination papers for G481 and G482. In addition to the main content in each chapter, there are also How Science Works boxes. These describe issues or events related to physics that have been included as learning outcomes in the specification. The How Science Works boxes explore the impact of scientific enquiry on individuals and society.

Self-assessment questions (SAQs) in each chapter provide opportunities to check understanding and to make links back to earlier work. The questions are written using appropriate command words used in examination papers. These questions often address misunderstandings that commonly appear in examination answers, and will help students to avoid such errors. Past examination questions at the end of each chapter allow students to practise answering exam-style questions. The answers to these, along with exam-style mark schemes and hints on answering questions, are found on the accompanying CD-ROM.

Acknowledgements

We would like to thank the following for permission to reproduce images:

p. 1*t* Edward Kinsman/Photo Researchers, Inc.; p. 1*b* Kingston Museum and Heritage Service; pp. 2, 73, 79*r* AFP/Getty Images; p. 3 © Dominic Burke/Alamy; p.13 Nigel Luckhurst; p. 15 David Scharf/Science Photo Library; p. 17*l* TRH Pictures/US Department of Defense; p. 17*r* Starstem/Science Photo Library; p. 23 © POPPERFOTO/Alamy; p. 27*t* © Aidan Gill; p. 27*b* TRH Pictures/E. Nevill; p.32 Michel Pissotte/Action-Plus; p.35 George Holton/Photo Researchers, Inc.; p. 36 Particolare della Tribuna di Galileo, Museo di Storia Naturale – Università di Firenze; p. 38*l* Keith Kent/Science Photo Library; p. 38*r* Didier Klein/Allsport; pp. 39*t*, 62*l* Glyn Kirk/Action-Plus; pp. 39*b*, 173*r* © Mira/Alamy; p. 43 Wayne Shakell/Life File; p. 52*t* Anne Ronan Picture Library/Image Select International; p. 52*b* Science Museum; p. 54 Professor Harold Edgerton/Science Photo Library; p. 59*l* Gustoimages/Science Photo Library; p. 59*r* Getty Images; p. 61 TRH Pictures/BAe; p. 62*r* Collections/Keith Pritchard; p. 71 Matthias Clamer; p. 72 HMSO *Highway Code*, reproduced under the terms of the Click-Use Licence; p. 74 TRL LTD./Science Photo Library; p. 75 David Parker/Science Photo Library; p. 76 ESA/CE/Eurocontrol/Science Photo Library; p. 79*l* Popperfoto; p. 80 Peter Tarry/Action-Plus; p. 85 Images Colour Library; p. 87*l* Bob Martin/Allsport; pp. 87*r*, 159*t*, 216*l* Science Photo Library; p. 90 © Britstock-IFA/Kohlhas; p. 95*l* Graham Burns/Life File; p. 95*r* Philippe Plailly/Eurelios/Science Photo Library; p. 102 © Bruno Lucas/Britstock-IFA; pp. 109, 138 Adam Hart-Davis/Science Photo Library; pp. 118, 130, 141, 142, 148 Andrew Lambert; p. 120 Richard Megna/Fundamental Photos/Science Photo Library; p. 131 Andrew Brookes, National Physical Laboratory/Science Photo Library; pp. 132, 199, 216 Andrew Lambert Photography/Science Photo Library; p. 133 Maximillian Stock LTD/Science Photo Library; p. 151*l* © Leslie Garland Picture Library/Alamy; p. 151*r* © Stock Connection Blue/Alamy; p. 159*b* Douglas W. Johnson/Science Photo Library; p. 160 Hermann Eisenbeiss/Science Photo Library; p.163*l* UC Regents, Natl. information service for earthquake engineering/Science Photo Library; p. 163*r* Popperfotos/Reuters; p. 164 © Lebrecht Music and Arts Photo Library/Alamy; p. 170*l* Dr Morley Read/Science Photo Library; p. 170*r* Physics Today collection/American Institute of Physics/Science Photo Library; p. 172 James King-Holmes/Toshiba Research Europe/Science Photo Library; pp. 173*l*, 179 © ImageState/Alamy; p. 175 Michael Brooke; p. 176 Peter Aprahamian/Sharples Stress Engineers LTD/Science Photo Library; p. 181 Edward Kinsman/Science Photo Library; p. 182 © superclic/Alamy; p. 184 © BRUCE COLEMAN INC./Alamy; p. 187 © PHOTOTAKE Inc./Alamy; p. 190 Daniel Sambraus/Science Photo Library; p. 196 Tim Ridley; p. 200 © Keith Leighton/Alamy; p. 206*l* © The Print Collector/Alamy; p. 206*r* © David R. Frazier Photolibrary, Inc./Alamy; p. 207 © Stockbyte/Alamy; p. 208 Sergei Verein/Life File; p. 211 Volker Steger/Science Photo Library; p. 217 Prof. Dr Hannes Lichte, Technische Universitat, Dresden; p. 219*l* Dr David Wexler, coloured by Dr Jeremy Burgess/Science Photo Library; p. 219*r* Dr Tim Evans/Science Photo Library; p. 224*tl* NMeM; p. 224*tr* Royal Astronomical Society/Science Photo Library; p. 224*b* © sciencephotos/Alamy; p. 225 *white light, mercury, helium, cadmium* Dept. of Physics, Imperial College/Science Photo Library; p. 225*tr* © Phil Degginger/Alamy; p. 225*br* Physics Dept., Imperial College/Science Photo Library; extension ch. 15 Dr Najeeb Layyous/Science Photo Library; extension ch. 20 Cambridge University Press.

We would like to thank OCR for permission to reproduce questions from past examination questions.

Chapter 1

Kinematics – describing motion

Background

e-Learning

Objectives

Describing movement

Our eyes are good at detecting movement. We notice even quite small movements out of the corners of our eyes. It's important for us to be able to judge movement – think about crossing the road, cycling or driving, or catching a ball.

Photography has played a big part in helping us to understand movement. The Victorian photographer Eadweard Muybridge used several cameras to take sequences of photographs of moving animals and people. He was able to show that, at some times, a trotting horse has all four feet off the ground (Figure 1.1). This had been the subject of much argument, and even of a $25 000 bet.

Figure 1.2 shows another way in which movement can be recorded on a photograph. This is a stroboscopic photograph of a boy juggling three balls. As he does so, a bright lamp flashes several times a second so that the camera records the positions of the balls at equal intervals of time.

If we knew the time between flashes, we could measure the photograph and calculate the speed of a ball as it moves through the air.

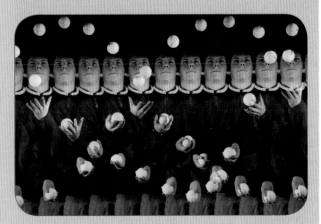

Figure 1.2 This boy is juggling three balls. A stroboscopic lamp flashes at regular intervals; the camera is moved to one side at a steady rate to show separate images of the boy.

Figure 1.1 Muybridge's sequence of photographs of a horse trotting.

Speed

We can calculate the **average speed** of something moving if we know the distance it moves and the time it takes:

$$\text{average speed} = \frac{\text{distance}}{\text{time}}$$

In symbols, this is written as: $v = \dfrac{x}{t}$

where v is the average speed and x is the distance travelled in time t. The photograph (Figure 1.3) shows the US team that set a new world record in the men's 4×400 m relay. The clock shows the time they took to cover 1600 m – they did it in less than 3 minutes. The photograph contains enough information to enable us to work out the runners' average speed.

Figure 1.3 The winning team in the men's 4×400 m relay at the World Athletics Championships.

If the object is moving at a constant speed, this equation will give us its speed during the time taken. If its speed is changing, then the equation gives us its **average speed**. Average speed is calculated over a period of time.

If you look at the speedometer in a car, it doesn't tell you the car's average speed; rather, it tells you its speed at the instant when you look at it. This is the car's **instantaneous speed**.

SAQ

1 Look at Figure 1.3. Each of the four runners ran 400 m, and the clock shows the total time taken. Calculate the team's average speed during the race.

Answer

Units

In Système Internationale d'Unités (SI system), distance is measured in metres (m) and time in seconds (s). Therefore, speed is in metres per second. This is written as $m\,s^{-1}$ (or as m/s). Here, s^{-1} is the same as 1/s, or 'per second'.

There are many other units used for speed. The choice of unit depends on the situation. You would probably give the speed of a snail in different units from the speed of a racing car. Table 1.1 includes some alternative units of speed.

Note that in many calculations it is necessary to work in SI units ($m\,s^{-1}$).

$m\,s^{-1}$	metres per second
$cm\,s^{-1}$	centimetres per second
$km\,s^{-1}$	kilometres per second
$km\,h^{-1}$ or km/h	kilometres per hour
mph	miles per hour

Table 1.1 Units of speed.

SAQ

2 Here are some units of speed:
  $m\,s^{-1}$ $mm\,s^{-1}$ $km\,s^{-1}$ $km\,h^{-1}$ mph
  Which of these units would be appropriate when stating the speed of each of the following?
  a a tortoise
  b a car on a long journey
  c light
  d a sprinter
  e an aircraft

Answer

3 A snail crawls 12 cm in one minute. What is its average speed in $mm\,s^{-1}$?

Hint

Answer

Determining speed

You can find the speed of something moving by measuring the time it takes to travel between two fixed points. For example, motorways and major roads often have marker posts every 100 m. Using a stopwatch you can time a car over a distance of, say, 500 m. Note that this can only tell you the car's average speed between the two points. You cannot tell whether it was increasing its speed, slowing down, or moving at a constant speed.

Laboratory measurements of speed

Here are some different ways to measure the speed of a trolley in the laboratory as it travels along a straight line. They can be adapted to measure the speed of other moving objects, such as a glider on an air track, or a falling mass.

Drive slower, live longer

Modern cars are designed to travel at high speeds – they can easily exceed the national speed limit (70 mph or $112\,km\,h^{-1}$ in the UK). However, road safety experts are sure that driving at lower speeds increases safety and saves the lives of drivers, passengers and pedestrians in the event of a collision. The police must identify speeding motorists. They have several ways of doing this.

On some roads, white squares are painted at intervals on the road surface. By timing a car between two of these markers, the police can determine whether the driver is speeding.

Speed cameras can measure the speed of a passing car. The camera shown in Figure 1.4 is of the type known as a 'Gatso'. The camera is usually mounted in a yellow box, and the road has characteristic markings painted on it.

The camera sends out a radar beam (radio waves) and detects the radio waves reflected by a car. The frequency of the waves is changed according to the instantaneous speed of the car. If the car is travelling above the speed limit, two photographs are taken of the car. These reveal how far the car has moved in the time interval between the photographs, and these can provide the necessary evidence for a prosecution. Note that the radar 'gun' data is not itself sufficient; the device may be confused by multiple reflections of the radio waves, or when two vehicles are passing at the same time.

Note also that the radar gun provides a value of the vehicle's instantaneous speed, but the photographs give the average speed.

Figure 1.4 A typical 'Gatso' speed camera (named after its inventor, Maurice Gatsonides). The box contains a radar speed gun which triggers a camera when it detects a speeding vehicle.

Extension

Using two light gates

The leading edge of the card in Figure 1.5 breaks the light beam as it passes the first light gate. This starts the timer. The timer stops when the front of the card breaks the second beam. The trolley's speed is calculated from the time interval and the distance between the light gates.

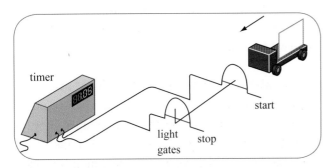

Figure 1.5 Using two light gates to find the average speed of a trolley.

Using one light gate

The timer in Figure 1.6 starts when the leading edge of the card breaks the light beam. It stops when the trailing edge passes through. In this case, the time shown is the time taken for the trolley to travel a distance equal to the length of the card. The computer software can calculate the speed directly by dividing the distance by the time taken.

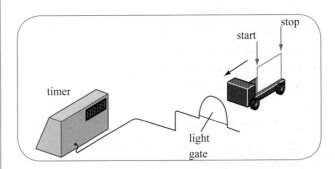

Figure 1.6 Using a single light gate to find the average speed of a trolley.

Using a ticker-timer

The ticker-timer (Figure 1.7) marks dots on the tape at regular intervals, usually 1/50 s (i.e. 0.02 s). (This is because it works with alternating current, and the frequency of the alternating mains is 50 Hz.) The pattern of dots acts as a record of the trolley's movement.

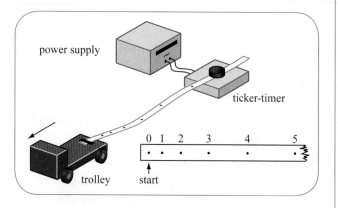

Figure 1.7 Using a ticker-timer to investigate the motion of a trolley.

Start by inspecting the tape. This will give you a description of the trolley's movement. Identify the start of the tape. Then look at the spacing of the dots:
● even spacing – constant speed
● increasing spacing – increasing speed.
Now you can make some measurements. Measure the distance of every fifth dot from the *start* of the tape. This will give you the trolley's distance at intervals of 0.1 s. Put the measurements in a table. Now you can draw a distance against time graph.

Using a motion sensor

The motion sensor (Figure 1.8) transmits regular pulses of ultrasound at the trolley. It detects the reflected waves and determines the time they took for the trip to the trolley and back. From this, the computer can deduce the distance to the trolley from the motion sensor. It can generate a distance against time graph. You can determine the speed of the trolley from this graph.

Choosing the best method

Each of these methods for finding the speed of a trolley has its merits. In choosing a method, you might think about the following points.

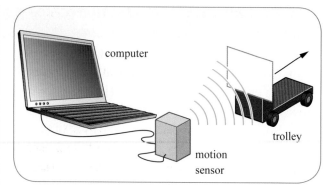

Figure 1.8 Using a motion sensor to investigate the motion of a trolley.

● Does the method give an average value of speed or can it be used to give the speed of the trolley at different points along its journey?
● How precisely does the method measure time – to the nearest millisecond?
● How simple and convenient is the method to set up in the laboratory?

SAQ

4 A trolley with a 5.0 cm long card passed through a single light gate. The time recorded by a digital timer was 0.40 s. What was the average speed of the trolley in $m s^{-1}$? [Answer]

5 Figure 1.9 shows two ticker-tapes. Describe the motion of the trolleys which produced them. [Hint]

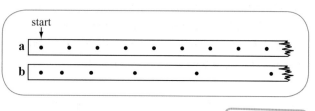

Figure 1.9 Ticker-tapes; for SAQ 5. [Answer]

6 Four methods for determining the speed of a moving trolley are described above. Each could be adapted to investigate the motion of a falling mass. Choose two methods which you think would be suitable, and write a paragraph for each to say how you would adapt it for this purpose. [Answer]

Distance and displacement, scalar and vector

In physics, we are often concerned with the distance moved by an object in a particular direction. This is called its **displacement**. Figure 1.10 illustrates the difference between distance and displacement. It shows the route followed by walkers as they went from Ayton to Seaton. Their winding route took them through Beeton, so that they covered a total distance of 15 km. However, their displacement was much less than this. Their finishing position was just 10 km from where they started. To give a complete statement of their displacement, we need to give both distance and direction:

displacement = 10 km 30° E of N

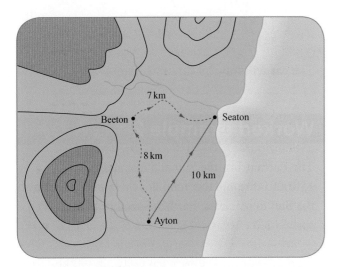

Figure 1.10 If you go on a long walk, the distance you travel will be greater than your displacement. In this example, the walkers travel a distance of 15 km, but their displacement is only 10 km, because this is the distance from the start to the finish of their walk.

Displacement is an example of a **vector quantity**. A vector quantity has both magnitude (size) and direction. Distance, on the other hand, is a **scalar quantity**. Scalar quantities have magnitude only.

Speed and velocity

It is often important to know both the speed of an object and the direction in which it is moving. Speed and direction are combined in another quantity, called **velocity**. The velocity of an object can be thought of as its speed in a particular direction. So, like displacement, velocity is a *vector* quantity. Speed is the corresponding scalar quantity, because it does not have a direction.

So, to give the velocity of something, we have to state the direction in which it is moving. For example: the aircraft flew with a velocity of $300\,\text{m s}^{-1}$ due north.

Since velocity is a vector quantity, it is defined in terms of displacement:

$$\text{velocity} = \frac{\text{change in displacement}}{\text{time taken}}$$

Alternatively, we can say that velocity is the rate of change of an object's displacement. From now on, you need to be clear about the distinction between velocity and speed, and between displacement and distance. Table 1.2 shows the standard symbols and units for these quantities.

Quantity	Symbol for quantity	Symbol for unit
distance	x	m
displacement	s	m
time	t	s
speed, velocity	v	m s^{-1}

Table 1.2 Standard symbols and units. (Take care not to confuse italic *s* for displacement with s for seconds. Notice also that *v* is used for both speed and velocity.)

SAQ

7 Which of these gives speed, velocity, distance or displacement? (Look back at the definitions of these quantities.)
   a The ship sailed south-west for 200 miles.
   b I averaged 7 mph during the marathon.
   c The snail crawled at $2\,\text{mm s}^{-1}$ along the straight edge of a bench.
   d The sales representative's round trip was 420 km.

Answer

Speed and velocity calculations

We can write the equation for velocity in symbols:

$$v = \frac{\Delta s}{\Delta t}$$

The word equation for velocity is:

$$\text{velocity} = \frac{\text{change in displacement}}{\text{time taken}}$$

Note that we are using Δs to mean 'change in displacement s'. The symbol Δ, Greek letter delta, means 'change in'. It does not represent a quantity (in the way that s does); it is simply a convenient way of representing a change in a quantity. Another way to write Δs would be $s_2 - s_1$, but this is more time-consuming and less clear.

The equation for velocity $v = \frac{\Delta s}{\Delta t}$ can be rearranged as follows, depending on which quantity we want to determine:

$$\text{change in displacement } \Delta s = v \times \Delta t$$

$$\text{change in time } \Delta t = \frac{\Delta s}{v}$$

Note that each of these equations is balanced in terms of units. For example, consider the equation for displacement. The units on the right-hand side are $\text{m s}^{-1} \times \text{s}$, which simplifies to m, the correct unit for displacement.

Note also that we can, of course, use the same equations to find speed and distance, that is:

$$\text{speed } v = \frac{x}{t}$$

$$\text{distance } x = v \times t$$

$$\text{time } t = \frac{x}{v}$$

Worked example 1

A car is travelling at $15\,\text{m s}^{-1}$. How far will it travel in 1 hour?

Step 1 It is helpful to start by writing down what you know and what you want to know:

$$v = 15\,\text{m s}^{-1}$$
$$t = 1\,\text{h} = 3600\,\text{s}$$
$$x = ?$$

Step 2 Choose the appropriate version of the equation and substitute in the values. Remember to include the units:

$$\begin{aligned} x &= v \times t \\ &= 15 \times 3600 \\ &= 5.4 \times 10^4\,\text{m} \\ &= 54\,\text{km} \end{aligned}$$

The car will travel 54 km in 1 hour.

Worked example 2

The Earth orbits the Sun at a distance of $150\,000\,000\,\text{km}$. How long does it take light from the Sun to reach the Earth? (Speed of light in space $= 3.0 \times 10^8\,\text{m s}^{-1}$.)

Step 1 Start by writing what you know. Take care with units; it is best to work in m and s. You need to be able to express numbers in scientific notation (using powers of 10) and to work with these on your calculator.

$$v = 3.0 \times 10^8\,\text{m s}^{-1}$$
$$\begin{aligned} x &= 150\,000\,000\,\text{km} \\ &= 150\,000\,000\,000\,\text{m} \\ &= 1.5 \times 10^{11}\,\text{m} \end{aligned}$$

Step 2 Substitute the values in the equation for time:

$$t = \frac{x}{v} = \frac{1.5 \times 10^{11}}{3.0 \times 10^8} = 500\,\text{s}$$

Guidance

Light takes 500 s (about 8.3 minutes) to travel from the Sun to the Earth.

Making the most of units

In Worked example 1 and Worked example 2 above, units have been omitted in intermediate steps in the calculations. However, at times it can be helpful to include units as this can be a way of checking that you have used the correct equation; for example, that you have not divided one quantity by another when you should have multiplied them. The units of an equation must be balanced, just as the numerical values on each side of the equation must be equal.

If you take care with units, you should be able to carry out calculations in non-SI units, such as kilometres per hour, without having to convert to metres and seconds.

For example, how far does a spacecraft travelling at $40\,000\,\text{km}\,\text{h}^{-1}$ travel in one day? Since there are 24 hours in one day, we have:

distance travelled $= 40\,000\,\text{km}\,\text{h}^{-1} \times 24\,\text{h}$

$= 960\,000\,\text{km}$

SAQ

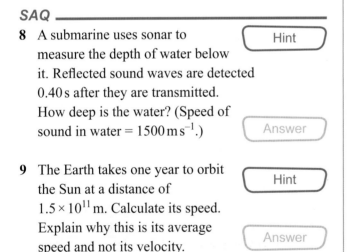

8 A submarine uses sonar to measure the depth of water below it. Reflected sound waves are detected $0.40\,\text{s}$ after they are transmitted. How deep is the water? (Speed of sound in water $= 1500\,\text{m}\,\text{s}^{-1}$.)

Hint

Answer

9 The Earth takes one year to orbit the Sun at a distance of $1.5 \times 10^{11}\,\text{m}$. Calculate its speed. Explain why this is its average speed and not its velocity.

Hint

Answer

Displacement against time graphs

We can represent the changing position of a moving object by drawing a displacement against time graph. The gradient (slope) of the graph is equal to its velocity (Figure 1.11). The steeper the slope, the greater the velocity. A graph like this can also tell us if an object is moving forwards or backwards. If the gradient is negative, the object's velocity is negative – it is moving backwards.

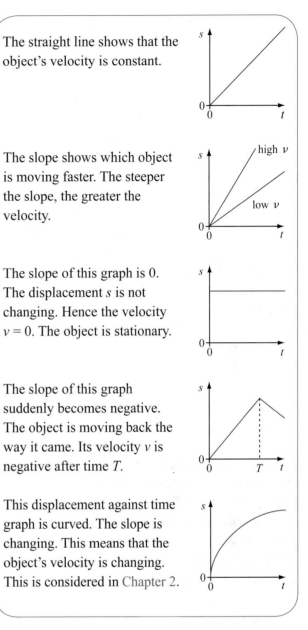

The straight line shows that the object's velocity is constant.

The slope shows which object is moving faster. The steeper the slope, the greater the velocity.

The slope of this graph is 0. The displacement s is not changing. Hence the velocity $v = 0$. The object is stationary.

The slope of this graph suddenly becomes negative. The object is moving back the way it came. Its velocity v is negative after time T.

This displacement against time graph is curved. The slope is changing. This means that the object's velocity is changing. This is considered in Chapter 2.

Figure 1.11 The slope of a displacement (s) against time (t) graph tells us about how fast an object is moving.

SAQ

10 The displacement against time sketch graph in Figure 1.12 represents the journey of a bus along a town's High Street. What does the graph tell you about the bus's journey?

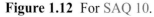

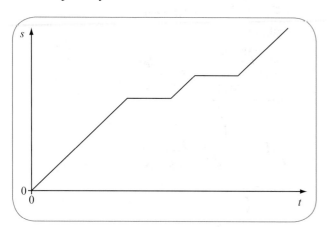

Figure 1.12 For SAQ 10.

11 Sketch a displacement against time graph to show your motion for the following event.

You are walking at a constant speed across a field after jumping off a gate. Suddenly you see a bull and stop. Your friend says there's no danger, so you walk on at a reduced constant speed. The bull bellows, and you run back to the gate.

Explain how each section of the walk relates to a section of your graph.

Answer

Deducing velocity from a displacement against time graph

A toy car moves along a straight track. Its displacement at different times is shown in Table 1.3. This data can be used to draw a displacement against time graph from which we can deduce the car's velocity.

Displacement s/m	1.0	3.0	5.0	7.0	7.0	7.0
Time t/s	0.0	1.0	2.0	3.0	4.0	5.0

Table 1.3 Displacement and time data for a toy car.

It is useful to inspect the data first, to see what we can deduce about the pattern of the car's movement. In this case, the displacement increases steadily at first, but after 3.0 s it becomes constant. In other words, initially the car is moving at a steady velocity, but then it stops.

Now we can plot the displacement against time graph (Figure 1.13).

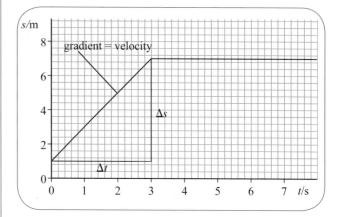

Figure 1.13 Displacement against time graph for a toy car; data as shown in Table 1.3.

We want to work out the velocity of the car over the first 3.0 seconds. To do this we need to work out the gradient of the graph, because:

velocity = gradient of displacement against time graph

We draw a right-angled triangle as shown. Now, to find the car's velocity, we need to divide a change in displacement by a time. These are given by the two sides of the triangle labelled Δs and Δt.

$$\text{velocity } v = \frac{\text{change in displacement}}{\text{change in time}}$$

$$= \frac{\Delta s}{\Delta t}$$

$$= \frac{(7.0-1.0)}{(3.0-0)} = \frac{6.0}{3.0} = 2.0 \text{ m s}^{-1}$$

If you are used to finding the gradient of a graph, you may be able to reduce the number of steps in this calculation.

Extension

SAQ

12 Table 1.4 shows the displacement of a racing car at different times as it travels along a straight track during a speed trial.

   a By inspecting the data, deduce the car's velocity.

   b Draw a displacement against time graph and use it to find the car's velocity.

Answer

Displacement *s*/m	0	85	170	255	340
Time *t*/s	0	1.0	2.0	3.0	4.0

Table 1.4 Data for SAQ 12.

13 A veteran car travels due south from London to Brighton. The distance it has travelled at hourly intervals is shown in Table 1.5.

   a Draw a distance against time graph to represent the car's journey.

   b From the graph, deduce the car's speed in km h^{-1} during the first three hours of the journey.

   c What is the car's average speed in km h^{-1} during the whole journey?

Answer

Time/h	Distance/km
0 (London)	0
1	23
2	46
3	69
4 (Brighton)	84

Table 1.5 Data for SAQ 13.

Summary

Glossary

- Displacement is the distance travelled in a particular direction.

- Velocity is defined by the following word equation:
$$\text{velocity} = \frac{\text{change in displacement}}{\text{time taken}}$$

- The gradient of a displacement against time graph is equal to velocity:
$$v = \frac{\Delta s}{\Delta t}$$

- A scalar quantity has only magnitude. A vector quantity has both magnitude and direction.

- Distance and speed are scalar quantities. Displacement and velocity are vector quantities.

Questions

1 The diagram shows the path of a
ball as it is passed between three
players. Player A passes a ball to player B. When
player B receives the ball, she immediately passes
the ball to player C. The distances for each pass
are shown on the diagram. The ball takes 2.4 s to
travel from player A to player C.
  a Calculate, for the total journey of the ball:
    i the average speed of the ball [2]
    ii the magnitude of the average velocity
      of the ball. [2]
  b Explain why the values for the *average
    speed* and *average velocity* are different. [2]

OCR Physics AS (2821) January 2005 [Total 6]

Hint

Answer

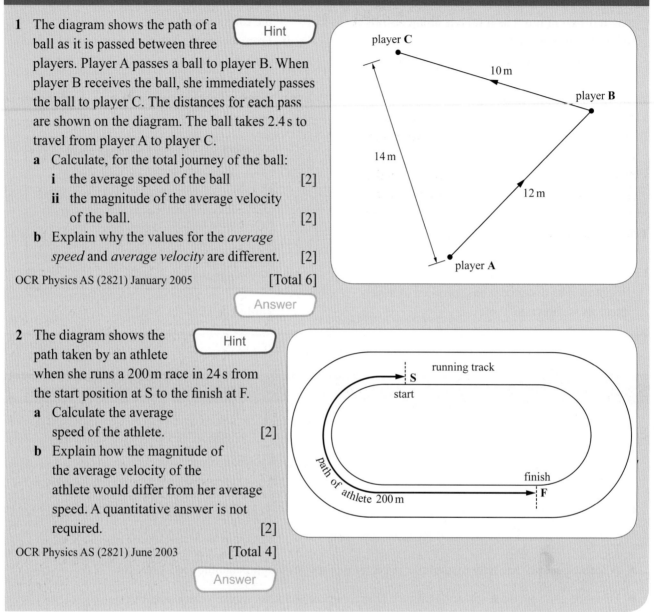

2 The diagram shows the
path taken by an athlete
when she runs a 200 m race in 24 s from
the start position at S to the finish at F.
  a Calculate the average
    speed of the athlete. [2]
  b Explain how the magnitude of
    the average velocity of the
    athlete would differ from her average
    speed. A quantitative answer is not
    required. [2]

OCR Physics AS (2821) June 2003 [Total 4]

Hint

Answer

Chapter 2

Accelerated motion

Background

e-Learning

Objectives

Defining acceleration

A sprinter can outrun a car – but only for the first couple of seconds of a race! Figure 2.1 shows how.

The sprinter gets off to a flying start. She accelerates rapidly from a standing start and reaches top speed after 2 s. The car cannot rapidly increase its speed like this. However, after about 3 s, it is travelling faster than the sprinter, and moves into the lead.

Figure 2.1 The sprinter has a greater acceleration than the car, but her top speed is less.

The meaning of acceleration

In everyday language, the term *accelerating* means 'speeding up'. Anything whose speed is increasing is accelerating. Anything whose speed is decreasing is decelerating.

To be more precise in our definition of acceleration, we should think of it as *changing velocity*. Any object whose speed is changing or which is changing its *direction* has **acceleration**. Because acceleration is linked to velocity in this way, it follows that it is a *vector* quantity.

Some examples of objects accelerating are shown in Figure 2.2.

A car speeding up as it leaves the town. The driver presses on the accelerator pedal to increase the car's velocity.

A car setting off from the traffic lights. There is an instant when the car is both stationary *and* accelerating. Otherwise it would not start moving.

A car travelling round a bend at a steady speed. The car's speed is constant, but its velocity is changing as it changes direction.

A ball being hit by a tennis racket. Both the ball's speed and direction are changing. The ball's velocity changes.

A stone dropped over a cliff. Gravity makes the stone go faster and faster (see Chapter 3). The stone accelerates as it falls.

Figure 2.2 Examples of objects accelerating.

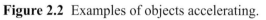

Calculating acceleration

The acceleration of something indicates the rate at which its velocity is changing. Language can get awkward here. Looking at the sprinter in Figure 2.1, we might say, 'The sprinter accelerates *faster* than the car'. However, 'faster' really means 'greater speed'. So it is better to say, 'The sprinter has a greater acceleration than the car'. Acceleration is defined as follows:

acceleration = rate of change of velocity

$$\text{acceleration} = \frac{\text{change in velocity}}{\text{time taken}}$$

So to calculate acceleration a, we need to know two quantities – the change in velocity Δv and the time taken Δt:

$$a = \frac{\Delta v}{\Delta t}$$

Sometimes this equation is written differently. We write u for the *initial velocity*, and v for the *final velocity* (because u comes before v in the alphabet). The moving object accelerates from u to v in a time t (this is the same as the time represented by Δt above). Then the acceleration is given by the equation:

$$a = \frac{v-u}{t}$$

Units of acceleration

The unit of acceleration is ms^{-2} (metres per second squared). The sprinter might have an acceleration of $5\,ms^{-2}$; her velocity increases by $5\,ms^{-1}$ every second.

You could express acceleration in other units. For example, an advertisement might claim that a car accelerates from 0 to 60 miles per hour (mph) in 10 s. Its acceleration would then be $6\,mph\,s^{-1}$ (6 miles per hour per second). However, mixing together hours and seconds is not a good idea, and so acceleration is almost always given in the standard SI units of ms^{-2}.

Worked example 1

Leaving a bus stop, the bus reaches a velocity of $8.0\,ms^{-1}$ after 10 s. Calculate the acceleration of the bus.

Step 1 Note that the bus's initial velocity is $0\,ms^{-1}$. Therefore:

change in velocity $\Delta v = (8.0-0)\,ms^{-1}$
time taken $= \Delta t = 10\,s$

Step 2 Substitute these values in the equation for acceleration:

$$\text{acceleration } a = \frac{\Delta v}{\Delta t} = \frac{8.0}{10} = 0.8\,ms^{-2}$$

Worked example 2

A sprinter starting from rest has an acceleration of $5.0\,ms^{-2}$ during the first 2.0 s of a race. Calculate her velocity after 2.0 s.

Step 1 Rearranging the equation $a = \frac{v-u}{t}$ gives:

$$v = u + at$$

Step 2 Substituting the values and calculating gives:

$$v = 0 + (5.0 \times 2.0) = 10\,ms^{-1}$$

Worked example 3

A train slows down from $60\,ms^{-1}$ to $20\,ms^{-1}$ in 50 s. Calculate the magnitude of the deceleration of the train.

Step 1 Write what you know:

> Guidance

$$u = 60\,ms^{-1} \quad v = 20\,ms^{-1} \quad t = 50\,s$$

Step 2 Take care! Here the train's final velocity is less than its initial velocity. To ensure that we arrive at the correct answer, we will use the alternative form of the equation to calculate a.

$$a = \frac{v-u}{t}$$
$$= \frac{(20-60)}{50} = \frac{-40}{50} = -0.8\,ms^{-2}$$

continued

The minus sign (negative acceleration) indicates that the train is slowing down. It is decelerating. The magnitude of the deceleration is $0.8\,\mathrm{m\,s^{-2}}$.

SAQ

1 A car accelerates from a standing start and reaches a velocity of $18\,\mathrm{m\,s^{-1}}$ after $6.0\,\mathrm{s}$. Calculate its acceleration.

   Answer

2 A car driver brakes gently. Her car slows down from $23\,\mathrm{m\,s^{-1}}$ to $11\,\mathrm{m\,s^{-1}}$ in $20\,\mathrm{s}$. Calculate the magnitude (size) of her deceleration. (Note that, because she is slowing down, her acceleration is negative.)

   Answer

3 A stone is dropped from the top of a cliff. Its acceleration is $9.81\,\mathrm{m\,s^{-2}}$. How fast will it be travelling:

   Hint

   a after $1\,\mathrm{s}$?

   b after $3\,\mathrm{s}$?

   Answer

Describing motion using graphs

A tachograph (Figure 2.3) is a device for drawing speed against time graphs. Tachographs are fitted behind the speedometers of goods vehicles and coaches. They provide a permanent record of the speed of the vehicle, so that checks can be made to ensure that the driver has not been speeding or driving for too long without a break. To many drivers, the tachograph is known as 'the spy in the cab'.

Figure 2.3 The tachograph chart takes 24 hours to complete one rotation. The outer section plots speed (increasing outwards) against time.

Deducing acceleration

The gradient of a velocity against time graph tells us whether the object's velocity has been changing at a high rate or a low rate, or not at all (Figure 2.4).

We can deduce the value of the acceleration from the gradient of the graph:

acceleration = gradient of velocity against time graph

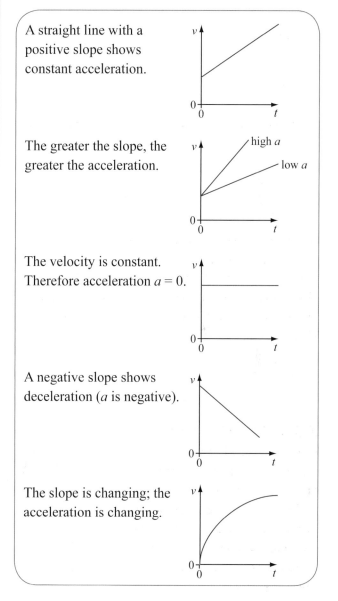

Figure 2.4 The gradient of a velocity against time graph is equal to acceleration.

The graph (Figure 2.5) shows how the velocity of a cyclist changed during the start of a sprint race. We can find his acceleration during the first section of the graph (where the line is straight) using the triangle as shown.

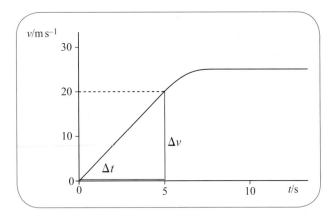

Figure 2.5 Deducing acceleration from a velocity against time graph.

The change in velocity Δv is given by the vertical side of the triangle. The time taken Δt is given by the horizontal side.

$$\text{acceleration} = \frac{\text{change in velocity}}{\text{time taken}}$$

$$= \frac{(20-0)}{5}$$

$$= 4.0\,\text{m}\,\text{s}^{-2}$$

Extension

Deducing displacement

We can also find the displacement of a moving object from its velocity against time graph. This is given by the area under the graph:

displacement = area under velocity against time graph

It is easy to see why this is the case for an object moving at a constant velocity. The displacement is simply velocity × time, which is the area of the shaded rectangle (Figure 2.6a).

For changing velocity, again the area under the graph gives displacement (Figure 2.6b). The area of each square of the graph represents a distance travelled: in this case, $1\,\text{m}\,\text{s}^{-1} \times 1\,\text{s}$, or 1 m. So, for this simple case in which the area is a triangle, we have:

$$\text{displacement} = \tfrac{1}{2}\,\text{base} \times \text{height}$$

$$= \tfrac{1}{2} \times 5.0 \times 10 = 25\,\text{m}$$

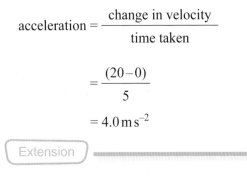

Figure 2.6 The area under the velocity against time graph is equal to the displacement of the object.

For more complex graphs, you may have to use other techniques such as counting squares to deduce the area, but this is still equal to the displacement. Take care when counting squares: it is easiest when the sides of the squares stand for one unit. Check the axes, as the sides may represent 2 units, or 5 units, or some other number.

It is easy to confuse displacement against time graphs and velocity against time graphs. Check by looking at the quantity marked on the vertical axis.

Extension

SAQ

4   A lorry driver is travelling at the speed limit on a motorway. Ahead, he sees hazard lights and gradually slows down. He sees that an accident has occurred, and brakes suddenly to a halt. Sketch a velocity against time graph to represent the motion of this lorry.

Answer

5 Look at the tachograph chart shown in Figure 2.3 and read the panel on page 13. How could you tell from such a chart when the vehicle was:
   a stationary?
   b moving slowly?
   c moving at a steady speed?
   d decelerating?

6 Table 2.1 shows how the velocity of a motorcyclist changed during a speed trial along a straight road.
   a Draw a velocity against time graph for this motion.
   b From the table, deduce the motorcyclist's acceleration during the first 10 s.
   c Check your answer by finding the gradient of the graph during the first 10 s.
   d Determine the motorcyclist's acceleration during the last 15 s.
   e Use the graph to find the total distance travelled during the speed trial.

Hint

Answer

Velocity/m s^{-1}	0	15	30	30	20	10	0
Time/s	0	5	10	15	20	25	30

Table 2.1 Data for SAQ 6.

Determining velocity and acceleration in the laboratory

In Chapter 1, we looked at ways of finding the velocity of a trolley moving in a straight line. These involved measuring distance and time, and deducing velocity. Now we will see how these techniques can be extended to find the acceleration of a trolley.

One light gate

The computer records the time for the first 'interrupt' section of the card to pass through the light beam of the light gate (Figure 2.8). Given the length of the interrupt, it can work out the trolley's initial velocity u. This is repeated for the second interrupt to give final velocity v. The computer also records the time interval $t_3 - t_1$ between these two velocity measurements. Now it can calculate the acceleration a as shown below:

$$u = \frac{l_1}{t_2 - t_1}$$ (l_1 = length of first section of the interrupt card)

and

$$v = \frac{l_2}{t_4 - t_3}$$ (l_2 = length of second section of the interrupt card)

Therefore

$$a = \frac{\text{change in velocity}}{\text{time taken}} = \frac{v - u}{t_3 - t_1}$$

Measuring velocity and acceleration

In a car crash, the occupants of the car may undergo a very rapid deceleration. This can cause them serious injury, but can be avoided if an air-bag is inflated within a fraction of a second. Figure 2.7 shows the tiny accelerometer at the heart of the system, which detects large accelerations and decelerations.

The acceleration sensor consists of two rows of interlocking teeth. In the event of a crash, these move relative to one another, and this generates a voltage which triggers the release of the air-bag.

At the top of the photograph, you can see a second sensor which detects sideways accelerations. This is important in the case of a side impact.

These sensors can also be used to detect when a car swerves or skids, perhaps on an icy road. In this case, they activate the car's stability-control systems.

Figure 2.7 A micro-mechanical acceleration sensor is used to detect sudden accelerations and decelerations as a vehicle travels along the road. This electron microscope image shows the device magnified about 1000 times.

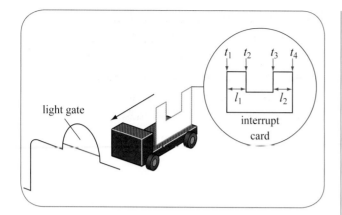

Figure 2.8 Determining acceleration using a single light gate.

Using a ticker-timer

The practical arrangement is the same as for measuring velocity. Now we have to think about how to interpret the tape produced by an accelerating trolley (Figure 2.9).

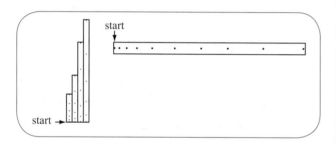

Figure 2.9 Ticker-tape for an accelerating trolley.

The tape is divided into sections, as before, every five dots. Remember that the time interval between adjacent dots is 0.02 s. Each section has five gaps and represents 0.10 s.

You can get a picture of the trolley's motion by placing the sections of tape side-by-side. This is in effect a velocity against time graph.

The length of each section gives the trolley's displacement in 0.10 s, from which the average velocity during this time can be found. This can be repeated for each section of the tape, and a velocity against time graph drawn. The gradient of this graph is equal to the acceleration. Table 2.2 and Figure 2.10 show some typical results.

Section of tape	Time at start /s	Time interval /s	Length of section /cm	Velocity /m s^{-1}
1	0.0	0.10	5.2	0.52
2	0.10	0.10	9.8	0.98
3	0.20	0.10	14.5	1.45

Table 2.2 Data for Figure 2.10.

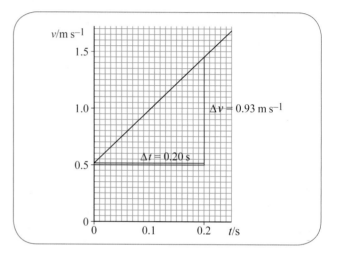

Figure 2.10 Deducing acceleration from measurements of a ticker-tape.

The acceleration is calculated to be:

$$a = \frac{\Delta v}{\Delta t}$$

$$= \frac{0.93}{0.20} \approx 4.7 \, \text{m s}^{-2}$$

Using a motion sensor

The computer software which handles the data provided by the motion sensor can calculate the acceleration of a trolley. However, because it deduces velocity from measurements of position, and then calculates acceleration from values of velocity, its precision is relatively poor.

Accelerometers

An accelerometer card (Figure 2.11) can be fitted to a trolley. When the trolley accelerates forwards, the pendulum swings backwards. When the trolley is moving at a steady speed (or is stationary), its acceleration is zero, and the pendulum remains at the midpoint.

In a similar way, a simple pendulum can act as an accelerometer. If it hangs down inside a car, it will swing backwards as the car accelerates forwards. It will swing forwards as the car decelerates. The greater the acceleration, the greater the angle to the vertical at which it hangs. More complex accelerometers are used in aircraft (Figure 2.12).

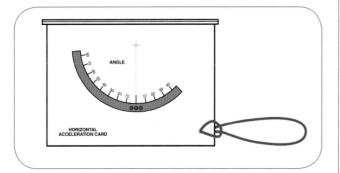

Figure 2.11 An accelerometer card uses a pendulum to give direct measurements of the acceleration of a trolley.

Figure 2.12 Practical accelerometers are important in aircraft. By continuously monitoring a plane's acceleration, its control systems can calculate its speed, direction and position.

SAQ

7 Figure 2.13 shows the dimensions of an interrupt card, together with the times recorded as it passed through a light gate. Use these measurements to calculate the acceleration of the card. (Follow the steps outlined on page 15.)

> Answer

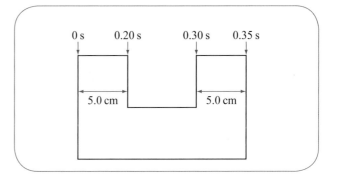

Figure 2.13 For SAQ 7.

8 Sketch a section of ticker-tape for a trolley which travels at a steady velocity and which then decelerates.

> Answer

9 Two adjacent five-dot sections of a ticker-tape measure 10 cm and 16 cm, respectively. The interval between dots is 0.02 s. Deduce the acceleration of the trolley which produced the tape.

> Hint

> Answer

The equations of motion

As a space rocket rises from the ground, its velocity steadily increases. It is accelerating (Figure 2.14). Eventually it will reach a speed of several kilometres per second. Any astronauts aboard find themselves pushed back into their seats while the rocket is accelerating.

Figure 2.14 A rocket accelerates as it lifts off from the ground.

The engineers who have planned the mission must be able to calculate how fast the rocket will be travelling and where it will be at any point in its journey. They have sophisticated computers to do this, using more elaborate versions of the equations given below.

There is a set of equations which allows us to calculate the quantities involved when an object is moving with a constant acceleration. The quantities we are concerned with are:

s displacement
u initial velocity
v final velocity
a acceleration
t time taken

Here are the four **equations of motion**. Take care when you use them. They only apply:

- to motion in a straight line
- to an object moving with a constant acceleration.

Equation 1: $v = u + at$

Equation 2: $s = \dfrac{(u+v)}{2} \times t$

Equation 3: $s = ut + \dfrac{1}{2}at^2$

Equation 4: $v^2 = u^2 + 2as$

To get a feel for how to use these equations, we will consider some worked examples. In each example, we will follow the same procedure.

Step 1 We write down the quantities which we know, and the quantity we want to find.

Step 2 Then we choose the equation which links these quantities, and substitute in the values.

Step 3 Finally, we calculate the unknown quantity.

We will look at where these equations come from in the next section.

Worked example 4

The rocket shown in Figure 2.14 lifts off from rest with an acceleration of $20\,\mathrm{m\,s^{-2}}$. Calculate its velocity after $50\,\mathrm{s}$.

Step 1 What we know: $u = 0\,\mathrm{m\,s^{-1}}$
     $a = 20\,\mathrm{m\,s^{-2}}$
     $t = 50\,\mathrm{s}$

and what we want to know: $v = ?$

Step 2 The equation linking u, a, t and v is equation 1:
$$v = u + at$$
Substituting gives: $v = 0 + (20 \times 50)$

Step 3 Calculation then gives:
$$v = 1000\,\mathrm{m\,s^{-1}}$$
So the rocket will be travelling at $1000\,\mathrm{m\,s^{-1}}$ after $50\,\mathrm{s}$. This makes sense, since its velocity increases by $20\,\mathrm{m\,s^{-1}}$ every second, for $50\,\mathrm{s}$.

You could use the same equation to work out how long the rocket would take to reach a velocity of $2000\,\mathrm{m\,s^{-1}}$, or the acceleration it must have to reach a speed of $1000\,\mathrm{m\,s^{-1}}$ in $40\,\mathrm{s}$, and so on.

Worked example 5

The car shown in Figure 2.15 is travelling along a straight road at $8.0\,\mathrm{m\,s^{-1}}$. It accelerates at $1.0\,\mathrm{m\,s^{-2}}$ for a distance of $18\,\mathrm{m}$. How fast is it then travelling?

In this case, we will have to use a different equation, because we know the distance during which the car accelerates, not the time.

Step 1 What we know: $u = 8.0\,\mathrm{m\,s^{-1}}$
     $a = 1.0\,\mathrm{m\,s^{-2}}$
     $s = 18\,\mathrm{m}$

and what we want to know: $v = ?$

Step 2 The equation we need is equation 4:
$$v^2 = u^2 + 2as$$
Substituting gives: $v^2 = 8.0^2 + (2 \times 1.0 \times 18)$

Step 3 Calculation then gives:
$$v^2 = 64 + 36 = 100\,\mathrm{m^2\,s^{-2}}$$
$$v = 10\,\mathrm{m\,s^{-1}}$$
So the car will be travelling at $10\,\mathrm{m\,s^{-1}}$ when it stops accelerating.

continued

(You may find it easier to carry out these calculations without including the units of quantities when you substitute in the equation. However, including the units can help to ensure that you end up with the correct units for the final answer.)

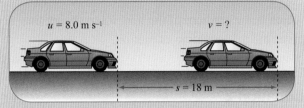

Figure 2.15 For Worked example 5. This car accelerates for a short distance as it travels along the road.

Worked example 6

A train (Figure 2.16) travelling at $20\,\mathrm{m\,s^{-1}}$ accelerates at $0.50\,\mathrm{m\,s^{-2}}$ for 30 s. Calculate the distance travelled by the train in this time.

Step 1 What we know:
$$u = 20\,\mathrm{m\,s^{-1}}$$
$$t = 30\,\mathrm{s}$$
$$a = 0.50\,\mathrm{m\,s^{-2}}$$
and what we want to know: $s = ?$

Step 2 The equation we need is equation 3:
$$s = ut + \tfrac{1}{2}\,at^2$$
Substituting gives: $s = (20 \times 30) + \tfrac{1}{2} \times 0.5 \times (30)^2$

Step 3 Calculation then gives:
$$s = 600 + 225 = 825\,\mathrm{m}$$
So the train will travel 825 m while it is accelerating.

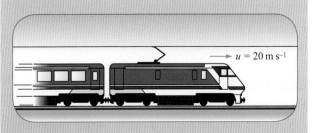

Figure 2.16 For Worked example 6. This train accelerates for 30 s.

Worked example 7

The cyclist in Figure 2.17 is travelling at $15\,\mathrm{m\,s^{-1}}$. She brakes so that she doesn't collide with the wall. Calculate the magnitude of her deceleration.

This example shows that it is sometimes necessary to rearrange an equation, to make the unknown quantity its subject. It is easiest to do this before substituting in the values.

Step 1 What we know:
$$u = 15\,\mathrm{m\,s^{-1}}$$
$$v = 0\,\mathrm{m\,s^{-1}}$$
$$s = 18\,\mathrm{m}$$
and what we want to know: $a = ?$

Step 2 The equation we need is equation 4:
$$v^2 = u^2 + 2as$$
Rearranging gives:
$$a = \frac{v^2 - u^2}{2s}$$

$$a = \frac{0^2 - 15^2}{2 \times 18} = \frac{-225}{36}$$

Step 3 Calculation then gives:
$$a = -6.25\,\mathrm{m\,s^{-2}} \approx -6.3\,\mathrm{m\,s^{-2}}$$
So the cyclist will have to brake hard to achieve a deceleration of magnitude $6.3\,\mathrm{m\,s^{-2}}$. The minus sign shows that her acceleration is negative, i.e. a deceleration.

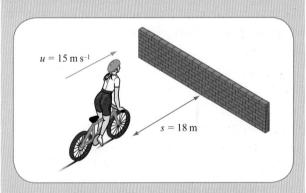

Figure 2.17 For Worked example 7. The cyclist brakes to stop herself colliding with the wall.

SAQ

10 A car is initially stationary. It has
a constant acceleration of $2.0\,\mathrm{m\,s^{-2}}$.

Hint

  a Calculate the velocity of the car after 10 s.
  b Calculate the distance travelled by the car at
  the end of 10 s.
  c Calculate the time taken by
  the car to reach a velocity
  of $24\,\mathrm{m\,s^{-1}}$.

Answer

11 A train accelerates steadily from
$4.0\,\mathrm{m\,s^{-1}}$ to $20\,\mathrm{m\,s^{-1}}$ in 100 s.

Hint

  a Calculate the acceleration of the train.
  b From its initial and final velocities, calculate
  the average velocity of the train.
  c Calculate the distance
  travelled by the train in
  this time of 100 s.

Answer

12 A car is moving at $8.0\,\mathrm{m\,s^{-1}}$. The driver makes
it accelerate at $1.0\,\mathrm{m\,s^{-2}}$ for a
distance of 18 m. What is the
final velocity of the car?

Answer

Deriving the equations of motion

On the previous pages, we have seen how to make
use of the equations of motion. But where do these
equations come from? We can find the first two
equations from the velocity against time graph shown
in Figure 2.18. The graph represents the motion of an
object. Its initial velocity is u. After time t, its final
velocity is v.

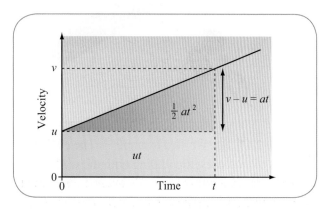

Figure 2.18 This graph shows the variation of
velocity of an object with time. The object has
constant acceleration.

Equation 1

The graph of Figure 2.18 is a straight line, therefore
the object's acceleration a is constant. The gradient
(slope) of the line is equal to acceleration.

The acceleration is given by:

$$a = \frac{(v-u)}{t}$$

which is the gradient of the line. Rearranging this
gives the first equation of motion:

$$v = u + at \qquad \text{(equation 1)}$$

Equation 2

Displacement is given by the area under the velocity
against time graph. Figure 2.19 shows that the
object's average velocity is half-way between u and
v. So the object's average velocity, calculated by
averaging its initial and final velocities, is

$$\frac{(u+v)}{2}$$

The object's displacement is the shaded area in
Figure 2.19. This is a rectangle, and so we have:

displacement = average velocity × time taken

and hence:

$$s = \frac{(u+v)}{2} \times t \qquad \text{(equation 2)}$$

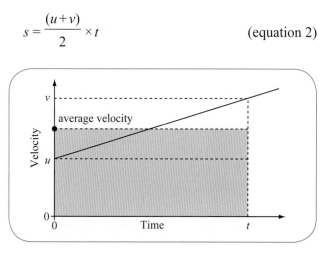

Figure 2.19 The average velocity is half-way
between u and v.

Equation 3

From equations 1 and 2, we can derive equation 3:

$$v = u + at \qquad \text{(equation 1)}$$

$$s = \frac{(u+v)}{2} \times t \qquad \text{(equation 2)}$$

Substituting v from equation 1 gives:

$$s = \left(\frac{u+u+at}{2} \right) \times t$$

$$= \frac{2ut}{2} + \frac{at^2}{2}$$

So

$$s = ut + \frac{1}{2}at^2 \qquad \text{(equation 3)}$$

Looking at Figure 2.18, you can see that the two terms on the right of the equation correspond to the *areas* of the rectangle and the triangle which make up the area under the graph. Of course, this is the same area as the rectangle in Figure 2.19.

Equation 4

Equation 4 is also derived from equations 1 and 2.

$$v = u + at \qquad \text{(equation 1)}$$

$$s = \frac{(u+v)}{2} \times t \qquad \text{(equation 2)}$$

Substituting for time t from equation 1 gives:

$$s = \frac{(u+v)}{2} \times \frac{(v-u)}{a}$$

Rearranging this gives:

$$2as = (u+v)(v-u)$$

$$= v^2 - u^2$$

Or simply:

$$v^2 = u^2 + 2as \qquad \text{(equation 4)}$$

Extension

Investigating road traffic accidents

The police frequently have to investigate road traffic accidents. They make use of many aspects of Physics, including the equations of motion. The next two questions will help you to apply what you have learned to situations where police investigators have used evidence from skid marks on the road.

SAQ

13 Trials on the surface of a new road show that, when a car skids to a halt, its acceleration is $-7.0\,\mathrm{m\,s^{-2}}$. Estimate the skid-to-stop distance of a car travelling at the speed limit of $30\,\mathrm{m\,s^{-1}}$ (approx. $110\,\mathrm{km\,h^{-1}}$ or $70\,\mathrm{mph}$).

Answer

14 At the scene of an accident on a French country road, police find skid marks stretching for $50\,\mathrm{m}$. Tests on the road surface show that a skidding car decelerates at $6.5\,\mathrm{m\,s^{-2}}$. Was the car which skidded exceeding the speed limit of $25\,\mathrm{m\,s^{-1}}$ ($90\,\mathrm{km\,h^{-1}}$) on this stretch of road?

Answer

Uniform and non-uniform acceleration

It is important to note that the equations of motion only apply to an object which is moving with a constant acceleration. If the acceleration a was changing, you wouldn't know what value to put in the equations. Constant acceleration is often referred to as **uniform acceleration**.

The velocity against time graph in Figure 2.20 shows *non-uniform* acceleration. It is not a straight line; its gradient is changing (in this case, decreasing). Clearly we could not derive such simple equations from this graph.

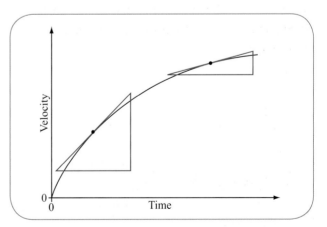

Figure 2.20 This curved velocity against time graph might show how a car accelerates until it reaches its top speed. A graph like this cannot be analysed using the equations of motion.

The acceleration at any instant in time is given by the gradient of the velocity against time graph. The triangles in Figure 2.20 show how to find the acceleration.

● At the time of interest, mark a point on the graph.
● Draw a *tangent* to the curve at that point.
● Make a large right-angled triangle, and use it to find the gradient.

In a similar way, you can find the instantaneous velocity of an object from the gradient of its displacement against time graph. Figure 2.21 shows a numerical example. At time $t = 20\,$s:

$$v = \frac{\Delta s}{\Delta t} = \frac{10}{20} = 0.50\,\text{m s}^{-1}$$

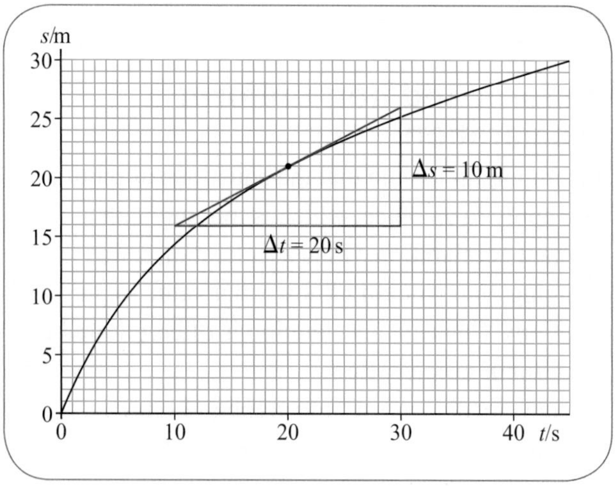

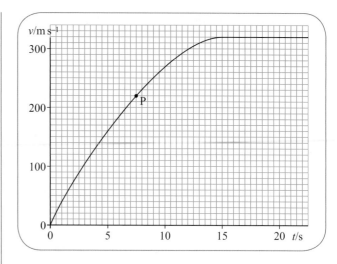

Figure 2.22 For SAQ 15.

16 The velocity against time graph (Figure 2.23) represents the motion of a car along a straight road for a period of 30 s.

  a Describe motion of the car.

  b From the graph, determine the car's initial and final velocities over the time of 30 s.

  c Determine the acceleration of the car.

  d By calculating the area under the graph, determine the displacement of the car.

  e Check your answer to part **d** by calculating the car's displacement using

$$s = ut + \tfrac{1}{2}at^2$$

[Answer]

Figure 2.21 This curved displacement against time graph shows that the object's velocity is changing. The graph can be used to find the velocity of the object; draw a tangent to the graph, and find its gradient.

[Extension]

SAQ

15 The graph shown in Figure 2.22 represents the motion of an object moving with varying acceleration. Lay your ruler on the diagram so that it is tangential to the graph at point P.

  a What are the values of time and velocity at this point?

  b Estimate the object's acceleration at this point.

[Answer]

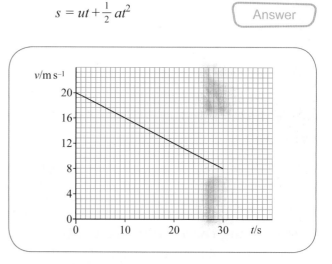

Figure 2.23 For SAQ 16.

17 In a 200 m race, run on a straight track, the displacement of an athlete after each second was found from analysis of a video film (Figure 2.24). From the values of displacement, the average velocity of the athlete during each second was calculated. This information is shown in Table 2.3. Use the data to plot a velocity against time graph for the athlete during this race, and answer the following questions.

a How were the values of velocity calculated?

b State the maximum velocity of the athlete.

c Calculate the acceleration of the athlete between $t = 1.0$ s and $t = 2.0$ s, and between $t = 8.0$ s and $t = 9.0$ s.

d Sketch a graph of the athlete's acceleration against time.

e State what is represented by the total area under the velocity against time graph. Determine the area and explain your answer. [Answer]

Time/s	Displacement/m	Average velocity during each second/m s^{-1}
0	0	
1	3.0	3.0
2	10.1	7.1
3	18.3	8.2
4	27.4	9.1
5	36.9	9.5
6	46.7	9.8
7	56.7	10.0
8	66.8	10.1
9	77.0	10.2
10	87.0	10.0
11	97.0	10.0
12	106.9	9.9
13	116.8	9.9
14	126.8	10.0
15	136.6	9.8
16	146.4	9.8

Table 2.3 Data for SAQ 17.

18 A motorway designer can assume that cars approaching a motorway enter a slip road with a velocity of $10\,\mathrm{m\,s^{-1}}$ and need to reach a velocity of $30\,\mathrm{m\,s^{-1}}$ before joining the motorway. Calculate the minimum length for the slip road, assuming that vehicles have an acceleration of $4.0\,\mathrm{m\,s^{-2}}$. [Answer]

19 A train is travelling at $50\,\mathrm{m\,s^{-1}}$ [Hint] when the driver applies the brakes and gives the train a constant deceleration of magnitude $0.50\,\mathrm{m\,s^{-2}}$ for 100 s. Describe what happens to the train. Calculate the distance travelled by the train in 100 s. [Answer]

Figure 2.24 Debbie Ferguson competing in a 200 m race. The time taken to complete the race is usually the only physical quantity measured – but the athlete's speed changes throughout the race.

20 The graph in Figure 2.25 shows the variation of velocity with time of two cars A and B, which are travelling in the same direction over a period of time of 40 s. Car A, travelling at a constant velocity of 40 m s⁻¹, overtakes car B at time $t = 0$. In order to catch up with car A, car B immediately accelerates uniformly for 20 s to reach a constant velocity of 50 m s⁻¹. Calculate:

a how far A travels during the first 20 s

b the acceleration and distance of travel of B during the first 20 s

c the additional time taken for B to catch up with A

d the distance each car will have then travelled since $t = 0$.

Answer

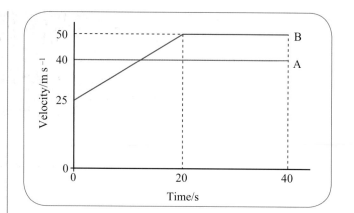

Figure 2.25 Speed against time graphs for two cars, A and B. For SAQ 20.

Summary

Glossary

- Acceleration is equal to the rate of change of velocity.

- Acceleration is a vector quantity.

- The gradient of a velocity against time graph is equal to acceleration: $a = \dfrac{\Delta v}{\Delta t}$

- The area under a velocity against time graph is equal to displacement (or distance travelled).

- The equations of motion (for constant acceleration in a straight line) are:

$$v = u + at$$

$$s = \dfrac{(u+v)}{2} \times t$$

$$s = ut + \dfrac{1}{2}at^2$$

$$v^2 = u^2 + 2as$$

Questions

1 a Define *acceleration*. [1]

b The diagram shows the variation of the velocity *v*, with time *t*, of a train as it travels from one station to the next.

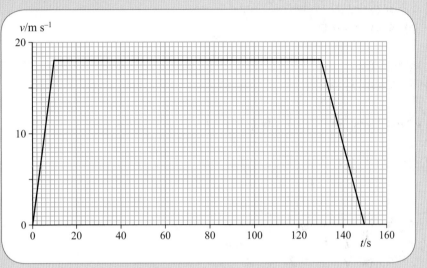

i Use the diagram to calculate the acceleration of the train in the first 10.0 s. [2]

ii Use the diagram to calculate the distance between the two stations. [3]

Hint

OCR Physics AS (2821) January 2002 [Total 6]

Answer

2 a i Define *speed*. [1]

ii Distinguish between speed and velocity. [2]

b Use the equations given below, which represent uniformly accelerated motion in a straight line, to obtain an expression for *v* in terms of *u*, *a* and *s* only.

$$v = u + at$$

$$s = \frac{(u+v)}{2} \times t$$ [2]

Hint

OCR Physics AS (2821) June 2001 [Total 5]

Answer

continued

3 **a** Define *acceleration*. [2] Hint

   b The diagram shows a graph of velocity v against time t for a train that stops at a station.

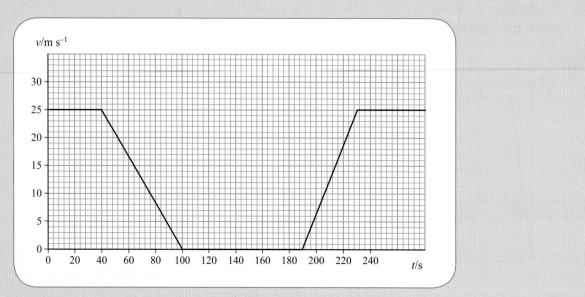

     For the time interval $t = 40\,\text{s}$ to $t = 100\,\text{s}$, calculate:

     i the acceleration of the train [3] Hint

     ii the distance travelled by the train. [2]

   c Calculate the distance travelled by the train during its acceleration from rest to $25\,\text{m s}^{-1}$. [2]

   d Calculate the journey time that would be saved if the train did not stop at the station but continued at a constant speed of $25\,\text{m s}^{-1}$. [4]

OCR Physics AS (2821) January 2001   [Total 13]

Answer

Chapter 3

Dynamics – explaining motion

Background

e-Learning

Objectives

Force and acceleration

Figure 3.1 shows two electric trains. One is a high-speed express train that runs between London and Paris. The other runs on the Singapore Metro. Each has powerful electric motors which provide the force needed to get it up to speed – the force that makes the train accelerate.

Figure 3.1 The Eurostar train has a greater top speed than the Metro train, but its acceleration is smaller.

There is a difference between these two trains. The Metro train has many stops along its route. It must get up to speed in a matter of seconds – it must have greater acceleration. The express train has few stops along its route. It doesn't matter if it takes several minutes to reach its top speed – its acceleration is quite small. If you have travelled on the Underground or a similar rapid-transit system, you will have felt the sudden changes in speed as the train accelerates and decelerates. The other train gives a much smoother ride.

Force and acceleration

In Chapter 1 and Chapter 2, we saw how motion can be *described* in terms of displacement, velocity, acceleration and so on. This is known as **kinematics**. Now we are going to look at how we can *explain* how an object moves, in terms of the forces which change its motion. This is known as **dynamics**.

Calculating the acceleration

Figure 3.2a shows how we represent the force which the motors provide to cause the train to accelerate. The net force is represented by an arrow. The direction of the arrow shows the direction of the net force, and the magnitude (size) of the net force of 20 000 N is also shown.

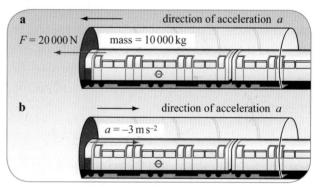

Figure 3.2 A force is needed to make the train **a** accelerate, and **b** decelerate.

To calculate the acceleration a produced by the net force F, we must also know the train's mass m (Table 3.1). These quantities are related by:

$$a = \frac{F}{m} \quad \text{or} \quad F = ma$$

Quantity	Symbol	Unit
net force	F	N (newtons)
mass	m	kg (kilograms)
acceleration	a	$\mathrm{m\,s^{-2}}$ (metres per second squared)

Table 3.1 The quantities related by $F = ma$.

27

In this case, we have $F = 20\,000\,\text{N}$ and $m = 10\,000\,\text{kg}$, and so:

$$a = \frac{F}{m} = \frac{20\,000}{10\,000} = 2\,\text{m s}^{-2}$$

In Figure 3.2b, the train is decelerating as it comes into a station. Its acceleration is $-3.0\,\text{m s}^{-2}$. What force must be provided by the braking system of the train?

$$F = ma = 10\,000 \times -3 = -30\,000\,\text{N}$$

Here, the minus sign shows that the force must act towards the right in the diagram, in the opposite direction to the motion of the train.

Force, mass and acceleration

The equation we used above, $F = ma$, is a simplified version of *Newton's second law* of motion. It applies to objects that have a constant mass. Hence this equation can be applied to a train whose mass remains constant during its journey.

The equation $a = \dfrac{F}{m}$ relates acceleration, net force and mass. In particular, it shows that the bigger the force, the greater the acceleration it produces. You will probably feel that this is an unsurprising result. For a given object, the acceleration is directly proportional to the net force:

$$a \propto F$$

The equation also shows that the acceleration produced by a force depends on the mass of the object. The **mass** of an object is a measure of its **inertia**, or its ability to resist any change in its motion. The greater the mass, the smaller the acceleration which results. If you push your hardest against a Smart car, you will have a greater effect than if you push against a more massive Rolls-Royce (Figure 3.3). So for a constant force, the acceleration is inversely proportional to the mass:

$$a \propto \frac{1}{m}$$

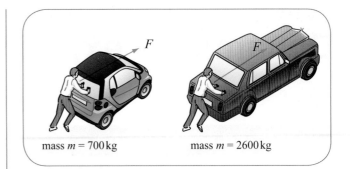

mass $m = 700\,\text{kg}$ mass $m = 2600\,\text{kg}$

Figure 3.3 It is easier to make a small mass accelerate than a large mass.

The Underground train driver knows that, when the train is full during the rush hour, it has a smaller acceleration. This is because its mass is greater when it is full of people. Similarly, it is more difficult to stop the train once it is moving. The brakes must be applied earlier if the train isn't to overshoot the platform at the station.

Extension

Worked example 1

A cyclist of mass 60 kg rides a bicycle of mass 20 kg. When starting off, the cyclist provides a force of 200 N. Calculate the initial acceleration.

Step 1 This is a straightforward example. First, we must calculate the combined mass m of the bicycle and its rider:

$$m = 20 + 60 = 80\,\text{kg}$$

We are given the force F:

force causing acceleration $F = 200\,\text{N}$

Step 2 Substituting these values gives:

$$a = \frac{F}{m} = \frac{200}{80} = 2.5\,\text{m s}^{-2}$$

So the cyclist's acceleration is $2.5\,\text{m s}^{-2}$.

Worked example 2

A car of mass 500 kg is travelling at 20 m s^{-1}. The driver sees a red traffic light ahead, and slows to a halt in 10 s. Calculate the braking force provided by the car.

Step 1 In this example, we must first calculate the acceleration required. The car's final velocity is 0 m s^{-1}, so its change in velocity Δv is –20 m s^{-1}. The time taken Δt is 10 s.

$$\text{acceleration } a = \frac{\text{change in velocity}}{\text{time taken}}$$

$$= \frac{\Delta v}{\Delta t} = \frac{-20}{10} = -2 \text{ m s}^{-2}$$

Step 2 To calculate the force, we use:

$$F = ma = 500 \times -2 = -1000 \text{ N}$$

So the brakes must provide a force of 1000 N. (The minus sign shows a force decreasing the velocity of the car.)

SAQ ───────────────

1 Calculate the force needed to give a car of mass 800 kg an acceleration of 2.0 m s^{-2}. [Answer]

2 A rocket has a mass of 5000 kg. At a particular instant, the net force acting on the rocket is 200 000 N. Calculate its acceleration. [Answer]

3 (In this question, you will need to make use of the equations of motion which you studied in Chapter 2.) [Hint]
A motorcyclist of mass 40 kg rides a bike of mass 60 kg. As she sets off from the lights, the forward force on the bike is 200 N. Assuming the net force on the bike remains constant, calculate the bike's velocity after 5.0 s. [Answer]

Defining the newton

Isaac Newton (1642–1727) played a significant part in developing the scientific idea of *force*. Building on Galileo's earlier thinking, he explained the relationship between force, mass and acceleration, which we now write as $F = ma$. For this reason, the SI unit of force is named after him.

We can use the equation $F = ma$ to define the **newton** (N).

One newton is the force that will give a 1 kg mass an acceleration of 1 m s^{-2} in the direction of the force.

$$1 \text{ N} = 1 \text{ kg} \times 1 \text{ m s}^{-2} \quad \text{or} \quad 1 \text{ N} = 1 \text{ kg m s}^{-2}$$

SAQ ───────────────

4 The pull of the Earth's gravity on an apple (its weight) is about 1 newton. We could devise a new international system of units by defining our unit of force as the weight of an apple. State as many reasons as you can why this would not be a very useful definition. [Answer]

Acceleration caused by gravity

If you drop a ball or stone, it falls to the ground. Figure 3.4, based on a multiflash photograph, shows the ball at equal intervals of time. You can see that the ball's velocity increases as it falls. You can see this from the way the spaces between the images of the ball increase steadily. The ball is accelerating.

A multiflash photograph is useful to demonstrate that the ball accelerates as it falls. Usually, objects fall too quickly for our eyes to be able to observe them speeding up. It is easy to imagine that the ball moves quickly as soon as you let it go, and falls at a steady speed to the ground. Figure 3.4 shows that this is not the case.

The force which causes the ball to accelerate is the pull of the Earth's gravity. Another name for this force is the **weight** of the ball. The force is shown as an arrow, pulling vertically downwards on the ball (Figure 3.5). It is usual to show the arrow coming from the centre of the ball – its **centre of gravity**. The centre of gravity of an object is defined as the point where its entire weight appears to act.

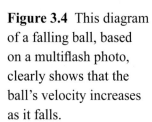

Figure 3.4 This diagram of a falling ball, based on a multiflash photo, clearly shows that the ball's velocity increases as it falls.

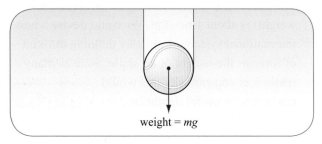

weight = *mg*

Figure 3.5 The weight of an object is a force caused by the Earth's gravity. It acts vertically down on the object.

Large and small

A large rock has a greater weight than a small rock, but if you push them over a cliff at the same time, they will fall at the same rate. In other words, they have the *same* acceleration, regardless of their mass. This is a surprising result. Common sense may suggest that a heavier object will fall faster than a lighter one. It is said that Galileo dropped a large cannon ball and a small cannon ball from the top of the Leaning Tower of Pisa, and showed that they landed simultaneously. He may never have done this, but the story does illustrate that the result is not intuitively obvious – if everyone thought that the two cannon balls would accelerate at the same rate, there would not have been any experiment or story.

In fact, we are used to lighter objects falling more slowly than heavy ones. A feather drifts down to the floor, while a stone falls quickly. However, we are being misled by the presence of *air resistance*. The force of air resistance has a large effect on the falling feather, and almost no effect on the falling stone. When astronauts visited the Moon (where there is virtually no atmosphere and so no air resistance), they were able to show that a feather and a stone fell side-by-side to the ground.

If we measure the acceleration of a freely falling object on the surface of the Earth (see pages 32–34), we find a value of $9.81\,\text{m}\,\text{s}^{-2}$. This is known as the *acceleration of free fall*, and is given the symbol g:

acceleration of free fall, $g = 9.81\,\text{m}\,\text{s}^{-2}$

The value of g depends on where you are on the Earth's surface, but for examination purposes we take $g = 9.81\,\text{m}\,\text{s}^{-2}$.

We can find the force causing this acceleration of free fall using $F = ma$. This force is the object's *weight*. Hence the weight W of an object is given by

weight = mass × acceleration of free fall

or

$$W = mg$$

On the Moon

The Moon is smaller and has less mass than the Earth, and so its gravity is weaker. If we were to drop a stone on the Moon, it would have a smaller acceleration. Your hand is about 1 m above ground level; a stone takes about 0.45 s to fall through this distance on the Earth, but about 1.1 s on the surface of the Moon. The acceleration of free fall on the Moon is about one-sixth of that on the Earth:

$$g_{\text{Moon}} = 1.6\,\text{m}\,\text{s}^{-2}$$

It follows that objects weigh less on the Moon than on the Earth. They are not completely weightless, because the Moon's gravity is not zero. In fact, the Moon would be a good place to observe an object accelerating as it falls, as shown in Figure 3.6. Table 3.2 shows the displacement of a falling object at intervals of 1 s. These have been calculated as follows:

initial velocity $u = 0\,\text{m}\,\text{s}^{-1}$

acceleration $a = 1.6\,\text{m}\,\text{s}^{-2}$

Substituting in $s = ut + \frac{1}{2}at^2$ gives displacement s:

$$s = \frac{1}{2} \times 1.6 \times t^2$$

$$= 0.8 \times t^2$$

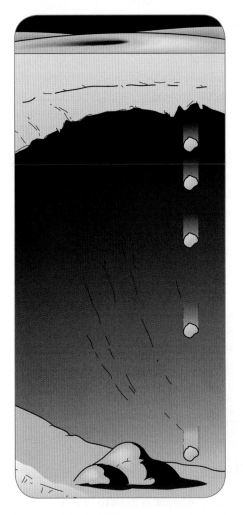

Figure 3.6 A falling moon rock has less acceleration than a similar rock on the Earth, so it takes longer to fall a given distance. This would make it easier to see the rock accelerating as it fell.

Time t/s	0	1.0	2.0	3.0	4.0
Displacement s/m	0	0.8	3.2	7.2	12.8

Table 3.2 Displacement of an object falling close to the surface of the Moon.

Mass and weight

We have now considered two related quantities, mass and weight. It is important to distinguish carefully between these (Table 3.3).

Quantity	Symbol	Unit	Comment
mass	m	kg	this does not vary from place to place
weight	mg	N	this a force – it depends on the strength of gravity

Table 3.3 Distinguishing between mass and weight.

If your moon-buggy breaks down (Figure 3.7), it will be no easier to push it along on the Moon than on the Earth. This is because its mass does not change, because it is made from just the same atoms and molecules wherever it is. From $F = ma$, it follows that if m doesn't change, you will need the same force F to start it moving.

However, your moon-buggy will be easier to lift on the Moon, because its weight will be less. From $W = mg$, since g is less on the Moon, it has a smaller weight than when on the Earth.

Figure 3.7 The mass of a moon-buggy is the same on the Moon as on the Earth, but its weight is smaller.

Gravitational field strength

Here is another way to think about the significance of g. This quantity indicates how strong gravity is at a particular place. The Earth's gravitational field is stronger than the Moon's. On the Earth's surface, gravity gives an acceleration of free fall of about $9.81\,\mathrm{m\,s^{-2}}$. On the Moon, gravity is weaker; it only gives an acceleration of free fall of about $1.6\,\mathrm{m\,s^{-2}}$. So g indicates the strength of the gravitational field at a particular place:

$g =$ gravitational field strength

and

weight = mass × gravitational field strength

(Gravitational field strength has unit $\mathrm{N\,kg^{-1}}$. This unit is equivalent to $\mathrm{m\,s^{-2}}$.)

Extension

SAQ

5 Estimate the mass and weight of each of the following at the surface of the Earth:

   a a kilogram of potatoes

   b this book

   c an average student

   d a mouse

   e a 40-tonne truck.

   (For estimates, use $g = 10\,\mathrm{m\,s^{-2}}$; 1 tonne = 1000 kg.)

Hint

Answer

6 If you drop a stone from the edge of a cliff, its initial velocity $u = 0$, and it falls with acceleration $g = 9.81\,\mathrm{m\,s^{-2}}$. You can calculate the distance s it falls in a given time t using an equation of motion.

   a Copy and complete Table 3.4, which shows how s depends on t.

   b Draw a graph of s against t.

   c Use your graph to find the distance fallen by the stone in 2.5 s.

   d Use your graph to find how long it will take the stone to fall to the bottom of a cliff 40 m high. Check your answer using the equations of motion.

Answer

Time t/s	0	1.0	2.0	3.0	4.0
Displacement s/m	0	4.9			

Table 3.4 For SAQ 6.

7 An egg falls off a table. The floor is 0.8 m from the table-top.

   a Calculate the time taken to reach the ground.

   b Calculate the velocity of impact with the ground.

Hint

Answer

Determining g

One way to measure the acceleration of free fall g would be to try bungee-jumping (Figure 3.8). You would need to carry a stopwatch, and measure the time between jumping from the platform and the moment when the elastic rope begins to slow your fall. If you knew the length of the unstretched rope, you could calculate g.

Figure 3.8 A bungee-jumper falls with initial acceleration g.

There are easier methods for finding g which can be used in the laboratory. We will look at three of these and compare them.

Method 1: Using an electronic timer

In this method, a steel ball-bearing is held by an electromagnet (Figure 3.9). When the current to the magnet is switched off, the ball begins to fall and an electronic timer starts. The ball falls through a trapdoor, and this breaks a circuit to stop the timer. So now we know the time taken for the ball to fall from rest through the distance h between the bottom of the ball and the trapdoor.

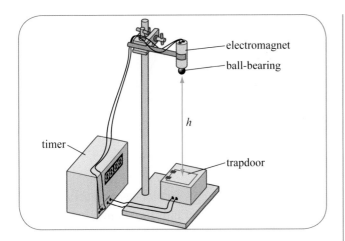

Figure 3.9 The timer records the time for the ball to fall through the distance h.

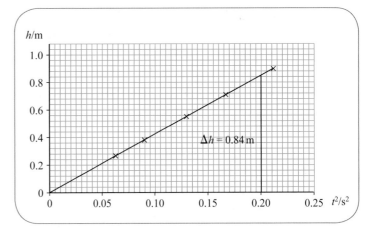

Figure 3.10 The acceleration of free fall can be determined from the gradient.

Here is how we can use one of the equations of motion to find g:

    displacement $s = h$
    time taken $= t$
    initial velocity $u = 0$
    acceleration $a = g$

Substituting in $s = ut + \frac{1}{2}at^2$ gives:

$$h = \frac{1}{2}gt^2$$

and for any values of h and t we can calculate a value for g.

A more satisfactory procedure is to take measurements of t for several different values of h. The height of the ball bearing above the trapdoor is varied systematically, and the time of fall measured several times to calculate an average for each height. Table 3.5 and Figure 3.10 show some typical results. We can deduce g from the gradient of the h against t^2 graph.

h/m	t/s	t^2/s^2
0.27	0.25	0.063
0.39	0.30	0.090
0.56	0.36	0.130
0.70	0.41	0.168
0.90	0.46	0.212

Table 3.5 Data for Figure 3.10. These are mean values.

The equation for a straight line through the origin is:

    $y = mx$

In our experiment we have:

$$\underset{y}{h} = \underset{m}{\tfrac{1}{2}g}\ \underset{x}{t^2}$$

The gradient of the straight line of a graph of h against t^2 is equal to $\frac{g}{2}$. Therefore:

$$\text{gradient} = \frac{g}{2} = \frac{0.84}{0.20} = 4.2$$

$$g = 4.2 \times 2 = 8.4\,\text{m s}^{-2}$$

Sources of uncertainty

The electromagnet may retain some magnetism when it is switched off, and this may tend to slow the ball's fall. Consequently, the time t recorded by the timer may be longer than if the ball were to fall completely freely. From $h = \frac{1}{2}gt^2$, it follows that, if t is too great, the experimental value of g will be too small. This is an example of a *systematic error* – all the results are systematically distorted so that they are too great (or too small) as a consequence of the experimental design.

Measuring the height h is awkward. You can probably only find the value of h to within ± 1 mm at best. So there is a *random error* in the value of h, and this will result in a slight scatter of the points on the graph, and a degree of uncertainty in the final value of g. For more about errors, see the Appendix.

Method 2: Using a ticker-timer

Figure 3.11 shows a weight falling. As it falls, it pulls a tape through a ticker-timer. The spacing of the dots on the tape increases steadily, showing that the weight is accelerating. You can analyse the tape to find the acceleration, as discussed in Chapter 2.

This is not a very satisfactory method of measuring *g*. The main problem arises from friction between the tape and the ticker-timer. This slows the fall of the weight and so its acceleration is less than *g*. (This is another example of a systematic error.)

The effect of friction is less of a problem for a large weight, which falls more freely. If measurements are made for increasing weights, the value of acceleration gets closer and closer to the true value of *g*.

Method 3: Using a light gate

Figure 3.12 shows how a weight can be attached to a card 'interrupt'. The card is designed to break the light beam twice as the weight falls. The computer can then calculate the velocity of the weight twice as it falls, and hence find its acceleration.

$$\text{initial velocity } u = \frac{x}{t_2 - t_1}$$

$$\text{final velocity } v = \frac{x}{t_4 - t_3}$$

Therefore

$$\text{acceleration } a = \frac{v - u}{t_3 - t_1}$$

The weight can be dropped from different heights above the light gate. This allows you to find out whether its acceleration is the same at different points in its fall. This is an advantage over Method 1, which can only measure the acceleration from a stationary start.

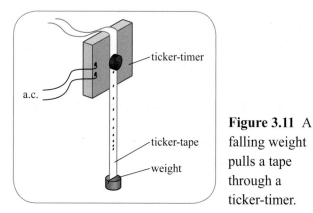

Figure 3.11 A falling weight pulls a tape through a ticker-timer.

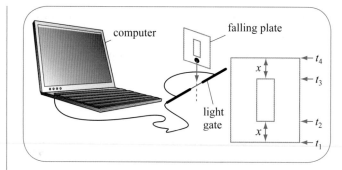

Figure 3.12 The weight accelerates as it falls. The upper section of the card falls more quickly through the light gate.

Worked example 3

To get a rough value for *g*, a student dropped a stone from the top of a cliff. A second student timed the stone's fall using a stopwatch. Here are their results:

estimated height of cliff = 30 m

time of fall = 2.6 s

Use the results to estimate a value for *g*.

Step 1 Calculate the average speed of the stone:

$$\text{average speed of stone during fall} = \frac{30}{2.6}$$

$$= 11.5 \, \text{m s}^{-1}$$

Step 2 Find the values of *v* and *u*:

final speed $v = 2 \times 11.5 \, \text{m s}^{-1} = 23.0 \, \text{m s}^{-1}$

initial speed $u = 0 \, \text{m s}^{-1}$

Step 3 Substitute these values into the equation for acceleration:

$$a = \frac{v - u}{t} = \frac{23.0}{2.6} = 8.8 \, \text{m s}^{-2}$$

Note that you can reach the same result more directly using $s = ut + \frac{1}{2}at^2$, but you may find it easier to follow what is going on using the method given here. (Guidance)

We should briefly consider why the answer is *less* than the expected value of $g = 9.81 \, \text{m s}^{-2}$. It might be that the cliff was higher than the student's estimate. The timer may not have been accurate in switching the stopwatch on and off. There will have been air resistance which slowed the stone's fall.

SAQ

8 A steel ball falls from rest through a height of 2.10 m. An electronic timer records a time of 0.67 s for the fall.

   a Calculate the average acceleration of the ball as it falls.

   b Suggest reasons why the answer is not exactly 9.81 m s^{-2}.

9 In an experiment to determine the acceleration due to gravity, a ball was timed electronically as it fell from rest through a height h. The times t shown in Table 3.6 were obtained.

   a Plot a graph of h against t^2.

   b From the graph, determine the acceleration of free fall, g.   **Hint**

   c Comment on your answer.   **Answer**

Height h/m	0.70	1.03	1.25	1.60	1.99
Time t/s	0.99	1.13	1.28	1.42	1.60

Table 3.6 For SAQ 9.

10 In Chapter 1, we looked at how to use a motion sensor to measure the speed and position of a moving object. Suggest how a motion sensor could be used to determine g.   **Answer**

Mass and inertia

It took a long time for scientists to develop correct ideas about forces and motion. We will start by thinking about some wrong ideas, and then consider why Galileo, Newton and others decided new ideas were needed.

Observations and ideas

Here are some observations to think about.

● The large tree trunk shown in Figure 3.13 is being dragged from a forest in Sri Lanka. The elephant provides the force needed to pull it along. If the elephant stops pulling, the tree trunk will stop moving.

Figure 3.13 An elephant provides the force needed to drag this tree from the forest.

● A horse is pulling a cart. If the horse stops pulling, the cart soon stops.

● You are riding a bicycle. If you stop pedalling, the bicycle will come to a halt.

● You are driving along the road. You must keep your foot on the accelerator pedal, otherwise the car will not keep moving.

● You are playing snooker. Your cue pushes the white ball across the table. It gradually stops.

In each of these cases, there is a force which makes something move – the pull of the elephant or the horse, your push on the bicycle pedals, the force of the car engine, the push of your snooker cue. Without the force, the moving object comes to a halt. So what conclusion might we draw?

   '*A moving object needs a force to keep it moving.*'

This might seem a sensible conclusion to draw, but it is wrong. We have not thought about *all* the forces involved. The missing force is friction.

In each example above, friction (or air resistance) makes the object slow down and stop when there is no force pushing or pulling it forwards. For example, if you stop pedalling your cycle, air resistance will slow you down. There is also friction at the axles of the wheels and this too will slow you down. If you could lubricate your axles and cycle in a vacuum, you could travel along at a steady speed for ever, without pedalling!

The game of bowls provides an interesting example. On a bowling green, it takes a while for the wooden ball to roll to a halt, because there is little friction between the wood and the grass. In the past people imagined that the force of the thrower's hand travelled along with the wooden ball, gradually weakening, until the ball stopped. We no longer imagine that we can push a ball when we are not touching it.

From Galileo to Einstein

In the 17th century, astronomers began to use telescopes to observe the heavens. They saw that objects such as the planets could move freely through space. They weren't attached to crystal spheres, as had previously been suggested. They simply kept on moving, without anything providing a force to push them. Galileo came to the conclusion that this was the natural motion of objects.

- An object at rest will stay at rest, unless a force causes it to start moving.
- A moving object will continue to move at a steady speed in a straight line, unless a force acts on it.

So objects move with a constant velocity, unless a force acts on them. (Being stationary is simply a particular case of this, where the velocity is zero.) Nowadays it is much easier to appreciate this law of motion, because we have more experience of objects moving with little or no friction – roller-skates with low-friction bearings, ice skates, and spacecraft in empty space. In Galileo's day, people's everyday experience was of dragging things along the ground, or pulling things on carts with high-friction axles. Before Galileo, the orthodox scientific idea was that a force must act all the time to keep an object moving – this had been handed down from the time of the ancient Greek philosopher Aristotle. So it was a great achievement when scientists were able to develop a picture of a world without friction.

Galileo devised several experiments to illustrate his ideas. In one (Figure 3.14) a ball rolls down a ramp, speeding up as it goes. It then runs up a second, hinged ramp. If there is no friction at all, it reaches the same height as it started from. Now the second ramp is lowered to a less steep angle. The ball again reaches the same height as before, but now it has travelled further horizontally.

Figure 3.14 Galileo's demonstration that a ball accelerates as it rolls down a ramp.

What happens if the ramp is lowered to a horizontal position? Galileo suggested that it will roll for ever, because it will not stop until it reaches the height from which it started.

If Galileo had lived another three centuries, he would have witnessed another revolution in our understanding of forces and motion. Albert Einstein, in his theories of Relativity, showed that Newton's laws could be relied on when objects are moving slowly, but they need to be modified when objects are moving fast.

What do we mean by 'moving fast'? In Einstein's Special Theory of Relativity, the speed of light c is a sort of universal 'speed limit'. This comes about because, as an object moves faster, its mass increases. This makes it harder to accelerate. (Think of the equation $F=ma$. If the mass m has increased, a given force F will produce a smaller acceleration a.) Why does mass increase with speed? You should know that an object's kinetic energy increases as it moves faster. Einstein said that an object's mass was an indication of its total energy; hence, if its kinetic energy increases, its mass also increases.

continued

Experiments have confirmed Einstein's predictions. For example, in particle accelerators that produce beams of high-energy particles (such as electrons and protons), we cannot simply apply $F = ma$. We have to use a version of the equation which takes account of the particles' increasing mass. A particle moving at $0.9c$ (90% of the speed of light) has a mass which is 2.3 times its mass when it is stationary. At $0.99c$, its mass is 7.1 times its stationary mass.

Experiment shows that, as particles are pushed closer and closer to the speed of light, their mass increases more and more, making it even harder to accelerate them, and so on. They can never quite reach this limit.

An object moving at a speed which is an appreciable fraction of the speed of light is described as *relativistic*. For relativistic motion, Special Relativity suggests that equations such as $F = ma$ must be modified.

The idea of inertia

The tendency of a moving object to carry on moving is sometimes known as **inertia**.

- An object with a large mass is difficult to stop moving – think about catching a cricket ball, compared with a tennis ball.
- Similarly, a stationary object with a large mass is difficult to start moving – think about pushing a car to get it started.
- It is difficult to make a massive object change direction – think about the way a fully laden supermarket trolley tries to keep moving in a straight line.

All of these examples suggest another way to think of an object's mass; it is a measure of its inertia – how difficult it is to change the object's motion. Uniform motion is the natural state of motion of an object. Here, **uniform motion** means 'moving with constant velocity or moving at a steady speed in a straight line'.

Now we can summarise these findings as *Newton's first law of motion*.

An object will remain at rest or in a state of uniform motion unless it is acted on by an external force.

In fact, this is already contained in the simple equation we have been using to calculate acceleration, $F = ma$. If no net force acts on an object ($F = 0$), it will not accelerate ($a = 0$). The object will either remain stationary or it will continue to travel at a constant velocity.

If we rewrite the equation as $a = \dfrac{F}{m}$, we can see that, the greater the mass m, the smaller the acceleration a produced by a force F.

SAQ

11 Use the idea of inertia to explain why some large cars have power-assisted brakes.

Answer

12 A car crashes head-on into a brick wall. Use the idea of inertia to explain why the driver is more likely to come out through the windscreen if he or she is not wearing a seat belt.

Answer

Top speed

The vehicle shown in Figure 3.15 is capable of speeds as high as 760 mph, greater than the speed of sound. Its streamlined shape is designed to cut down air resistance and its jet engines provide a strong forward force to accelerate it up to top speed. All vehicles have a top speed. But why can't they go any faster? Why can't a car driver keep pressing on the accelerator pedal, and simply go faster and faster?

To answer this, we have to think about the two forces mentioned above: air resistance and the forward thrust (force) of the engine. The vehicle will accelerate so long as the thrust is greater than the air resistance. When the two forces are equal, the net force on the vehicle is zero, and the vehicle moves at a steady velocity.

Figure 3.15 The Thrust SSC rocket car broke the world land-speed record in 1997. It achieved a top speed of 763 mph (just over $340\,\mathrm{m\,s^{-1}}$) over a distance of 1 mile (1.6 km).

Balanced and unbalanced forces

If an object has two or more forces acting on it, we have to consider whether or not they are 'balanced' (Figure 3.16). Forces on an object are balanced when the *net force* on the object is zero. The object will either remain at rest or have a constant velocity.

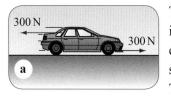

Two equal forces acting in opposite directions cancel each other out. We say they are *balanced*. The car will continue to move at a steady velocity in a straight line.

resultant force = 0 N

These two forces are unequal, so they do not cancel out. They are *unbalanced*. The car will accelerate.

resultant force
= 400 N – 300 N
= 100 N to the *right*

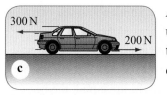

Again the forces are unbalanced. This time, the car will slow down or decelerate.

resultant force
= 200 N – 300 N
= –100 N to the *left*

Figure 3.16 Balanced and unbalanced forces.

We can calculate the **resultant force** by adding up two (or more) forces which act in the same straight line. We must take account of the direction of each force. In the examples above, forces to the right are positive and forces to the left are negative.

When a car travels slowly, it encounters little air resistance. However, the faster it goes, the more air it has to push out of the way each second, and so the greater the air resistance. Eventually the backward force of air resistance equals the forward force provided between the tyres and the road, and the forces on the car are balanced. It can go no faster – it has reached top speed.

Free fall

Skydivers (Figure 3.17) are rather like cars – at first, they accelerate freely. At the start of the fall, the only force acting on the diver is his or her weight. The acceleration of the diver at the start must therefore be *g*. Then increasing air resistance opposes their fall and their acceleration decreases. Eventually they reach a maximum velocity, known as the **terminal velocity**. At the terminal velocity the air resistance is equal to the weight. The terminal velocity is approximately 120 miles per hour (about $50\,\mathrm{m\,s^{-1}}$), but it depends on the diver's weight and orientation. Head-first is fastest.

Figure 3.17 A skydiver falling freely.

The idea of a parachute is to greatly increase the air resistance. Then terminal velocity is reduced, and the parachutist can land safely. Figure 3.18 shows how a parachutist's velocity might change during descent.

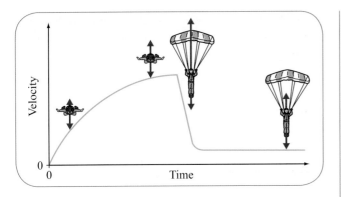

Figure 3.18 The velocity of a parachutist varies during a descent.

Terminal velocity depends on the weight and surface area of the object. For insects, air resistance is much more important than for a human being and so their terminal velocity is quite low. Insects can be swept up several kilometres into the atmosphere by rising air streams. Later, they fall back to Earth uninjured. It is said that mice can survive a fall from a high building for the same reason.

Moving through fluids

Air resistance is just one example of the resistive forces which objects experience when they move through a fluid – a liquid or a gas. If you have ever run down the beach and into the sea, or tried to wade quickly through the water of a swimming pool, you will have experienced the force of drag. The deeper the water gets, the more it resists your movement and the harder you have to work to make progress through it. In deep water, it is easier to swim than to wade.

You can observe the effect of drag on a falling object if you drop a key or a coin into the deep end of a swimming pool. For the first few centimetres, it speeds up, but for the remainder of its fall, it has a steady speed. (If it fell through the same distance in air, it would accelerate all the way.) The drag of water means that the falling object reaches its terminal velocity very soon after it is released. Compare this with a skydiver, who has to fall hundreds of metres before reaching terminal velocity.

Moving through air

We rarely experience drag in air. This is because air is much less dense than water; its density (see Chapter 5) is roughly $\frac{1}{800}$th that of water. At typical walking speed, we do not notice the effects of drag. However, if you want to move faster, they can be important. Racing cyclists, like the one shown in Figure 3.19, wear tight-fitting clothing and streamlined helmets. Some are even said to shave their legs so that they cause less disturbance to the air as they move through it.

Other athletes may take advantage of the drag of air. The runner in Figure 3.20 is undergoing resistance training. The parachute provides a backward force against which his muscles must work. This should help to develop his muscles.

Figure 3.19 A racing cyclist adopts a posture which helps to reduce drag. Clothing, helmet and even the cycle itself are designed to allow them to go as fast as possible.

Figure 3.20 A runner making use of air resistance to build up his muscles.

continued

For small creatures, such as tiny insects, air resistance is much more important. For an insect like an aphid (a greenfly), flying through the air is hard work, much like wading through water is for us. This is because an aphid is very light and has a large surface area compared to its volume. The advantage is that, if the aphid should fall towards the ground, its speed never exceeds a few millimetres per second, so it is unlikely to be damaged when it lands. Compare this to what happens if a human falls from a high building – air resistance does little to reduce their speed of impact.

Worked example 4

A car of mass $500\,\text{kg}$ is travelling along a flat road. The forward force provided between the car tyres and the road is $300\,\text{N}$ and the air resistance is $200\,\text{N}$. Calculate the acceleration of the car.

Step 1 Start by drawing a diagram of the car, showing the forces mentioned in the question (Figure 3.21). Calculate the resultant force on the car; the force to the right is taken as positive:

resultant force $= 300 - 200 = 100\,\text{N}$

Step 2 Now use $F = ma$ to calculate the car's acceleration:

$$a = \frac{F}{m} = \frac{100}{500} = 0.20\,\text{m\,s}^{-2}$$

So the car's acceleration is $0.20\,\text{m\,s}^{-2}$.

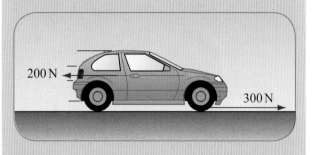

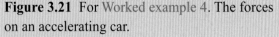

Figure 3.21 For Worked example 4. The forces on an accelerating car.

Worked example 5

The maximum forward force a car can provide is $500\,\text{N}$. The air resistance F which the car experiences depends on its speed according to $F = 0.2v^2$, where v is the speed in $\text{m\,s}^{-1}$. Determine the top speed of the car.

Step 1 From the equation $F = 0.2v^2$, you can see that the air resistance increases as the car goes faster. Top speed is reached when the forward force equals the air resistance. So, at top speed:

$500 = 0.2v^2$

Step 2 Rearranging gives:

$$v^2 = \frac{500}{0.2} = 2500$$

$$v = 50\,\text{m\,s}^{-1}$$

So the car's top speed is $50\,\text{m\,s}^{-1}$ (this is about $180\,\text{km\,h}^{-1}$).

SAQ

13 If you drop a large stone and a small stone from the top of a tall building, which one will reach the ground first? Explain your answer. 〔Answer〕

14 In a race, downhill skiers want to travel as quickly as possible. They are always looking for ways to increase their top speed. Explain how they might do this. Think about:
   a their skis   d the slope.
   b their clothing
   c their muscles   〔Answer〕

15 Skydivers jump from a plane at intervals of a few seconds. If two divers wish to join up as they fall, the second must catch up with the first.
   a If one diver is more massive than the other, which should jump first? Use the idea of forces and terminal velocity to explain your answer.
   b If both divers are equally massive, suggest what the second might do to catch up with the first. 〔Answer〕

Summary

Glossary

- Net force F, mass m and acceleration a are related by the equation $F=ma$. This is a form of Newton's second law of motion.

- The acceleration produced by a force is in the same direction as the force. Where there are two or more forces, we must determine the resultant force.

- A newton (N) is the force required to give a mass of 1 kg an acceleration of $1\,m\,s^{-2}$ in the direction of the force.

- The greater the mass of an object, the more it resists changes in its motion. Mass is a measure of the object's inertia.

- The centre of gravity of an object is a point where its entire weight appears to act.

- The weight of an object is a result of the pull of gravity on it:
  weight = mass × acceleration of free fall   ($W=mg$)
  weight = mass × gravitational field strength

- An object falling freely under gravity has a constant acceleration provided the gravitational field strength is constant. However, fluid resistance (such as air resistance) reduces its acceleration. Terminal velocity is reached when the fluid resistance is equal to the weight of the object.

- According to the Special Theory of Relativity, the mass of an object increases as it approaches the speed of light, so that we can no longer use the equation $F=ma$.

Questions

1 The diagram shows a gannet hovering above a water surface.

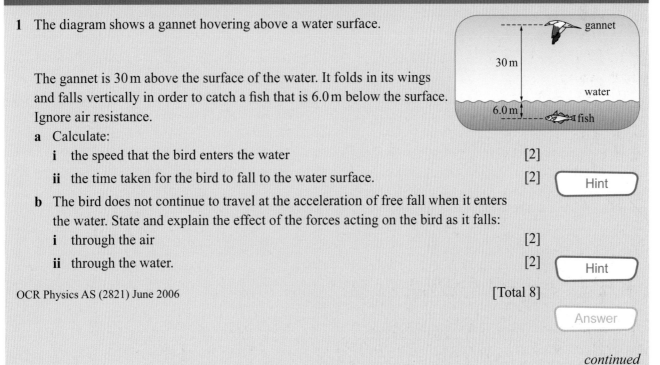

The gannet is 30 m above the surface of the water. It folds in its wings and falls vertically in order to catch a fish that is 6.0 m below the surface. Ignore air resistance.

a Calculate:

   i   the speed that the bird enters the water   [2]

   ii the time taken for the bird to fall to the water surface.   [2]   Hint

b The bird does not continue to travel at the acceleration of free fall when it enters the water. State and explain the effect of the forces acting on the bird as it falls:

   i   through the air   [2]

   ii through the water.   [2]   Hint

OCR Physics AS (2821) June 2006   [Total 8]

Answer

continued

2 **a** Define *acceleration*. [2]

   b An aircraft of total mass 1.5×10^5 kg accelerates, at maximum thrust from the engines, from rest along a runway for 25 s before reaching the required speed for take-off of 65 m s^{-1}.

   Assume that the acceleration of the aircraft is constant.

   Calculate:

   i   the acceleration of the aircraft [3]

   ii the force acting on the aircraft to produce this acceleration [2]

   iii the distance travelled by the aircraft in this time. [2]

   c The length of runways at some airports is less than the required distance for take-off by this aircraft calculated in **b iii**.

   State and explain <u>one</u> method that could be adopted for this aircraft so that it could reach the required take-off speed on shorter runways. [2]

OCR Physics AS (2821) June 2003 [Total 11]

Hint

Answer

3 **a** An object falls vertically through a large distance from rest in air. Describe and explain the motion of the object as it descends in terms of the forces that act and its resulting acceleration. [6]

   b Explain how a free-fall diver can increase the speed at which she descends through the air. [2]

OCR Physics AS (2821) May 2002 [Total 8]

Hint

Answer

Chapter 4

Working with vectors

e-Learning

Objectives

Magnitude and direction

In Chapter 1, we discussed the distinction between distance and displacement.

- *Distance* has magnitude (size) only. It is a scalar quantity.
- *Displacement* has both magnitude and direction. It is a vector quantity.

You should recall that a scalar quantity has magnitude only. A vector quantity has both magnitude and direction. We also looked at another example of a scalar/vector pair: speed and velocity. To define the velocity of a moving object, you have to say how fast it is moving and the direction it is moving in.

Here are some more examples of scalar and vector quantities; vector quantities are usually represented by arrows on diagrams.

- Examples of scalar quantities: distance, speed, mass, energy and temperature.
- Examples of vector quantities: displacement, velocity, acceleration and force (or weight).

Combining displacements

The walkers shown in Figure 4.1 are crossing difficult ground. They navigate from one prominent point to the next, travelling in a series of straight lines. From the map, they can work out the distance that they travel and their displacement from their starting point.

distance travelled = 25 km

(Lay thread along route on map; measure thread against map scale.)

displacement = 15 km north-east

(Join starting and finishing points with straight line; measure line against scale.)

A map is a scale drawing. You can find your displacement by measuring the map. But how can you *calculate* your displacement? You need to use ideas from geometry and trigonometry. Worked example 1 and Worked example 2 show how.

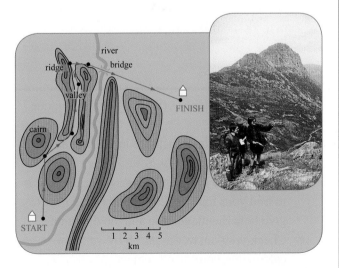

Figure 4.1 In rough terrain, walkers head straight for a prominent landmark.

Worked example 1

A spider runs along two sides of a table (Figure 4.2). Calculate its final displacement.

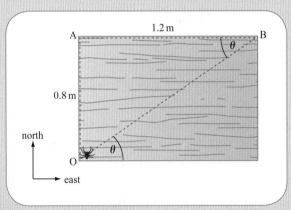

Figure 4.2 The spider runs a distance of 2.0 m, but what is its displacement?

Step 1 Because the two sections of the spider's run (OA and AB) are at right angles, we can *add* the two displacements using Pythagoras's theorem:

$$OB^2 = OA^2 + AB^2$$

$$= 0.8^2 + 1.2^2 = 2.08$$

$$OB = \sqrt{2.08} = 1.44\,\text{m} \approx 1.4\,\text{m}$$

continued

Step 2 Displacement is a vector. We have found the *magnitude* of this vector, but now we have to find its direction. The angle θ is given by:

$$\tan\theta = \frac{\text{opp}}{\text{adj}} = \frac{0.8}{1.2}$$

$$= 0.667$$

$$\theta = \tan^{-1}(0.667)$$

$$= 33.7° \approx 34°$$

So the spider's displacement is 1.4 m at an angle of 34° north of east.

Worked example 2

An aircraft flies 30 km due east and then 50 km north-east (Figure 4.3). Calculate the final displacement of the aircraft.

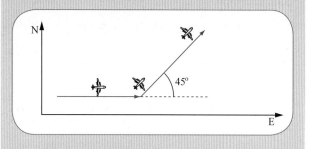

Figure 4.3 What is the aircraft's final displacement?

Here, the two displacements are not at 90° to one another, so we can't use Pythagoras's theorem. We can solve this problem by making a scale drawing, and measuring the final displacement. (This is often an adequate technique. However, you could solve the same problem using trigonometry.)

Step 1 Choose a suitable scale. Your diagram should be reasonably large; in this case, a scale of 1 cm to represent 5 km is reasonable.

Step 2 Draw a line to represent the first vector. North is at the top of the page. The line is 6 cm long, towards the east (right).

continued

Step 3 Draw a line to represent the second vector, starting at the end of the first vector. The line is 10 cm long, and at an angle of 45° (Figure 4.4).

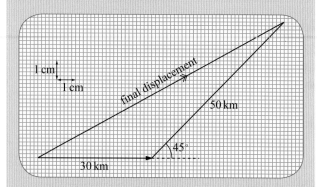

Figure 4.4 Scale drawing for Worked example 2. Using graph paper can help you to show the vectors in the correct directions.

Step 4 To find the final displacement, join the start to the finish. You have created a **vector triangle**. Measure this displacement vector, and use the scale to convert back to kilometres:

length of vector = 14.8 cm

final displacement = $14.8 \times 5 = 74$ km

Step 5 Measure the angle of the final displacement vector:

angle = 28° N of E

Therefore the aircraft's final displacement is 74 km at 28° N of E.

SAQ

1 You walk 3.0 km due north, and then 4.0 km due east.

  a Calculate the total distance in km you have travelled.

  b Make a scale drawing of your walk, and use it to find your final displacement. Remember to give both the magnitude and the direction.

  c Check your answer to part **b** by calculating your displacement.

Answer

Combining velocities

Imagine that you are attempting to swim across a river. You want to swim directly across to the opposite bank, but the current moves you sideways at the same time as you are swimming forwards. The outcome is that you will end up on the opposite bank, but downstream of your intended landing point. In effect, you have two velocities:

- the velocity due to your swimming, which is directed straight across the river
- the velocity due to the current, which is directed downstream, at right angles to your swimming velocity.

These combine to give a resultant (or net) velocity, which will be diagonally downstream. When any two or more vectors are added together, their combined effect is known as the **resultant** of the vectors.

In order to swim directly across the river, you would have to aim upstream. Then your resultant velocity could be directly across the river.

Worked example 3

An aircraft is flying due north with a velocity of $200\,\mathrm{m\,s^{-1}}$. A side wind of velocity $50\,\mathrm{m\,s^{-1}}$ is blowing due east. What is the aircraft's resultant velocity (give the magnitude and direction)?

Here, the two velocities are at 90°. A sketch diagram and Pythagoras's theorem will suffice to solve the problem.

Step 1 Draw a sketch of the situation – this is shown in Figure 4.5a.

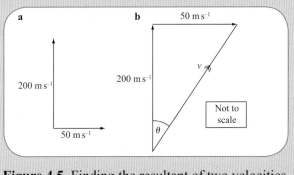

Figure 4.5 Finding the resultant of two velocities – for Worked example 3.

continued

Step 2 Now sketch a vector triangle. Remember that the second vector starts where the first one ends. This is shown in Figure 4.5b.

Step 3 Join the start and end points to complete the triangle.

Step 4 Calculate the magnitude of the resultant vector v (the hypotenuse of the right-angled triangle).

$$v^2 = 200^2 + 50^2 = 40\,000 + 2500 = 42\,500$$

$$v = \sqrt{42\,500} = 206\,\mathrm{m\,s^{-1}}$$

Step 5 Calculate the angle θ:

$$\tan\theta = \frac{50}{200} = 0.25$$

$$\theta = \tan^{-1}0.25 = 14°$$

So the aircraft's resultant velocity is $206\,\mathrm{m\,s^{-1}}$ at 14° east of north.

SAQ

2   A swimmer can swim at $2.0\,\mathrm{m\,s^{-1}}$ in still water. She aims to swim directly across a river which is flowing at $0.80\,\mathrm{m\,s^{-1}}$. Calculate her resultant velocity. (You must give both the magnitude and the direction.)

Hint

Answer

Combining forces

There are several forces acting on the car (Figure 4.6) as it struggles up the steep hill. They are:

- its weight $W\,(=mg)$
- the contact force N of the road (its normal reaction)
- air resistance R
- the forward force F caused by friction between the car tyres and the road.

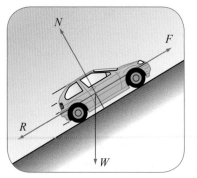

Figure 4.6 Four forces act on this car as it moves uphill.

If we knew the magnitude and direction of each of these forces, we could work out their combined effect on the car. Will it accelerate up the hill? Or will it slide backwards down the hill? The combined effect of several forces is known as the *resultant force*. To see how to work out the resultant of two or more forces, we will start with a relatively simple example.

Two forces in a straight line

We have seen some examples earlier of two forces acting in a straight line. For example, a falling tennis ball may be acted on by two forces: its weight mg, downwards, and air resistance R, upwards (Figure 4.7). The resultant force is then:

resultant force $= mg - R = 1.0 - 0.2 = 0.8\,\text{N}$

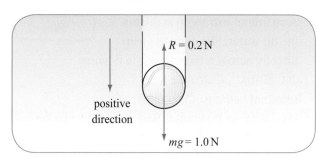

Figure 4.7 Two forces on a falling tennis ball.

When adding two or more forces which act in a straight line, we have to take account of their directions. A force may be positive or negative; we adopt a *sign convention* to help us decide which is which.

If you apply a sign convention correctly, the sign of your final answer will tell you the direction of the resultant force (and hence acceleration).

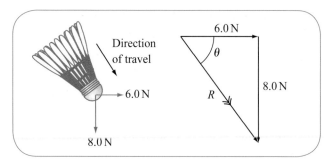

Figure 4.8 Two forces act on this shuttlecock as it travels through the air; the vector triangle shows how to find the resultant force.

Two forces at right angles

Figure 4.8 shows a shuttlecock falling on a windy day. There are two forces acting on the shuttlecock: weight vertically downwards, and the horizontal push of the wind. (It helps if you draw the force arrows of different lengths, to show which force is greater.) We must add these two forces together to find the resultant force acting on the shuttlecock.

We add the forces by drawing two arrows, end-to-end, as shown on the right of Figure 4.8.

- First, a horizontal arrow is drawn to represent the 6.0 N push of the wind.
- Next, starting from the *end* of this arrow, we draw a second arrow, downwards, representing the weight of 8.0 N.
- Now we draw a line from the start of the first arrow to the end of the second arrow. This arrow represents the resultant force R, in both magnitude and direction.

The arrows are added by drawing them end-to-end; the end of the first arrow is the start of the second arrow. Compare this with the way in which the two displacements of the aircraft in Figure 4.4 were added together.

Now we can find the resultant force either by scale drawing, or by calculation. In this case, we have a 3–4–5 right-angled triangle, so calculation is simple:

$$R^2 = 6.0^2 + 8.0^2 = 36 + 64 = 100$$

$$R = 10\,\text{N}$$

$$\tan \theta = \frac{\text{opp}}{\text{adj}} = \frac{8.0}{6.0} = \frac{4}{3}$$

$$\theta = \tan^{-1}\frac{4}{3} = 53°$$

So the resultant force is 10 N, at an angle of 53° below the horizontal. This is a reasonable answer; the weight is pulling the shuttlecock downwards and the wind is pushing it to the right. The angle is greater than 45° because the downward force is greater than the horizontal force.

Three or more forces

The spider shown in Figure 4.9 is hanging by a thread. It is blown sideways by the wind. The diagram shows the three forces acting on it:

- weight acting downwards
- the tension in the thread along the thread
- the push of the wind.

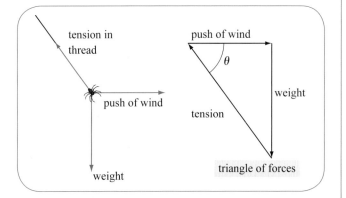

Figure 4.9 Blowing in the wind – this spider is hanging in equilibrium.

The diagram also shows how these can be added together. In this case, we arrive at an interesting result. Arrows are drawn to represent each of the three forces, end-to-end. The end of the third arrow coincides with the start of the first arrow, so the three arrows form a closed triangle. This tells us that the resultant force R on the spider is zero, that is $R=0$. The closed triangle in Figure 4.9 is known as a **triangle of forces**.

So there is no resultant force. The forces on the spider balance each other out, and we say that the spider is in **equilibrium**. If the wind blew a little harder, there would be an unbalanced force on the spider, and it would move off to the right.

We can use this idea in two ways.

- If we work out the resultant force on an object, and find that it is zero, this tells us that the object is in equilibrium.

- If we know that an object is in equilibrium, we know that the forces on it must add up to zero. We can use this to work out the values of one or more unknown forces.

Vector addition

The process of adding up forces by drawing arrows end-to-end is an example of **vector addition**. We can use the same technique for adding up any other vector quantities – displacements, for example (page 43).

Adding two forces together gives a vector triangle, like the one in Figure 4.8. Adding more than two forces gives a vector polygon, like the one in Figure 4.10. Remember: the vectors are always drawn end-to-end, so that the end of one is the starting point of the next; the resultant is found by joining the starting point of the first vector to the end of the last one.

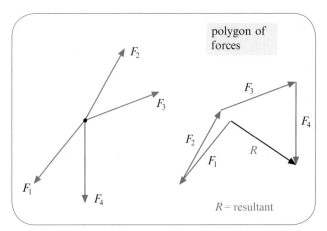

Figure 4.10 Adding four vectors gives a vector polygon. Note that the resultant is the same no matter what order we add the forces in.

Extension —————————————————————

SAQ

3 A parachutist weighs 1000 N. When she opens her parachute, it pulls upwards on her with a force of 2000 N.

   a Draw a diagram to show the forces acting on the parachutist.

   b Calculate the resultant force acting on her.

   c What effect will this force have on her?

Hint

Answer

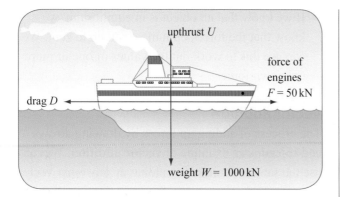

Figure 4.11 For SAQ 4. The force D is the frictional drag of the water on the boat. Like air resistance, drag is always in the opposite direction to the object's motion.

4 The ship shown in Figure 4.11 is travelling at a constant velocity.
  a Is the ship in equilibrium (in other words, is the resultant force on the ship equal to zero)? How do you know?
  b What is the upthrust U of the water?
  c What is the drag D of the water?

  [Answer]

5 A stone is dropped into a fast-flowing stream. It does not fall vertically, because of the sideways push of the water (Figure 4.12).

  [Hint]

  a Calculate the resultant force on the stone.
  b Is the stone in equilibrium?

  [Answer]

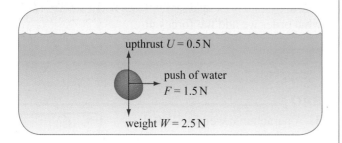

Figure 4.12 For SAQ 5.

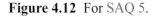

Components of vectors

Look back to Figure 4.9. The spider is in equilibrium, even though three forces are acting on it. We can think of the tension in the thread as having two effects:

● it is pulling upwards, to counteract the downward effect of gravity
● it is pulling to the left, to counteract the effect of the wind.

We can say that this force has two effects or **components**: an upwards (vertical) component and a sideways (horizontal) component. It is often useful to split up a vector quantity into components like this.

The components are in two directions at right angles to each other, often horizontal and vertical. The process is called *resolving* the vector. Then we can think about the effects of each component separately; we say that the perpendicular components are *independent* of one another. Because the two components are at 90° to each other, a change in one will have no effect on the other.

Figure 4.13 shows how to resolve a force F into its horizontal and vertical components. These are:

horizontal component of $F = F_x = F\cos\theta$
vertical component of $F = F_y = F\sin\theta$

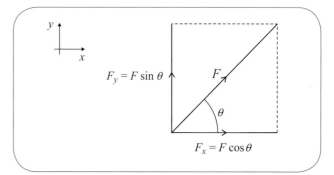

Figure 4.13 Resolving a vector into two components at right angles.

To find the component of any vector (e.g. displacement, velocity, acceleration, etc.) in a particular direction, we can use the following strategy:

Step 1 Find the angle between the vector and the direction of interest: angle $= \theta$

Step 2 Multiply the vector by the cosine of the angle. So the component of an object's velocity v at angle θ to v is equal to $v\cos\theta$, and so on (see Figure 4.14).

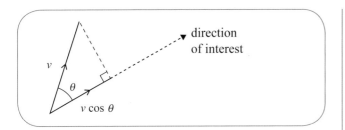

Figure 4.14 The component of the velocity v is $v\cos\theta$.

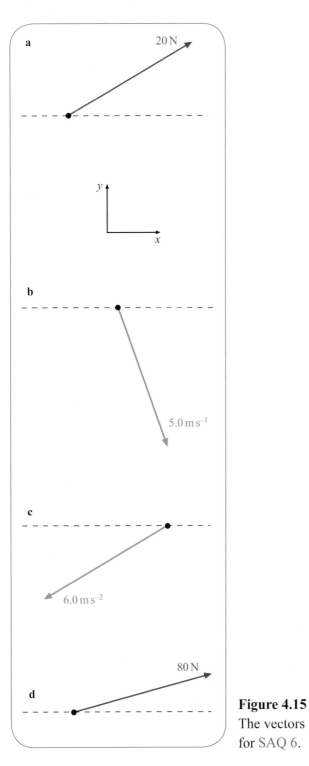

Figure 4.15
The vectors
for SAQ 6.

SAQ

6 Find the x and y components of each of the vectors shown in Figure 4.15. (You will need to use a protractor to measure angles from the diagram.)

> Answer

Making use of components

When the trolley shown in Figure 4.16 is released, it accelerates down the ramp. This happens because of the weight of the trolley. The weight acts vertically downwards. However, it does have a *component* which acts down the slope. By calculating the component of the trolley's weight down the slope, we can determine its acceleration.

Figure 4.17 shows the forces acting on the trolley. To simplify the situation, we will assume there is no friction. The forces are:

● W, the weight of the trolley, which acts vertically downwards
● R, the contact force of the ramp, which acts at right angles to the ramp.

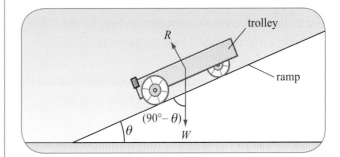

Figure 4.16 These students are investigating the acceleration of a trolley down a sloping ramp.

Figure 4.17 A force diagram for a trolley on a ramp.

49

You can see at once from the diagram that the forces cannot be balanced, since they do not act in the same straight line.

To find the component of W down the slope, we need to know the angle between W and the slope. The slope makes an angle θ with the horizontal, and from the diagram we can see that the angle between the weight and the ramp is $(90° - \theta)$. Using the rule for calculating the component of a vector given on page 48, we have:

component of W down slope $= W \cos (90° - \theta)$
$= W \sin \theta$

(A very helpful mathematical trick is $\cos (90° - \theta) = \sin \theta$; you can see this from Figure 4.17.)

Does the contact force R help to accelerate the trolley down the ramp? To answer this, we must calculate its component down the slope. The angle between R and the slope is $90°$. So:

component of R down slope $= R \cos 90° = 0$

The cosine of $90°$ is zero, and so R has no component down the slope. This shows why it is useful to think in terms of the components of forces; we don't know the value of R, but, since it has no effect down the slope, we can ignore it.

(There's no surprise about this result. The trolley runs down the slope because of the influence of its weight, not because it is pushed by the contact force R.)

Changing the slope

If the students in Figure 4.16 increase the slope of their ramp, the trolley will move down the ramp with greater acceleration. They have increased θ, and so the component of W down the slope will have increased.

Now we can work out the trolley's acceleration. If the trolley's mass is m, its weight is mg. So the force F making it accelerate down the slope is:

$F = mg \sin \theta$

Since from Newton's second law for constant mass we have $a = \dfrac{F}{m}$, the trolley's acceleration a is given by:

$$a = \frac{mg \sin \theta}{m} = g \sin \theta$$

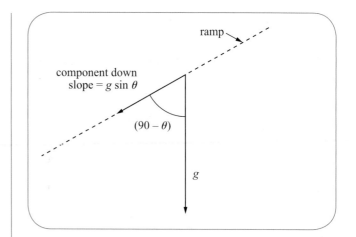

Figure 4.18 Resolving g down the ramp.

In fact, we could have arrived at this result simply by saying that the trolley's acceleration would be the component of g down the slope (Figure 4.18). The steeper the slope, the greater the value of $\sin \theta$, and hence the greater the trolley's acceleration.

SAQ

7 The person in Figure 4.19 is pulling a large box using a rope. Use the idea of components of a force to explain why they are more likely to get the box to move if the rope is horizontal (as in **a**) than if it is sloping upwards (as in **b**).

Answer

Figure 4.19 Why is it easier to move the box with the rope horizontal? See SAQ 7.

8 A crate is sliding down a slope. The weight of the crate is 500 N. The slope makes an angle of $30°$ with the horizontal.

a Draw a diagram to show the situation. Include arrows to represent the forces which act on the crate: the weight and the contact force of the slope.

b Calculate the component of the weight down the slope.

c Explain why the contact force of the slope has no component down the slope.

d What third force might act to oppose the motion? In which direction would it act?

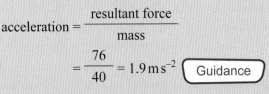

Solving problems by resolving forces

A force can be resolved into two components at right angles to each other; these can then be treated independently of one another. This idea can be used to solve problems, as illustrated in Worked example 4.

Worked example 4

A girl of mass 40 kg slides down a flume. The flume slopes at 30° to the horizontal. The frictional force up the slope is 120 N. Calculate the girl's acceleration down the slope. Take acceleration of free fall g to be 9.81 m s⁻².

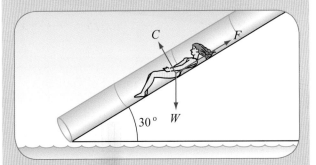

Figure 4.20 For Worked example 4.

Step 1 It is often helpful to draw a diagram showing all the forces acting (Figure 4.20). The forces are:

the girl's weight $W = 40 \times 9.81 = 392\,\text{N}$
the frictional force up the slope $F = 120\,\text{N}$
the contact force C at 90° to the slope

Step 2 We are trying to find the resultant force on the girl which makes her accelerate down the

continued

slope. We resolve the forces down the slope, i.e. we find their components in that direction.

$$\text{component of } W \text{ down slope} = 392 \times \cos 60°$$
$$= 196\,\text{N}$$

$$\text{component of } F \text{ down slope} = -120\,\text{N}$$
(negative because F is directed up the slope)

$$\text{component of } C \text{ down slope} = 0$$
(because it is at 90° to the slope)

It is convenient that C has no component down the slope, since we do not know the value of C.

Step 3 Calculate the resultant force on the girl:

$$\text{resultant force} = 196 - 120 = 76\,\text{N}$$

Step 4 Calculate her acceleration:

$$\text{acceleration} = \frac{\text{resultant force}}{\text{mass}}$$
$$= \frac{76}{40} = 1.9\,\text{m s}^{-2}$$

So the girl's acceleration down the slope is 1.9 m s⁻². We could have arrived at the same result by resolving vertically and horizontally, but that would have led to two simultaneous equations from which we would have had to eliminate the unknown force C. It often helps to resolve forces at 90° to an unknown force.

SAQ

9 A child of mass 40 kg slides down a water-flume. The flume slopes down at 25° to the horizontal. The acceleration of free fall is 9.81 m s⁻². Calculate the child's acceleration down the slope:

a when there is no friction and the only force acting on the child is her weight

b if a frictional force of 80 N acts up the slope.

Projectiles

Figure 4.21 This medieval illustration from 1561 shows how soldiers thought their cannon balls travelled through the air.

The illustration of Figure 4.21 is from a medieval manual. Soldiers were unsure of the paths their artillery shells followed through the air. They imagined that a cannon ball followed an almost straight path until it 'ran out of force', and then it dropped to the ground. This way of thinking derived from the ideas of Aristotle and his followers, discussed in Chapter 3.

It was not unreasonable to think that a cannon ball might behave like this – it's difficult to follow the path of a cannon ball or a bullet. The paths shown in the drawing are similar to the way a shuttlecock or a ball of crumpled paper moves. Air resistance is much more important for a shuttlecock than for a bullet. If we ignore air resistance, the only force which determines the path of a moving ball or bullet is its weight.

An object which is given an initial push, and which then moves freely through the air, is called a **projectile**. Early in the 17th century, Galileo studied the motion of projectiles. He believed that experiments were the correct way to find out about nature, rather than pondering how nature ought to be. Figure 4.22 shows a model of one of his experiments. The ball rolled down the curved slope and flew off the end. Galileo could adjust the metal rings so that the ball passed through them as it curved downwards. Thus he was able to show that the ball followed a curved path, rather than dropping suddenly when it 'ran out of force'.

Figure 4.22 An 18th century model of Galileo's projectile experiment by means of which he showed that a projectile follows a parabolic path. Compare this with the medieval idea shown in Figure 4.21.

Understanding projectiles

We will first consider the simple case of a projectile thrown straight up in the air, so that it moves vertically. Then we will look at projectiles which move horizontally and vertically at the same time.

Up and down

A stone is thrown upwards with an initial velocity of $20\,\text{m s}^{-1}$. Figure 4.23 shows the situation.

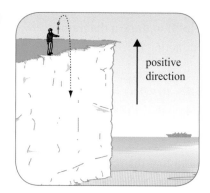

positive direction

Figure 4.23 Standing at the edge of the cliff, you throw a stone vertically upwards. The height of the cliff is 25 m.

It is important to use a consistent sign convention here. We will take upwards as positive, and downwards as negative. So the stone's initial velocity is positive, but its acceleration g is negative. We can solve various problems simply using the equations of motion which we studied in Chapter 2.

How high?

How high will the stone rise above ground level of the cliff?

As the stone rises upwards, it moves more and more slowly – it decelerates, because of the force of gravity. At its highest point, the stone's velocity is zero. So the quantities we know are:

initial velocity = $u = 20\,\text{m}\,\text{s}^{-1}$
final velocity = $v = 0\,\text{m}\,\text{s}^{-1}$
acceleration = $a = -9.81\,\text{m}\,\text{s}^{-2}$
displacement = $s = ?$

The relevant equation of motion is $v^2 = u^2 + 2as$, and substituting values gives:

$$0^2 = 20^2 + 2 \times (-9.81) \times s$$

$$0 = 400 - 19.62s$$

$$s = \frac{400}{19.62} = 20.4\,\text{m} \approx 20\,\text{m}$$

The stone rises 20 m upwards, before it starts to fall again.

How long?

How long will it take from leaving your hand for the stone to fall back to the clifftop?

When the stone returns to the point from which it was thrown, its displacement s is zero. So:

$$s = 0 \quad u = 20\,\text{m}\,\text{s}^{-1} \quad a = -9.81\,\text{m}\,\text{s}^{-2} \quad t = ?$$

Substituting in $s = ut + \frac{1}{2}at^2$ gives:

$$0 = 20t \times \frac{1}{2}(-9.81) \times t^2$$

$$= 20t - 4.905t^2 = (20 - 4.905t) \times t$$

There are two possible solutions to this:
- $t = 0\,\text{s}$, i.e. the stone had zero displacement at the instant it was thrown
- $t = 4.1\,\text{s}$, i.e. the stone returned to zero displacement after 4.1 s, which is the answer we are interested in.

Falling further

The height of the cliff is 25 m. How long will it take the stone to reach the foot of the cliff?

This is similar to the last example, but now the stone's final displacement is 25 m below its starting point. By our sign convention, this is a negative displacement, and $s = -25\,\text{m}$.

SAQ

10 Read the section on 'Understanding projectiles' again on page 52. Calculate the time it will take for the stone to reach the foot of the cliff.

> Answer

11 A ball is fired upwards with an initial velocity of $30\,\text{m}\,\text{s}^{-1}$. Table 4.1 shows how the ball's velocity changes. (Take $g = 9.81\,\text{m}\,\text{s}^{-2}$.)
   a Copy and complete the table.
   b Draw a graph to represent the data in the table.
   c Use your graph to deduce how long the ball took to reach its highest point.
   d Use $v = u + at$ to check your answer to c.

> Answer

Velocity/m s^{-1}	30	20.19				
Time/s	0	1.0	2.0	3.0	4.0	5.0

Table 4.1 For SAQ 11.

A curved trajectory

A multiflash photograph can reveal details of the path, or trajectory, of a projectile. Figure 4.24 shows the trajectories of a projectile – a bouncing ball. Once the ball has left the child's hand and is moving through the air, the only force acting on it is its weight.

The ball has been thrown at an angle to the horizontal. It speeds up as it falls – you can see that the images of the ball become farther and farther apart. At the same time, it moves steadily to the right. You can see this from the even spacing of the images across the picture. The ball's path has a mathematical shape known as a *parabola*. After it bounces, the ball is moving more slowly. It slows down, or decelerates, as it rises – the images get closer and closer together.

Figure 4.24 A bouncing ball is an example of a projectile. This multiflash photograph shows details of its motion which would escape the eye of an observer.

We interpret this picture as follows. The vertical motion of the ball is affected by the force of gravity, that is, its weight. It has a vertical deceleration of magnitude g, which slows it down as it rises, and speeds it up as it falls when the acceleration is g. The ball's horizontal motion is unaffected by gravity. In the absence of air resistance, the ball has a constant horizontal component of velocity. We can treat the ball's vertical and horizontal motions separately, because they are independent of one another. We can use these ideas to calculate details of a projectile's trajectory.

Here is an example to illustrate these ideas. In a toy, a ball-bearing is fired horizontally from a point 0.4 m above the ground. Its initial velocity is 2.5 m s^{-1}. Its position at equal intervals of time have been calculated and are shown in Table 4.2. These results are also shown in Figure 4.25. Study the table and the graph. You should notice the following.

- The horizontal distance increases steadily. This is because the ball's horizontal motion is unaffected by the force of gravity. It travels at a steady velocity horizontally.
- The vertical distances do not show the same pattern. The ball is accelerating downwards. (These figures have been calculated using $g = 9.81$ m s^{-2}.)

You can calculate the distance s fallen using the equation of motion $s = ut + \frac{1}{2}at^2$. (The initial vertical velocity $u = 0$.)

The horizontal distance is calculated using:

horizontal distance $= 2.5 \times t$

The vertical distance is calculated using:

vertical distance $= \frac{1}{2} \times 9.81 \times t^2$

(Extension)

Time/s	Horizontal distance/m	Vertical distance/m
0.00	0.00	0.00
0.04	0.10	0.008
0.08	0.20	0.031
0.12	0.30	0.071
0.16	0.40	0.126
0.20	0.50	0.196
0.24	0.60	0.283
0.28	0.70	0.385

Table 4.2 Data for the example of a moving ball, as shown in Figure 4.25.

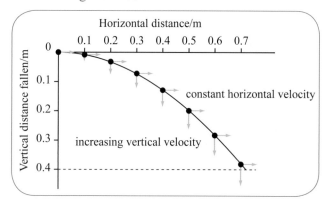

Figure 4.25 This sketch shows the path of the ball projected horizontally. The arrows represent the horizontal and vertical components of its velocity.

Worked example 5

A ball is thrown with an initial velocity of $20\,\mathrm{m\,s^{-1}}$ at an angle of 30° to the horizontal (Figure 4.26). Calculate the horizontal distance travelled by the ball (its **range**).

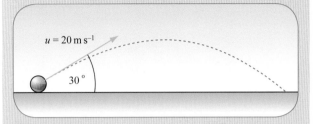

Figure 4.26 Where will the ball land?

Step 1 Split the ball's initial velocity into horizontal and vertical components:

initial velocity $= u = 20\,\mathrm{m\,s^{-1}}$

horizontal component of initial velocity

$= u\cos\theta = 20\times\cos30° = 17.3\,\mathrm{m\,s^{-1}}$

vertical component of initial velocity

$= u\sin\theta = 20\times\sin30° = 10\,\mathrm{m\,s^{-1}}$

Step 2 Consider the ball's vertical motion. How long will it take to return to the ground? In other words, when will its displacement return to zero?

$u = 10\,\mathrm{m\,s^{-1}} \quad a = -9.81\,\mathrm{m\,s^{-2}} \quad s = 0 \quad t = ?$

continued

Using $s = ut + \frac{1}{2}at^2$, we have $0 = 10t - 4.905t^2$, and $t = 0\,\mathrm{s}$ or $t = 2.04\,\mathrm{s}$. So the ball is in the air for $2.04\,\mathrm{s}$.

Step 3 Consider the ball's horizontal motion. How far will it travel horizontally in the 2.04 s before it lands? This is simple to calculate, since it moves with a constant horizontal velocity of $17.3\,\mathrm{m\,s^{-1}}$.

horizontal displacement $s = 17.3 \times 2.04$

$= 35.3\,\mathrm{m}$

Hence the horizontal distance travelled by the ball (its range) is about 35 m.

SAQ

12 The range of a projectile is the horizontal distance it travels before it reaches the ground. The greatest range is achieved if the projectile is thrown at 45° to the horizontal.
A ball is thrown with an initial velocity of $40\,\mathrm{m\,s^{-1}}$. Calculate its greatest possible range when air resistance is considered to be negligible.

Hint

Answer

Summary

Glossary

- Vectors are quantities that must have a direction associated with them.

- Vectors can be added if direction is taken into account. Two vectors can be added by means of a vector triangle. Their resultant can be determined using trigonometry or by scale drawing.

- Vectors can be resolved into components. Components at right angles to one another can be treated independently of one another. For a force F at an angle θ to the x-direction, the components are
  x-direction: $F\cos\theta$
  y-direction: $F\sin\theta$

- For projectiles, the horizontal and vertical components of velocity can be treated independently. In the absence of air resistance, the horizontal component of velocity is constant while the vertical component of velocity downwards increases at a rate of $9.81\,\mathrm{m\,s^{-2}}$.

Questions

1 a i Below is a list of five quantities. Which of these are scalar quantities?

acceleration   energy   force   power   speed   [1]

  ii What is a vector quantity?   [2]

  b The diagram shows the direction of two forces of 16 N and 12 N acting at
an angle of 50° to each other.

Hint

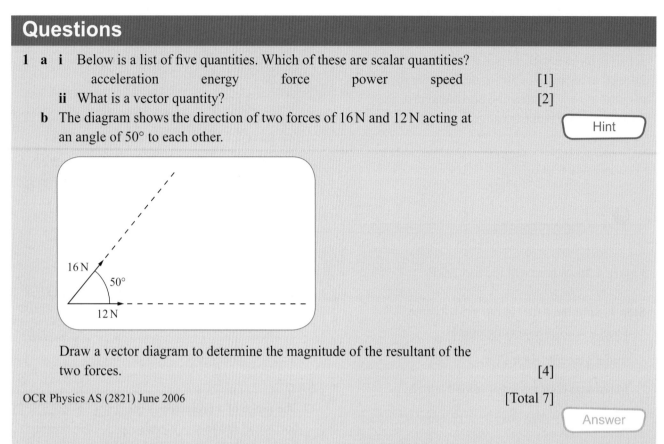

Draw a vector diagram to determine the magnitude of the resultant of the
two forces.   [4]

OCR Physics AS (2821) June 2006   [Total 7]

Answer

2 A girl travels down a pulley–rope system that is set up in an adventure playground. Figure 1 shows the girl
at a point on her run where she has come to rest.

The girl exerts a vertical force of 500 N on the pulley wheel. All the forces acting on the pulley wheel are
shown in Figure 2.

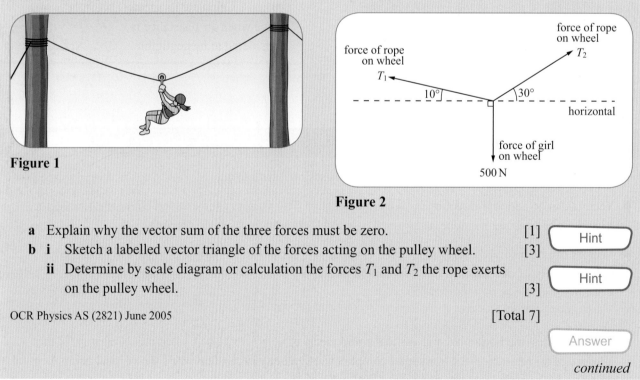

Figure 1

Figure 2

  a Explain why the vector sum of the three forces must be zero.   [1]   Hint

  b i Sketch a labelled vector triangle of the forces acting on the pulley wheel.   [3]

  ii Determine by scale diagram or calculation the forces T_1 and T_2 the rope exerts
on the pulley wheel.   [3]   Hint

OCR Physics AS (2821) June 2005   [Total 7]

Answer

continued

3 Figure 1 shows a boy on a sledge travelling down a slope. The boy and sledge have a total mass of 60 kg and are travelling at a constant speed. The angle of the slope to the horizontal is 35°. All the forces acting on the boy and sledge are shown on Figure 1 and in a force diagram in Figure 2.

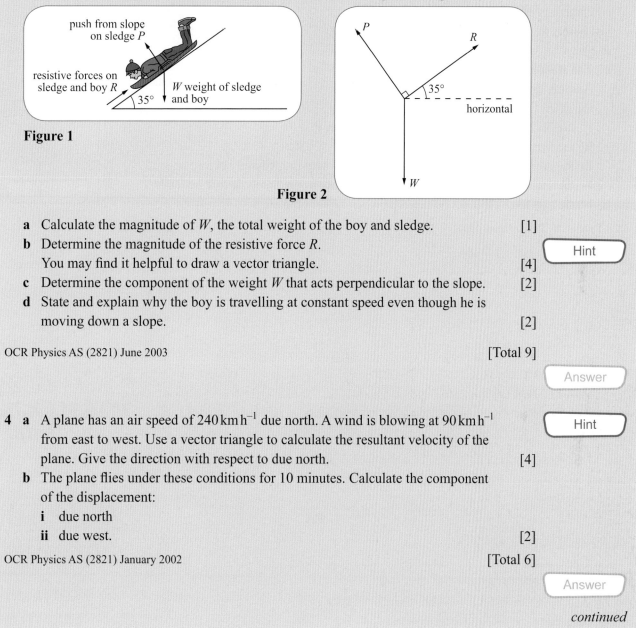

Figure 1

Figure 2

    a Calculate the magnitude of W, the total weight of the boy and sledge. [1]

    b Determine the magnitude of the resistive force R.
       You may find it helpful to draw a vector triangle. [4]

    c Determine the component of the weight W that acts perpendicular to the slope. [2]

    d State and explain why the boy is travelling at constant speed even though he is moving down a slope. [2]

OCR Physics AS (2821) June 2003   [Total 9]

Hint

Answer

4 **a** A plane has an air speed of 240 km h^{-1} due north. A wind is blowing at 90 km h^{-1} from east to west. Use a vector triangle to calculate the resultant velocity of the plane. Give the direction with respect to due north. [4]

    b The plane flies under these conditions for 10 minutes. Calculate the component of the displacement:

       i due north

      ii due west. [2]

OCR Physics AS (2821) January 2002   [Total 6]

Hint

Answer

continued

5   A ski jumper skis down a runway and projects
    himself into the air, landing on the ground a short
    time later. The mass of the ski jumper and his
    equipment is 80 kg. The diagram shows the skier
    just before he leaves the runway where his velocity
    is 20 m s⁻¹ in a horizontal direction.

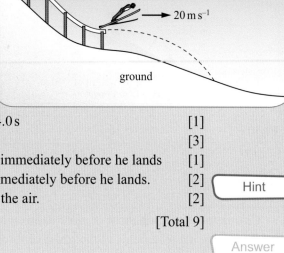

a   The skier lands 4.0 s after leaving the runway.
    Assume that only a gravitational force acts on
    the skier. Calculate:

    i   the horizontal distance travelled by the skier in 4.0 s   [1]

    ii the vertical fall of the skier in this 4.0 s   [3]

    iii the horizontal component of the skier's velocity immediately before he lands   [1]

    iv the vertical component of the skier's velocity immediately before he lands.   [2]

b   Name <u>two</u> forces that act on the skier when he is in the air.   [2]

OCR Physics AS (2821) January 2002   [Total 9]

Hint

Answer

Chapter 5

Forces, moments and pressure

Objectives

Experiencing forces

From the day we are born (if not before), we learn to live with the forces that act upon us – such as our weight, friction, or the push of the wind. We do not have to make any calculations to know when the forces acting on us are likely to make us fall over.

Human beings are innately unstable. We are tall and thin, and we stand on two smallish feet. We ought to fall over all the time, but as children we learn to remain upright as we move around. Without thinking, we can walk, run and pick up heavy loads without toppling.

The basketball player in Figure 5.1 is expert at keeping forces balanced. You can see that he can run and turn through 360° while keeping the ball bouncing. At the right, he is standing on his left foot and leaning over; his weight is in danger of pulling him down to the ground. He will swing his right foot forwards so that it reaches the ground before he can fall. This is what people do as they walk around, but basketball players are more skilled at it than the average person.

Engineers, too, have to take account of the turning effects of forces. For example, a wind turbine like that shown in Figure 5.2 will experience powerful forces when the wind blows hard. These forces will tend to tip or bend the turbine, and its designers must be sure that it can withstand them.

Figure 5.2 A wind turbine has a heavy mass attached to the top of a tall mast. The engineers who design these structures must take account of the turning forces which act on them – and on the crane which is used to erect them in the first place.

Figure 5.1 A skilful basketball player can perform exotic twists and turns without falling over.

Diagram	Force	Important situations
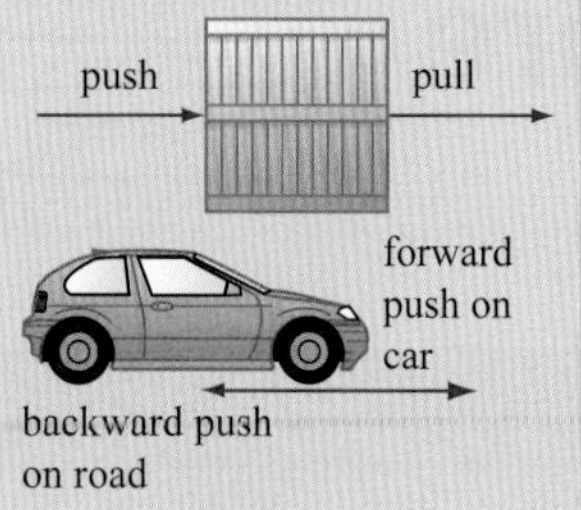 push ⟶ pull ⟶ forward push on car — backward push on road	**Pushes and pulls**. You can make an object accelerate by pushing and pulling it. Your force is shown by an arrow pushing (or pulling) the object. The engine of a car provides a force to push backwards on the road. Frictional forces from the road on the tyre push the car forwards.	• pushing and pulling • lifting • force of car engine • attraction and repulsion by magnets and by electric charges
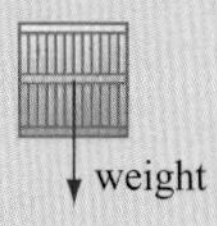 ↓ weight	**Weight**. This is the force of gravity acting on the object. It is usually shown by an arrow pointing vertically downwards from the object's centre of gravity.	• any object in a gravitational field • less on the Moon
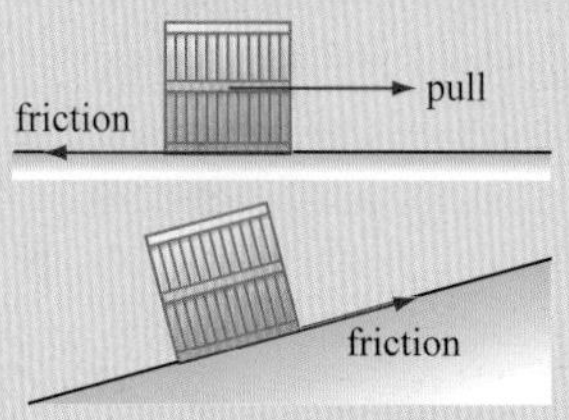 friction ⟵ ⟶ pull — friction	**Friction**. This is the force which arises when two surfaces rub over one another. If an object is sliding along the ground, friction acts in the opposite direction to its motion. If an object is stationary, but *tending* to slide – perhaps because it is on a slope – the force of friction acts up the slope to stop it from sliding down. Friction always acts along a surface, never at an angle to it.	• pulling an object along the ground • vehicles cornering or skidding • sliding down a slope
 ⟵ drag	**Drag**. This force is similar to friction. When an object moves through air, there is friction between it and the air. Also, the object has to push aside the air as it moves along. Together, these effects make up drag. Similarly, when an object moves through a liquid, it experiences a drag force. Drag acts to oppose the motion of an object; it acts in the opposite direction to the object's velocity. It can be reduced by giving the object a streamlined shape.	• vehicles moving • aircraft flying • parachuting • objects falling through air or water • ships sailing
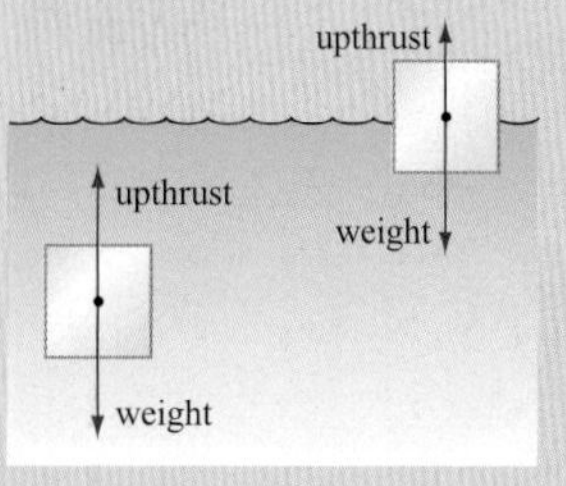 upthrust ↑ — upthrust ↑ weight ↓ — weight ↓	**Upthrust**. Any object placed in a fluid such as water or air experiences an upwards force. This is what makes it possible for something to float in water. Upthrust arises from the pressure which a fluid exerts on an object. The deeper you go, the greater the pressure. So there is more pressure on the lower surface of an object than on the upper surface, and this tends to push it upwards. If upthrust is greater than the object's weight, it will float up to the surface.	• boats and icebergs floating • people swimming • divers surfacing • a hot air balloon rising
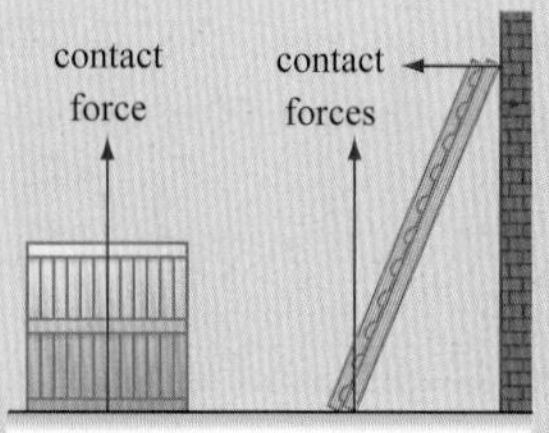 contact force ↑ — contact forces ↖	**Contact force**. When you stand on the floor or sit on a chair, there is usually a force which pushes up against your weight, and which supports you so that you do not fall down. The contact force is sometimes known as the *normal reaction* of the floor or chair. (In this context, *normal* means 'perpendicular'.) The contact force always acts at right angles to the surface which produces it. The floor pushes straight upwards; if you lean against a wall, it pushes back against you horizontally.	• standing on the ground • one object sitting on top of another • leaning against a wall • one object bouncing off another
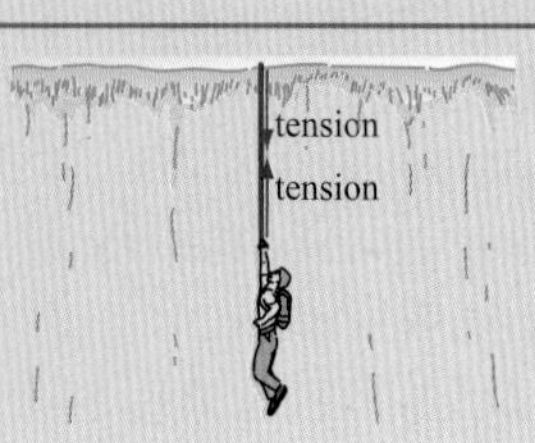 tension tension	**Tension**. This is the force in a rope or string when it is stretched. If you pull on the ends of a string, it tends to stretch. The tension in the string pulls back against you. It tries to shorten the string. Tension can also act in springs. If you stretch a spring, the tension pulls back to try to shorten the spring. If you squash (compress) the spring, the tension acts to expand the spring.	• pulling with a rope • squashing or stretching a spring

Figure 5.3 Some important forces.

Some important forces

It is important to be able to identify the forces which act on an object. When we know what forces are acting, we can predict how it will move. Figure 5.3 (opposite) shows some important forces, how they arise, and how we represent them in diagrams.

Two or more forces

It is important to be able to identify the forces which are acting on an object if we are going to predict how it will move. Often, two or more forces are acting, and we have to think clearly about what they are.

Figure 5.4a shows an aircraft travelling at top speed through the air. Figure 5.4b shows the four forces acting on it:

- its downward weight and the upward lift force on its wings,
- the forward thrust of its engines and the backward air resistance or drag.

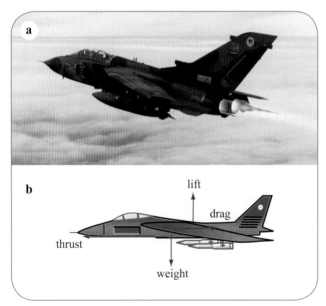

Figure 5.4 a An aircraft in flight; **b** the four forces which act on it – these have turning effects (moments) which also must be considered.

SAQ

1 Name these forces:
  a the upward push of water on a submerged object
  b the force which wears away two surfaces as they move over one another
  c the force which pulled the apple off Isaac Newton's tree
  d the force which stops you falling through the floor
  e the force in the creeper as Tarzan swings from tree to tree
  f the force which makes it difficult to run through shallow water.

  Answer

2 Draw a diagram to show the forces which act on a car as it travels along a level road at its top speed.

  Answer

3 Imagine throwing a shuttlecock straight up in the air. Air resistance is important for shuttlecocks, more important than for a tennis ball. Air resistance always acts in the opposite direction to the velocity of an object.
  Draw diagrams to show the two forces, weight and air resistance, acting on the shuttlecock:
  a as it moves upwards
  b as it falls back downwards.

  Answer

Centre of gravity

We have weight because of the force of gravity of the Earth on us. Each part of our body – arms, legs, head, for example – experiences a force, caused by the force of gravity. However, it is much simpler to picture the overall effect of gravity as acting at a single point. This is our **centre of gravity**. The centre of gravity of an object is defined as a point where the entire weight of the object appears to act. For a person standing upright, it is roughly in the middle of the body, behind the navel. For a sphere, it is at the centre. It is much easier to solve problems if we simply indicate an object's weight by a single force acting at the centre of gravity, rather than a large number of forces acting on each part of the object.

Figure 5.5 illustrates this point. The athlete performs a complicated manoeuvre. However, we can see that her centre of gravity follows a smooth, parabolic path through the air, just like the paths of projectiles we discussed in Chapter 4.

Finding the centre of gravity

The centre of gravity of a thin sheet, or lamina, of cardboard or metal can be found by suspending it freely from two or three points (Figure 5.6).

Figure 5.5 The dots indicate the athlete's centre of gravity, which follows a smooth trajectory through the air. With her body curved like this, the athlete's centre of gravity is actually outside her body, just below the small of her back. At no time is the whole of her body above the bar.

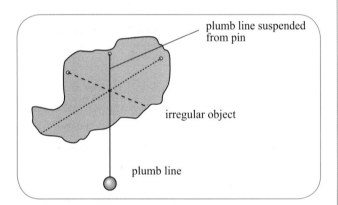

Figure 5.6 The centre of gravity is located at the intersection of the lines.

Small holes are made round the edge of the irregularly shaped object. A pin is put through one of the holes and held firmly in a clamp and stand so the object can swing freely. A length of string is attached to the pin. The other end of the string has a heavy mass attached to it. This arrangement is known as a *plumb line*. The object will stop swinging when its centre of gravity is vertically below the point of suspension. A line is drawn on the object along the vertical string of the plumb line. The centre of gravity must lie on this line. To find the position of the centre of gravity, the process is repeated with the object suspended from different holes. The centre of gravity will be at the point of intersection of the lines drawn on the object.

The turning effect of forces

Forces can make things accelerate. They can do something else as well: they can make an object turn round. We say that they can have a *turning effect*. The lock gate shown in Figure 5.7 turns on its pivot when the operator pushes against the arm of the gate.

Figure 5.7 To open the canal lock gate, you have to push hard on the long wooden arm. You are pushing against the weight of the water behind the gate.

This arm is made of a long piece of wood. It must be long so that the pushing force has a large turning effect. To maximise the effect, the operator pushes close to the end of the arm, as far as possible from the pivot (the fixed point at which the arm is hinged).

Moment of a force

The quantity which tells us about the turning effect of a force is its **moment**. The moment of a force depends on two quantities:

- the *magnitude* of the force (the bigger the force, the greater its moment)
- the *perpendicular distance* of the force from the pivot (the further the force acts from the pivot, the greater its moment).

The moment of a force is defined as follows.

> The moment of a force = force × perpendicular distance of the pivot from the line of action of the force.

Figure 5.8a shows these quantities. The force F_1 is pushing down on the lever, at a perpendicular distance x_1 from the pivot. The moment of the force F_1 about the pivot is then given by:

$$\text{moment} = \text{force} \times \text{distance from pivot}$$
$$= F_1 \times x_1$$

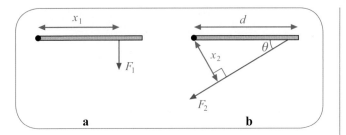

Figure 5.8 The quantities involved in calculating the moment of a force.

The unit of moment is the newton metre (N m). This is a unit which does not have a special name. You can also determine the moment of a force in N cm.

Figure 5.8b shows a slightly more complicated situation. F_2 is pushing at an angle θ to the lever, rather than at 90°. This makes it have less turning effect. There are two ways to calculate the moment of the force.

Method 1
Draw a perpendicular line from the pivot to the line of the force. Find the distance x_2. Calculate the moment of the force, $F_2 \times x_2$. From the right-angled triangle, we can see that
$$x_2 = d \sin \theta$$
Hence:
moment of force $= F_2 \times d \sin \theta = F_2 d \sin \theta$

Method 2
Calculate the component of F_2 which is at 90° to the lever. This is $F_2 \sin \theta$. Multiply this by d.
moment $= F_2 \sin \theta \times d$

We get the same result as Method 1:
moment of force $= F_2 d \sin \theta$

Note that any force (such as the component $F_2 \cos \theta$) which passes *through* the pivot has no turning effect, because the distance from the pivot to the line of the force is zero.

Balanced or unbalanced?
We can use the idea of the moment of a force to solve two sorts of problem.
- We can check whether an object will remain balanced or start to rotate.
- We can calculate an unknown force or distance if we know that an object is balanced.

We can use the **principle of moments** to solve problems. The principle of moments states that:

> For any object that is in **equilibrium**, the sum of the clockwise moments about any point provided by the forces acting on the object equals the sum of the anticlockwise moments about that same point.

Worked example 1

Is the see-saw shown in Figure 5.9 in equilibrium (balanced), or will it start to rotate?

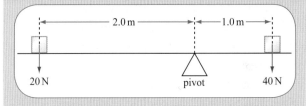

Figure 5.9 Will these forces make the see-saw rotate, or are their moments balanced?

The see-saw will remain balanced, because the 20 N force is twice as far from the pivot as the 40 N force.

To prove this, we need to think about each force individually. Which direction is each force trying to turn the see-saw, clockwise or anticlockwise? The 20 N force is tending to turn the see-saw anticlockwise, while the 40 N force is tending to turn it clockwise.

Step 1 Determine the anticlockwise moment:

moment of
anticlockwise force $= 20 \times 2.0 = 40$ N m

Step 2 Determine the clockwise moment:

moment of
clockwise force $= 40 \times 1.0 = 40$ N m

Step 3 We can see that:

clockwise moment $=$ anticlockwise moment

So the see-saw is balanced and therefore does not rotate. The see-saw is in equilibrium.

Worked example 2

The beam shown in Figure 5.10 is in equilibrium Determine the force X.

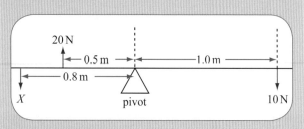

Figure 5.10 For Worked example 2.

The unknown force X is tending to turn the beam anticlockwise. The other two forces (10 N and 20 N) are tending to turn the beam clockwise. We will start by calculating their moments and adding them together.

Step 1 Determine the clockwise moments:

sum of moments
of clockwise forces $= (10 \times 1.0) + (20 \times 0.5)$

$$= 10 + 10 = 20 \, \mathrm{N\,m}$$

Step 2 Determine the anticlockwise moment:

moment of
anticlockwise force $= X \times 0.8$

Step 3 Since we know that the beam must be balanced, we can write:

sum of clockwise moments
= sum of anticlockwise moments

$20 = X \times 0.8$

$$X = \frac{20}{0.8} = 25 \, \mathrm{N}$$

So a force of 25 N at a distance of 0.8 m from the pivot will keep the beam still and prevent it from rotating (keep it balanced).

Worked example 3

Figure 5.11 shows the internal structure of a human arm holding an object. The biceps are muscles attached to one of the bones of the forearm. These muscles provide an upward force.

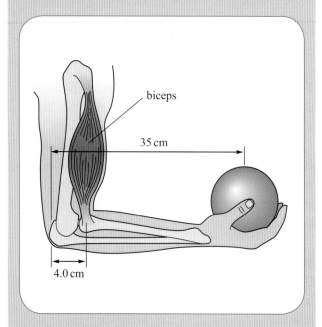

Figure 5.11 The human arm. For Worked example 3.

An object of weight 50 N is held in the hand with the forearm at right angles to the upper arm. Use the principle of moments to determine the muscular force F provided by the biceps, given the following data:

weight of forearm = 15 N

distance of biceps from the elbow = 4.0 cm

distance of centre of gravity of forearm from
elbow = 16 cm

distance of object in the hand from elbow = 35 cm

Step 1 There is a lot of information in this question. It is best to draw a simplified diagram of the forearm that shows all the forces and the relevant distances (Figure 5.12). All distances must be from the pivot, which in this case is the elbow.

continued

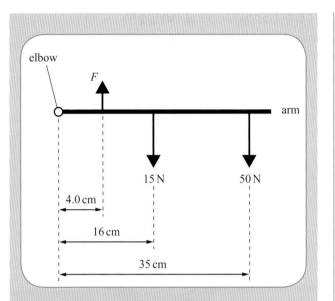

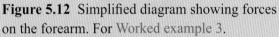

Figure 5.12 Simplified diagram showing forces on the forearm. For Worked example 3.

Step 2 Determine the clockwise moments:

sum of moments of
clockwise forces = $(15 \times 0.16) + (50 \times 0.35)$

$$= 19.9\,\text{Nm}$$

Step 3 Determine the anticlockwise moment:

moment of anticlockwise force = $F \times 0.04$

Step 4 Since the arm is in balance, according to the principle of moments we have:

sum of clockwise moments
= sum of anticlockwise moments

$19.9 = 0.04F$

$$F = \frac{19.9}{0.04} = 497.5\,\text{N} \approx 500\,\text{N}$$

The biceps provide a force of 500 N – a force large enough to lift 500 apples!

SAQ

4   A wheelbarrow is loaded as shown in Figure 5.13.
   a   Calculate the force that the gardener needs to exert to hold the wheelbarrow's legs off the ground.   *Hint*
   b   Calculate the force exerted by the ground on the legs of the wheelbarrow (taken both together) when the gardener is not holding the handles.   *Answer*

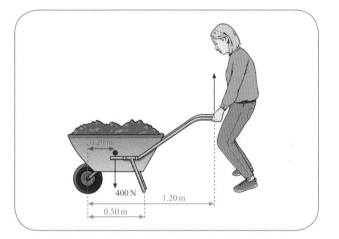

Figure 5.13 For SAQ 4.

5   An old-fashioned pair of scales uses sliding masses of 10 g and 100 g to achieve a balance. A diagram of the arrangement is shown in Figure 5.14. The bar itself is supported with its centre of gravity at the pivot.   *Hint*
   a   Calculate the value of the mass M, attached at X.
   b   State *one* advantage of this method of measuring mass.   *Answer*

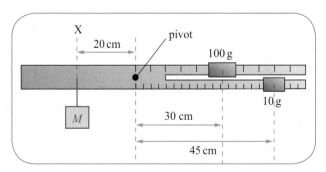

Figure 5.14 For SAQ 5.

6 Figure 5.15 shows a beam with four forces acting on it.

   a For each force, calculate the moment of the force about point P.

   b State whether each moment is clockwise or anticlockwise.

   c State whether or not the moments of the forces are balanced.

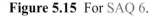

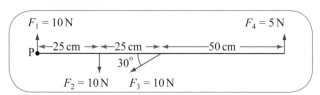

Figure 5.15 For SAQ 6.

7 The force F shown in Figure 5.16 has a moment of 40 N m about the pivot. Calculate the magnitude of the force F.

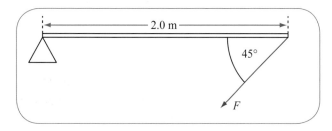

Figure 5.16 For SAQ 7.

8 The asymmetric bar shown in Figure 5.17 has a weight of 7.6 N and a centre of gravity that is 0.040 m from the wider end, on which there is a load of 3.3 N. It is pivoted a distance of 0.060 m from its centre of gravity. Calculate the force P that is needed at the far end of the bar in order to maintain equilibrium.

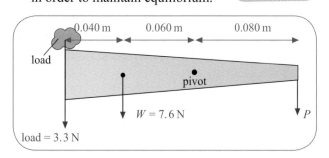

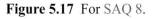

Figure 5.17 For SAQ 8.

The torque of a couple

Figure 5.18 shows the forces needed to turn a car's steering wheel. The two forces balance up and down (15 N up and 15 N down), so the wheel will not move up, down or sideways. However, the wheel is not in equilibrium. The pair of forces will cause it to rotate.

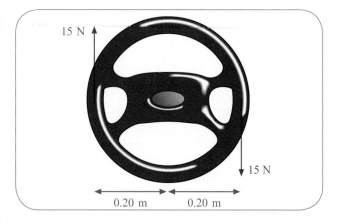

Figure 5.18 Two forces act on this steering wheel to make it turn.

A pair of forces like that in Figure 5.18 is known as a *couple*. A couple has a turning effect, but does not cause an object to accelerate. To form a couple, the two forces must be:

● equal in magnitude

● parallel, but opposite in direction

● separated by a distance d.

The turning effect or moment of a couple is known as its **torque**. We can calculate the torque of the couple in Figure 5.18 by adding the moments of each force about the centre of the wheel:

$$\text{torque of a couple} = (15 \times 0.20) + (15 \times 0.20)$$
$$= 6.0 \, \text{N m}$$

We could have found the same result by multiplying *one* of the forces by the perpendicular distance between them:

$$\text{torque of a couple} = 15 \times 0.4 = 6.0 \, \text{N m}$$

The torque of a couple is defined as follows:

> torque of a couple
> = one of the forces × perpendicular distance
>   between the forces

Extension

SAQ

9 The driving wheel of a car travelling at a constant velocity has a torque of 137 N m applied to it by the axle that drives the car (Figure 5.19). The radius of the tyre is 0.18 m. Calculate the driving force provided by this wheel.

Answer

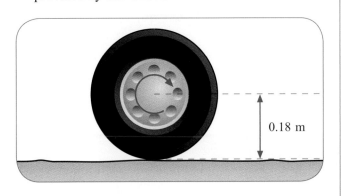

0.18 m

Figure 5.19 For SAQ 9.

Pure turning effect

When we calculate the moment of a single force, the result depends on the point or pivot about which the moment acts. The farther the force is from the pivot, the greater the moment. A couple is different; the moment of a couple does not depend on the point about which it acts, only on the perpendicular distance between the two forces.

A single force acting on an object will tend to make the object accelerate (unless there is another force to balance it). A couple, however, is a pair of equal and opposite forces, so it will not make the object accelerate.

This means we can think of a couple as a pure 'turning effect', the size of which is given by its torque.

> For an object to be in equilibrium, two conditions must be met at the same time.
> ● The resultant force acting on the object is zero.
> ● The resultant torque must be zero.

Density

Density is a macroscopic property of matter. It is something we can measure and use without having to think about microscopic particles. It tells us about how concentrated the matter is. Density is a constant for a given material. Density is defined as follows:

$$\text{density} = \frac{\text{mass}}{\text{volume}}$$

$$\rho = \frac{m}{V}$$

The symbol used here for density, ρ, is the Greek letter rho.

The standard unit for density in the SI system is kg m^{-3}; you may also find values quoted in g cm^{-3}. It is useful to remember that these units are related by:

$$1000 \, \text{kg m}^{-3} = 1 \, \text{g cm}^{-3}$$

and that the density of water is approximately $1000 \, \text{kg m}^{-3}$.

Pressure

Often it is convenient to think of a force acting at a point on a body. For example, we picture the weight of an object acting at its centre of gravity, even though every part of the object is acted on by gravity. There are other forces which clearly do not act at a point. When you stand on the floor, the contact force (normal reaction) of the floor acts all over your feet. When you are swimming, the upthrust of the water pushes upwards on the underside of your body.

In cases such as these, it is often useful to think about the **pressure** that the force exerts on an object. Pressure tells you about how the force is shared out over the area it acts on. For example, a flat shoe exerts a smaller pressure on the ground than a stiletto heel. The larger the area, the smaller the pressure, for a given force.

Pressure is defined as the normal force acting per unit cross-sectional area. We can write this as the following word equation:

$$\text{pressure} = \frac{\text{normal force}}{\text{cross-sectional area}}$$

$$p = \frac{F}{A}$$

The units of pressure are newtons per square metre ($N\,m^{-2}$), which are given the special name of pascals (Pa).

$$1\,Pa = 1\,N\,m^{-2}$$

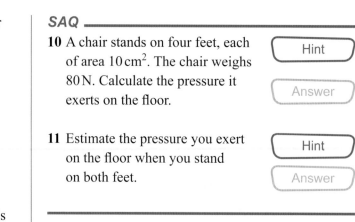

SAQ

10 A chair stands on four feet, each of area $10\,cm^2$. The chair weighs $80\,N$. Calculate the pressure it exerts on the floor.

Hint

Answer

11 Estimate the pressure you exert on the floor when you stand on both feet.

Hint

Answer

Summary

Glossary

- The centre of gravity of an object is defined as the point through which the entire weight of the object may be considered to act.

- The moment of a force is defined by:

  moment of a force = force × perpendicular distance of the pivot from the line of action of the force.

- For any object that is in equilibrium, the sum of the clockwise moments about a point is equal to the sum of the anticlockwise moments about that same point (principle of moments).

- A pair of equal and opposite forces, not acting in the same straight line, is called a couple, and the turning effect that they cause is called a torque.

- The torque of a couple is defined by:

  torque of a couple = one of the forces × perpendicular distance between the two forces.

- Equilibrium of a body is achieved when the resultant force and the resultant torque on the body are both zero.

- Density is defined as the mass per unit volume:

  $$\text{density} = \frac{\text{mass}}{\text{volume}}$$

  $$\rho = \frac{m}{V}$$

- Pressure is defined as the normal force per unit cross-sectional area.

  $$\text{pressure} = \frac{\text{normal force}}{\text{cross-sectional area}}$$

  $$p = \frac{F}{A}$$

Questions

1 The diagram shows two forces, each of magnitude 1200 N, acting on the edge of a disc of radius 0.20 m.

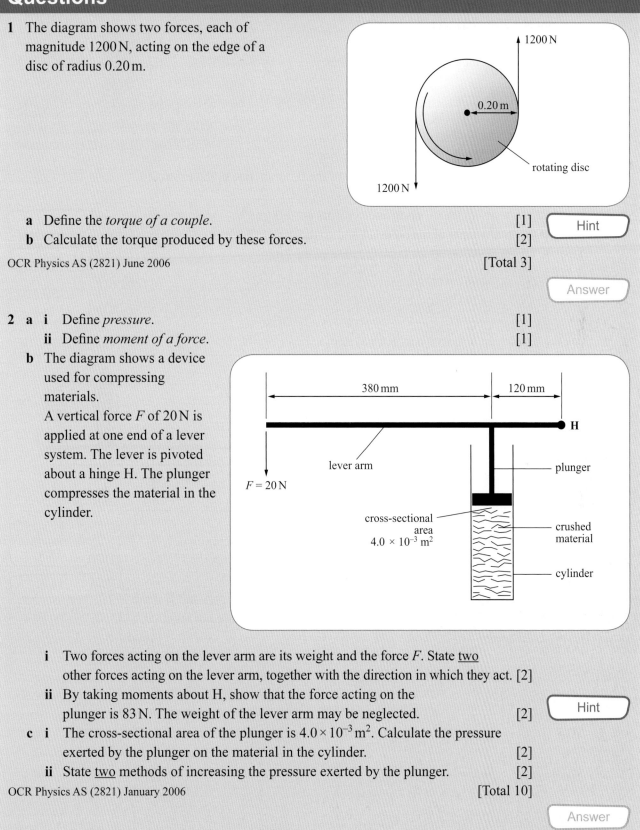

   a Define the *torque of a couple*. [1]

   b Calculate the torque produced by these forces. [2]

OCR Physics AS (2821) June 2006   [Total 3]

Hint

Answer

2 a i Define *pressure*. [1]

     ii Define *moment of a force*. [1]

   b The diagram shows a device used for compressing materials.
A vertical force *F* of 20 N is applied at one end of a lever system. The lever is pivoted about a hinge H. The plunger compresses the material in the cylinder.

     i Two forces acting on the lever arm are its weight and the force *F*. State <u>two</u> other forces acting on the lever arm, together with the direction in which they act. [2]

     ii By taking moments about H, show that the force acting on the plunger is 83 N. The weight of the lever arm may be neglected. [2]

   c i The cross-sectional area of the plunger is 4.0×10^{-3} m^2. Calculate the pressure exerted by the plunger on the material in the cylinder. [2]

     ii State <u>two</u> methods of increasing the pressure exerted by the plunger. [2]

OCR Physics AS (2821) January 2006   [Total 10]

Hint

Answer

continued

3 The diagram shows a stationary oil drum floating in water.
The oil drum is 0.75 m long and
has a cross-sectional area of 0.25 m².
The air pressure above the oil drum is 1.0×10^5 Pa.

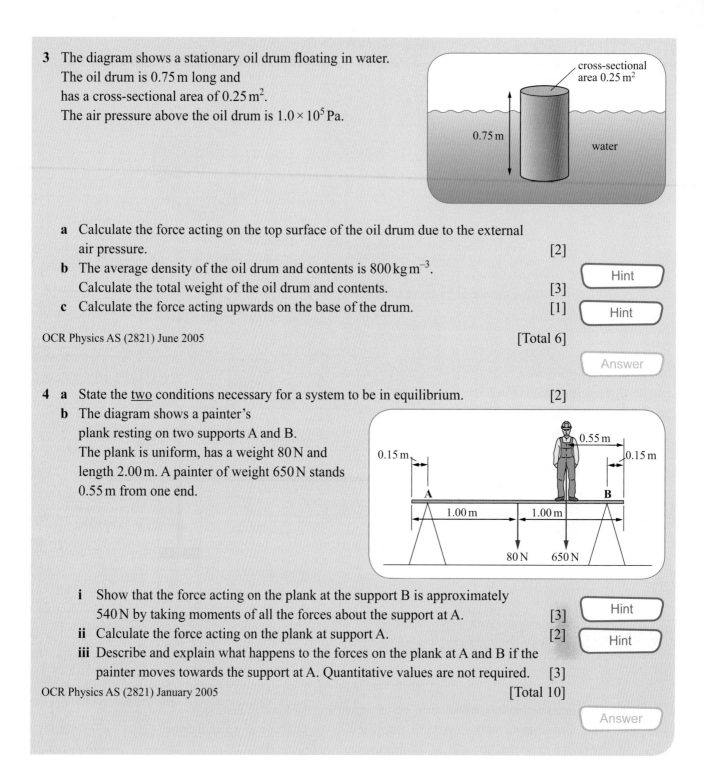

a Calculate the force acting on the top surface of the oil drum due to the external air pressure. [2]

b The average density of the oil drum and contents is 800 kg m⁻³.
Calculate the total weight of the oil drum and contents. [3]

Hint

c Calculate the force acting upwards on the base of the drum. [1]

Hint

OCR Physics AS (2821) June 2005 [Total 6]

Answer

4 a State the <u>two</u> conditions necessary for a system to be in equilibrium. [2]

b The diagram shows a painter's
plank resting on two supports A and B.
The plank is uniform, has a weight 80 N and
length 2.00 m. A painter of weight 650 N stands
0.55 m from one end.

i Show that the force acting on the plank at the support B is approximately
540 N by taking moments of all the forces about the support at A. [3]

Hint

ii Calculate the force acting on the plank at support A. [2]

Hint

iii Describe and explain what happens to the forces on the plank at A and B if the
painter moves towards the support at A. Quantitative values are not required. [3]

OCR Physics AS (2821) January 2005 [Total 10]

Answer

Chapter 6

Forces, vehicles and safety

Background

e-Learning

Objectives

Stopping distances

In the previous chapters, we have looked at how the motion of an object is affected by the forces acting on it. In this chapter, we will apply those ideas to the particular case of vehicles, such as cars, trucks and trains. In particular, we will think about how driving can be made safer through an understanding of dynamics.

Roads are dangerous places (Figure 6.1). However, as you can see from Figure 6.2, the number of deaths on the roads in the UK has been declining more or less steadily over a period of decades. Science and engineering have played a big part in this.

A number of factors have helped to reduce the toll of death on the roads.

Figure 6.1 A lucky escape from a head-on collision. (In fact, the motorist in this photograph is a stuntman.)

- Vehicles are designed so that, in the event of a collision, the occupants are less likely to be badly injured.
- Roads are better designed, with better surfaces and clearer markings and road signs, so that motorists understand better how to drive in heavy traffic.
- Changes in the law have compelled motorists to wear seat belts and motorcyclists to wear safety helmets, while road safety campaigns have made people aware of the dangers of driving while affected by alcohol and other drugs.
- At the same time, crowded roads have made it harder for people to travel at dangerous speeds, and cyclists and pedestrians have been scared off the roads.

Young people who are new to driving often overestimate their ability to control a powerful car, and they underestimate the harm that may come to them. For some, it is more important to impress their friends than to worry about other road-users who may be affected by their dangerous driving. This explains why those under 25 are prominent among road death statistics. At the same time, elderly people may continue to drive when their reactions and their eyesight are not up to the job. All drivers need a realistic understanding of their own limitations.

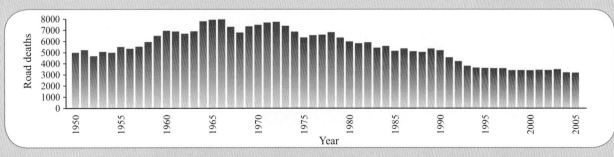

Figure 6.2 A graph showing the declining numbers of road casualties in the UK. The slight rise in 2003 was due to the increased use of high-power motorbikes, particularly by middle-aged men.

Stopping safely

The *Highway Code* is the guidebook for drivers which can answer most questions about the rules of the road and how to drive safely. In particular, it indicates the shortest stopping distances which can realistically be achieved by drivers. These are shown in Table 6.1 and Figure 6.3. **Stopping distance** is made up of two parts: the distance travelled by the car in the time it takes the driver to react to a particular situation (**thinking distance**) and the distance travelled by the car whilst the brakes are being applied and the car is decelerating to a halt (**braking distance**).

    stopping distance
       = thinking distance + braking distance

The figures given are for a well-maintained car in good road conditions. A car with bad brakes, travelling on a poor or wet road surface, could take much longer to stop.

You should notice two features of the data in Table 6.1:

- *Thinking distance* is directly proportional to the speed of the car. This is because the time taken to react is constant, about two-thirds of a second. At twice the speed, you will travel twice the thinking distance. Hence

    thinking distance ∝ speed of car

- *Braking distance* is directly proportional to the *square* of the speed. So braking distance at 40 mph (24 m) is four times as much as at 20 mph (6 m). You will find the same relationship if you compare

Speed	Thinking distance /m	Braking distance /m	Stopping distance /m
20 mph = 8.9 m s^{-1}	6	6	12
30 mph – 13.3 m s^{-1}	9	14	23
40 mph = 17.8 m s^{-1}	12	24	36
50 mph = 22.2 m s^{-1}	15	38	53
60 mph = 26.7 m s^{-1}	18	55	73
70 mph = 31.1 m s^{-1}	21	75	96

Table 6.1 Stopping distances, from the *Highway Code*.

braking distances at 60 mph and 30 mph. Hence

    braking distance ∝ speed^2

We can understand the relationship between braking distance and speed by using one of the equations of motion (Chapter 2):

$$v^2 = u^2 + 2as$$

The final speed *v* is 0. Rearranging the equation gives:

$$s = \frac{-u^2}{2a}$$

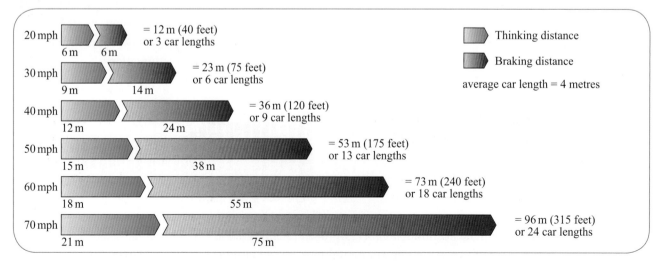

Figure 6.3 Typical stopping distances – data from the *Highway Code*.

The car is decelerating and therefore a will be negative. So, for a given deceleration a, the braking distance is directly proportional to the square of the initial speed u of the car. That is:

$$s \propto u^2$$

SAQ

1 Plot a graph of thinking distance against speed (in $m\,s^{-1}$), using data from Table 6.1. From the gradient, deduce the thinking time.

2 The values of braking distances in Table 6.1 are deduced assuming a realistic value for the magnitude of the deceleration a of a car as it stops in an emergency. You can deduce the value of a as follows:

   a Draw up a table of values of speed^2 (u^2) and braking distance (s).

   b Plot a graph of u^2 against s.

   c Rearranging the equation $s = \dfrac{u^2}{2a}$ for the magnitude of the acceleration a gives $u^2 = 2as$. Determine a from the gradient of the graph.

3 A driver is travelling at $30\,m\,s^{-1}$. She sees an incident on the road, $150\,m$ ahead. After a thinking time of $0.60\,s$, she presses on the brake pedal. The magnitude of the car's deceleration is $3.0\,m\,s^{-2}$. Will it stop before it reaches the incident site?

Factors affecting stopping distances

Thinking distance depends on speed, but it may also be affected by the condition of the driver. A driver who is affected by alcohol or drugs may react slowly (which means that the driver's reaction time has increased) and this will increase the driver's thinking distance. In the UK, over 20% of drivers involved in accidents are found to have traces of illegal drugs in their bloodstream, although it has yet to be established how much this can be considered a cause of accidents. Older people also tend to have slower reactions, so their thinking distance is also likely to be greater.

Braking distances are affected by factors which govern the deceleration of the car. A poorly maintained car may have faulty brakes which cannot provide the necessary braking force. Similarly, on a wet, icy or greasy road surface (Figure 6.4), the tyres may slip so that there is a danger of the car skidding if the brakes are applied too firmly. If the deceleration is less than on a good road surface, the braking distance will be greater. The braking distance increases when:

● the mass of the car is increased
● the road is wet or icy (the friction between tyre and road decreases, hence the braking distance is greater)
● the car has worn tyres or brakes
● the tyres have little or no tread (the surface water cannot be pressed out between the road and tyre, which leads to reduced friction and slipping)
● the car travels at greater speed (remember that the braking distance is directly proportional to speed^2).

Figure 6.4 An accident on a snow-covered road – drivers need to proceed slowly and maintain a good distance from the car in front in these conditions. It only takes one driver to misjudge the conditions to produce mayhem like this.

Drivers must take account of other aspects of the conditions they find themselves in. For example, if the road has many bends, or if it is foggy, the driver will not be able to see far ahead. To avoid colliding with a vehicle in front, they should keep their speed down to a safe level where their stopping distance is within the distance they can see ahead of them.

SAQ

4 Driving close to the car in front is known as 'tail-gating'. Explain why this practice may lead to a collision if the driver in front decides to brake.

Answer

Car safety features

Today's cars are much safer than those of 20 or 30 years ago. This is because designers now include several different features which can help to protect the driver and passengers during an impact. Nevertheless, there is still a 1 in 200 chance that you will eventually die in a road accident.

Passenger cells

Many modern cars are designed so that the people using them are protected in a passenger cell or safety cage (Figure 6.5). This is a rigid 'box' which is more likely to survive an impact. The front compartment of the car is the *crumple zone*, which squashes up in a crash. This absorbs a lot of the energy of the moving car. At the same time, the heavy engine is directed downwards so that it is not pushed into the passenger cell.

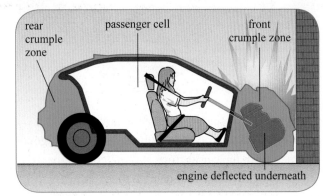

Figure 6.5 In a car, you may be protected by a reinforced passenger cell and a collapsible crumple zone.

Seat belts

When a car crashes, its occupants may be thrown about. The car stops, but the people keep on moving. They are likely to be thrown forwards, colliding with the windscreen or steering wheel. Seat belts help to keep the passengers in their seats. The inertia reels come into operation whenever a sudden force acts to pull on the belt. The end of each belt is wound round an inertia reel. You can pull the belt slowly from the reel; pull it fast, and the reel clamps it firmly. A seat belt is slightly stretchy so that the passenger isn't brought to a halt too suddenly, which would involve a large force that could break bones.

Air bags

Some cars are fitted with air bags to protect the occupants. If the car suddenly decelerates, the bag inflates and the person is cushioned as they move forwards. There are holes in the air bag so that it deflates almost immediately, preventing the person from bouncing back (Figure 6.6).

If you look back to Figure 2.7 in Chapter 2, you will see the tiny accelerometer which triggers the release of the bag. Part of the accelerometer is free to move forwards during an impact, in the same way that the driver tends to be thrown forwards if unrestrained. A magnetic detector senses this movement and generates an electrical signal which releases the bag. A more massive device would respond more slowly to a sudden deceleration, perhaps too slowly to save the motorist.

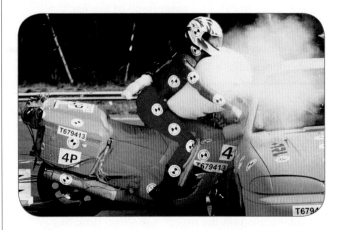

Figure 6.6 Motorcyclists can also benefit from air bags. Here, in a test collision, the dummy driver is saved by the air bag which bursts out of the body of the machine.

Controlling impact forces

These three examples of car safety features all rely on controlling the impact forces which arise during a collision. In particular, they ensure that the occupants of the car are brought slowly to a halt. This increases the time taken to stop, leading to a smaller deceleration. According to $F = ma$, this means that the impact force is reduced. A sudden stop which happens in a shorter time results in bigger and more damaging impact forces.

Where on Earth?

In 2006, the UK Government proposed a system of road pricing to replace the standard road tax, paid by all vehicle owners. The idea was that motorists would be charged according to their use of the roads. Using the main roads which become congested at peak periods would cost more, so motorists would be encouraged to travel at less busy, cheaper times of day. Such a system would require the position of every vehicle to be known at all times, so that the correct charge could be levied. A public outcry forced the Government to withdraw this plan.

At the heart of such a road pricing system (which operates in one or two other parts of the world) is the Global Positioning System (GPS). This is a satellite-based system which allows the location of a vehicle to be determined with great accuracy. Many cars have a GPS device fitted (Figure 6.7) which is used for navigation. It can be programmed with a destination and it guides the driver along a suitable route.

GPS has other uses.

- Vehicle tracking – if a car is stolen, a beacon in the car is activated, signalling its location so that police can trace it quickly.
- Aircraft navigation – since the information from GPS is in three dimensions, pilots can determine precisely their latitude, longitude and altitude.
- Exploration – hikers can enjoy a trek in the wilderness without having to worry about getting lost. More importantly, geological surveyors searching for useful mineral deposits make use of GPS.

- Mobile phones – many mobile phones have GPS systems built in. This means that they can be located in an emergency. Some commercial companies use this facility to track their sales representatives and delivery lorries as they travel about from place to place. There are even some parents who track their children – a website shows where the phone-owner is at any time, and where they have been.

Figure 6.7 This motorist is using a hand-held GPS unit to find his way around a difficult route.

GPS navigation – how it works

The Global Positioning System was originally set up for military purposes, to guide US aircraft and missiles. It consists of 30 or so satellites in high orbits around the Earth; there are six of these orbits, each with four or more satellites positioned at intervals around it (Figure 6.8). At any point on the Earth's surface it is likely that several of these satellites will be above the horizon and so a GPS receiver on the ground will be able to pick up their signals.

Figure 6.8 The orbits of the GPS satellites ensure that, at any point on the Earth's surface, between three and six spacecraft are above the horizon.

GPS satellites act as 'beacons' in space, sending out regular signals containing information about their identity and the time of transmission (based on a high-precision on-board atomic clock). The receiver compares these signals with its own built-in clock and measures the time lag. This is used to determine the time which has elapsed between the signal being sent and received. From this, knowing the speed of radio waves in space ($3.0 \times 10^8 \, \text{m s}^{-1}$), the receiving system can calculate its distance from each of the satellites.

The GPS satellite signal also includes precise coordinates giving its position at the time of transmission. Now the receiver knows its distance from each of three or more satellites and also the positions of the satellites, and so it can work out its own position. Because this requires three satellites, the procedure is known as *trilateration*. Figure 6.9 shows how this works.

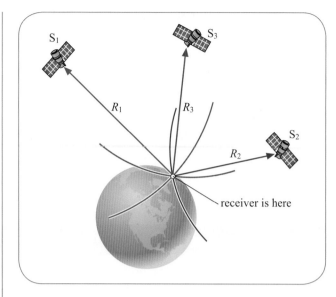

Figure 6.9 A GPS receiver uses information about its distance from three known satellites to deduce its position on the Earth's surface.

If the receiver knows that it is at a distance R_1 from satellite S_1, it must lie somewhere on a sphere of radius R_1 centred on S_1.

Similarly, knowing that it is at a distance R_2 from S_2 means that it must lie on a second sphere. The two spheres intersect to produce a circle on which the receiver must lie.

The distance from satellite S_3 tells the receiver the precise point at which it must lie on the circle. (In fact, there will be two points, but one is far out in space and so can be rejected.)

In practice, three satellite signals will allow a receiver to determine its position to within a few metres. This can be made more precise using the signal from a fourth satellite. In this way, a GPS-based tracker system can even tell in which lane of a motorway a vehicle is travelling.

The GPS system uses a transmission frequency of 10.23 MHz. However, the GPS satellites orbit high above the Earth where the Earth's gravitational field is weaker than on the surface. Einstein's Theory of General Relativity predicts that, in weaker gravity, a clock will run faster. To compensate for this, the transmission frequency must be set slightly below 10.23 MHz, at 10.229 999 995 43 MHz. This tiny difference in frequency is needed to give correct results, and it provides an everyday test of the accuracy of Einstein's Theory of General Relativity.

SAQ

6 Calculate the percentage difference in GPS transmission frequency which is required to take account of the relativistic effect of a weaker gravitational field.

Answer

Worked example 1

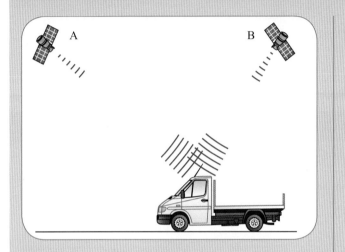

Figure 6.10 For Worked example 1.

Figure 6.10 shows a truck which makes use of a satellite positioning system to determine its position on the surface of the Earth. The truck receives a timing signal from each satellite, and compares their arrival times with its own on-board clock.

time delay for satellite A = 73.180 ms

time delay for satellite B = 68.205 ms

Calculate the distance of the truck from each satellite. (Take the speed of radio waves as $299\,792\,458\,\mathrm{m\,s^{-1}}$.) What other information would be needed to determine the position of the truck on the Earth's surface?

Step 1 Use

$$\text{distance} = \text{speed} \times \text{time}$$

to determine the distances; the question gives the speed of radio waves = $299\,792\,458\,\mathrm{m\,s^{-1}}$.

Step 2: Calculate the distances:

distance from satellite A
$$= 73.180 \times 10^{-3} \times 299\,792\,458 = 21\,939\,\mathrm{km}$$

distance from satellite B
$$= 68.205 \times 10^{-3} \times 299\,792\,458 = 20\,447\,\mathrm{km}$$

Note that we can only give the result to five significant figures because the time delays are given to this precision. This means that the distances are to the nearest kilometre. To give measurements to the nearest metre requires time measurements to eight or nine significant figures.

To determine the truck's position, the GPS device will need to receive signals from at least one other satellite, and to know the positions of all three satellites.

Summary

- Thinking distance is the distance travelled by the car in the time the driver reacts to a particular situation.

- Braking distance is the distance travelled by the car as the brakes are engaged and the car comes to a stop.

- Stopping distance = thinking distance + braking distance

- Cars are made safer by incorporating safety features such as seat belts, air bags and crumple zones. Tyres should have good tread to ensure that they grip the road. Smooth or wet road surfaces provide poor grip.

- Seat belts, air bags and crumple zones all increases the time taken for the driver to come to a halt. This makes both the deceleration and the impact forces smaller.

Questions

1 a State and explain <u>two</u> factors that affect the braking distance of a car. [4]

   b State and explain <u>two</u> safety features in a car that are designed to protect the driver during a collision. [4]

OCR Physics AS (2821) January 2006 [Total 8]

2 The diagram shows a crate resting on the flat bed of a moving lorry.

a The lorry brakes and decelerates to rest.
   i Describe and explain what happens to the crate if the flat bed of the lorry is smooth. [2]
   ii A rough flat bed allows the crate to stay in the same position on the lorry when the lorry brakes. State the direction of the force that must act on the crate to allow this. [1]
   b Using your answers to a or otherwise, explain how seat belts worn by rear seat passengers can reduce injuries when a car is involved in a head-on crash. [3]

OCR Physics AS (2821) June 2005 [Total 6]

Chapter 7

Work, energy and power

Background

e-Learning

Objectives

The idea of energy

The Industrial Revolution started in England (though many of the pioneers of industrial technology came from other parts of the British Isles). Engineers developed new machines which were capable of doing the work of hundreds of craftsmen and labourers. At first, they made use of the traditional techniques of water power and wind power. Water stored behind a dam was used to turn a wheel, which turned many machines. By developing new mechanisms, the designers tried to extract as much as possible of the energy stored in the water.

Steam engines were developed, initially for pumping water out of mines. Steam engines use a fuel such as coal; there is much more energy stored in 1 kg of coal than in 1 kg of water behind a dam. Steam engines soon powered the looms of the textile mills (Figure 7.1), and the British industry came to dominate world trade in textiles.

Nowadays, most factories and mills in the UK rely on electrical power, generated by burning coal at a power station. The fuel is burnt to release its store of energy. High-pressure steam is generated, and this turns a turbine which turns a generator. Even in the most efficient coal-fired power station, only about 40% of the energy from the fuel is transferred to the electrical energy that the station supplies to the grid.

Engineers strove to develop machines which made the most efficient use of the energy supplied to them. At the same time, scientists were working out the basic ideas of energy transfer and energy transformations. The idea of energy itself had to be developed; it was not obvious at first that heat, light, electrical energy and so on could all be thought of as being, in some way, forms of the same thing. In fact, steam engines had been in use for 150 years before it was realised that their energy came from the heat supplied to them from their fuel. Previously it had been thought that the heat was necessary only as a 'fluid' through which energy was transferred.

The earliest steam engines had very low efficiencies – many converted less than 1% of the energy supplied to them into useful work. The understanding of the relationship between work and energy developed by physicists and engineers in the 19th century led to many ingenious ways of making the most of the energy supplied by fuel. This improvement in energy efficiency has led to the design of modern engines such as the jet engines which have made long distance air travel a commercial possibility (Figure 7.2).

Figure 7.2 The jet engines of this aeroplane are designed to make efficient use of their fuel. If they were less efficient, their thrust might only be sufficient to lift the empty aircraft, and the passengers would have to be left behind.

Figure 7.1 At one time, smoking chimneys like these were prominent landmarks in the industrial regions of the UK.

Doing work, transferring energy

The weight-lifter shown in Figure 7.3 has powerful muscles. They can provide the force needed to lift a large weight above her head – about 2 m above the ground. The force exerted by the weight-lifter transfers energy from her to the weights. We know that the weights have gained energy because, when the athlete releases them, they come crashing down to the ground.

Figure 7.3 It is hard work being a weight-lifter.

As the athlete lifts the weights and transfers energy to them, we say that her lifting force is doing work. 'Doing work' is a way of transferring energy from one object to another. In fact, if you want to know the scientific meaning of the word 'energy', we have to say it is 'that which is transferred when a force moves through a distance'. So work and energy are two closely linked concepts.

In Physics, we often use an everyday word but with a special meaning. *Work* is an example of this. Table 7.1 describes some situations which illustrate the meaning of *doing work* in Physics.

It is important to appreciate that our bodies sometimes mislead us. If you hold a heavy weight above your head for some time, your muscles will get tired. However, you are not doing any work *on the weights*, because you are not transferring energy to the weights once they are above your head. Your muscles get tired because they are constantly relaxing and contracting, and this uses energy, but none of the energy is being transferred to the weights.

Doing work	Not doing work
Pushing a car to start it moving: your force transfers energy to the car. The car's kinetic energy (i.e. 'movement energy') increases.	Pushing a car but it would not budge: no energy is transferred, because your force does not move. The car's kinetic energy does not change.
Lifting weights: you are doing work as the weights move upwards. The gravitational potential energy of the weights increases.	Holding weights above your head: you are not doing work on the weights (even though you may find it tiring) because the force you apply on them is not moving. The gravitational potential energy of the weights is not changing.
A falling stone: the force of gravity is doing work. The stone's kinetic energy is increasing.	The Moon orbiting the Earth: the force of gravity is not doing work. The Moon's kinetic energy is not changing.
Writing an essay: you are doing work because you need a force to move your pen across the page, or to press the keys on the keyboard.	Reading an essay: this may seem like 'hard work', but no force is involved, so you are not doing any work.

Table 7.1 The meaning of 'doing work' in Physics.

Calculating work done

Because *doing work* defines what we mean by *energy*, we start this chapter by considering how to calculate *work done*. There is no doubt that you do work if you push a car along the road. A force transfers energy from you to the car. But how much work do you do? Figure 7.4 shows the two factors involved:

- the size of the force F – the bigger the force, the greater the amount of work you do
- the distance x you push the car – the further you push it, the greater the amount of work done.

Figure 7.4 You have to do work to start the car moving.

So, the bigger the force, and the further it moves, the greater the amount of work done. The **work done** by a force is defined as follows:

work done = force × distance moved in the
direction of the force

$$W = F \times x$$

In the example shown in Figure 7.4, $F = 300\,\text{N}$ and $x = 5.0\,\text{m}$, so:

work done $W = F \times x = 300 \times 5.0 = 1500\,\text{J}$

Energy transferred

Doing work is a way of transferring energy. For both energy and work the correct SI unit is the joule (J). The amount of work done, calculated using

$$W = F \times x$$

shows the amount of energy transferred:

work done = energy transferred

Newtons, metres and joules

From the equation

$$W = F \times x$$

we can see how the unit of force (the newton), the unit of distance (the metre) and the unit of work or energy (the joule) are related:

1 joule = 1 newton × 1 metre
$$1\,\text{J} = 1\,\text{Nm}$$

The joule is defined as the amount of work done when a force of 1 newton moves a distance of 1 metre in the direction of the force. Since *work done = energy transferred*, it follows that a joule is also the amount of energy transferred when a force of 1 newton moves a distance of 1 metre in the direction of the force.

SAQ

1 In each of the following examples, explain whether or not any work is done by the force mentioned.
   a You pull a heavy sack along rough ground.
   b The force of gravity pulls you downwards when you fall off a wall.
   c The tension in a string pulls on a conker when you whirl it around in a circle at a steady speed.
   d The contact force of the bedroom floor stops you from falling into the room below.

   Hint

   Answer

2 A man of mass 70 kg climbs stairs of vertical height 2.5 m. Calculate the work done against the force of gravity. (Take $g = 9.81\,\text{m s}^{-2}$.)

   Hint

   Answer

3 A stone of weight 10 N falls from the top of a 250 m high cliff.
   a Calculate how much work is done by the force of gravity in pulling the stone to the foot of the cliff.
   b How much energy is transferred to the stone?

   Answer

Force, distance and direction

It is important to appreciate that, for a force to do work, there must be movement *in the direction of the force*. Both force F and distance x moved in the direction of the force are vector quantities, so you should know that their directions are likely to be important. To illustrate this, we will consider three examples involving force of gravity (Figure 7.5).

In the equation for work done, $W = F \times x$, the distance moved x is thus the displacement in the direction of the force.

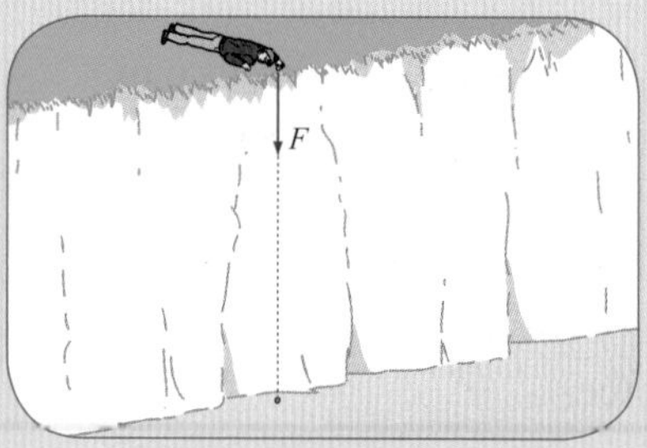

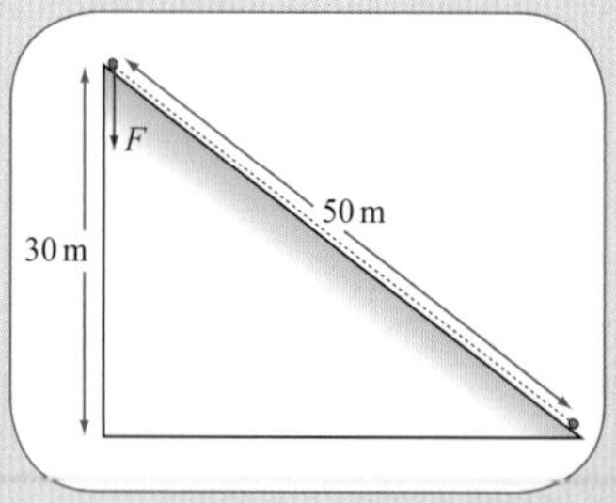

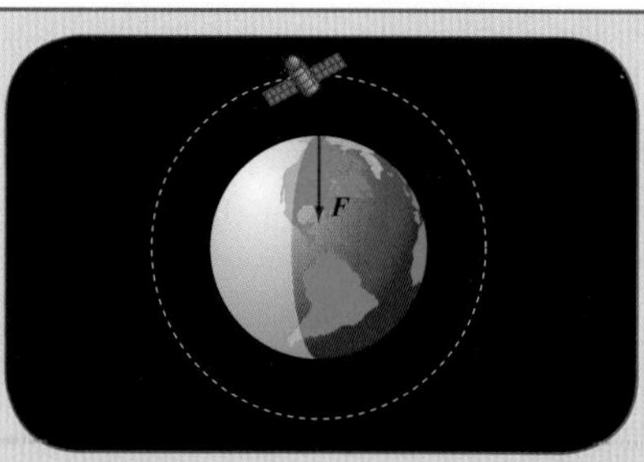

1 You drop a stone weighing 5.0 N from the top of a 50 m high cliff. What is the work done by the force of gravity?	2 A stone weighing 5.0 N rolls 50 m down a slope. What is the work done by the force of gravity?	3 A satellite orbits the Earth at a constant height and at a constant speed. The weight of the satellite at this height is 500 N. What is the work done by the force of gravity?
force on stone = pull of gravity = weight of stone = 5.0 N vertically downwards	force on stone = pull of gravity = weight of stone = 5.0 N vertically downwards	force on satellite = pull of gravity = weight of satellite = 500 N towards centre of Earth
distance moved by stone x = 50 m vertically downwards	distance moved by stone down slope is 50 m, but distance moved in direction of force is 30 m.	distance moved by satellite towards centre of Earth (i.e. in the direction of force) x = 0
Since F and x are in the same direction, there is no problem: work done = $F \times x$ $\qquad$ = 5.0 × 50 $\qquad$ = 250 J	The work done by the force of gravity is: work done = 5.0 × 30 $\qquad$ = 150 J	The satellite remains at a constant distance from the Earth. It does not move in the direction of F. The work done by the Earth's pull on the satellite is zero because F = 500 N but x = 0: work done = 500 × 0 $\qquad$ = 0 J

Figure 7.5 Three examples involving gravity.

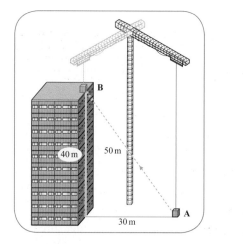

Figure 7.6 For SAQ 4. The dotted line shows the track of the load as it is lifted by the crane.

SAQ

4 The crane shown in Figure 7.6 lifts its 500 N load to the top of the building from A to B. Distances are as shown on the diagram. Calculate how much work is done by the crane.

Hint

Answer

Suppose that the force F moves through a distance x which is at an angle θ to F, as shown in Figure 7.7. To determine the work done by the force, it is simplest to determine the component of F in the direction of x. This component is $F\cos\theta$, and so we have:

$\qquad$ work done = $(F\cos\theta) \times x$

Or simply:

$\qquad$ work done = $Fx\cos\theta$

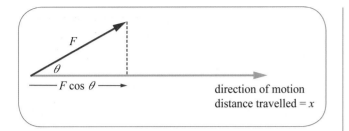

Figure 7.7 The work done by a force depends on the angle between the force and the distance it moves.

Worked example 1 shows how to use this.

Worked example 1

A man pulls a box along horizontal ground using a rope (Figure 7.8). The force provided by the rope is 200 N, at an angle of 30° to the horizontal. Calculate the work done if the box moves 5.0 m along the ground.

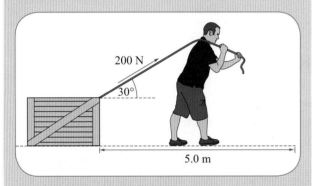

Figure 7.8 For Worked example 1.

Step 1 Calculate the component of the force in the direction in which the box moves. This is the horizontal component of the force:

horizontal component of force
$= 200 \cos 30° = 173 \, \text{N}$

Step 2 Now calculate the work done:

work done = force × distance moved
$= 173 \times 5.0 = 865 \, \text{J}$

Note that we could have used the equation

work done $= Fx \cos \theta$

to combine the two steps into one.

SAQ

5 Figure 7.9 shows the forces acting on a box which is being pushed up a slope. Calculate the work done by each force if the box moves 0.50 m up the slope.

Answer

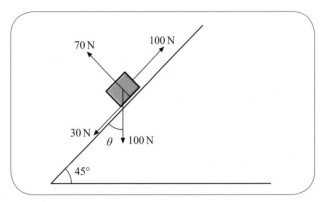

Figure 7.9 For SAQ 5.

Gravitational potential energy

If you lift a heavy object, you do work. You are providing an upward force to overcome the downward force of gravity on the object. The force moves the object upwards, so the force is doing work.

In this way, energy is transferred from you to the object. You lose energy, and the object gains energy. We say that the **gravitational potential energy** E_p of the object has increased. Worked example 2 shows how to calculate a change in gravitational potential energy – or GPE for short.

Worked example 2

A weight-lifter raises weights with a mass of 200 kg from the ground to a height of 1.5 m. Calculate how much work he does. By how much does the GPE of the weights increase?

Step 1 It helps to draw a diagram of the situation (Figure 7.10). The downward force on the weights is their weight $W = mg$. An equal, upward force F is required to lift them.

$W = F = mg = 200 \times 9.81 = 1962 \, \text{N}$

continued

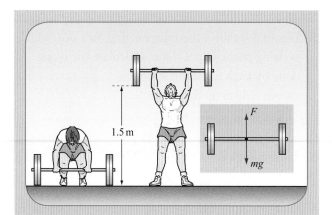

Figure 7.10 For Worked example 2.

Step 2 Now we can calculate the work done by the force F:

work done = force × distance moved

$$= 1962 \times 1.5 \approx 2940\,\text{J}$$

Note that the distance moved is in the same direction as the force. So the work done on the weights is about 2940 J. This is also the value of the increase in their GPE.

An equation for gravitational potential energy

The change in the gravitational potential energy (GPE) of an object, E_p, depends on the change in its height, h. We can calculate E_p using this equation:

change in GPE = weight × change in height

$$E_p = (mg) \times h$$

or simply

$$E_p = mgh$$

It should be clear where this equation comes from. The force needed to lift an object is equal to its weight mg, where m is the mass of the object and g is the acceleration of free fall or the gravitational field strength on the Earth's surface. The work done by this force is given by force × distance moved, or weight × change in height. You might feel that it takes a force *greater than* the weight of the object being raised to lift it upwards, but this is not so. Provided the force is *equal to* the weight, the object will move upwards at a steady speed.

Note that h stands for the *vertical height* through which the object moves. Note also that we can only use the equation $E_p = mgh$ for relatively small changes in height. It would not work, for example, in the case of a satellite orbiting the Earth. Satellites orbit at a height of at least 200 km and g has a smaller value at this height.

SAQ

6 Calculate how much gravitational potential energy is gained if you climb a flight of stairs. Assume that you have a mass of 52 kg and that the height you lift yourself is 2.5 m. [Answer]

7 A climber of mass 100 kg (including the equipment he is carrying) ascends from sea level to the top of a mountain 5500 m high. Calculate the change in his gravitational potential energy. [Answer]

Kinetic energy

As well as lifting an object, a force can make it accelerate. Again, work is done by the force and energy is transferred to the object. In this case, we say that it has gained **kinetic energy**, E_k. The faster an object is moving, the greater its kinetic energy (KE). For an object of mass m travelling at a speed v, we have:

kinetic energy = $\frac{1}{2}$ × mass × speed^2

$$E_k = \frac{1}{2}mv^2$$

Worked example 3

Calculate the increase in kinetic energy of a car of mass 800 kg when it accelerates from 20 m s^{-1} to 30 m s^{-1}.

Step 1 Calculate the initial KE of the car:

$$E_k = \frac{1}{2}mv^2 = \frac{1}{2} \times 800 \times (20)^2 = 160\,000\,\text{J}$$

$$= 160\,\text{kJ}$$

continued

Step 2 Calculate the final KE of the car:

$$E_k = \tfrac{1}{2}mv^2 = \tfrac{1}{2} \times 800 \times (30)^2 = 360\,000\,\text{J}$$

$$= 360\,\text{kJ}$$

Step 3 Calculate the change in the car's KE:

change in KE = 360 − 160 = 200 kJ

Take care! You can't calculate the change in KE by squaring the change in speed. In this example, the change in speed is 10 m s⁻¹, and this would give an incorrect value for the change in KE.

SAQ

8 Which has more KE, a car of mass 500 kg travelling at 15 m s⁻¹ or a motorcycle of mass 250 kg travelling at 30 m s⁻¹? *Answer*

9 Calculate the change in kinetic energy of a ball of mass 200 g when it bounces. Assume that it hits the ground with a speed of 15.8 m s⁻¹ and leaves it at 12.2 m s⁻¹. *Hint* *Answer*

Extension

GPE–KE transformations

A motor drags the roller coaster car to the top of the first hill. The car runs down the other side, picking up speed as it goes (see Figure 7.11). It is moving just fast enough to reach the top of the second hill, slightly lower than the first. It accelerates downhill again. Everybody screams!

The motor provides a force to pull the roller coaster car to the top of the hill. It transfers energy to the car. But where is this energy when the car is waiting at the top of the hill? The car now has gravitational potential energy; as soon as it is given a small push to set it moving, it accelerates. It gains kinetic energy and at the same time it loses GPE.

Figure 7.11 The roller coaster car accelerates as it comes downhill. It's even more exciting if it runs through water.

As the car runs along the roller coaster track (Figure 7.12), its energy changes.

1 At the start, it has GPE.

2 As it runs downhill, its GPE decreases and its KE increases.

3 At the bottom of the hill, all of its GPE has been changed to KE.

4 As it runs back uphill, the force of gravity slows it down. KE is being changed to GPE.

Inevitably, some energy is lost by the car. There is friction with the track, and air resistance. So the car cannot return to its original height. That is why the second hill must be slightly lower than the first.

It is fun if the car runs through a trough of water, but that takes even more energy, and the car cannot rise so high.

There are many situations where an object's energy changes between gravitational potential energy and kinetic energy. For example:

● a high diver falling towards the water – GPE changes to KE

● a ball is thrown upwards – KE changes to GPE

● a child on a swing – energy changes back and forth between GPE and KE.

continued

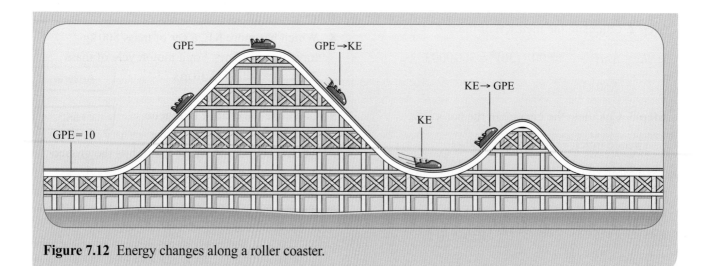

Figure 7.12 Energy changes along a roller coaster.

Down, up, down – energy changes

When an object falls, it speeds up. Its GPE decreases and its KE increases. Energy is being transformed from gravitational potential energy to kinetic energy. Some energy is likely to be lost, usually as heat because of air resistance. However, if no energy is lost in the process, we have:

decrease in GPE = gain in KE

We can use this idea to solve a variety of problems, as illustrated by Worked example 4.

Worked example 4

A pendulum consists of a brass sphere of mass 5.0 kg hanging from a long string (see Figure 7.13). The sphere is pulled to the side so that it is 0.15 m above is lowest position. It is then released. How fast will it be moving when it passes through the lowest point along its path?

Step 1 Calculate the loss in GPE as the sphere falls from its highest position.

$$E_p = mgh = 5.0 \times 9.81 \times 0.15 = 7.36\,\text{J}$$

Step 2 The gain in the sphere's KE is 7.36 J. We can use this to calculate the sphere's speed. First calculate v^2, then v:

$$\tfrac{1}{2}mv^2 = 7.36$$

$$\tfrac{1}{2} \times 5.0 \times v^2 = 7.36$$

continued

$$v^2 = \frac{2 \times 7.36}{5.0} = 2.944$$

$$v = \sqrt{2.944} = 1.72\,\text{m s}^{-1} \approx 1.7\,\text{m s}^{-1}$$

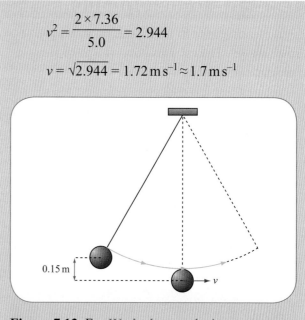

Figure 7.13 For Worked example 4.

Note that we would obtain the same result in Worked example 4 no matter what the mass of the sphere. This is because both KE and GPE depend on mass m. If we write:

change in GPE = change in KE

$$mgh = \tfrac{1}{2}mv^2$$

we can cancel m from both sides. Hence:

$$gh = \frac{v^2}{2}$$

$$v^2 = 2gh$$

Therefore

$$v = \sqrt{2gh}$$

The final speed v only depends on g and h. The mass m of the object is irrelevant. This is not surprising; we could use the same equation to calculate the speed of an object falling from height h. An object of small mass gains the same speed as an object of large mass, provided air resistance has no effect.

SAQ _____

10 Rework Worked example 4 above; take the mass of the brass sphere as 10 kg, and show that you get the same result. Repeat with any other value of mass. Answer

11 Calculate how much gravitational [Hint] potential energy is lost by an aircraft of mass 80 000 kg if it descends from an altitude of 10 000 m to an altitude of 1000 m. What happens to this energy if the pilot keeps its speed constant? [Answer]

12 A high diver (see Figure 7.14) [Hint] reaches a highest point in her jump where her centre of gravity is 10 m above the water. Assuming that all her gravitational potential energy becomes kinetic energy during the dive, calculate her speed just before she enters the water. [Answer]

Figure 7.14 A high dive is an example of converting (transforming) gravitational potential energy to kinetic energy.

Energy conservation

When we use the idea that GPE is changing to KE, we are using the idea that energy is conserved; that is to say, there is as much energy at the end of the process as there was at the beginning. Where did this idea come from?

Figure 7.15 shows James Joule, the English scientist after whom the unit of energy is named. Joule is famous among physicists for having taken a thermometer on his honeymoon in the Alps. He knew that water at the top of a waterfall had gravitational potential energy; it lost this energy as it fell. Joule was able to show that the water was warmer at the foot of the waterfall than at the top and so he was able to explain where the water's energy went to when it fell.

The idea of energy can be difficult to grasp. When Newton was working on his theories of mechanics, more than three centuries ago, the idea did not exist. It took several generations of physicists to develop the concept fully. So far, we have considered two forms of energy (kinetic and gravitational potential), and one way of transferring energy (by doing work). You are no doubt aware that energy takes other forms such as electrical, heat and sound, and the idea that energy is conserved extends to these, too. For the moment, we will consider how the idea of energy conservation relates to KE and GPE.

Figure 7.15 James Prescott Joule; he helped to develop our idea of energy.

Energy transfers

Climbing bars

If you are going to climb a mountain, you will need a supply of energy. This is because your gravitational potential energy is greater at the top of the mountain than at the base. A good supply of energy would be some bars of chocolate. Each bar supplies 1200 kJ.

Suppose your weight is 600 N and you climb a 2000 m high mountain. The work done by your muscles is:

work done = Fx = 600 × 2000 = 1200 kJ

So one bar of chocolate will do the trick. Of course, in reality, it would not. Your body is inefficient. It cannot convert 100% of the energy from food into gravitational potential energy. A lot of energy is wasted as your muscles warm up, you perspire, and your body rises and falls as you walk along the path. Your body is perhaps only 5% efficient as far as climbing is concerned, and you will need to eat 20 chocolate bars to get you to the top of the mountain. And you will need to eat more to get you back down again.

Many energy transfers are inefficient. That is, only part of the energy is transferred to where it is wanted. The rest is wasted, and appears in some form that is not wanted (such as waste heat), or in the wrong place. You can determine the **efficiency** of any device or system using the following equation:

$$\text{efficiency} = \frac{\text{useful output energy}}{\text{total input energy}} \times 100\%$$

A car engine is more efficient than a human body, but not much more. Figure 7.16 shows how this can be represented by a *Sankey diagram*. The width of the arrow represents the fraction of the energy which is transformed to each new form. In the case of a car engine, we want it to provide kinetic energy to turn the wheels. In practice, 80% of the energy is transformed into heat: the engine gets hot, and heat escapes into the surroundings. So the car engine is only 20% efficient.

We have previously considered situations where an object is falling, and all of its gravitational potential energy changes to kinetic energy. In Worked example 5, we will look at a similar situation, but in this case the energy change is not 100% efficient.

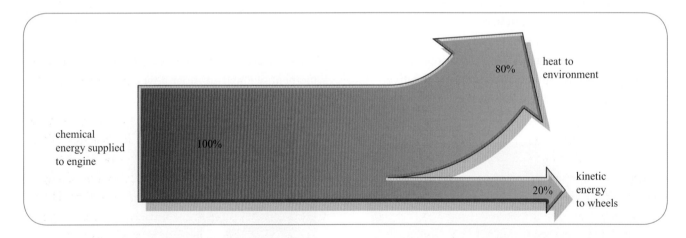

Figure 7.16 We want a car engine to supply kinetic energy. This Sankey diagram shows that only 20% of the energy supplied to the engine ends up as kinetic energy – it is 20% efficient.

Worked example 5

Figure 7.17 shows a dam which stores water. The outlet of the dam is 20 m below the surface of the water in the reservoir. Water leaving the dam is moving at 16 m s^{-1}. Calculate the percentage of the gravitational potential energy converted into kinetic energy.

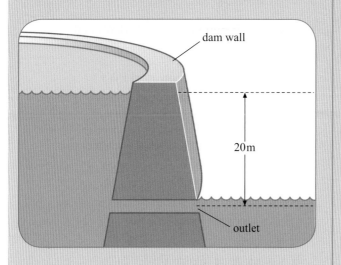

Figure 7.17 Water stored behind the dam has gravitational potential energy; the fast-flowing water leaving the foot of the dam has kinetic energy.

Step 1 We will picture 1 kg of water, starting at the surface of the lake (where it has GPE, but no KE) and flowing downwards and out at the foot (where it has KE, but less GPE). Then:

$$\text{change in GPE of water between surface and outflow} = mgh = 1 \times 9.81 \times 20 = 196 \text{ J}$$

Step 2 Calculate the KE of 1 kg of water as it leaves the dam:

$$\text{KE of water leaving dam}$$
$$= \tfrac{1}{2}mv^2 = \tfrac{1}{2} \times 1 \times (16)^2 = 128 \text{ J}$$

Step 3 For each kilogram of water flowing out of the dam, the loss of energy is:

$$\text{loss} = 196 - 128 = 68 \text{ J}$$

$$\text{percentage loss} = \frac{68}{196} \times 100\% \approx 35\%$$

If you wanted to use this moving water to generate electricity, you would have already lost more than a third of the energy which it stores when it is behind the dam.

Conserving energy

Where does the lost energy from the water in the reservoir go? Most of it ends up warming the water, or warming the pipes that the water flows through. The outflow of water is probably noisy, so some sound is produced.

Here, we are assuming that all of the energy ends up somewhere. None of it disappears. We assume the same thing when we draw a Sankey diagram. The total thickness of the arrow remains constant. We could not have an arrow which got thinner (energy disappearing) or thicker (energy appearing out of nowhere).

We are assuming that *energy is conserved*. This is a principle which we expect to apply in all situations. We should always be able to add up the total amount of energy at the beginning, and be able to account for it all at the end. We cannot be sure that this is always the case, but we expect it to hold true.

We have to think about energy changes *within a*

closed system; that is, we have to draw an imaginary boundary around all of the interacting objects which are involved in an energy transfer.

Sometimes, applying the Principle of Conservation of Energy can seem like a scientific fiddle. When physicists were investigating radioactive decay involving beta particles, they found that the particles after the decay had less energy in total than the particles before. They guessed that there was another, invisible particle which was carrying away the missing energy. This particle, named the neutrino, was proposed by the theoretical physicist Wolfgang Pauli in 1931. The neutrino was not detected by experimenters until 25 years later.

Although we cannot prove that energy is always conserved, this example shows that the Principle of Conservation of Energy can be a powerful tool in helping us to understand what is going on in nature, and that it can help us to make fruitful predictions about future experiments.

SAQ

13 A stone falls from the top of a cliff, 80 m high. When it reaches the foot of the cliff, its speed is 38 m s⁻¹.

   a Calculate the fraction of the stone's initial GPE that is converted to KE.

   b What happens to the rest of the stone's initial energy?

Answer

Power

The word *power* has several different meanings – political power, powers of ten, electrical power from power stations. In Physics, it has a specific meaning which is related to these other meanings. Figure 7.18 illustrates what we mean by power in Physics.

The lift shown in Figure 7.18 can lift a heavy load of people. The motor at the top of the building provides a force to raise the lift car, and this force does work against the force of gravity. The motor transfers energy to the lift car. The **power** P of the motor is the rate at which it does work. Power is defined as the rate of work done. As a word equation, power is given by:

$$\text{power} = \frac{\text{work done}}{\text{time taken}}$$

or $P = \dfrac{W}{t}$

where W is the work done in a time t.

Figure 7.18 A lift needs a powerful motor to raise the car when it has a full load of people. The motor does many thousands of joules of work each second.

Units of power: the watt

Power is measured in watts, named after James Watt, the Scottish engineer famous for his development of the steam engine in the second half of the 18th century. The watt is defined as a rate of working of 1 joule per second. Hence:

    1 watt = 1 joule per second

or   1 W = 1 J s⁻¹

In practice we also use kilowatts (kW) and megawatts (MW).

    1000 watts = 1 kilowatt (1 kW)
   1000 000 watts = 1 megawatt (1 MW)

You are probably familiar with the labels on light bulbs which indicate their power in watts, for example 60 W or 100 W. The values of power on the labels tell you about the energy transferred by an electrical current, rather than by a force doing work

Take care not to confuse the two uses of the letter W:

W = watt (a unit)

W = work done (a quantity)

Extension

Worked example 6

The motor of the lift shown in Figure 7.18 provides a force of 20 kN; this force is enough to raise the lift by 18 m in 10 s. Calculate the output power of the motor.

Step 1 First, we must calculate the work done:

  work done = force × distance moved
            = 20 × 18 = 360 kJ

Step 2 Now we can calculate the motor's output power:

$$\text{power} = \frac{\text{work done}}{\text{time taken}} = \frac{360 \times 10^3}{10} = 36 \text{ kW}$$

So the lift motor's power is 36 kW. Note that this is its mechanical power output. The motor cannot be 100% efficient since some energy is bound to be wasted as heat due to friction, so the electrical power input must be more than 36 kW.

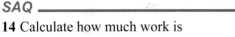

SAQ

14 Calculate how much work is done by a 50 kW car engine in a time of 1.0 minute.

Answer

15 A car engine does 4200 kJ of work in one minute. Calculate its output power, in kilowatts.

Answer

16 A particular car engine provides a force of 700 N when the car is moving at its top speed of 40 m s^{-1}.
a Calculate how much work is done by the car's engine in one second.
b State the output power of the engine.

Answer

Human power

Our energy supply comes from our food. A typical diet supplies 2000–3000 kcal (kilocalories) per day. This is equivalent (in SI units) to about 10 MJ of energy. We need this energy for our daily requirements – keeping warm, moving about, brainwork, and so on. We can determine the average power of all the activities of our body:

average power = 10 MJ per day

$$= \frac{10 \times 10^6}{86\,400} = 116\,\text{W}$$

So we dissipate energy at the rate of about 100 W. We supply roughly as much energy to our surroundings as a 100 W light bulb. Twenty people will keep a room as warm as a 2 kW electric heater.

Note that this is our average power. If you are doing some demanding physical task, your power will be greater. This is illustrated in Worked example 7.

Worked example 7

A person who weighs 500 N runs up a flight of stairs in 5.0 s (Figure 7.19). Their gain in height is 3.0 m. Calculate the rate at which work is done against the force of gravity.

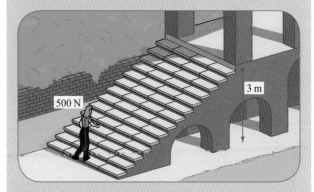

Figure 7.19 Running up stairs can require a high rate of doing work. You may have investigated your own power in this way.

Step 1 Calculate the work done against gravity:

work done $W = F \times x = 500 \times 3.0 = 1500\,\text{J}$

Step 2 Now calculate the power:

power $P = \dfrac{W}{t} = \dfrac{1500}{5.0} = 300\,\text{W}$

So, while the person is running up the stairs, they are doing work against gravity at a greater rate than their average power – perhaps three times as great. And, since our muscles are not very efficient, they need to be supplied with energy even faster, perhaps at a rate of 1 kW. This is why we cannot run up stairs all day long without greatly increasing the amount we eat. The inefficiency of our muscles also explains why we get hot when we exert ourselves.

SAQ

17 In an experiment to measure a student's power, she times herself running up a flight of steps. Use the data below to work out her useful power.

Hint

    number of steps = 28
    height of each step = 20 cm
    acceleration of free fall = 9.81 m s^{-2}
    mass of student = 55 kg
    time taken = 5.4 s

Answer

Summary

Glossary

- To calculate the work done W by a force, we need to know the size of the force F, and the displacement in the direction of the force, x. Then:

$$W = Fx \quad \text{or} \quad W = Fx \cos \theta$$

where θ is the angle between the force and the displacement.

- A joule is defined as the work done (or energy transferred) when a force of 1 N moves a distance of 1 m in the direction of the force.

- When an object of mass m rises through a height h, its gravitational potential energy E_p increases by an amount:

$$E_p = mgh$$

- The kinetic energy E_k of a body of mass m moving at speed v is:

$$E_k = \tfrac{1}{2} mv^2$$

- The Principle of Conservation of Energy states that, for a closed system, energy can be transformed to other forms but the total amount of energy remains constant.

- A Sankey diagram can be used to represent such energy transformations.

- The efficiency of a device or system is determined using the equation:

$$\text{efficiency} = \frac{\text{useful output energy}}{\text{total input energy}} \times 100\%$$

- Power is the rate at which work is done (or energy is transferred):

$$P = \frac{W}{t}$$

- A watt is defined as a transfer of energy of one joule per second.

Questions

1 a Explain the quantities:
   i gravitational potential energy [2]
   ii kinetic energy [2]
   iii power. [1]

  b Water leaves a reservoir and falls through a vertical height of 130 m and causes a water wheel to rotate. The rotating wheel is then used to produce 110 kW of electrical power.
   i Calculate the velocity of the water as it reaches the wheel, assuming that all the gravitational potential energy is converted to kinetic energy. [3]
   ii Calculate the mass of water flowing through the wheel per second, assuming that the production of electrical energy is 100% efficient. [3]
   iii State and explain <u>two</u> reasons why the mass of water flowing per second needs to be greater than the value in **ii** in order to produce this amount of electrical power. [2]

OCR Physics AS (2821) June 2004   [Total 13]

Hint

Hint

Answer

2 a Define:
   i power [1]
   ii a joule. [1]

  b The diagram shows part of a fairground ride with a carriage on rails.

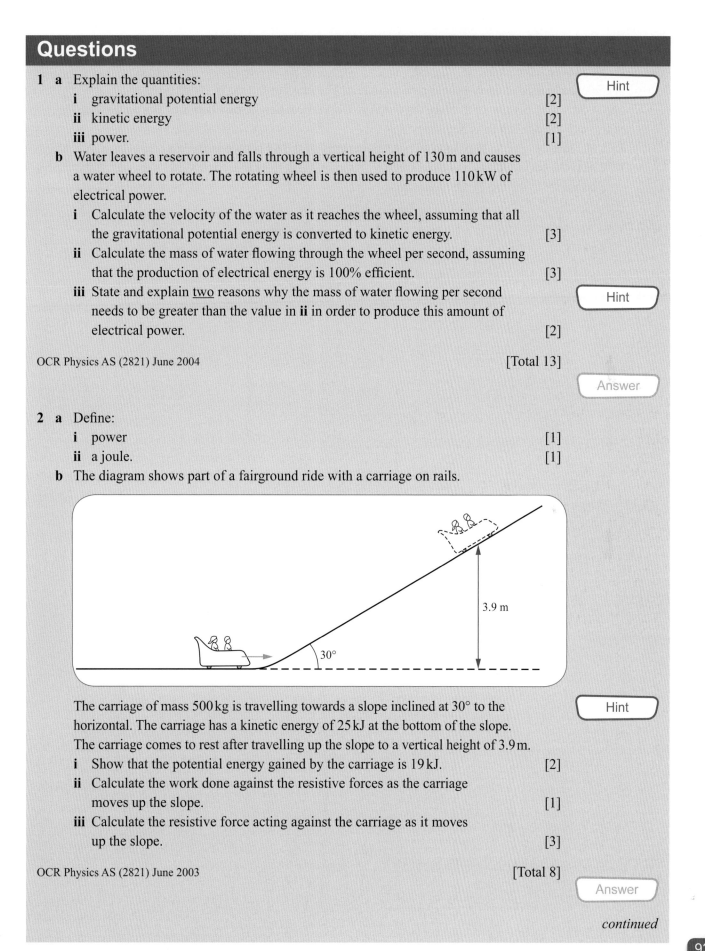

The carriage of mass 500 kg is travelling towards a slope inclined at 30° to the horizontal. The carriage has a kinetic energy of 25 kJ at the bottom of the slope. The carriage comes to rest after travelling up the slope to a vertical height of 3.9 m.
   i Show that the potential energy gained by the carriage is 19 kJ. [2]
   ii Calculate the work done against the resistive forces as the carriage moves up the slope. [1]
   iii Calculate the resistive force acting against the carriage as it moves up the slope. [3]

OCR Physics AS (2821) June 2003   [Total 8]

Hint

Hint

Answer

continued

3 a i Explain the concept of work and relate it to power.   [2]
      ii Define the joule.   [1]
    b A cable car is used to carry people up a mountain. The mass of the car is 2000 kg
       and it carries 80 people, of average mass 60 kg. The vertical height travelled is
       900 m and the time taken is 5 minutes.
      i Calculate the gain in gravitational potential energy of the 80 people in the car. [2]
      ii Calculate the minimum power required by a motor to lift the cable car and its
          passengers to the top of the mountain.   [3]

OCR Physics AS (2821) June 2001   [Total 8]

Hint

Answer

Chapter 8

Deforming solids

e-Learning

Objectives

Springy stuff

In everyday life, we make great use of elastic materials. The term elastic means *springy*; that is, the material deforms when a force is applied and returns to its original shape when the force is removed. Rubber is an elastic material. This is obviously important for a bungee jumper (Figure 8.1). The bungee rope must have the correct degree of elasticity. The jumper must be brought gently to a halt. If the rope is too stiff, the jumper will be jerked violently so that the deceleration is greater than their body can withstand. On the other hand, if the rope is too stretchy, they may bounce up and down endlessly, or even strike the ground.

Springs are elastic as long as the applied forces are not too large. They are usually made of metal. They help us to have a comfortable ride in a car and they contribute to a good night's sleep. They can be made of materials other than metals – plastic, rubber or even glass. Wood is a springy natural material, because trees must be able to bend in a high wind. We rely on wooden floors to bend very slightly when we stand on them; they then provide the necessary contact force to support us. Move away, and the floor returns to its original position.

Materials scientists use large 'tensile testing' machines to measure the elasticity and the strength of materials (Figure 8.2). Thick specimens of metals, polymers or ceramic materials are gradually stretched, and a graph shows how they extend in response to the forces acting on them.

Figure 8.1 The stiffness and elasticity of rubber are crucial factors in bungee jumping.

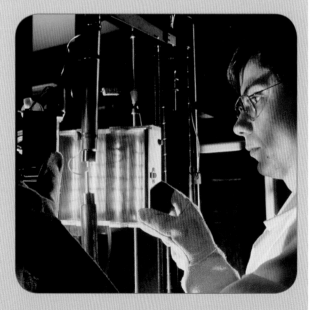

Figure 8.2 This tensile testing machine is being used to test the strength of a valve stem from a racing car engine.

Compressive and tensile forces

A pair of forces is needed to change the shape of a spring. If the spring is being squashed and shortened, we say that the forces are **compressive**. More usually, we are concerned with stretching a spring, in which case the forces are described as **tensile** (Figure 8.3).

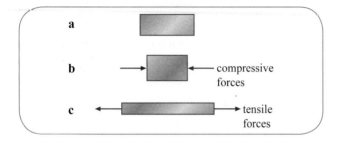

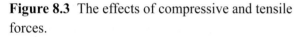

Figure 8.3 The effects of compressive and tensile forces.

It is simple to investigate how the length of the helical spring is affected by the applied force or load. The spring hangs freely with the top end clamped firmly (Figure 8.4). A load is added and gradually increased. For each value of the load, the extension of the spring is measured. Note that it is important to determine the increase in length of the spring, which we call the **extension**. We can plot a graph of force against extension to find the stiffness of the spring, as shown in Figure 8.5.

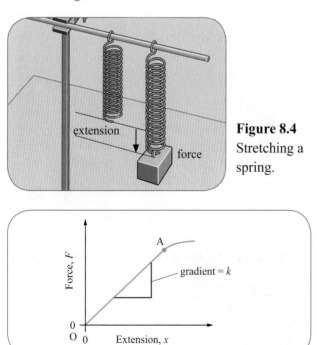

Figure 8.4
Stretching a spring.

Figure 8.5 Force against extension graph for a spring.

Hooke's law

The conventional way of plotting the results would be to have the force along the horizontal axis and the extension along the vertical axis. This is because we are changing the force (the independent variable) and this results in a change in the extension (the dependent variable). The graph shown in Figure 8.5 has extension on the horizontal axis and force on the vertical axis. This is a departure from the convention because the *gradient* of the straight section of this graph turns out to be an important quantity known as the **force constant** of the spring. For a typical spring, the first section of this graph OA is a straight line passing through the origin. The extension x is directly proportional to the applied force (load) F. The behaviour of the spring in the linear region OA of the graph can be expressed by the following equation:

$$x \propto F$$
$$\text{or} \quad F = kx$$

where k is the force constant of the spring (sometimes called either the stiffness or the spring constant of the spring). The force constant is the force per unit extension. The force constant k of the spring is given by the equation:

$$k = \frac{F}{x}$$

The SI unit for the force constant is newton per metre or $N\,m^{-1}$. We can find the force constant k from the gradient of section OA of the graph:

$$k = \text{gradient}$$

A stiffer spring will have a large value for the force constant k. Beyond point A, the graph is no longer a straight line. This is because the spring has become permanently deformed. It has been stretched beyond its **elastic limit**. The meaning of the term *elastic limit* is discussed further on pages 100–101.

If a spring or anything else responds to a pair of tensile forces in the way shown in section OA of Figure 8.5, we say that it obeys Hooke's law:

> A material obeys **Hooke's law** if the extension produced in it is proportional to the applied force (load). This is true as long as the elastic limit of the material is not exceeded.

SAQ

1 Figure 8.6 shows the force against extension graphs for four springs, A, B, C and D.

  a State which spring has the greatest value of force constant.

  b State which is the least stiff.

  c State which of the four springs does not obey Hooke's law.

Answer

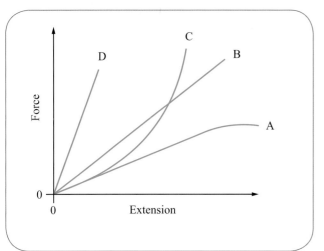

Figure 8.6 Force against extension graphs for four different springs.

Investigating springs

Springs can be combined in different ways (Figure 8.7): end-to-end (in series) and side-by-side (in parallel). Using identical springs, you can measure the force constant of a single spring, and of springs in series and in parallel. Before you do this, predict the outcome of such an experiment.

If the force constant of a single spring is k, what will be the equivalent force constant of:

● two springs in series?

● two springs in parallel?

This approach can be applied to combinations of three or more springs.

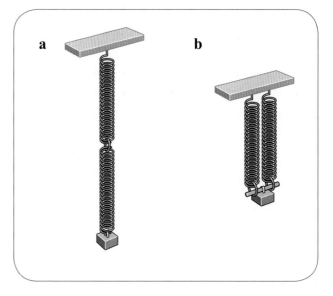

Figure 8.7 Two ways to combine a pair of springs: **a** in series; **b** in parallel.

Stretching materials

When we determine the force constant of a spring, we are only finding out about the stiffness of that particular spring. However, we can talk about the stiffnesses of different *materials*. For example, steel is stiffer than copper, but copper is stiffer than lead.

Stress and strain

Figure 8.8 shows a simple way of assessing the stiffness of a wire in the laboratory. As the long wire is stretched, the position of the sticky tape pointer can be read from the scale on the bench.

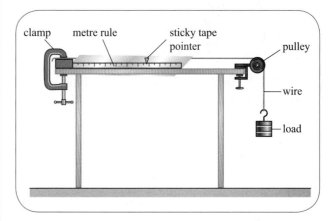

Figure 8.8 Stretching a wire in the laboratory. WEAR EYE PROTECTION and be careful not to overload the wire.

Why do we use a long wire? Obviously, this is because a short wire would not stretch as much as a long one. We need to take account of this in our calculations, and we do this by calculating the strain produced by the load. The **strain** is defined as the fractional increase in the original length of the wire. That is:

$$\text{strain} = \frac{\text{extension}}{\text{original length}}$$

This may be written as:

$$\text{strain} = \frac{x}{L}$$

where x is the extension of the wire and L is its original length.

Note that both extension and original length must be in the same units and so strain is a ratio, without units. Sometimes strain is given as a percentage. For example, a strain of 0.012 is equivalent to 1.2%.

Why do we use a thin wire? This is because a thick wire would not stretch as much for the same force. Again, we need to take account of this in our calculations, and we do this by calculating the stress produced by the load. The **stress** is defined as the force applied per unit cross-sectional area of the wire. That is:

$$\text{stress} = \frac{\text{force}}{\text{cross-sectional area}}$$

This may be written as:

$$\text{stress} = \frac{F}{A}$$

where F is the applied force on a wire of cross-sectional area A.

Force is measured in newtons and area is measured in square metres. Stress is similar to pressure, and has the same units: $N\,m^{-2}$ or pascals, Pa. If you imagine compressing a bar of metal rather than stretching a wire, you will see why stress or pressure is the important quantity.

The Young modulus

We can now find the *stiffness* of the *material* we are stretching. Rather than calculating the ratio of force to extension as we would for a spring or a wire, we calculate the ratio of stress to strain. This ratio is a constant for a particular material and does not depend on its shape or size. The ratio of stress to strain is called the **Young modulus** of the material. That is:

$$\text{Young modulus} = \frac{\text{stress}}{\text{strain}}$$

$$\text{or} \qquad E = \frac{\text{stress}}{\text{strain}}$$

where E is the Young modulus of the material.

The unit of the Young modulus is the same as that for stress, $N\,m^{-2}$ or Pa. In practice, values may be quoted in MPa or GPa, where

$$1\,\text{MPa} = 10^6\,\text{Pa}$$
$$1\,\text{GPa} = 10^9\,\text{Pa}$$

Usually, we plot a graph with stress on the vertical axis and strain on the horizontal axis (Figure 8.9). It is drawn like this so that the gradient is the Young modulus of the material. It is important to consider only the first, linear section of the graph. In the linear section

$$\text{stress} \propto \text{strain}$$

and the wire under test obeys Hooke's law.

Table 8.1 gives some values of the Young modulus for different materials.

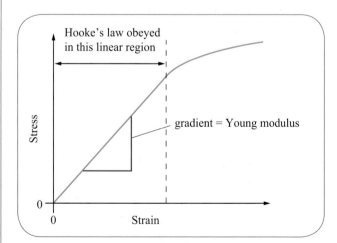

Figure 8.9 Stress against strain graph, and how to deduce the Young modulus.

Material	Young modulus/GPa
aluminium	70
brass	90–110
brick	7–20
concrete	40
copper	130
glass	70–80
iron (wrought)	200
lead	18
Perspex	3
polystyrene	2.7–4.2
rubber	0.01
steel	210
tin	50
wood	10 approx.

Table 8.1 The Young modulus of various materials. Many of these values depend on the precise composition of the material concerned. (Remember $1\,GPa = 10^9\,Pa$.)

SAQ

2 List the metals in Table 8.1 from stiffest to least stiff.

3 Which of the non-metals in Table 8.1 is the stiffest?

[Answer]

4 Figure 8.10 shows stress against strain graphs for two materials, A and B. Use the graphs to determine the Young modulus of each material.

[Answer]

5 A piece of steel wire, 200.0 cm long and having cross-sectional area 0.50 mm², is stretched by a force of 50 N. Its new length is found to be 200.1 cm. Calculate the stress and strain, and the Young modulus of steel.

[Hint]

[Answer]

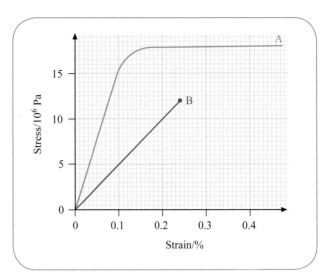

Figure 8.10 Stress against strain graphs for two different materials. For SAQ 4.

6 Calculate the extension of a copper wire of length 1.00 m and diameter 1.00 mm when a tensile force of 10 N is applied to the end of the wire. (Young modulus E of copper = 130 GPa.)

[Answer]

Determining the Young modulus

Metals are not very elastic. In practice, they can only be stretched by about 0.1% of their original length. Beyond this, they become permanently deformed. As a result, some careful thought must be given to getting results that are good enough to give an accurate value of the Young modulus.

First, the wire used must be long. The increase in length is proportional to the original length, and so a longer wire gives larger and more measurable extensions. Typically, extensions up to 1 mm must be measured for a wire of length 1 m. There are two possibilities: use a very long wire, or use a method that allows measurement of extensions that are a fraction of a millimetre.

Figure 8.11 shows an arrangement that incorporates a vernier scale, which can be read to ±0.1 mm. One part of the scale (the vernier) is attached to the wire that is stretched; this moves past the scale on the fixed reference wire.

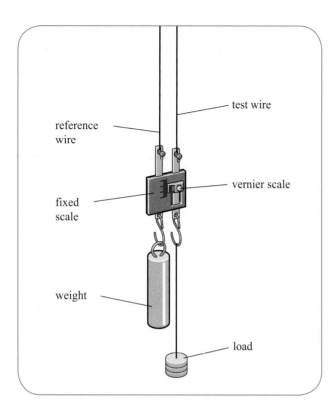

Figure 8.11 A more precise method for determining the Young modulus of a metal.

Secondly, the cross-sectional area of the wire must be known accurately. The diameter of the wire is measured using a micrometer screw gauge. This is reliable to within ±0.001 mm.

Once the wire has been loaded in increasing steps, the load must be gradually decreased to ensure that there has been no permanent deformation of the wire.

Other materials such as glass and many plastics are also quite stiff, and so it is difficult to measure their Young modulus. Rubber is not as stiff, and strains of several hundred per cent can be achieved. However, the stress against strain graph for rubber is not a straight line. This means the value of the Young modulus found is not very precise, because it only has a very small linear region on a stress against strain graph.

SAQ

7 In an experiment to measure the Young modulus of glass, a student draws out a glass rod to form a fibre 0.800 m in length. Using a travelling microscope, she estimates its diameter to be 0.40 mm. Unfortunately it proves impossible to obtain a series of readings for load and extension. The fibre snaps when a load of 1.00 N is hung on the end. The student judges that the fibre extended by no more than 1 mm before it snapped. Use these values to obtain an estimate for the Young modulus of the glass used. Explain how the actual or accepted value for the Young modulus might differ from this estimate.

Answer

Describing deformation

The Young modulus of a material describes its stiffness. This only relates to the initial, straight-line section of the stress against strain graph. In this region, the material is behaving in an elastic way and the straight line means that the material obeys Hooke's law. However, if we continue to increase the force beyond the elastic limit, the graph may cease to be a straight line. Figure 8.12, Figure 8.13 and Figure 8.14 show stress against strain graphs for some typical materials. We will discuss what these illustrate in the paragraphs below.

Glass, cast iron

These materials (Figure 8.12) behave in a similar way. If you increase the stress on them, they stretch slightly. However, there comes a point where the material breaks. Both glass and cast iron are **brittle**; if you apply a large stress, they shatter. They also show **elastic** behaviour up to the breaking point. If you apply a stress and then remove it, they return to their original length.

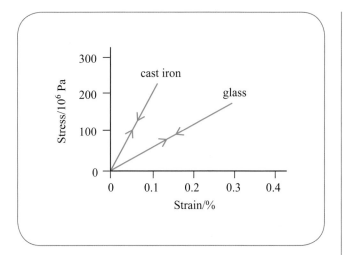

Figure 8.12 Stress against strain graphs for two brittle materials.

Copper, gold

These materials (Figure 8.13) show a different form of behaviour. If you have stretched a copper wire to determine its Young modulus, you will have noticed that, beyond a certain point (the elastic limit), the wire stretches more and more and will not return to its original length when the load is removed. It has become permanently deformed. We describe this as **plastic deformation**. Copper and gold are both metals that can be shaped by stretching, rolling, hammering and squashing. This makes them very useful for making wires, jewellery, and so on. They are described as **ductile** metals. Pure iron is also a ductile metal. Cast iron has carbon in it – it's really a form of steel – and this changes its properties so that it is brittle.

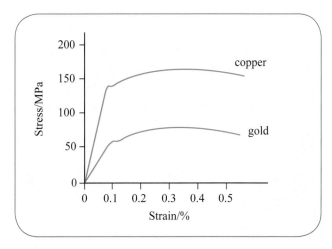

Figure 8.13 Stress against strain graphs for two ductile materials.

Polythene, Perspex

Different polymers behave differently, depending on their molecular structure and their temperature. This graph (Figure 8.14) shows two typical forms of stress against strain graph for polymers. Polythene is easy to deform, as you will know if you have ever tried to stretch a polythene bag. The material stretches (plastic deformation), and then eventually becomes much stiffer and snaps. This is rather like the behaviour of a ductile metal. Perspex behaves in a brittle way. It stretches elastically up to a point, and then it breaks. In practice, if Perspex is warmed slightly, it stops being brittle and can be formed into a desired shape.

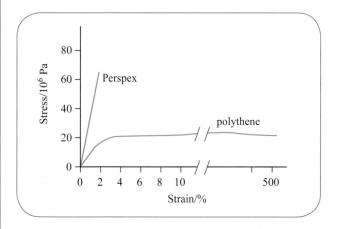

Figure 8.14 Stress against strain graphs for two polymeric materials.

We can summarise the way materials behave as follows:

- All materials show *elastic* behaviour up to the elastic limit; they return to their original length when the force is removed.
- *Brittle* materials break at the elastic limit.
- *Ductile* materials become permanently deformed if they are stretched beyond the elastic limit; they show *plastic* behaviour.

8 Use the words *elastic*, *plastic*, *brittle* and *ductile* to deduce what the following observations tell you about the materials described.

a If you tap a cast iron bath gently with a hammer, the hammer bounces off. If you hit it hard, the bath shatters.

b Aluminium drinks cans are made by forcing a sheet of aluminium into a mould at high pressure.

c 'Silly putty' can be stretched to many times its original length if it is pulled gently and slowly. If it is pulled hard and rapidly, it snaps.

Answer

Strength of a material

The *strength* of a material tells us about how much stress is needed to break the material. On a stress against strain graph (Figure 8.15), we look for the value of the stress at which the material breaks. The maximum stress a material can withstand is the **ultimate tensile strength (UTS)**. The term *ultimate* is used because this is the top of the graph and *tensile* because the material is being stretched. For brittle materials the UTS is the stress at the breaking point.

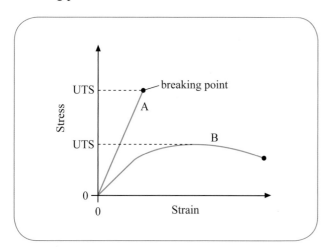

Figure 8.15 Material A has a greater UTS than material B. Material B's stress at the breaking point is lower than its UTS.

Extension

9 For each of the materials whose stress against strain graphs are shown in Figure 8.16, deduce the values of the Young modulus and the ultimate tensile strength (breaking stress).

Answer

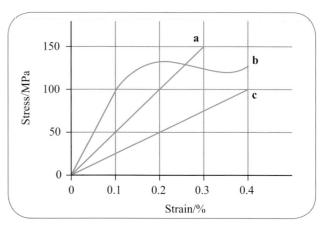

Figure 8.16 Stress against strain graphs for three materials.

Elastic potential energy

Whenever you stretch a material, you are doing work. This is because you have to apply a *force* and the material *extends* in the direction of the force. You will know this if you have ever used an exercise machine with springs intended to develop your muscles (Figure 8.17). Similarly, when you push down on the end of a springboard before diving, you are doing work. You transfer energy to the springboard, and you recover the energy when it pushes you up into the air.

Figure 8.17 Using an exercise machine is hard work.

We call the energy in a deformed solid the **elastic potential energy**. If the material has been strained elastically (the elastic limit has not been exceeded), the energy can be recovered. If the material has been plastically deformed, some of the work done has gone into moving atoms past one another, and the energy cannot be recovered. The material warms up slightly. We can determine how much elastic potential energy is involved from a force against extension graph, see Figure 8.18. We need to use the equation that defines the amount of work done by a force. That is:

work done = force × distance moved in the direction of the force

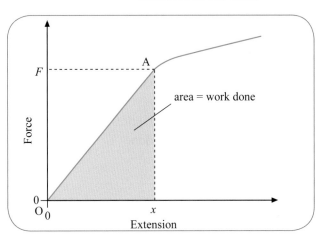

Figure 8.18 Elastic potential energy is equal to the area under the force against extension graph.

First, consider the linear region of the graph where Hooke's law is obeyed, OA. The graph in this region is a straight line through the origin. The extension x is directly proportional to the applied force F. There are two ways to find the work done.

- Method 1: We can think about the average force needed to produce an extension x. The average force is half the final force F, and so we can write:

elastic potential energy = work done

$$\text{elastic potential energy} = \frac{\text{final force}}{2} \times \text{extension}$$

$$\text{elastic potential energy} = \tfrac{1}{2}Fx$$

or $\qquad\qquad E = \tfrac{1}{2}Fx$

- Method 2: The other way to find the elastic potential energy is to recognise that we can get the same answer by finding the area under the graph. The area shaded in Figure 8.18 is a triangle whose area is

$$\tfrac{1}{2} \times \text{base} \times \text{height}$$

which again gives:

$$\text{elastic potential energy} = \tfrac{1}{2}Fx$$

or $\qquad\qquad E = \tfrac{1}{2}Fx$

The **work done** in *stretching* or *compressing* a material is always equal to the area under the force against distance graph. In fact, this is true whatever the shape of the graph. Take care: here we are drawing the graph with extension on the horizontal axis. If the graph is not a straight line, we cannot use the $\tfrac{1}{2}Fx$ relationship, so we have to resort to counting squares or some other technique to find the answer. However, the elastic potential energy relates to the elastic part of the graph (i.e. up to the elastic limit), so we can only consider the linear section of the force against extension graph.

There is an alternative equation for elastic potential energy. We know (page 96) that applied force F and extension x are related by $F = kx$, where k is the force constant. Substituting for F gives:

$$\text{elastic potential energy} = \tfrac{1}{2}Fx = \tfrac{1}{2} \times kx \times x$$

$$\text{elastic potential energy} = \tfrac{1}{2}kx^2$$

or $\qquad\qquad E = \tfrac{1}{2}Fx$

Extension

Worked example 1

Figure 8.19 shows a simplified version of a force against extension graph for a piece of metal. Find the elastic potential energy when the metal is stretched to its elastic limit and the total work that must be done to break the metal.

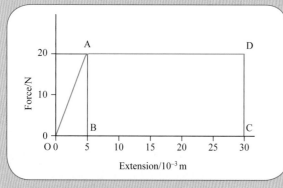

Figure 8.19 For Worked example 1.

Step 1 The elastic potential energy when the metal is stretched to its elastic limit is given by the area under the graph up to the elastic limit. The graph is a straight line up to $x = 5.0$ mm, $F = 20$ N, so the elastic potential energy is the area of triangle OAB:

$$\text{elastic potential energy} = \tfrac{1}{2}Fx$$

$$= \tfrac{1}{2} \times 20 \times 5.0 \times 10^{-3}$$

$$= 0.05 \text{ J}$$

Step 2 To find the work done to break the metal, we need to add on the area of the rectangle ABCD:

$$\text{work done} = \text{total area under the graph}$$

$$= 0.05 + (20 \times 25 \times 10^{-3})$$

$$= 0.05 + 0.50 = 0.55 \text{ J}$$

10 A force of 12 N extends a length of rubber band by 18 cm. Estimate the energy stored in this rubber band. Explain why your answer can only be an estimate.

11 A spring has a force constant of 4800 N m^{-1}. Calculate the elastic potential energy when it is compressed by 2.0 mm.

12 Figure 8.20 shows force against extension graphs for two pieces of polymer. For each of the following questions, explain how you deduce your answer from the graphs.
   a State which polymer has the greater stiffness.
   b State which polymer requires the greater force to break it.
   c State which polymer requires the greater amount of work to be done in order to break it.

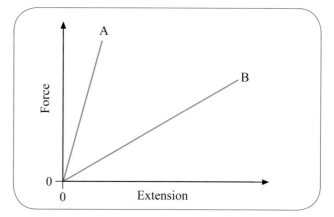

Figure 8.20 For SAQ 12.

Summary

- Hooke's law states that the extension of a material is directly proportional to the applied force as long as its elastic limit is not exceeded. A spring obeys Hooke's law.

- For a spring or a wire, $F = kx$, where k is the force constant. The force constant has unit $N\,m^{-1}$.

- Stress is defined as:

$$\text{stress} = \frac{\text{force}}{\text{cross-sectional area}} \quad \text{or} \quad \text{stress} = \frac{F}{A}$$

- Strain is defined as:

$$\text{strain} = \frac{\text{extension}}{\text{original length}} \quad \text{or} \quad \text{strain} = \frac{x}{L}$$

- To describe the behaviour of a material under tensile and compressive forces, we have to draw a graph of stress against strain. The gradient of the initial linear section of the graph is equal the Young modulus. The Young modulus is an indication of the *stiffness* of the material.

- The Young modulus E is given by:

$$E = \frac{\text{stress}}{\text{strain}}$$

The unit of the Young modulus is pascal (Pa) or $N\,m^{-2}$.

- Beyond the elastic limit, brittle materials break. Ductile materials show plastic behaviour and become permanently deformed.

- The area under a force against extension graph is equal to the work done by the force.

- For a spring or a wire obeying Hooke's law, the elastic potential energy E is given by:

$$E = \tfrac{1}{2}kx^2$$

Questions

1 Figure 1 shows part of the force against extension graph for a spring.
  The spring obeys Hooke's law for forces up to 5.0 N.

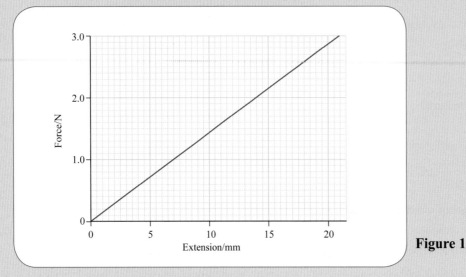

Figure 1

a Calculate the extension produced by a force of 5.0 N. [2]

b Figure 2 shows a second identical spring that has been put in parallel with the first spring. A force of 5.0 N is applied to this combination of springs.

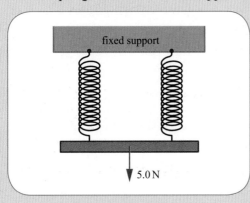

Figure 2

For the arrangement shown in Figure 2, calculate:
  i the extension of each spring [2]
  ii the elastic potential energy in the springs. [2]

c The Young modulus of the wire used in the springs is 2.0×10^{11} Pa. Each spring is made from a straight wire of length 0.40 m and cross-sectional area 2.0×10^{-7} m^2.
  Calculate the extension produced when a force of 5.0 N is applied to this straight wire. [3]

d Describe and explain, without further calculations, the difference in the elastic potential energies in the straight wire and in the spring when a 5.0 N force is applied to each. [2]

OCR Physics AS (2821) June 2006 [Total 11]

Hint

Hint

Answer

continued

2   The diagram shows a stress against strain graph up to the point of fracture for a rod of cast iron.

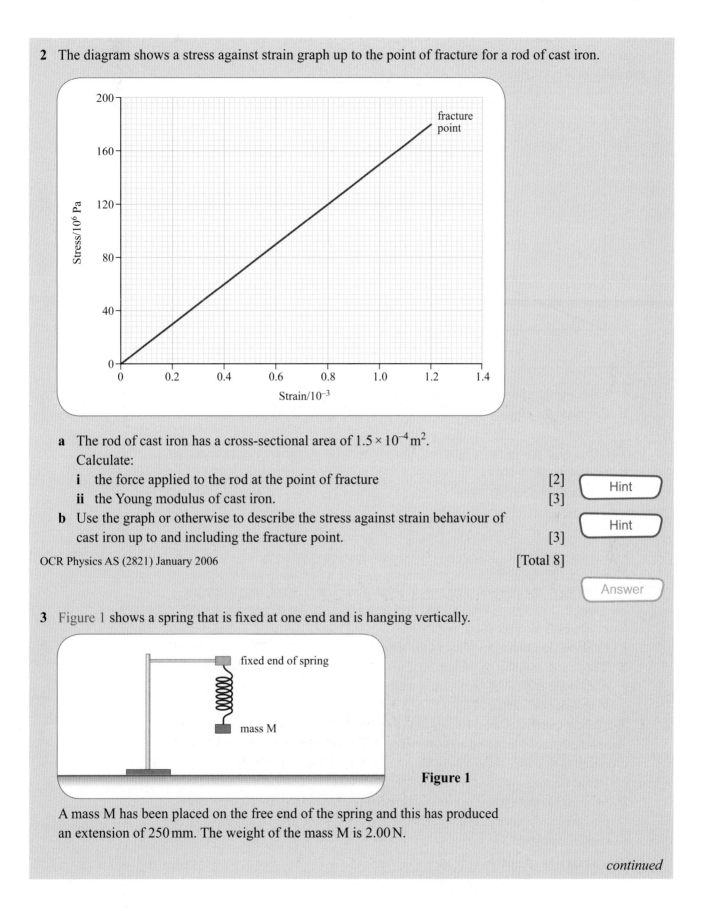

a   The rod of cast iron has a cross-sectional area of $1.5 \times 10^{-4}\,\text{m}^2$.
Calculate:
   i   the force applied to the rod at the point of fracture   [2]
   ii the Young modulus of cast iron.   [3]
b   Use the graph or otherwise to describe the stress against strain behaviour of cast iron up to and including the fracture point.   [3]

OCR Physics AS (2821) January 2006   [Total 8]

Hint

Hint

Answer

3   Figure 1 shows a spring that is fixed at one end and is hanging vertically.

fixed end of spring

mass M

Figure 1

A mass M has been placed on the free end of the spring and this has produced an extension of 250 mm. The weight of the mass M is 2.00 N.

continued

Figure 2 shows how the force F applied to the spring varies with extension x up to an extension of $x = 250\,\text{mm}$.

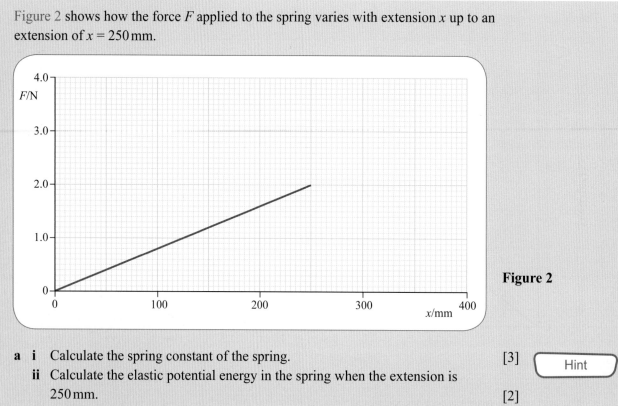

Figure 2

a i Calculate the spring constant of the spring. [3]
  ii Calculate the elastic potential energy in the spring when the extension is 250 mm. [2]

b The mass M is pulled down a further 150 mm by a force F additional to its weight.
  i Determine the force F. [1]
  ii State any assumption made. [1]

OCR Physics AS (2821) June 2005 [Total 7]

Hint

Answer

4 a Define the *Young modulus*. [1]

  b The wire used in a piano string is made from steel. The original length of wire used was 0.75 m. Fixing one end and applying a force to the other stretches the wire. The extension produced is 4.2 mm.
   i Calculate the strain produced in the wire. [2]
   ii The Young modulus of the steel is $2.0 \times 10^{11}\,\text{Pa}$ and the cross-sectional area of the wire is $4.5 \times 10^{-7}\,\text{m}^2$. Calculate the force required to produce the strain in the wire calculated in **i**. [3]

  c A different material is used for one of the other strings in the piano. It has the same length, cross-sectional area and force applied. Calculate the extension produced in this wire if the Young modulus of this material is half that of steel. [2]

  d i Define *density*. [1]
   ii State and explain what happens to the density of the material of a wire when it is stretched. Assume that when the wire stretches the cross-sectional area remains constant. [1]

OCR Physics AS (2821) June 2004 [Total 10]

Hint

Hint

Answer

Chapter 9

Electric current

e-Learning

Objectives

Developing ideas

Electricity plays a vital part in our lives. We use electricity as a way of transferring energy from place to place – for heating, lighting and making things move. For people in a developing nation, the arrival of a reliable electricity supply marks a great leap forward. In Kenya, a micro-hydroelectric scheme has been built on Kabiri Falls, on the slopes of Mount Kenya. Although this produces just 14 kW of power, it has given work to a number of people, as shown in Figure 9.1, Figure 9.2 and Figure 9.3.

Figure 9.2 A hairdresser can now work in the evenings, thanks to electrical lighting.

Figure 9.1 An operator controls the water inlet at the Kabiri Falls power plant. The generator is on the right.

Figure 9.3 A metal workshop uses electrical welding equipment. This allows rapid repairs to farmers' machinery.

What's in a word?

Electricity is a rather tricky word. In everyday life, its meaning may be rather vague – sometimes we use it to mean electric current; at other times, it may mean electrical energy or electrical power. In this chapter and the ones which follow, we will avoid using the word *electricity* and try to develop the correct usage of these more precise scientific terms.

Making a current

You will have carried out many practical activities involving electric current. For example, if you connect up a wire to a cell (Figure 9.4), there will be current in the wire. And of course you make use of electric currents every day of your life – when you switch on a lamp or a computer, for example.

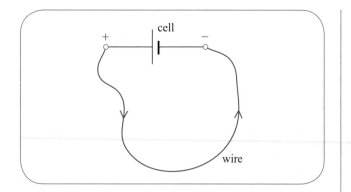

Figure 9.4 There is current in the wire when it is connected to a cell.

In the circuit of Figure 9.4, the direction of the current is from the positive terminal of the cell, around the circuit to the negative terminal. This is a scientific convention: the direction of current is from positive to negative, and hence the current may be referred to as *conventional current*. But what is going on inside the wire?

A wire is made of metal. Inside a metal, there are negatively charged electrons which are free to move about. We call these *conduction* or *free* electrons, because they are the particles which allow a metal to conduct an electric current. The atoms of a metal bind tightly together; they usually form a regular array, as shown in Figure 9.5. In a typical metal such as copper or silver, one electron from each atom breaks free to become a conduction electron. The atom remains as a positively charged ion. Since there are equal numbers of free electrons (negative) and ions (positive), the metal has no overall charge – it is neutral.

When the cell is connected to the wire, it exerts an electrical force on the conduction electrons that makes them travel along the length of the wire. Since electrons are negatively charged, they flow away from the negative terminal of the cell and towards the positive terminal. This is in the *opposite* direction to conventional current. This may seem a bit odd; it comes about because the direction of conventional current was chosen long before anyone had any idea what was going on inside a piece of metal when carrying a current.

Note that there is a current at all points in the circuit as soon as the circuit is completed. We do not have to wait for charge to travel around from the cell. This is because the charged electrons are already present throughout the metal before the cell is connected.

Sometimes a current is a flow of positive charges; for example, a beam of protons produced in a particle accelerator. The current is in the same direction as the particles. Sometimes a current is due to both positive and negative charges; for example, when charged particles flow through a solution. A solution which conducts is called an **electrolyte** and it contains both positive and negative ions. These move in opposite directions when the solution is connected to a cell (Figure 9.6). Any charged particles which contribute to an electric current are known as **charge carriers**; these can be electrons, protons or ions.

SAQ

1 Look at Figure 9.6 and state the direction of the conventional current in the electrolyte (towards the left, towards the right, or in both directions at the same time).

Answer

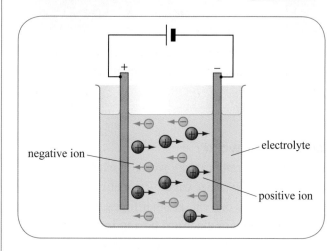

Figure 9.6 Both positive and negative charges are free to move in a solution. Both contribute to the electric current.

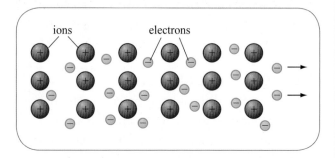

Figure 9.5 In a metal, conduction electrons are free to move around the fixed positive ions. A cell connected across the ends of the metal causes the electrons to drift towards its positive terminal.

2 Figure 9.7 shows a circuit with a conducting solution having both positive and negative ions. A cell is connected between points A and B. Copy the diagram and complete it as follows:

a Add an arrow to show the direction of the conventional current in the solution.

b Add arrows to show the direction of the conventional current in the two connecting wires.

c Add a cell between points A and B. Clearly indicate the positive and negative terminals of the cell.

Answer

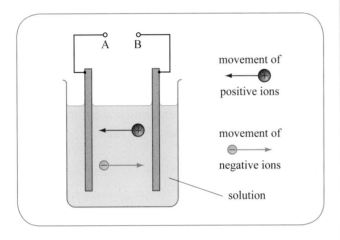

Figure 9.7 For SAQ 2.

Current and charge

When charged particles flow past a point in a circuit, we say that there is a current in the circuit. Electrical current is measured in **amperes** (A). So how much charge is moving when there is a current of 1 A?

Charge is measured in **coulombs** (C). For a current of 1 A, the charge flow past a point in a circuit is 1 C in a time of 1 s. Similarly, a current of 2 A gives a charge of 2 C in a time of 1 s. A current of 3 A gives a charge of 6 C in a time of 2 s, and so on. The relationship between charge, current and time may be written as the following word equation:

charge = current × time

From this the unit of charge, the coulomb is defined as follows:

One coulomb is the amount of charge which flows past a point in a circuit in a time of 1 s when the current is 1 A.

The amount of charge flowing past a point is given by the following relationship:

$$\Delta Q = I \Delta t$$

where ΔQ is the amount of charge which flows during a time interval Δt and I is the current. You should think of Δt as a single symbol, meaning 'a change in time t' or 'an interval of time'. It doesn't mean $\Delta \times t$. Similarly, ΔQ means 'change in charge Q'.

Worked example 1

There is a current of 10 A through a lamp for 1.0 hour. Calculate how much charge flows through the lamp in this time.

Step 1 We need to find the time interval Δt in seconds:

$$\Delta t = 60 \times 60 = 3600 \, \text{s}$$

Step 2 We know the current $I = 10 \, \text{A}$, so the charge which flows is:

$$\Delta Q = I \Delta t$$
$$= 10 \times 3600 = 36\,000 \, \text{C} = 3.6 \times 10^4 \, \text{C}$$

Worked example 2

Calculate the current in a circuit when a charge of 180 C passes a point in a circuit in 2.0 minutes.

Step 1 Rearranging $\Delta Q = I \Delta t$ gives:

$$I = \frac{\Delta Q}{\Delta t} \quad \left(\text{or current} = \frac{\text{charge}}{\text{time}} \right)$$

Step 2 With time in seconds we then have:

$$\text{current } I = \frac{180}{120} = 1.5 \, \text{A}$$

SAQ

3 The current in a circuit is 0.40 A. Calculate the charge flow past a point in the circuit in a period of 15 s.

Answer

4 Calculate the current that gives rise to a charge flow of 150 C in a time of 30 s.

Answer

5 In a circuit, a charge of 50 C passes a point in 20 s. Calculate the current in the circuit.

Answer

6 A car battery is labelled '50 Ah'. This means that it can supply a current of 50 A for one hour.

Hint

   a For how long could the battery supply a continuous current of 200 A needed to start the car?

   b Calculate the charge which flows past a point in the circuit in this time.

Answer

Charged particles

Electrons are charged particles. They have a tiny negative charge of approximately -1.6×10^{-19} C. This charge is represented by $-e$. The magnitude of the charge is known as the **elementary charge**. This charge is so tiny that you would need about six million million million electrons – that's 6 000 000 000 000 000 000 of them – to have a charge equivalent to one coulomb.

elementary charge $e = 1.6 \times 10^{-19}$ C

Protons are positively charged, with a charge $+e$. This is equal and opposite to that of an electron. As far as we know, it is impossible to have charge on its own; charge is always associated with particles having mass.

Extension

SAQ

7 Calculate the number of protons which would have a charge of one coulomb. (Proton charge $= +1.6 \times 10^{-19}$ C.)

Answer

Kirchhoff's first law

You should be familiar with the idea that current may divide up where a circuit splits into two separate branches. For example, a current of 5.0 A may split at a junction or a point in a circuit into two separate currents of 2.0 A and 3.0 A. The total amount of current remains the same after it splits. We would not expect some of the current to disappear, or extra current to appear from nowhere. This is the basis of **Kirchhoff's first law**, which states that:

> The sum of the currents entering any point in a circuit is equal to the sum of the currents leaving that same point.

This is illustrated in Figure 9.8. In the first part of the figure, the current into point P must equal the current out, so:

$$I_1 = I_2$$

In the second part of the figure, we have one current coming into point Q, and two currents leaving. The current divides at Q. Kirchhoff's first law gives:

$$I_1 = I_2 + I_3$$

Kirchhoff's first law is an expression of the *conservation of charge*. The idea is that the total amount of charge entering a point must exit the point. To put it another way, if a billion electrons enter a point in a circuit in a time interval of 1.0 s, then one billion electrons must exit this point in 1.0 s.

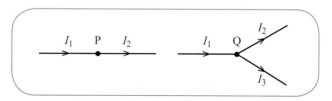

Figure 9.8 Kirchhoff's first law: current is conserved because charge is conserved.

The law can be tested by connecting ammeters at different points in a circuit where the current divides. You should recall that an ammeter must be connected in series so the current to be measured flows *through* it.

SAQ

8 Use Kirchhoff's first law to deduce the value of the current I in Figure 9.9.

Answer

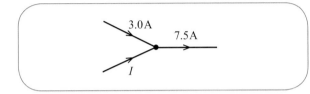

Figure 9.9 For SAQ 8.

9 In Figure 9.10, calculate the current in the wire X. State the direction of this current (towards P or away from P).

Answer

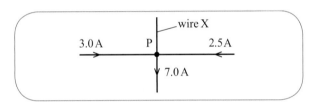

Figure 9.10 For SAQ 9.

An equation for current

Copper, silver and gold are good conductors of electric current. There are large numbers of conduction electrons in a copper wire – as many conduction electrons as there are atoms. The number of conduction electrons per unit volume (i.e. in $1\,m^3$ of the metal) is called the **number density** and has the symbol n. For copper, the value of n is about $10^{29}\,m^{-3}$.

Figure 9.11 shows a length of wire, cross-sectional area A, along which there is a current I. How fast do the electrons have to travel? The following equation allows us to answer this question:

$I = Anev$

Here, v is called the **mean drift velocity** of the electrons and e is the elementary charge. Worked example 3 shows how to use this equation to calculate a typical value of v.

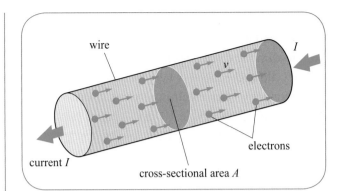

Figure 9.11 A current I in the wire of cross-sectional area A. The charge carriers are mobile conduction electrons with mean drift velocity v.

Worked example 3

Calculate the mean drift velocity of the electrons in a copper wire of cross-sectional area $5.0 \times 10^{-6}\,m^2$ when carrying a current of $1.0\,A$. The electron number density for copper is $8.5 \times 10^{28}\,m^{-3}$.

Step 1 Rearrange the equation $I = Anev$ to make v the subject:

$$v = \frac{I}{nAe}$$

Step 2 Substitute values and calculate v:

$$v = \frac{1.0}{8.5 \times 10^{28} \times 5.0 \times 10^{-6} \times 1.6 \times 10^{-19}}$$

$$= 1.47 \times 10^{-5}\,m\,s^{-1}$$

$$= 0.015\,mm\,s^{-1}$$

Extension

Slow flow

It may surprise you to find that, as suggested by the result of Worked example 3, electrons in a copper wire drift at a fraction of a millimetre per second. To understand this result fully, we need to closely examine how electrons behave in a metal. The conduction electrons are free to move around inside the metal. When connected to a battery or an external supply, each electron within the metal experiences an electrical force that causes it to move towards the positive end of the battery. The electrons randomly collide with the fixed but vibrating metal ions. Their journey along the metal is very haphazard. The actual velocity of an electron between collisions is of the order of magnitude $10^6\,\mathrm{m\,s^{-1}}$, but its haphazard journey causes it to have a *drift velocity* towards the positive end of the battery. Since there are billions of electrons, we use the term *mean drift velocity v* of the electrons.

Figure 9.12 shows how the mean drift velocity of electrons varies in different situations. We can understand this using the equation:

$$v = \frac{I}{nAe}$$

If the current increases, the drift velocity v must increase ($v \propto I$).

If the wire is thinner, the electrons move more quickly. That is:

$$v \propto \frac{1}{A}$$

There are fewer electrons in a thinner piece of wire, so an individual electron must travel more quickly.

In a material with a lower density of electrons (smaller n), the mean drift velocity must be greater. That is

$$v \propto \frac{1}{n}$$

It may help you to picture how the drift velocity of electrons changes by thinking about the flow of water in a river. For a high rate of flow, the water moves fast – this corresponds to a greater current I. If the course of the river narrows, it speeds up – this corresponds to a smaller cross-sectional area A.

Metals have a high electron number density – typically of the order of 10^{28} or $10^{29}\,\mathrm{m^{-3}}$. Semiconductors, such as silicon and germanium, have much lower values of n – perhaps $10^{23}\,\mathrm{m^{-3}}$. In a semiconductor, electron mean drift velocities are typically a million times greater than those in metals for the same current. Electrical insulators, such as rubber and plastic, have very few conduction electrons per unit volume to act as charge carriers.

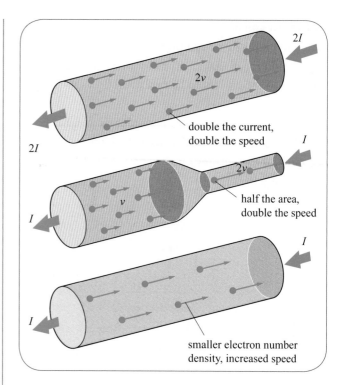

Figure 9.12 The mean drift velocity of electrons depends on the current, the cross-sectional area, and the electron density of the material.

SAQ

10 Calculate the current in a gold wire of cross-sectional area $2.0\,\mathrm{mm^2}$ when the mean drift velocity of the electrons in the wire is $0.10\,\mathrm{mm\,s^{-1}}$. The electron number density for gold is $5.9 \times 10^{28}\,\mathrm{m^{-3}}$.

Hint

Answer

11 Calculate the mean drift velocity of electrons in a copper wire of diameter $1.0\,\mathrm{mm}$ with a current of $5.0\,\mathrm{A}$. The electron number density for copper is $8.5 \times 10^{28}\,\mathrm{m^{-3}}$.

Hint

Answer

12 A length of copper wire is joined in series to a length of silver wire of the same diameter. Both wires have a current in them when connected to a battery. Explain how the mean drift velocity of the electrons will change as they travel from the copper into the silver. Electron number densities:
    copper $n = 8.5 \times 10^{28}\,\mathrm{m^{-3}}$
    silver $n = 5.9 \times 10^{28}\,\mathrm{m^{-3}}$.

Hint

Answer

Summary

Glossary

- An electric current is a flow of charge. In a metal this is due to the flow of electrons. In an electrolyte, the flow of positive and negative ions produces the current.

- The direction of conventional current is from positive to negative; the direction of electron flow is from negative to positive.

- The SI unit of charge is the coulomb (C). One coulomb is the charge which passes a point when a current of 1 A flows for 1 s.

- charge = current × time; $\Delta Q = I\Delta t$

- The elementary charge, $e = 1.6 \times 10^{-19}$ C

- Kirchhoff's first law states that the sum of the currents entering any point in a circuit is equal to the sum of the currents leaving that same point.

- The current I in a conductor of cross-sectional area A depends on the mean drift velocity v of the charge carriers and on their number density in the material n:
  $I = Anev$

Questions

1 a Explain what is meant by *electric current*. [1]
   b The SI unit of electric charge is the coulomb. Define the *coulomb*. [1]

   Hint

   c The diagram shows two strips of aluminium foil connected to a d.c. supply.

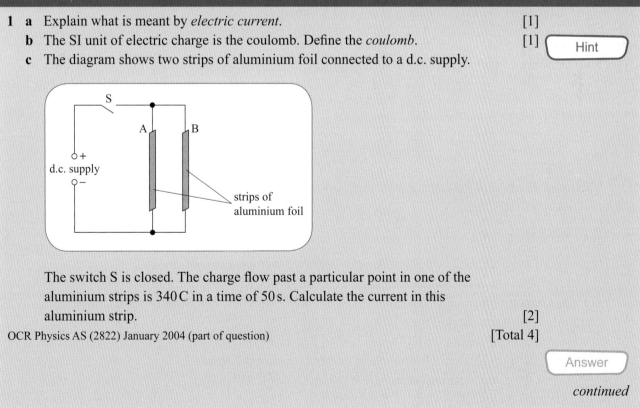

The switch S is closed. The charge flow past a particular point in one of the aluminium strips is 340 C in a time of 50 s. Calculate the current in this aluminium strip. [2]

OCR Physics AS (2822) January 2004 (part of question) [Total 4]

Answer

continued

2 a State Kirchhoff's first law. [2]

b The diagram shows part of an electrical circuit.

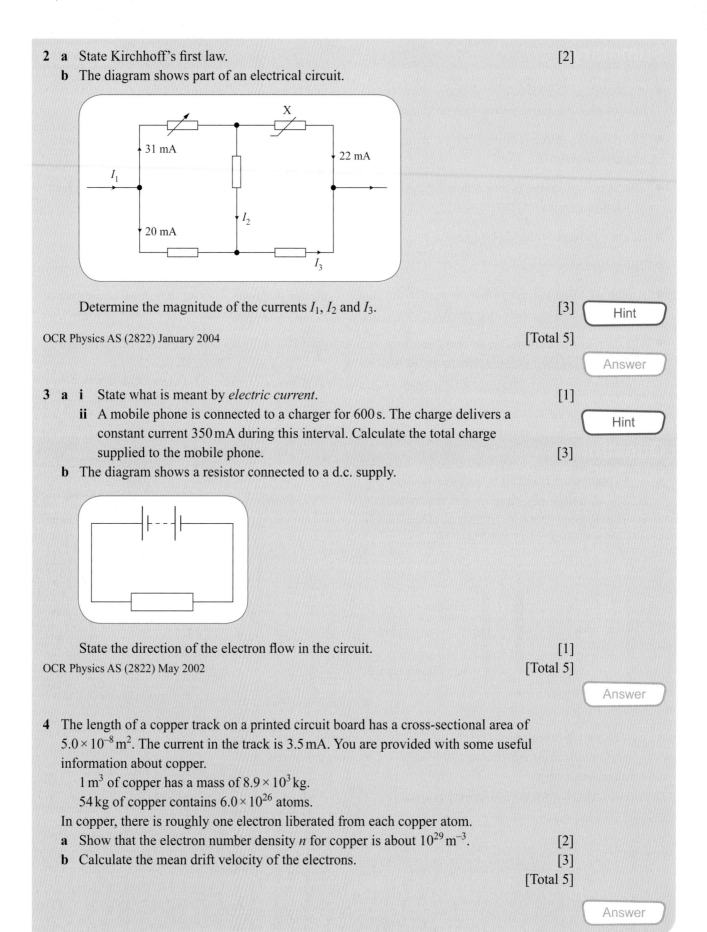

Determine the magnitude of the currents I_1, I_2 and I_3. [3]

OCR Physics AS (2822) January 2004 [Total 5]

Hint

Answer

3 a i State what is meant by *electric current*. [1]

   ii A mobile phone is connected to a charger for 600 s. The charge delivers a constant current 350 mA during this interval. Calculate the total charge supplied to the mobile phone. [3]

Hint

b The diagram shows a resistor connected to a d.c. supply.

State the direction of the electron flow in the circuit. [1]

OCR Physics AS (2822) May 2002 [Total 5]

Answer

4 The length of a copper track on a printed circuit board has a cross-sectional area of $5.0 \times 10^{-8}\,\text{m}^2$. The current in the track is 3.5 mA. You are provided with some useful information about copper.

    1 m^3 of copper has a mass of $8.9 \times 10^3\,\text{kg}$.

    54 kg of copper contains 6.0×10^{26} atoms.

In copper, there is roughly one electron liberated from each copper atom.

a Show that the electron number density n for copper is about $10^{29}\,\text{m}^{-3}$. [2]

b Calculate the mean drift velocity of the electrons. [3]

[Total 5]

Answer

Chapter 10

Resistance and resistivity

Objectives

Electrical resistance

If you connect a lamp to a battery, a current in the lamp causes it to glow. But what determines the size of the current? This depends on two factors:

- the potential difference or voltage V across the lamp – the greater the voltage, the greater the current for a given lamp
- the resistance R of the lamp – the greater the resistance, the smaller the current for a given voltage.

We will look more carefully at the meaning of voltage in Chapter 11. For the purpose of this chapter, you just need to know that we can measure the voltage (also known as *potential difference*) across a component by placing a voltmeter across the component.

Now we need to think about the meaning of **electrical resistance**. Different lamps have different resistances. It is easy to demonstrate this by connecting a torch bulb and a car headlamp in series to a battery. The current is the *same* in each component, but the voltage across the torch bulb will be greater than the voltage across the headlamp. The torch bulb has a larger resistance than the headlamp.

The resistance of any component is defined as the ratio of the voltage to the current. As a word equation, this is written as:

$$resistance = \frac{voltage}{current}$$

or

$$R = \frac{V}{I}$$

where R is the resistance of the component, V is the voltage across the component and I is the current in the component.

You can rearrange the equation above to give:

$$I = \frac{V}{R} \quad \text{and} \quad V = IR$$

Table 10.1 summarises these quantities and their units.

Quantity	Symbol for quantity	Unit	Symbol for unit
current	I	ampere (amp)	A
voltage	V	volt	V
resistance	R	ohm	Ω

Table 10.1 Basic electrical quantities, their symbols and SI units. Take care to understand the difference between V (in italics) meaning the quantity voltage and V meaning the unit volt.

Worked example 1

Calculate the current in a lamp given its resistance is $15\,\Omega$ and the potential difference across its ends is $3.0\,V$.

Step 1 Here we have $V = 3.0\,V$ and $R = 15\,\Omega$.

Step 2 Substituting in $I = \dfrac{V}{R}$ gives:

$$current\ I = \frac{3.0}{15} = 0.20\,A$$

So the current in the lamp is $0.20\,A$.

SAQ

1 A car headlamp bulb has a resistance of $36\,\Omega$. Calculate the current in the lamp when connected to a '12 V' battery.

Answer

2 You can buy lamps of different brightness to fit in light fittings at home (Figure 10.1). A '100 watt' lamp glows more brightly than a '60 watt' lamp. Which of the lamps has the higher resistance?

Hint

Answer

Figure 10.1 Both of these lamps work from the 230 V mains supply, but one has a higher resistance than the other. For SAQ 2.

Defining the ohm

The unit of resistance, the ohm, can be determined from the equation that defines resistance:

$$resistance = \frac{voltage}{current}$$

The ohm is equivalent to '1 volt per ampere'. That is:

$$1\,\Omega = 1\,V\,A^{-1}$$

> The ohm is the resistance of a component when a potential difference of 1 volt is produced per ampere of current.

SAQ

3 a Calculate the potential difference across a motor carrying a current of 1.0 A having a resistance of 50 Ω.

   b Calculate the potential difference across the same motor when the current is doubled. Assume its resistance remains constant.

   Answer

4 Calculate the resistance of a lamp carrying a current of 0.40 A when connected to a 230 V supply.

   Answer

Determining resistance

As we have seen, the equation for resistance is:

$$R = \frac{V}{I}$$

To determine the resistance of a component, we therefore need to measure both the voltage *V* across it and the current *I* through it. To measure the current we need an ammeter. To measure the voltage, we need a voltmeter. Figure 10.2a shows how these meters should be connected to determine the resistance of a metallic conductor, such as a length of wire.

- The ammeter is connected in *series* with the conductor, so that there is the same current in both.
- The voltmeter is connected across (in *parallel* with) the conductor, to measure the voltage across it.

The voltage across the metal conductor can be altered using a variable power supply or by having a variable resistor placed in series with the conductor. This gives currents at different voltages. The results of such a series of measurements is shown graphically in Figure 10.2b.

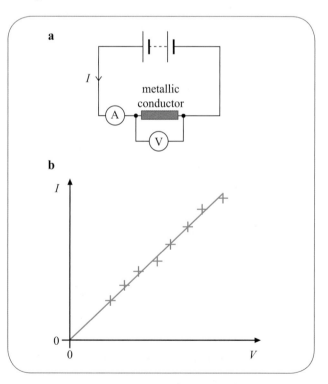

Figure 10.2 To determine the resistance of a component, you need to measure both current and potential difference.

Look at the graph of Figure 10.2b. Such a graph is known as an *I–V* **characteristic**. The points are slightly scattered, but they clearly lie on a straight line. A line of best fit has been drawn. If you extend this line downwards, you will see that it passes through the origin of the graph. In other words, the current *I* is directly proportional to the voltage *V*. The straight-line graph passing through the origin shows that the resistance of the conductor remains constant. If you double the current, the voltage will also double. However, its resistance, which is the ratio of the voltage to the current, remains the same. Instead of using:

$$R = \frac{V}{I}$$

to determine the resistance, for a graph of *I* against *V* which is a straight line passing through the origin, you can also use:

$$\text{resistance} = \frac{1}{\text{gradient of graph}}$$

(Take care! This is only true for an *I–V* graph which is a straight line through the origin.)

You get results similar to those shown in Figure 10.2b for a commercial **resistor**. Resistors have different resistances, hence the gradient of the *I–V* graph will be different for different resistors.

SAQ

5 Table 10.2 shows the results of an experiment to measure the resistance of a carbon resistor whose resistance is given by the manufacturer as $47\,\Omega \pm 10\%$.

   a Plot a graph to show the *I–V* characteristic of this resistor.

   b Do the points appear to fall on a straight line which passes through the origin of the graph?

   c Use the graph to determine the resistance of the resistor.

   d Does the value of the resistance fall within the range given by the manufacturer?

> Answer

Voltage *V*/V	Current *I*/A
2.1	0.040
4.0	0.079
6.3	0.128
7.9	0.192
10.0	0.202
12.1	0.250

Table 10.2 Data for SAQ 5.

Ohm's law

For the metallic conductor whose *I–V* characteristic is shown in Figure 10.2b, the current through it is directly proportional to the voltage across it. This is only true if the temperature of the conductor does not change. This means that its resistance is independent of both the current and the voltage. This is because the ratio $\frac{V}{I}$ is a constant. Any component which behaves like this is described as an *ohmic component*, and we say that it obeys **Ohm's law**. The statement of Ohm's law is very precise and you must not confuse this with the equation '*V = IR*'.

> *Ohm's law*
> For a metallic conductor at constant temperature, the current in the conductor is directly proportional to the potential difference across its ends.

It is easier to see the significance of this if we consider a non-ohmic component. An example is a **semiconductor diode**. This is a component which allows electric current in only one direction. Nowadays, most diodes are made of semiconductor materials. One type, the **light-emitting diode** or LED, gives out light when it conducts.

Figure 10.3 shows the *I–V* characteristic for a light-emitting diode. There are some points you should notice about this graph:

- We have included positive and negative values of current and voltage. This is because, when connected one way round (positively biased), the diode conducts and has a fairly low resistance. Connected the other way round (negatively biased), it allows only a tiny current through and has almost infinite resistance.
- For positive voltages less than about 2 V, the current is almost zero and hence the LED has almost infinite resistance. The LED starts to conduct suddenly at its *threshold voltage*. This depends on the colour of light it emits, but may be taken to be about 2 V. The resistance of the LED decreases dramatically for voltages greater than 2 V.

The resistance of a light-emitting diode depends on the potential difference across it. From this we can conclude that the LED does not obey Ohm's law; it is a *non-ohmic component*.

LEDs have traditionally been used as indicator lamps to show when an appliance is switched on. Newer versions, some of which produce white light, are replacing filament lamps, for example in traffic lights. This is because, although they are more expensive to manufacture, they are more energy-efficient and hence cheaper to run, so that the overall cost is less.

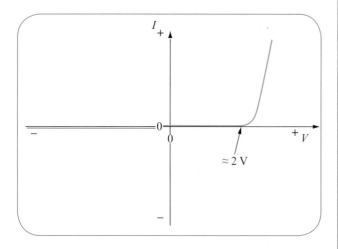

Figure 10.3 The current against voltage (*I–V*) characteristic for a light-emitting diode. The graph is not a straight line. An LED does not obey Ohm's law.

SAQ

6 An electrical component allows a current of 10 mA through it when a voltage of 2.0 V is applied. When the voltage is increased to 8.0 V, the current becomes 60 mA. Does the component obey Ohm's law? Give numerical values for the resistance to justify your answer.

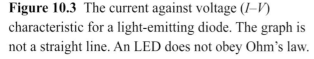 Hint

Answer

Resistance and temperature

You should have noted earlier that, for a component to obey Ohm's law, the temperature must remain constant. You can see why this must be the case by considering the characteristics of a filament lamp. Figure 10.4 shows such a lamp; you can clearly see the wire filament glowing as the current passes through it. Figure 10.5 shows the *I–V* characteristic for a similar lamp.

Figure 10.4 The metal filament in a lamp glows as the current passes through it. It also feels warm. This shows that the lamp produces both heat and light.

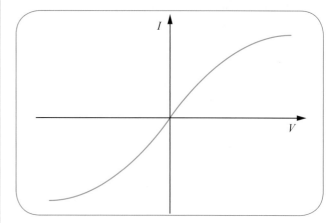

Figure 10.5 The *I–V* characteristic for a filament lamp.

There are some points you should notice about the graph in Figure 10.5:

- The line passes through the origin (as for an ohmic component).
- For very small currents and voltages, the graph is roughly a straight line.
- At higher voltages, the line starts to curve. The current is a bit less than we would have expected from a straight line. This suggests that the lamp's resistance has increased. You can also tell that the resistance has increased because the ratio $\frac{V}{I}$ is larger for higher voltages than for low voltages.

The fact that the graph of Figure 10.5 is not a straight line shows that the resistance of the lamp depends on the temperature of its filament. Its resistance may increase by a factor as large as ten between when it is cold and when it is brightest (when its temperature may be as high as $1750\,°C$).

SAQ

7 The two graphs in Figure 10.6 show the $I–V$ characteristics of a metal wire at two different temperatures, θ_1 and θ_2.

   a Calculate the resistance of the wire at each temperature.

   b State which is the higher temperature, θ_1 or θ_2.

8 The graph of Figure 10.7 shows the $I–V$ characteristics for two electrical components, a filament lamp and a length of steel wire.

   a Identify which curve relates to each component.

   b State at what voltage both have the same resistance.

   c Determine the resistance at the voltage stated in **b**.

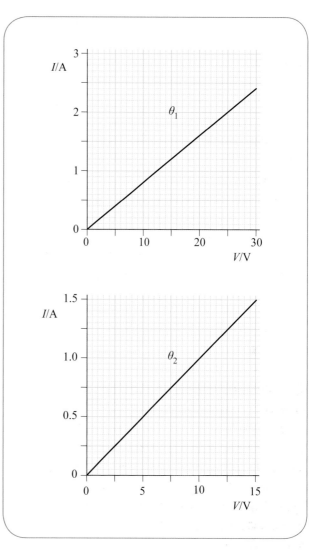

Figure 10.6 $I–V$ graphs for a wire at two different temperatures. For SAQ 7.

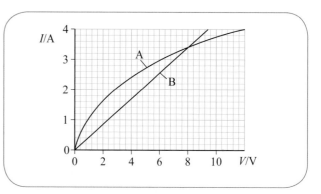

Figure 10.7 For SAQ 8.

Thermistors

These are components that are designed to have a resistance which changes rapidly with temperature. Thermistors ('*therm*al res*istors*') are made from metal oxides such as those of manganese and nickel. There are two distinct types of thermistor.

- Negative temperature coefficient (NTC) thermistors – the resistance of this type of thermistor decreases with increasing temperature. Those commonly used in schools and colleges may have a resistance of many thousands of ohms at room temperature, falling to a few tens of ohms at 100 °C. You are expected to recall the properties of NTC thermistors.
- Positive temperature coefficient (PTC) thermistors – the resistance of this type of thermistor rises abruptly at a definite temperature, usually around 100–150 °C.

Thermistors at work

The change in their resistance with temperature gives thermistors many uses.

- Water temperature sensors in cars and ice sensors on aircraft wings – if ice builds up on the wings, the thermistor 'senses' this temperature drop and a small heater is activated to melt the ice.
- Baby alarms – the baby rests on an air-filled pad, and as he or she breathes, air from the pad passes over a thermistor, keeping it cool; if the baby stops breathing, the air movement stops, the thermistor warms up and an alarm sounds.
- Fire sensors – the rise in temperature activates an alarm.
- Overload protection in electric razor sockets – if the razor overheats, the thermistor's resistance rises rapidly and cuts off the circuit.

SAQ

9 The graph in Figure 10.8 was obtained by measuring the resistance R of a particular thermistor as its temperature θ changed.

   a Determine its resistance at
      i 20 °C
      ii 45 °C.
   b Determine the temperature when its resistance is
      i 5000 Ω
      ii 2000 Ω.
   c The *sensitivity* of the thermistor is defined as $\frac{\Delta R}{\Delta \theta}$. This is the gradient of the graph. Use the graph to estimate the sensitivity at
      i 20 °C
      ii 45 °C
      iii 70 °C.

   Answer

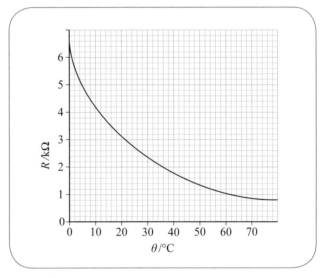

Figure 10.8 The resistance of an NTC thermistor decreases as the temperature increases. For SAQ 9.

10 A student connects a circuit with an NTC thermistor, a filament lamp and a battery in series. The lamp glows dimly. The student warms the thermistor with a hair dryer. What change will the student notice in the brightness of the lamp? Explain your answer.

   Answer

Understanding the origin of resistance

To understand a little more about the origins of resistance, it is helpful to look at how the resistance of a pure metal wire changes as its temperature is increased. This is shown in the graph of Figure 10.9. You will see that the resistance of the pure metal increases linearly as the temperature increases from 0 °C to 100 °C. Compare this with the graph of Figure 10.8 for an NTC thermistor; the thermistor's resistance decreases very dramatically over a narrow temperature range.

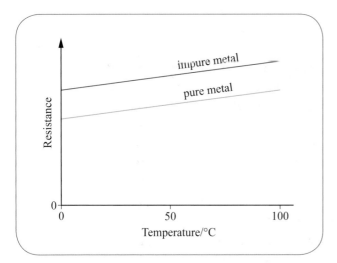

Figure 10.9 The resistance of a metal increases gradually as its temperature is increased. The resistance of an impure metal wire is greater than that of a pure metal wire of the same dimensions.

Figure 10.9 also shows how the resistance of the metal changes if it is slightly impure. The resistance of an impure metal is greater than that of the pure metal and follows the same gradual upward slope. The resistance of a metal changes in this gradual way over a wide range of temperatures – from close to absolute zero up to its melting point, which may be over 2000 °C.

This suggests that there are two factors which affect the resistance of a metal:

- the temperature
- the presence of impurities.

Here is what we picture is happening in a metal when electrons flow through it (Figure 10.10).

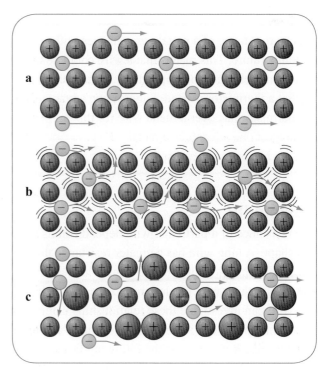

Figure 10.10 The origins of resistance in a metal. **a** At low temperatures, electrons flow relatively freely. **b** At higher temperatures, the electrons are obstructed by the vibrating ions and they make very frequent collisions with the ions. **c** Impurity atoms can also obstruct the free flow of electrons.

In a metal, a current is due to the movement of free electrons. At low temperatures, they can move easily past the positive ions (Figure 10.10a). However, as the temperature is raised, the ions vibrate with larger amplitudes. The electrons collide more frequently with the vibrating ions, and this decreases their mean drift velocity. They lose energy to the vibrating ions (Figure 10.10b).

If the metal contains impurities, some of the atoms will be of different sizes (Figure 10.10c). Again, this disrupts the free flow of electrons. In colliding with impurity atoms, the electrons lose energy to the vibrating atoms.

You can see that electrons tend to lose energy when they collide with vibrating ions or impurity atoms. They give up energy to the metal, so it gets hotter. The resistance of the metal increases with the temperature of the wire because of the decrease in the mean drift velocity of the electrons.

SAQ

11 The resistance of a metal wire changes with temperature. This means that a wire could be used to sense changes in temperature, in the same way that a thermistor is used. Suggest one advantage a thermistor has over a metal wire for this purpose; suggest one advantage a metal wire has over a thermistor.

Answer

Resistivity

The resistance of a particular wire depends on its size and shape. A long wire has a greater resistance than a short one, provided it is of the same thickness and material. A thick wire has less resistance than a thin one. You can investigate these relationships using conducting putty. For a metal in the shape of a wire, its resistance R depends on the following factors:

- its length L
- its cross-sectional area A
- the material the wire is made from
- its temperature.

At a constant temperature, the resistance is directly proportional to the length of the wire and inversely proportional to its cross-sectional area. That is:

$$\text{resistance} \propto \text{length}$$

and

$$\text{resistance} \propto \frac{1}{\text{cross-sectional area}}$$

Therefore:

$$\text{resistance} \propto \frac{\text{length}}{\text{cross-sectional area}}$$

or

$$R \propto \frac{L}{A}$$

The resistance of a wire also depends on the material it is made of. Copper is a better conductor than steel, steel is a better conductor than silicon, and so on. So if we are to determine the resistance R of a particular wire, we need to take into account its length, its cross-sectional area and the material. The relevant property of the material is its **resistivity**, for which the symbol is ρ (Greek letter *rho*).

The word equation for resistance is:

$$\text{resistance} = \frac{\text{resistivity} \times \text{length}}{\text{cross-sectional area}}$$

$$R = \frac{\rho L}{A}$$

We can rearrange this equation to give an equation for resistivity. The resistivity of a material is defined by the following word equation:

$$\text{resistivity} = \frac{\text{resistance} \times \text{cross-sectional area}}{\text{length}}$$

$$\rho = \frac{RA}{L}$$

Values of the resistivities of some typical materials are shown in Table 10.3. Notice that the units of resistivity are ohm metres ($\Omega\,\text{m}$); this is not the same as ohms per metre.

Material	Resistivity/ $\Omega\,\text{m}$	Material	Resistivity/ $\Omega\,\text{m}$
silver	1.60×10^{-8}	mercury	69.0×10^{-8}
copper	1.69×10^{-8}	graphite	800×10^{-8}
nichrome[a]	1.30×10^{-8}	germanium	0.65
aluminium	3.21×10^{-8}	silicon	2.3×10^{3}
lead	20.8×10^{-8}	Pyrex glass	10^{12}
manganin[b]	44.0×10^{-8}	PTFE[d]	$10^{13} - 10^{16}$
eureka[c]	49.0×10^{-8}	quartz	5×10^{16}

Table 10.3 Resistivities of various materials at 20 °C.

[a] Nichrome – an alloy of nickel, copper and aluminium used in electric fires because it does not oxidise at 1000 °C.

[b] Manganin – an alloy of 84% copper, 12% manganese and 4% nickel.

[c] Eureka (constantan) – an alloy of 60% copper and 40% nickel.

[d] Poly(tetrafluoroethene) or Teflon.

Extension

Worked example 2

Find the resistance of a 2.6 m length of eureka wire with cross-sectional area 2.5×10^{-7} m².

Step 1 Using the equation for resistance, and taking the value for ρ from Table 10.3:

$$\text{resistance} = \frac{\text{resistivity} \times \text{length}}{\text{area}}$$

$$R = \frac{\rho L}{A}$$

Step 2 Substituting values:

$$R = \frac{49.0 \times 10^{-8} \times 2.6}{2.5 \times 10^{-7}}$$

$$= 5.1 \,\Omega$$

So the wire has a resistance of $5.1 \,\Omega$.

SAQ

12 Use the resistivity value quoted in Table 10.3 to calculate the lengths of 0.50 mm diameter manganin wire needed to make resistance coils with resistances of:

  a $1.0 \,\Omega$

  b $5.0 \,\Omega$

  c $10 \,\Omega$.

  Hint   Answer

13 1.0 cm³ of copper is drawn out into the form of a long wire of cross-sectional area 4.0×10^{-7} m². Calculate its resistance. (Use the resistivity value from Table 10.3.)

Hint   Answer

14 A 1.0 m length of copper wire has a resistance of $0.50 \,\Omega$.

  a   Calculate the resistance of a 5.0 m length of the same wire.

  b   What will be the resistance of a 1.0 m length of copper wire having half the diameter of the original wire?

Answer

15 A piece of steel wire has a resistance of $10 \,\Omega$. It is stretched to twice its original length. Compare its new resistance with its original resistance.

Hint   Answer

Resistivity and temperature

Resistivity, like resistance, depends on temperature. For a metal, resistivity increases with temperature. As we saw above, this is because there are more frequent collisions between the conduction electrons and the vibrating ions of the metal.

For a semiconductor, the picture is different. The resistivity of a semiconductor *decreases* with temperature. This is because, as the temperature increases, more electrons can break free of their atoms to become conduction electrons. The number density n of electrons thus increases and so the material becomes a better conductor. At the same time, there are more electron–ion collisions, but this effect is small compared with the increase in n.

Summary

Glossary

- Resistance is defined as the ratio of voltage to current. That is:

  $$\text{resistance} = \frac{\text{voltage}}{\text{current}} \qquad (R = \frac{V}{I})$$

- Another term for voltage is *potential difference*.

- The ohm is the resistance of a component when a potential difference of 1 volt is produced per ampere.

- Ohm's law can be stated as:
  For a metallic conductor at constant temperature, the current in the conductor is directly proportional to the potential difference (voltage) across its ends.

- Ohmic components include a wire at constant temperature and a resistor.

- Non-ohmic components include a filament lamp and a light-emitting diode.

- A semiconductor diode allows current in one direction only. A light-emitting diode (LED) emits light when it conducts.

- As the temperature of a metal increases, so does its resistance.

- A thermistor is a component which shows a rapid change in resistance over a narrow temperature range. The resistance of an NTC thermistor decreases as its temperature is increased.

- The resistivity ρ of a material is defined as $\rho = \frac{RA}{L}$, where R is the resistance of a wire of that material, A is its cross-sectional area and L is its length. The unit of resistivity is the ohm metre ($\Omega\,m$).

Questions

1 **a** A wire has length L, cross-sectional area A and is made of material of resistivity ρ.
Write an equation for the electrical resistance R of the wire in terms of L, A and ρ.   [1]

b A second wire is made of the same material as the wire in **a**, has the same length but twice the diameter. State how the resistance of this wire compares with the resistance of the wire in **a**.   [2]

Hint

c The diagram shows a resistor made by depositing a thin layer of carbon onto a plastic base.

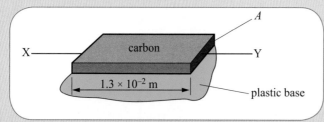

The resistance of the carbon layer between X and Y is $2200\,\Omega$. The length of the carbon layer is $1.3 \times 10^{-2}\,m$. The resistivity of carbon is $3.5 \times 10^{-5}\,\Omega\,m$.
Show that the cross-sectional area A of the carbon layer is about $2 \times 10^{-10}\,m^2$.   [2]

OCR Physics AS (2822) January 2006   [Total 5]

Answer

continued

2 a The electrical resistance of a wire depends upon its temperature and on the resistivity of the material. List <u>two</u> other factors that affect the resistance of a wire. [2]

b The diagram shows an electrical circuit that contains a thin insulated copper wire formed as a bundle.

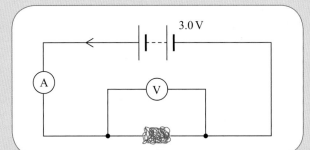

The ammeter and the battery have negligible resistance and the voltmeter has an infinite resistance.

The copper wire has length 1.8 m and diameter 0.27 mm. The resistance of the wire is 0.54 Ω.

i Calculate the resistivity of copper. [4]

ii State and explain the effect on the ammeter reading and the voltmeter reading when the temperature of the copper wire bundle is increased. [4]

OCR Physics AS (2822) June 2005 [Total 10]

Answer

3 a State the difference between the directions of conventional current and electron flow. [1]

b State Ohm's law. [2]

c Current against voltage (*I–V*) characteristics are shown in Figure 1 for a metallic conductor at a constant temperature and in Figure 2 for a particular thermistor.

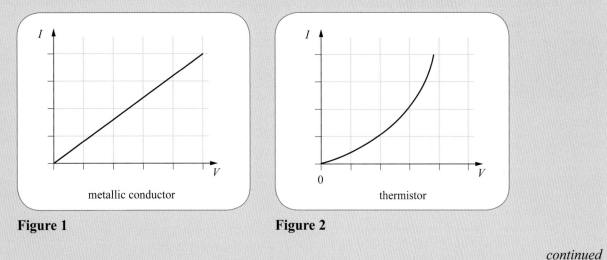

Figure 1 metallic conductor

Figure 2 thermistor

continued

    i Sketch the variation of resistance R with voltage V for:

       1 the metallic conductor at constant temperature

       2 the thermistor.   [3]

   ii State and explain the change, if any, to the graph of resistance against voltage for the metallic conductor:

       1 when the temperature of the metallic conductor is kept constant at a higher temperature

       2 when the length of the conductor is doubled but the material, temperature and the cross-sectional area of the conductor remain the same.   [4]

OCR Physics AS (2822) January 2005   [Total 10]

Answer

4 **a** State Ohm's law.   [2]

    b The I–V characteristic for a particular component is shown in the diagram.

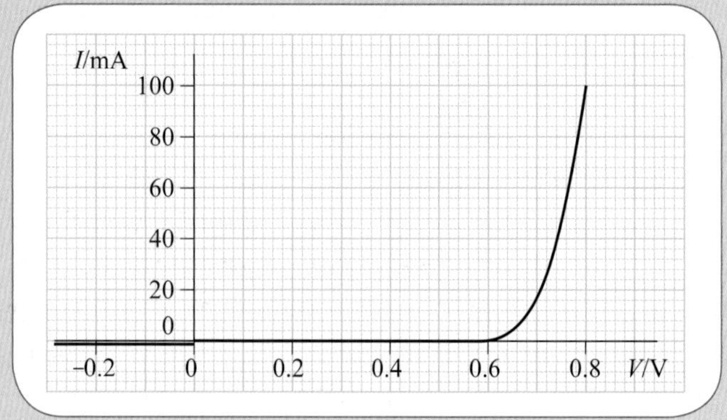

     i Name the component with the I–V characteristic shown in the diagram.   [1]

    ii Describe, making reference to the diagram, how the resistance of the component depends on the potential difference V across it. You are advised to show any calculations.   [5]

Hint

OCR Physics AS (2822) January 2004   [Total 8]

Answer

Voltage, energy and power

Objectives

The meaning of voltage

So far, we have used the term *voltage* in a rather casual way. You may think of a voltage simply as something measured by a voltmeter. In everyday life, the word is used in a less scientific sense – for example, 'A big voltage can go through you and kill you.' In this chapter, we will consider a bit more carefully just what we mean by voltage in relation to electric circuits.

Look at the simple circuit in Figure 11.1. The power supply has negligible internal resistance. (We look at internal resistance later in Chapter 13). The three voltmeters are measuring three voltages. With the switch open, the voltmeter placed across the supply measures 12 V. With the switch closed, the voltmeter across the power supply still measures 12 V and the voltmeters placed across the resistors measure 8 V and 4 V. You will not be surprised to see that the voltage across the power supply is equal to the sum of the voltages across the resistors.

In Chapter 9 we saw that electric current is the rate of flow of electric charge. Figure 11.2 shows the same circuit as in Figure 11.1, but here we are looking at the movement of one coulomb (1 C) of charge round

the circuit. Electrical energy is transferred to the charge by the power supply. The charge flows round the circuit, transferring some of its electrical energy to heat in the first resistor, and the rest to the second resistor.

The voltmeter readings indicate the energy transferred to the component by each unit of charge. The voltmeter placed across the power supply measures the electromotive force (e.m.f.) of the supply, whereas the voltmeters placed across the resistors measure the potential difference (p.d.) or voltage across these components. Electromotive force and potential difference have different meanings – so you have to be very vigilant.

● The term **potential difference** is used when charges *lose* energy by transferring electrical energy to other forms of energy in a component. Potential difference, V, is defined as the energy transferred per unit charge.

● The term **electromotive force** is used when charges *gain* electrical energy from a power supply or a battery. Electromotive force, E, is also defined as the energy transferred per unit charge.

Electromotive force is a misleading term. It has nothing at all to do with force. This term is a legacy from the past and we are stuck with it!

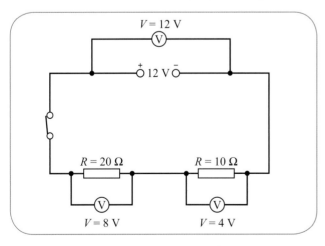

Figure 11.1 Measuring voltages in a circuit. Note that each voltmeter is connected *across* the component.

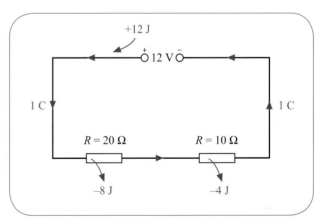

Figure 11.2 Energy transfers as 1 C of charge flows round a circuit. This circuit is the same as that shown in Figure 11.1.

Voltage and energy

By comparing Figure 11.1 and Figure 11.2, you will see the relationship between volts and joules. A 12 V power supply gives 12 J of electrical energy to each coulomb of charge that passes through it. This electrical energy is dissipated as heat as the charge moves through the resistors connected in the circuit. Each coulomb of charge dissipates 8 J of energy as heat in the 20 Ω resistor and 4 J of energy as heat in the 10 Ω resistor. All the energy gained by the one coulomb of charge is transferred to the components in the circuit.

The potential difference across a component and the electromotive force of a battery (or power supply) are defined as follows:

$$\text{potential difference} = \frac{\text{energy lost by charge}}{\text{charge}}$$

or

$$V = \frac{W}{Q}$$

where V is the potential difference, and W is the energy lost by a charge Q as it moves through a component.

$$\text{electromotive force} = \frac{\text{energy gained by charge}}{\text{charge}}$$

or

$$E = \frac{W}{Q}$$

where E is the e.m.f. of the battery (or power supply) and W is the energy gained by a charge Q moving through the battery.

From the definitions above, we can see how the volt is related to the joule and the coulomb:

1 volt = 1 joule per coulomb

or

$$1\,\text{V} = 1\,\text{J}\,\text{C}^{-1}$$

So perhaps we should now also think of voltmeters as devices that measure the amount of 'joules transferred per coulomb'.

Sources of e.m.f. (Figure 11.3) are often labelled with their e.m.f. For example, a 1.5 V chemical cell transfers 1.5 J of energy to each coulomb of charge

that it passes through it. All sources of e.m.f. change energy *to* electrical energy. For example, a chemical cell changes chemical energy into electrical energy and a solar cell changes light energy into electrical energy.

Figure 11.3 Some sources of e.m.f. – cells, batteries, a power supply and a dynamo.

SAQ

1 Calculate how much energy is transferred to 1.0 C of charge:
   a by a 6.0 V battery, and
   b by a 5.0 kV high-voltage supply.

Answer

2 A 12 V battery drives a current of 2.0 A round a circuit for one minute. Calculate:
   a how much charge flows through the battery in this time
   b how much energy is transferred to the charge by the battery
   c how much energy this charge transfers to the components in the circuit.

Answer

3 Describe the energy transfers that occur in 1.0 s in the resistor shown in Figure 11.4.

Hint

Answer

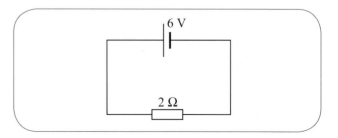

Figure 11.4 For SAQ 3.

Naming units

Volt, ampere, ohm – these are all electrical units from the SI system, established over 50 years ago. SI, which stands for *Système Internationale d'Unités*, is the system of units which is used in most scientific applications. The ampere (or simply the amp) is one of the seven base units in the SI system, from which all other SI units (including the volt and ohm) are derived.

These three units are named after pioneers in the study of electricity.

- Alessandro Volta (1745–1827) was an Italian physicist who invented the first reliable battery. He also invented a device for producing electricity.
- André-Marie Ampère (1775–1836) was a French pioneer of the study of electromagnetism. He produced a detailed study of the magnetic field produced by an electric current.
- Georg Ohm (1789–1854) was a German physicist who discovered the relationship between voltage and current, long before the invention of ammeters and voltmeters.

These three physicists' working lives covered a revolutionary century in the field of electricity and magnetism. It is fitting that their names have come down to us in the form of units. However, other pioneers have been less lucky. The names of Maxwell, Gauss, Oersted and the Curies were used as units in earlier systems of units, only to be abandoned when the SI system became established.

The International Committee for Weights and Measures is the body which ratifies decisions about the naming of units. Its headquarters is near Paris; the French have had a powerful influence on this area of international cooperation, largely because the metric system was first developed and adopted in France, shortly after Napoleon came to power in 1799.

It is not just in science that it is important to have agreement about units. International trade requires that manufacturers produce goods to agreed standards, and this requires a shared system of measurement. Although some countries (notably the USA) still use non-SI units, these are now based on the definitions of SI units. In the UK, the National Physical Laboratory (Figure 11.5) at Teddington, near London, is the body with responsibility for ensuring that scientific and commercial measurements meet international standards.

Figure 11.5 The National Physical Laboratory near London is home to a team of scientists working to improve the precision of measurement in the UK and further afield.

Electrical power

The rate at which energy is transferred is known as **power**. Power P is measured in watts (W). (If you are not sure about this, refer back to Chapter 7, where we looked at the concept of power in relation to forces and work done.)

$$\text{power} = \frac{\text{energy transferred}}{\text{time taken}}$$

$$P = \frac{W}{t}$$

where P is the power and W is the energy transferred in a time t. (Take care not to confuse W for energy transferred or work done with W for watts.)

The rate at which energy is transferred in an electrical component is related to two quantities:
- the current I in the component
- the potential difference V across the component.

We can derive an equation for electrical power from the equations we have met so far.

The amount of energy transferred W by a charge Q travelling through a potential difference V is given by:

$$W = VQ$$

Hence:

$$P = \frac{VQ}{t} = V\left(\frac{Q}{t}\right)$$

The ratio of charge to time, $\frac{Q}{t}$, is the current I in the component. Therefore:

$$P = VI$$

As a word equation, we have:

power = potential difference × current

Worked example 1

Calculate the rate at which energy is transferred by a 230 V mains supply which provides a current of 8.0 A to an electric heater. Guidance

Step 1 Use the equation for power:

$P = VI$ with $V = 230$ V and $I = 8.0$ A

Step 2 Substitute values:

$P = 8 \times 230 = 1840$ W (1.84 kW)

4 Calculate the current in a 60 W light bulb when it is connected to a 230 V supply. Answer

5 A large power station supplies electrical energy to the grid at a voltage of 25 kV. Calculate the output power of the station when the current it supplies is 40 kA. Hint Answer

Fuses

A fuse is a device which is fitted in an electric circuit; it is usually there to protect the wiring from excessive currents. For example, the fuses in a domestic fuse box will 'blow' if the current is too large. High currents cause wires to get hot, and this can lead to damaged wires, fumes from melting insulation, and even fires.

Fuses (Figure 11.6) are usually marked with their current rating; that is, the *maximum current* which they will permit. Inside the fuse cartridge is a thin wire which gets hot and melts if the current exceeds this value. This breaks the circuit and stops any hazardous current. Worked example 2 shows how an appropriate fuse is chosen.

Figure 11.6 Fuses of different current ratings.

Worked example 2

An electric kettle is rated at 2.5 kW, 230 V. Determine a suitable current rating of the fuse to put in the three-pin plug. Choose from 1 A, 5 A, 13 A, 30 A.

Step 1 Calculate the current through the kettle in normal operation. Rearranging $P = VI$ to make I the subject gives:

$$I = \frac{P}{V}$$

So: $I = \dfrac{2500}{230} = 10.9\,\text{A}$

Step 2 Now we know that the normal current through the kettle is 10.9 A. We must choose a fuse with a *slightly higher* rating than this. Therefore the value of the fuse rating is 13 A.

Note that a 5 A fuse would not be suitable because it would melt as soon as the kettle is switched on. A 30 A fuse would allow more than twice the normal current before blowing, which would not provide suitable protection.

SAQ

6 An electric cooker is usually connected to the mains supply in a separate circuit from other appliances, because it draws a high current. A particular cooker is rated at 10 kW, 230 V.
   a Calculate the current through the cooker when it is fully switched on.
   b Suggest a suitable current rating for the fuse for this cooker.

<small>Answer</small>

Power and resistance

A current I in a resistor of resistance R transfers energy to it. The resistor dissipates heat. The p.d. V across the resistor is given by $V = IR$. Combining this with the equation for power, $P = VI$, gives us two further forms of the equation for power:

$$P = I^2 R$$

$$P = \frac{V^2}{R}$$

Which form of the equation we use in any particular situation depends on the information we have available to us. This is illustrated in Worked example 3a and Worked example 3b, which relate to a power station and to the grid cables which lead from it (Figure 11.7).

Worked example 3a

A power station produces 20 MW of power at a voltage of 200 kV. Calculate the current supplied to the grid cables.

Step 1 Here we have P and V and we have to find I, so we can use $P = VI$.

Step 2 Rearranging the equation and substituting the values we know gives:

$$\text{current } I = \frac{P}{V} = \frac{20 \times 10^6}{200 \times 10^3} = 100\,\text{A}$$

So the power station supplies a current of 100 A.

Figure 11.7 A power station and electrical transmission lines. How much electrical power is lost as heat in these cables? (See Worked example 3a and Worked example 3b.)

Worked example 3b

The grid cables are 15 km long, with a resistance per unit length of $0.20\,\Omega\,km^{-1}$. How much power is wasted as heat in these cables?

Step 1 First we must calculate the resistance of the cables:

$$\text{resistance } R = 15\,km \times 0.20\,\Omega\,km^{-1} = 3.0\,\Omega$$

Step 2 Now we know I and R and we want to find P. We can use $P = I^2R$.

$$\text{power wasted as heat, } P = I^2R$$
$$= (100)^2 \times 3.0$$
$$= 3.0 \times 10^4\,W$$
$$= 30\,kW$$

Hence, of the 20 MW of power produced by the power station, 30 kW is wasted – just 0.15%.

SAQ

7 A calculator is powered by a 3.0 V battery. The calculator's resistance is 20 kΩ. Calculate the power transferred to the calculator.

8 A light bulb is labelled '230 V, 150 W'. This means that when connected to the 230 V mains supply it is fully lit and changes electrical energy to heat and light at the rate of 150 W. Calculate:
   a the current which flows through the bulb when fully lit
   b its resistance when fully lit.

9 Calculate the resistance of a 100 W light bulb that draws a current of 0.43 A from a power supply.

Calculating energy

Since

$$\text{power} = \text{current} \times \text{voltage}$$

and

$$\text{energy} = \text{power} \times \text{time}$$

we have:

$$\text{energy transferred} = \text{current} \times \text{voltage} \times \text{time}$$
$$W = IVt$$

Working in SI units, this gives energy transferred in joules.

SAQ

10 A 12 V car battery can supply a current of 10 A for 5.0 hours. Calculate how many joules of energy the battery transfers in this time.

   Hint

   Answer

11 A lamp is operated for 20 s. The current in the lamp is 10 A. In this time, it transfers 400 J of energy to the lamp. Calculate:
   a how much charge flows through the lamp
   b how much energy each coulomb of charge transfers to the lamp
   c the p.d. across the lamp.

   Answer

Energy units

We are used to energy transfers given in joules (J), the SI unit of energy. However, this is a rather small unit for many practical purposes – the energy transferred to you by your daily diet is of the order of 10 MJ, and many hundreds of megajoules are supplied by the electricity, gas and other fuels you use in your daily activities.

A more practical unit for many purposes is the **kilowatt-hour** (kWh). If you operate a 1 kW electric heater for one hour, the energy it transfers to the surroundings is 1 kWh. If you use a 2 kW heater for 3 hours, it transfers 6 kWh, and so on. Therefore

$$\text{energy transferred (kWh)} = \text{power (kW)} \times \text{time (h)}$$

Domestic and industrial electricity consumption is measured in kWh, sometimes simply known as 'units'. Domestic gas bills also show the cost of energy in kWh, to allow the consumer to make comparisons. Elsewhere you may come across many other practical energy units: kilocalories for the energy content of foods, barrels or tonnes of oil, and so on.

Since one kilowatt is 1000 joules per second and an hour is 3600 s, it follows that:

$$1\,kWh = 1000 \times 3600 = 3.6 \times 10^6\,J = 3.6\,MJ$$

It is the large size of this value that makes it easier to work in kWh for everyday purposes.

You can calculate the cost of the energy consumption if the cost for each kWh is given. That is,

cost (p) = number of kWh × cost of each kWh (p)

SAQ

12 A 100 W lamp is guaranteed to run for 1000 hours. Calculate the number of kilowatt-hours transferred in this time.

Hint

Answer

Extension

Summary

Glossary

- The term potential difference (p.d.) is used when charges *lose* energy in a component. It is defined as the energy transferred per unit charge.

  $$V = \frac{W}{Q} \quad \text{or} \quad W = VQ$$

- The term electromotive force (e.m.f.) is used when charges *gain* electrical energy from a battery or similar device. It is also defined as the energy transferred per unit charge.

  $$E = \frac{W}{Q} \quad \text{or} \quad W = EQ$$

- A volt is a joule per coulomb. That is, $1\,V = 1\,J\,C^{-1}$.

- A fuse is selected so that its current rating is slightly higher than the normal operating current of the device which it is protecting.

- Power is the rate of energy transfer. In electrical terms, power is the product of voltage and current. That is, $P = VI$.

- For a resistance R, we also have:

  $$P = I^2R \quad \text{and} \quad P = \frac{V^2}{R}$$

- Energy transferred is given by the equation:

  $$W = IVt$$

- One kilowatt-hour is defined as the energy transferred by a 1 kW device operating for a time of 1 hour.

  energy (kWh) = power (kW) × time (h)

Questions

1 **a** Define the *kilowatt-hour* (kWh). [1]

  b On average, a student uses a computer of power rating 110 W for 4.0 hours every day. The computer draws a current of 0.48 A.

    i For a period of <u>one</u> week, calculate:

      1 the number of kilowatt-hours supplied to the computer [2]

      2 the cost of operating the computer if the cost of each kWh is 7.5p. [1]

    ii Calculate the electric charge drawn by the computer for a period of <u>one</u> week. [3]

OCR Physics AS (2822) January 2005 [Total 7]

Hint

Answer

2 A convenient unit of energy is the kilowatt-hour (kWh).

  a Define the *kilowatt-hour*. [1]

  b A 120 W filament lamp transforms 5.8 kWh. Calculate the time in seconds for which the lamp is operated. [2]

OCR Physics AS (2822) June 2004 [Total 3]

Answer

3 The diagram shows an electrical circuit for a small dryer used to blow warm air.

The 12 V supply has negligible internal resistance.

It may be assumed that coils X and Y have constant resistances of 2.0 Ω and 6.0 Ω, respectively.

  a Calculate the total resistance of the circuit with both switches closed. [3]

  b Calculate the power dissipated by the coil X with only switch A closed. [4]

OCR Physics AS (2822) May 2002 [Total 7]

Hint

Hint

Answer

4 **a** Use energy considerations to distinguish between potential difference (p.d.) and electromotive force (e.m.f.). [2]

  b Which of the following is the correct answer for an alternative unit for e.m.f. or p.d.?

    $J s^{-1}$ $J A^{-1}$ $J C^{-1}$ [1]

OCR Physics AS (2822) June 2001 [Total 3]

Answer

Chapter 12

DC circuits

Objectives

Circuit symbols and diagrams

Now that we have studied in some detail the nature of electric current, voltage and resistance, we can go on to solve a variety of problems involving electrical circuits. When representing circuits by circuit diagrams, we will use the standard circuit symbols shown in Figure 12.1. (We have used a few of these already in the previous three chapters.) Some of these components are shown in Figure 12.2.

These symbols are a small part of a set of internationally agreed conventional symbols for electrical components. It is essential that scientists, engineers, manufacturers and others around the world use the same symbol for a particular component. In addition, many circuits are now designed by computers and these need a universal language in which to work and to present their results.

Symbol	Component name	Symbol	Component name
	connecting lead	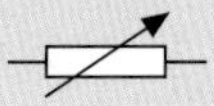	variable resistor
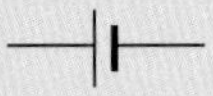	cell	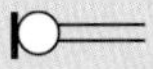	microphone
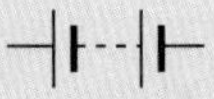	battery of cells		loudspeaker
	fixed resistor	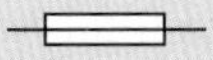	fuse
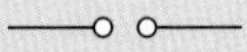	power supply	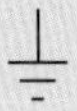	earth
	junction of conductors		alternating signal
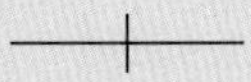	crossing conductors (no connection)	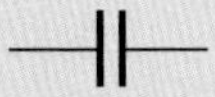	capacitor
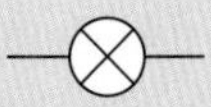	filament lamp	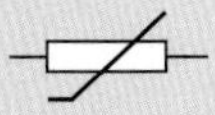	thermistor
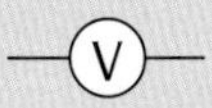	voltmeter	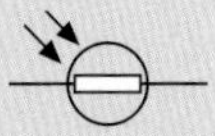	light-dependent resistor (LDR)
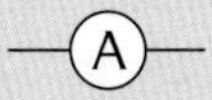	ammeter	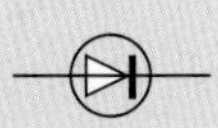	semi-conductor diode
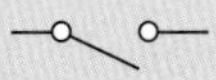	switch	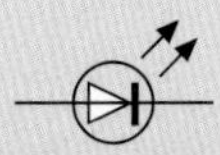	light-emitting diode (LED)

Figure 12.1 Names of electrical components and their circuit symbols. *continued*

In the UK, BSI (formerly the British Standards Institute) is the body which establishes agreements on such things as electrical symbols, as well as for safety standards, working practices and so on. The circuit symbols used here form part of a standard known as BS EN 60617 (formerly BS3939). Because this is a shared 'language', there is less likelihood that misunderstandings will arise between people working in different organisations and different countries.

Figure 12.2 A selection of electrical components, including resistors, fuses, capacitors and microchips.

Series circuits

In the circuit shown in Figure 12.3, the three components (the cell and the two lamps) are connected end-to-end, or in **series**. The direction of the conventional current I is shown. No current is lost at any point because electrons cannot escape from the wires. So the current is the same at all points round the circuit. The current transfers energy to the lamps; no energy is lost in the connecting wires if we assume that they have negligible resistance. The total potential difference V across the lamps is simply the sum of the p.d.s across the individual lamps:

$$V = V_1 + V_2$$

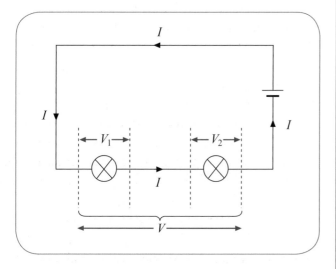

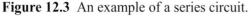

Figure 12.3 An example of a series circuit.

Similarly, if we have several cells in series, their e.m.f.s add up, as shown in Figure 12.4. Note that we have to be careful to take account of the polarity of each cell: if they are all connected in the same sense, their e.m.f.s add up, but if one is reversed, its e.m.f. must be subtracted.

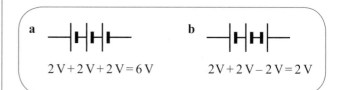

Figure 12.4 **a** For cells connected in series, e.m.f.s add up. **b** If one cell is reversed, its e.m.f. must be subtracted.

Lastly, the resistances of resistors in series also add up. A 6 Ω resistor in series with a 4 Ω resistor are equivalent to a 10 Ω resistor. It is clear why this should be the case: the current has to flow through one resistor and then the next (Figure 12.5), so the overall length of the resistors in the circuit has increased. According to the resistivity equation $R = \frac{\rho L}{A}$ met in Chapter 10, the resistance is directly proportional to the length. The total resistance of two resistors of resistances R_1 and R_2 connected in series is thus given by the formula:

$$R = R_1 + R_2$$

For three or more resistors in series this becomes:

$$R = R_1 + R_2 + R_3 + \ldots$$

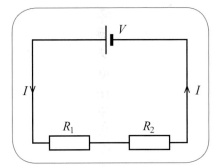

Figure 12.5 Two resistors in series.

Summarising

To summarise, for a series circuit:

- the current is the same at all points around the circuit
- the p.d.s add up
- the e.m.f.s add up
- the resistances add up.

SAQ

1 Calculate the combined resistance of two 5 Ω resistors and a 10 Ω resistor connected in series.

> Answer

2 The cell shown in Figure 12.3 provides an e.m.f. of 2.0 V. The p.d. across one lamp is 1.2 V. Determine the p.d. across the other lamp.

> Answer

3 You have five 1.5 V cells. How would you connect all five of them to give an e.m.f. of:

> Hint

   a 7.5 V, **b** 1.5 V, **c** 4.5 V?

> Answer

Parallel circuits

Figure 12.6 shows two lamps connected in **parallel** with one another. In this situation, the current I from the cell divides into two portions I_1 and I_2. Looking at the diagram, you should be able to see the point at which the current divides. Beyond the lamps, the currents recombine. Since current (or charge) cannot disappear or appear from nowhere, we can deduce:

$$I = I_1 + I_2$$

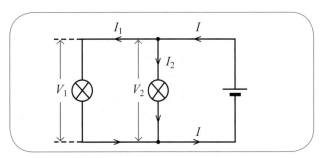

Figure 12.6 An example of a parallel circuit.

In other words, the total current is the sum of the currents at each point or junction in the circuit. This is Kirchhoff's first law, which was discussed in detail in Chapter 9.

What can we say about the p.d.s across the two lamps? If you trace the connections round, you will see that each lamp has one end connected to the positive terminal of the cell, and the other connected to the negative terminal. Components connected side-by-side in this way therefore have the same p.d. across them:

$$V_1 = V_2$$

Now we will consider what happens when two resistors are connected in parallel, as shown in Figure 12.7. The total resistance R of the two resistors of resistances R_1 and R_2 is given by the following equation:

$$\frac{1}{R} = \frac{1}{R_1} + \frac{1}{R_2}$$

For two resistors, this can also be written as:

$$R = \frac{R_1 R_2}{R_1 + R_2}$$

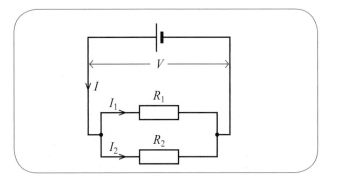

Figure 12.7 Two resistors connected in parallel.

For three or more resistors in parallel, the formula is:

$$\frac{1}{R} = \frac{1}{R_1} + \frac{1}{R_2} + \frac{1}{R_3} + \dots$$

In words: the reciprocal of the total resistance is found by adding the reciprocals of the individual resistances. We will refer to this later as the *reciprocal formula* for resistance. You can determine the total resistance easily using the 'x^{-1}' or the '$\frac{1}{x}$' button on your calculator. The total resistance R of three resistors can be determined as follows:

$$R = (R_1^{-1} + R_2^{-1} + R_3^{-1})^{-1}$$

Worked example 1

Two 10 Ω resistors are connected in parallel. Calculate the total resistance.

Step 1 We have $R_1 = R_2 = 10\ \Omega$, so:

$$\frac{1}{R} = \frac{1}{R_1} + \frac{1}{R_2}$$

$$\frac{1}{R} = \frac{1}{10} + \frac{1}{10} = \frac{2}{10} = \frac{1}{5}$$

Step 2 Inverting both sides of the equation gives:

$$R = 5\ \Omega$$

Note that we have to be careful with how we write this. Do *not* write $\frac{1}{R} = \frac{1}{5} = 5\ \Omega$. The calculation must be done in two steps, as shown above. You can also determine the resistance as follows:

$$R = (R_1^{-1} + R_2^{-1})^{-1}$$

$$R = (10^{-1} + 10^{-1})^{-1} = 5\ \Omega$$

It is worth noting that the total resistance of two identical resistors in parallel is equal to half the resistance value of a single resistor. This can be understood using the equation $R = \frac{\rho L}{A}$. For two identical resistors of the same length and cross-sectional area, connecting them in parallel doubles the cross-sectional area. Since the resistance is inversely proportional to the cross-sectional area, the resistance is halved.

Summarising

To summarise, when components are connected in parallel:
- all have the same p.d. across their ends
- the current is shared between them
- we use the reciprocal formula to calculate their combined resistance.

Extension

SAQ

4 Calculate the total resistance of four 10 Ω resistors connected in parallel.

Answer

5 Calculate the resistances of the following combinations:
   a 100 Ω and 200 Ω in series
   b 100 Ω and 200 Ω in parallel
   c 100 Ω and 200 Ω in series and this in parallel with 200 Ω.

Hint

Answer

6 Calculate the current drawn from a 12 V battery of negligible internal resistance connected to the ends of the following:
   a 500 Ω resistor
   b 500 Ω and 1000 Ω resistors in series
   c 500 Ω and 1000 Ω resistors in parallel.

Answer

7 You are given one 200 Ω resistor and two 100 Ω resistors. What total resistances can you obtain by connecting some, none, or all of these resistors in various combinations?

Answer

Solving problems

Here are some useful ideas which may prove helpful when you are solving problems (or checking your answers to see whether they seem reasonable).
- When two or more resistors are connected in parallel, their combined resistance is smaller than any of their individual resistances. For example, three resistors of 2 Ω, 3 Ω and 6 Ω connected together in parallel have a combined resistance of 1 Ω. This is less than

even the smallest of the individual resistances. This comes about because, by connecting the resistors in parallel, you are providing extra pathways for the current. Since the combined resistance is lower than the individual resistances, it follows that connecting two or more resistors in parallel will increase the current drawn from a supply. Figure 12.8 shows a hazard which can arise when electrical appliances are connected in parallel.

- When components are connected in parallel, they all have the same p.d. across them. This means that you can often ignore parts of the circuit which are not relevant to your calculation.
- Similarly, for resistors in parallel, you may be able to calculate the current in each one individually, then add them up to find the total current. This

may be easier than working out their combined resistance using the reciprocal formula. (This is illustrated in SAQ 10.)

SAQ

8 Three resistors of resistances 20 Ω, 30 Ω and 60 Ω are connected together in parallel. Select which of the following gives their combined resistance: 110 Ω, 50 Ω, 20 Ω, 10 Ω.

Hint

Answer

9 In the circuit in Figure 12.9 the battery of e.m.f. 10 V has negligible internal resistance. Calculate the current in the 20 Ω resistor shown in the circuit.

Answer

10 Determine the current drawn from the battery in Figure 12.9.

Answer

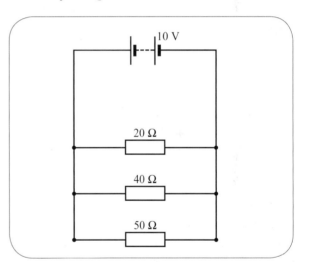

Figure 12.9 Circuit diagram for SAQ 9 and SAQ 10.

11 What value of resistor must be connected in parallel with a 20 Ω resistor so that their combined resistance is 10 Ω?

Answer

12 You are supplied with a number of 100 Ω resistors. Describe how you could combine the minimum number of these to make a 250 Ω resistor.

Answer

Figure 12.8 a Correct use of an electrical socket. **b** Here, too many appliances (resistances) are connected in parallel. This reduces the total resistance and increases the current drawn, to the point where it becomes dangerous.

13 Calculate the current at each point
(**A–E**) in the circuit shown
in Figure 12.10.

Hint

Answer

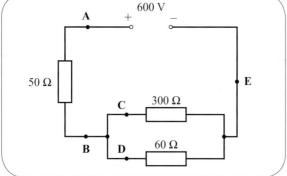

Figure 12.10 For SAQ 13.

Ammeters and voltmeters

Ammeters and voltmeters are connected differently
in circuits (Figure 12.11). Ammeters are always
connected in *series*, since they measure the current
through a circuit. For this reason, an ammeter should
have as low a resistance as possible so that as little

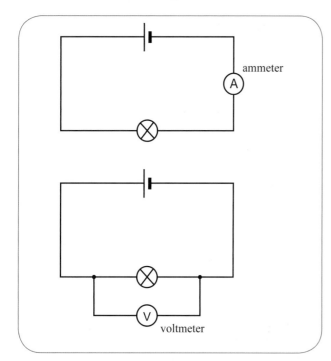

Figure 12.11 How to connect up an ammeter and
a voltmeter.

energy as possible is transferred in the ammeter itself.
Inserting an ammeter with a higher resistance could
significantly reduce the current flowing in the circuit.
The ideal internal resistance of an ammeter is zero.
Digital ammeters have very low resistances.

Voltmeters measure the potential difference between
two points in the circuit. For this reason, they are
connected in parallel (i.e. between the two points), and
they should have a very high resistance to take as little
current as possible. The ideal resistance of a voltmeter
would be infinity. In practice, voltmeters have typical
resistance of about 1 MΩ. A voltmeter with a resistance
of 10 MΩ measuring a p.d. of 2.5 V will take a current
of 2.5×10^{-7} A and dissipate just 0.625 µJ of heat
energy from the circuit every second.

Some measuring instruments are shown in
Figure 12.12.

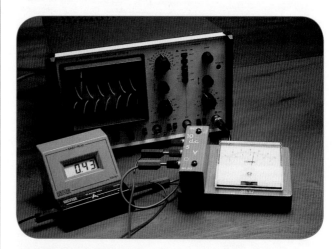

Figure 12.12 Electrical measuring instruments:
an ammeter, a voltmeter and an oscilloscope. The
oscilloscope can display rapidly changing voltages.

SAQ

14 a   A 10 V power supply of negligible internal
resistance is connected to a 100 Ω resistor.
Calculate the current in the resistor.

   b   An ammeter is now connected in the circuit,
to measure the current. The resistance of the
ammeter is 5.0 Ω. Calculate
the ammeter reading.

Answer

Summary

- Components connected in series have the same current through them.

- Components connected in parallel have the same p.d. across them.

- Resistors connected in series have a total resistance R given by:

  $R = R_1 + R_2 + R_3 + \ldots$

- Resistors connected in parallel have a total resistance R given by:

  $\dfrac{1}{R} = \dfrac{1}{R_1} + \dfrac{1}{R_2} + \dfrac{1}{R_3} + \ldots$ or $R = (R_1^{-1} + R_2^{-1} + R_3^{-1} + \ldots)^{-1}$

- Ammeters measure current and are connected in series. An ammeter has very small resistance.

- Voltmeters measure potential difference and are connected in parallel. A voltmeter has very high resistance.

Questions

1 A filament lamp and a 220 Ω resistor are connected in series to a battery of e.m.f. 6.0 V. The battery has negligible internal resistance. A high-resistance voltmeter placed across the resistor measures 1.8 V. Calculate:

   a the current drawn from the battery   [2]   Hint

   b the p.d. across the lamp   [1]

   c the total resistance of the circuit   [3]   Hint

   d the number of electrons passing through the battery in a time of 1.0 minutes. The elementary charge is 1.6×10^{-19} C.   [3]

                                                          [Total 9]   Answer

2 The circuit diagram below shows a 12 V power supply connected to some resistors.

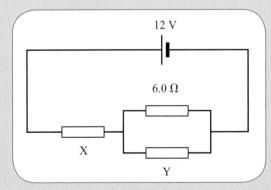

The current in the resistor X is 2.0 A and the current in the 6.0 Ω resistor is 0.5 A. Calculate:

   a the current in resistor Y   [2]   Hint

   b the resistance of resistor Y   [2]   Hint

   c the resistance of resistor X.   [3]

                                                          [Total 7]   Answer

Chapter 13

Practical circuits

e-Learning

Objectives

Internal resistance

You will be familiar with the idea that, when you use a power supply or other source of e.m.f., you cannot assume that it is providing you with the exact voltage across its terminals as suggested by its electromotive force (e.m.f.). There are two reasons for this. First, the supply may not be made to a high degree of precision, batteries become flat, and so on. However, there is a second, more important factor, which is that all sources of e.m.f. have an **internal resistance**. For a power supply, this may be due to the wires and components inside, whereas for a battery its internal resistance is due to its chemicals. Experiments show that the voltage across the terminals of the power supply depends on the circuit of which it is part. In particular, the voltage across the power supply terminals decreases if it is required to supply more current.

Figure 13.1 shows a circuit you can use to investigate this effect, and a sketch graph showing how the voltage across the terminals of a power supply might decrease as the current supplied increases.

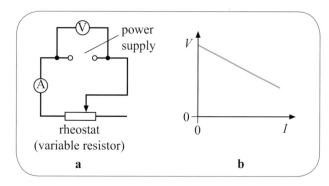

Figure 13.1 a A circuit for determining the e.m.f. and internal resistance of a supply; **b** typical form of results.

The charges moving round a circuit have to pass through the external components *and* through the internal resistance of the power supply. These charges gain electrical energy from the power supply. This energy is lost as heat as the charges pass through

the external components and through the internal resistance of the power supply. Power supplies and batteries get warm when they are being used. The reason for this is now clear. Heat is produced as charges lose energy within the internal resistance of the power supply or the battery.

It can often help to solve problems if we show the internal resistance r of a source of e.m.f. explicitly in circuit diagrams (Figure 13.2). Here, we are representing a cell as if it were a 'perfect' cell of e.m.f. E, together with a separate resistor of resistance r. The dashed line enclosing E and r represents the fact that these two are, in fact, a single component.

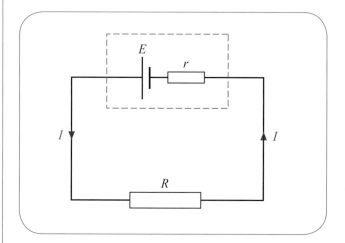

Figure 13.2 It can be helpful to show the internal resistance r of a cell (or a supply) explicitly in a circuit diagram.

Now we can determine the current when this cell is connected to an external resistor of resistance R. You can see that R and r are in series with each other. The current I is the same for both of these resistors. The combined resistance of the circuit is thus $R + r$, and we can write:

$$E = I(R + r) \quad \text{or} \quad E = IR + Ir$$

We cannot measure the e.m.f. E of the cell directly, because we can only connect a voltmeter across its terminals. This **terminal p.d.** V across the cell is always the same as the p.d. across the external resistor. Therefore, we have

$V = IR$

This will be less than the e.m.f. E by an amount Ir. The quantity Ir is the potential difference across the internal resistor and is referred to as the **lost volts**. If we combine these two equations, we get:

$V = E - Ir$

or

terminal p.d. = e.m.f. – 'lost volts'

The 'lost volts' indicates the energy transferred to the internal resistance of the supply. If you short-circuit a battery with a piece of wire, a large current will flow, and you may feel the battery getting warm as energy is transferred within it. This is also why you may damage a power supply by trying to make it supply a larger current than it is designed to give.

SAQ

1   A battery of e.m.f. 5.0 V and internal resistance 2.0 Ω is connected to an 8.0 Ω resistor. Draw a circuit diagram and calculate the current in the circuit.

Hint

Answer

2   Calculate the current in each circuit in Figure 13.3. Calculate also the 'lost volts' for each cell and the terminal p.d.

Answer

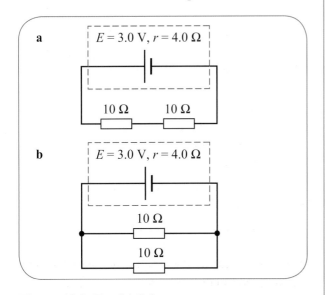

Figure 13.3 For SAQ 2.

3   Four identical cells, each of e.m.f. 1.5 V and internal resistance 0.10 Ω, are connected in series. A lamp of resistance 2.0 Ω is connected across the four cells. Calculate the current in the lamp.

Hint

Answer

Determining electromotive force and internal resistance

You can get a good idea of the e.m.f. of an isolated power supply or a battery by connecting a digital voltmeter across it. A digital voltmeter has a very high resistance (~1 MΩ), so only a tiny current will pass through it. The 'lost volts' will then only be a tiny fraction of the e.m.f. If you want to determine the internal resistance r as well as the e.m.f. E, you need to use a circuit like that shown in Figure 13.1. When the variable resistor is altered, the current in the circuit changes, and measurements can be recorded of the circuit current I and terminal p.d. V. The internal resistance r can be found from a graph of V against I (Figure 13.4).

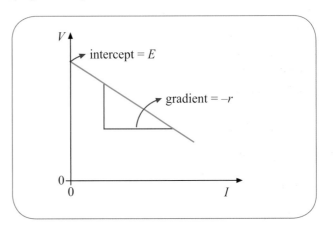

Figure 13.4 E and r can be found from this graph.

Compare the equation $V = E - Ir$ with the equation of a straight line $y = mx + c$. By plotting V on the y-axis and I on the x-axis, a straight line should result. The intercept on the y-axis is E, and the gradient is $-r$. In practice, you may find that the graph is curved. This is because r changes with current – we cannot simply describe the internal resistance as if there were an extra resistor inside the power supply.

SAQ

4   When a high-resistance voltmeter is placed across an isolated battery, its reading is 3.0 V. When a 10 Ω resistor is connected across the terminals of the battery, the voltmeter reading drops to 2.8 V. Use this information to determine the internal resistance of the battery.

[Answer]

5   The results of an experiment to determine the e.m.f. E and internal resistance r for a power supply are shown in the table below. Plot a suitable graph and use it to find E and r.

[Answer]

V/ V	1.43	1.33	1.18	1.10	0.98
I/A	0.10	0.30	0.60	0.75	1.00

The effects of internal resistance

You cannot ignore the effects of internal resistance. Consider a battery of e.m.f. 3.0 V and of internal resistance 1.0 Ω. The *maximum current* that can be drawn from this battery is when its terminals are shorted-out. (The external resistance $R \approx 0$.) The maximum current is given by:

$$\text{maximum current} = \frac{E}{r} = \frac{3.0}{1.0} = 3.0\,\text{A}$$

The *terminal p.d.* of the battery depends on the resistance of the external resistor. For an external resistor of resistance 1.0 Ω, the terminal p.d. is 1.5 V – half of the e.m.f. The terminal p.d. approaches the value of the e.m.f. when the external resistance R is very much greater than the internal resistance of the battery. For example, a resistor of resistance 1000 Ω connected to the battery gives a terminal p.d. of 2.997 V. This is almost equal to the e.m.f. of the battery.

The more current a battery supplies, the more its terminal p.d. will decrease. An example of this can be seen if a driver tries to start a car with the headlamps on. The starter motor requires a large current from the battery, the battery's terminal p.d. drops, and the headlamps dim.

In order to transfer *maximum power* or *energy* from the battery to an external circuit, the resistance R of this circuit must be equal to the internal resistance r of the battery. The sketch graph in Figure 13.5 shows how the power dissipated across the external resistor depends on the resistance R of this resistor. (For our battery of e.m.f. 3.0 V and internal resistance 1.0 Ω, maximum power is dissipated when $R = r = 1.0\,\Omega$.)

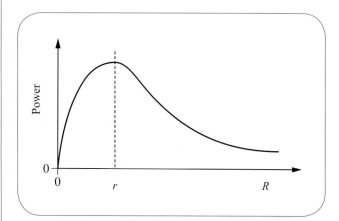

Figure 13.5 Maximum power is dissipated in an external circuit when its resistance R equals the internal resistance r.

[Extension]

SAQ

6   A car battery has an e.m.f. of 12 V and an internal resistance of 0.04 Ω. The starter motor draws a current of 100 A.
    a   Calculate the terminal p.d. of the battery when the starter motor is in operation.
    b   Each headlamp is rated as '12 V, 36 W'. Calculate its resistance.
    c   To what value will the power output of each headlamp decrease when the starter motor is in operation? (Assume that the resistance of the headlamp remains constant.)

[Answer]

Potential dividers

How can we get an output of 3.0 V from a battery of e.m.f. 6.0 V? Sometimes we want to use only part of the e.m.f. of a supply. To do this, we use an arrangement of resistors called a **potential divider** circuit.

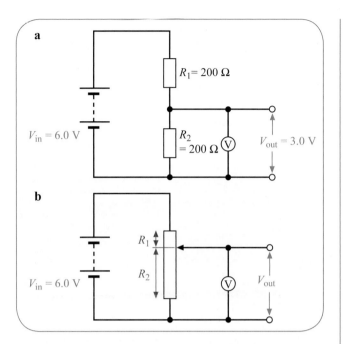

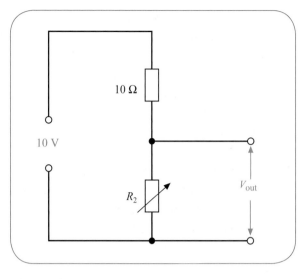

Figure 13.7 For SAQ 7.

Figure 13.6 Two potential divider circuits.

Figure 13.6 shows two potential divider circuits, each connected across a battery of e.m.f. 6.0 V and of negligible internal resistance. The high-resistance voltmeter measures the voltage across the resistor of resistance R_2. We refer to this voltage as the output voltage V_{out} of the circuit. The first circuit, **a**, consists of two resistors of resistances R_1 and R_2. The voltage across the resistor of resistance R_2 is half of the 6.0 V of the battery. The second potential divider, **b**, is more useful. It consists of a single variable resistor. By moving the sliding contact, we can achieve any value of V_{out} between 0.0 V (slider at the bottom) and 6.0 V (slider at the top).

The output voltage V_{out} depends on the relative values of R_1 and R_2. You can calculate the value of V_{out} using the following potential divider equation:

$$V_{out} = \left(\frac{R_2}{R_1 + R_2}\right) \times V_{in}$$

In this equation, V_{in} is the total voltage across the two resistors.

Potential dividers in use

Potential divider circuits are often used in electronic circuits. They are useful when a sensor is connected to a processing circuit. Suitable sensors include thermistors and light-dependent resistors (Figure 13.8). These can be used as sensors because:

- the resistance of a negative temperature coefficient (NTC) thermistor *decreases* as its temperature *increases*

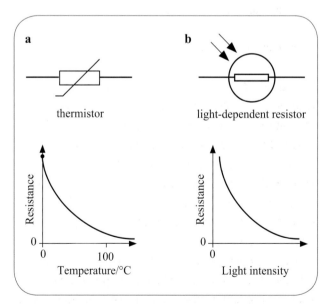

Figure 13.8 Two components with variable resistances: **a** the thermistor's resistance changes with temperature; **b** the light-dependent resistor's resistance depends on the intensity of light.

SAQ

7 Determine the range for V_{out} for the circuit in Figure 13.7 as the variable resistor R_2 is adjusted over its full range from 0 Ω to 40 Ω. (Assume the supply of e.m.f. 10 V has negligible internal resistance.)

Answer

147

- the resistance of a light-dependent resistor (LDR) *decreases* as the incident intensity of light *increases*.

This means that a thermistor can be used in a potential divider circuit to provide an output voltage V_{out} which depends on the temperature; a light-dependent resistor can be used in a potential divider circuit to provide an output voltage V_{out} which depends on the intensity of light.

Figure 13.9 shows how a sensor can be used in a potential divider circuit. Here, a thermistor is being used to detect temperature, perhaps the temperature of a fish tank. If the temperature rises, the resistance of the thermistor decreases and the output voltage V_{out} increases. If the output voltage V_{out} is across the thermistor, as shown in Figure 13.9b, it will decrease as the temperature rises. By changing the setting of the variable resistor R_2, you can control the range over which V_{out} varies. This would allow you to set the temperature at which a heater operates, for example.

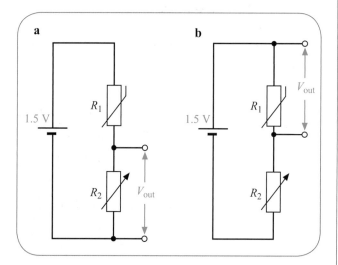

Figure 13.9 Using a thermistor in a potential divider circuit. The output voltage V_{out} may be **a** across the variable resistor, or **b** across the thermistor.

When designing a practical circuit like this, it is necessary to know how the voltage output depends on the temperature. You can investigate the voltage against temperature characteristics of such a circuit using a datalogger (Figure 13.10). The temperature probe of the datalogger records the temperature of the water bath and the second input to the datalogger records the voltage output of the potential divider circuit. The temperature can be raised rapidly by pouring amounts of water into the water bath. The datalogger then records both temperature and voltage and the computer gives a display of the voltage against temperature. Dataloggers are very good at processing the collected data.

Figure 13.10 Using a datalogger to investigate the characteristics of a thermistor in a potential divider circuit. During the experiment, the screen shows how temperature and output voltage change with time; after the experiment, the same data can be displayed as a graph of p.d. against temperature.

Potential divider circuits are especially useful in circuits with very small currents but where voltages are important. Electronic devices such as transistors and integrated circuits draw only very small currents, so potential dividers are very useful where these devices are used. Where large currents are involved, because there will be some current through both R_1 and R_2 (Figure 13.6), there will be wasted power in the resistors of the potential divider circuit.

SAQ

8 An NTC thermistor is used in the circuit shown in Figure 13.11. The supply has an e.m.f. of 10 V and negligible internal resistance. The resistance of the thermistor changes from 20 kΩ at 20 °C to 100 Ω at 60 °C. Calculate the output voltage V_{out} at these two temperatures.

Hint

Answer

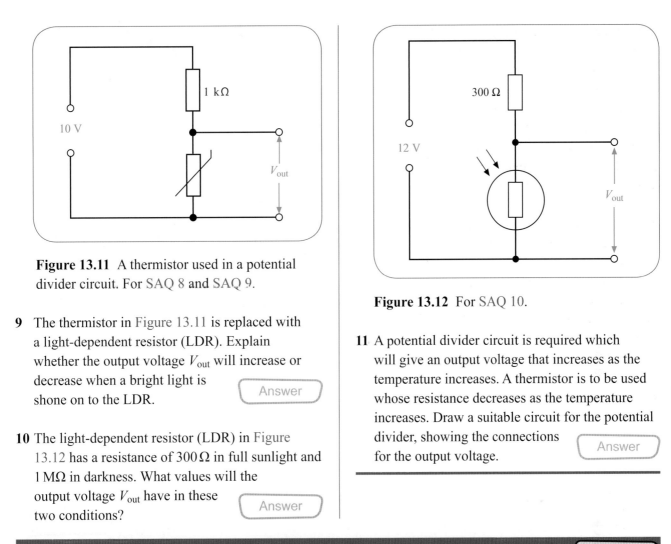

Figure 13.11 A thermistor used in a potential divider circuit. For SAQ 8 and SAQ 9.

Figure 13.12 For SAQ 10.

9 The thermistor in Figure 13.11 is replaced with a light-dependent resistor (LDR). Explain whether the output voltage V_{out} will increase or decrease when a bright light is shone on to the LDR.

Answer

10 The light-dependent resistor (LDR) in Figure 13.12 has a resistance of $300\,\Omega$ in full sunlight and $1\,M\Omega$ in darkness. What values will the output voltage V_{out} have in these two conditions?

Answer

11 A potential divider circuit is required which will give an output voltage that increases as the temperature increases. A thermistor is to be used whose resistance decreases as the temperature increases. Draw a suitable circuit for the potential divider, showing the connections for the output voltage.

Answer

Summary

Glossary

● A source of e.m.f., such as a battery, has an internal resistance. We can think of the source as having an internal resistance r in series with an e.m.f. E.

● The terminal p.d. of a source of e.m.f. is less than the e.m.f. because of 'lost volts' across the internal resistor:

terminal p.d. = e.m.f. – 'lost volts'

$$V = E - Ir$$

● A potential divider circuit consists of two or more resistors connected in series to a supply. The output voltage V_{out} across the resistor of resistance R_2 is given by:

$$V_{out} = \left(\frac{R_2}{R_1 + R_2}\right) \times V_{in}$$

● The resistance of a light-dependent resistor (LDR) decreases as the intensity of light falling on it increases. The resistance of a negative temperature coefficient (NTC) thermistor decreases as its temperature increases.

● Thermistors and light-dependent resistors can be used in potential divider circuits to provide output voltages that are dependent on temperature and light intensity, respectively.

Questions

1 A single cell of e.m.f. 1.5 V is connected across a 0.30 Ω resistor. The current in the circuit is 2.5 A.
   a Calculate the terminal p.d. and explain why it is not equal to the e.m.f. of
      the cell. [3]

      Hint

   b Show that the internal resistance r of the cell is 0.30 Ω. [3]

      Hint

   c It is suggested that the power dissipated in the external resistor is a maximum
      when its resistance R is equal to the internal resistance r of the cell.
      i Calculate the power dissipated when $R = r$. [1]
      ii Show that the power dissipated when $R = 0.50$ Ω and $R = 0.20$ Ω is less than
         that dissipated when $R = r$, as the statement above suggests. [2]

      [Total 9]

      Answer

2 The diagram shows a circuit used to monitor the variation of light intensity in a room.

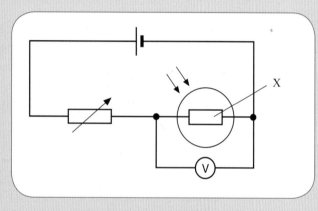

   a Identify the component X and describe how the circuit works. [4]

      Hint

   b Suggest the reason for including the variable resistor in the circuit. [1]

      [Total 5]

      Answer

Chapter 14

Kirchhoff's laws

e-Learning

Objectives

Circuit design

Over the years, electrical circuits have become increasingly complex, with more and more components combining to achieve very precise results (Figure 14.1). Such circuits typically include power supplies, sensing devices, potential dividers and output devices. At one time, circuit designers would start with a simple circuit and gradually modify it until the desired result was achieved. This is impossible today when circuits include many hundreds or thousands of components.

Instead, electronic engineers (Figure 14.2) rely on computer-based design software which can work out the effect of any combination of components. This is only possible because computers can be programmed with the equations which describe how current and voltage behave in a circuit. These equations, which include Ohm's law and Kirchhoff's two laws, were established in the 18th century, but they have come into their own in the 21st century through their use in computer-aided design (CAD) systems.

Figure 14.1 A complex electronic circuit – this is the circuit board which controls a computer's hard drive.

Figure 14.2 A computer engineer in California uses a computer-aided design (CAD) software tool to design a circuit which will form part of a microprocessor, the device at the heart of every computer.

Revisiting Kirchhoff's first law

This law has already been considered in Chapter 9. It relates to currents at a point in a circuit, and stems from the fact that electric charge is conserved. **Kirchhoff's first law** states that:

> The sum of the currents entering any point (or junction) in a circuit is equal to the sum of the currents leaving that same point.

As an equation, we can write Kirchhoff's first law as:

$$\Sigma I_{in} = \Sigma I_{out}$$

Here, the symbol Σ (Greek letter *sigma*) means 'the sum of all', so ΣI_{in} means 'the sum of all currents entering into a point' and ΣI_{out} means 'the sum of all currents leaving that point'. This is the sort of equation which a computer program can use to predict the behaviour of a complex circuit.

SAQ

1 Calculate ΣI_{in} and ΣI_{out} in Figure 14.3. Is Kirchhoff's first law satisfied?

Answer

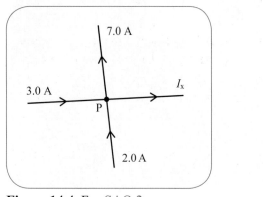

Figure 14.3 For SAQ 1.

2 Use Kirchhoff's first law to deduce the value and direction of the current I_x in Figure 14.4.

Answer

Figure 14.4 For SAQ 2.

Kirchhoff's second law

This law deals with e.m.f.s and voltages in a circuit. We will start by considering a simple circuit which contains a cell and two resistors of resistances R_1 and R_2 (Figure 14.5). Since this is a simple series circuit, the current I must be the same all the way around, and we need not concern ourselves further with Kirchhoff's first law. For this circuit, we can write the following equation:

$$E = IR_1 + IR_2$$

e.m.f. of battery = sum of p.d.s across the resistors

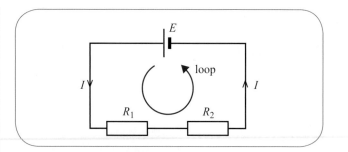

Figure 14.5 A simple series circuit.

You should not find these equations surprising. However, you may not realise that they are a consequence of applying **Kirchhoff's second law** to the circuit. This law states that:

> The sum of the e.m.f.s around any loop in a circuit is equal to the sum of the p.d.s around the loop.

You will see later (page 155) that Kirchhoff's second law is an expression of the conservation of energy.

We shall look at another example of how this law can be applied, and then look at how it can be applied in general.

Figure 14.6 shows a circuit with two batteries (connected back-to-front) and two resistors. Again, the current is the same all the way round the circuit. Using Kirchhoff's second law, we can find the value of the current I. First, we calculate the sum of the e.m.f.s, taking account of the way that the batteries are connected together:

$$\text{sum of e.m.f.s} = 6.0\,\text{V} - 2.0\,\text{V} = 4.0\,\text{V}$$

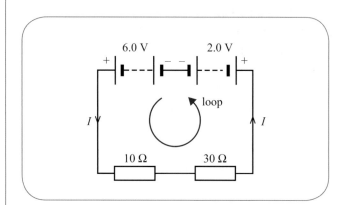

Figure 14.6 A circuit with two opposing batteries.

Second, we calculate the sum of the p.d.s:

sum of p.d.s $= (I \times 10) + (I \times 30) = 40I$

Equating these gives:

$4.0 = 40I$

and so $I = 0.1\,\text{A}$. No doubt, you could have solved this problem without formally applying Kirchhoff's second law.

SAQ

3 Use Kirchhoff's second law to deduce the p.d. across the resistor of resistance R in the circuit shown in Figure 14.7, and hence find the value of R. (Assume the battery of e.m.f. 10 V has negligible internal resistance.)

Hint

Answer

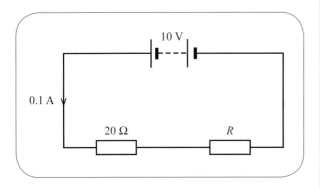

Figure 14.7 Circuit for SAQ 3.

Applying Kirchhoff's laws

Figure 14.8 shows a more complex circuit, with more than one 'loop'. Again there are two batteries and two resistors. The problem is to find the current in the resistors. There are several steps in this; Worked example 1 shows how such a problem is solved.

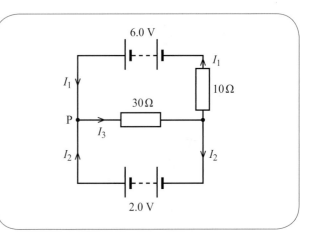

Figure 14.8 Kirchhoff's laws are needed to determine the currents in this circuit.

Worked example 1

Calculate the current in each of the resistors in the circuit shown in Figure 14.8.

Step 1 Mark the currents flowing. The diagram shows I_1, I_2 and I_3; note that it does *not* matter if we mark these flowing in the wrong directions, as they will simply appear as negative quantities in the solutions.

Step 2 Apply Kirchhoff's first law. At point P, this gives:

$$I_1 + I_2 = I_3 \qquad (1)$$

Step 3 Choose a loop and apply Kirchhoff's second law. Around the upper loop, this gives:

$$6.0 = (I_3 \times 30) + (I_1 \times 10) \qquad (2)$$

Step 4 Repeat step 3 around other loops until there are the same number of equations as unknown currents. Around the lower loop, this gives:

$$2.0 = I_3 \times 30 \qquad (3)$$

We now have three equations with three unknowns (the three currents).

continued

Step 5 Solve these equations as simultaneous equations. In this case, the situation has been chosen to give simple solutions. Equation 3 gives $I_3 = 0.067\,A$, and substituting this value in equation 2 gives $I_1 = 0.400\,A$. We can now find I_2 by substituting in equation 1:

$$I_2 = I_3 - I_1 = 0.067 - 0.400 = -0.333\,A \approx -0.33\,A$$

Thus I_2 is negative – it is in the opposite direction to the arrow shown in Figure 14.7.

Note that there is a third 'loop' in this circuit; we could have applied Kirchhoff's second law to the outermost loop of the circuit. This gives a fourth equation:

$$6 - 2 = I_1 \times 10$$

However, this is not an independent equation; we could have arrived at it by subtracting equation 3 from equation 2.

Signs and directions

Caution is necessary when applying Kirchhoff's second law. You need to take account of the ways in which the sources of e.m.f. are connected and the directions of the currents. Figure 14.9 shows a loop from a complicated circuit to illustrate this point. Only the components and currents within the loop are shown.

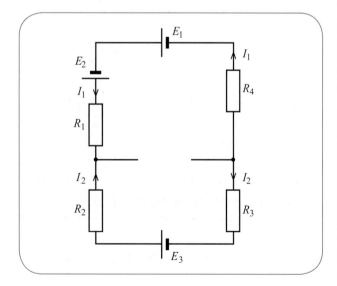

Figure 14.9 A loop extracted from a complicated circuit.

e.m.f.s

Starting with the cell of e.m.f. E_1 and working *anticlockwise* around the loop (because E_1 is 'pushing current' anticlockwise):

sum of e.m.f.s $= E_1 + E_2 - E_3$

Note that E_3 is opposing the other two e.m.f.s.

p.d.s

Starting from the same point, and working *anticlockwise* again:

sum of p.d.s $= I_1R_1 - I_2R_2 - I_2R_3 + I_1R_4$

Note that the direction of current I_2 is clockwise, so the p.d.s that involve I_2 are negative.

Extension

SAQ

4 You can use Kirchhoff's second law to find the current I in the circuit shown in Figure 14.10. Choosing the best loop can simplify the problem.
   a Which loop in the circuit should you choose?
   b Calculate the current I.

Answer

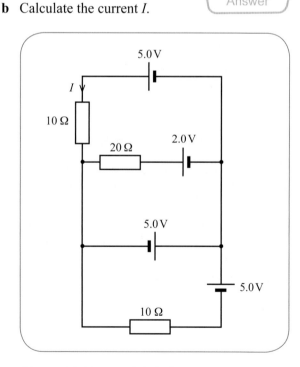

Figure 14.10 Careful choice of a suitable loop can make it easier to solve problems like this.

5 Use Kirchhoff's second law to deduce the resistance R of the resistor shown in the circuit loop of Figure 14.11.

Hint

Answer

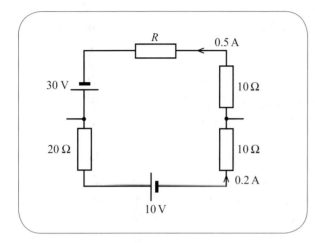

Figure 14.11 For SAQ 5.

Conservation of energy

Kirchhoff's second law is a consequence of the principle of conservation of energy. If a charge, say 1 C, moves around the circuit, it *gains* energy as it moves through each source of e.m.f. and loses energy as it passes through each p.d. If the charge moves all the way round the circuit, so that it ends up where it started, it must have the same energy at the end as at the beginning. (Otherwise we would be able to create energy from nothing simply by moving charges around circuits.) So:

energy gained passing through sources of e.m.f.
    = energy lost passing through components with p.d.s

You should recall that an e.m.f. in volts is simply the energy gained per 1 C of charge as it passes through a source. Similarly, a p.d. is the energy lost per 1 C as it passes through a component.

1 volt = 1 joule per coulomb

Hence we can think of Kirchhoff's second law as:

energy gained per coulomb around loop
        = energy lost per coulomb around loop

Here is another way to think of the meaning of e.m.f. A 1.5 V cell gives 1.5 J of energy to each coulomb of charge which passes through it. The charge then moves round the circuit, transferring the energy to components in the circuit. The consequence is that, by driving 1 C of charge around the circuit, the cell transfers 1.5 J of energy. Hence the e.m.f. of a source simply tells us the amount of energy (in J) transferred by the source in driving unit charge (1 C) around a circuit.

SAQ

6 Use the idea of the energy gained and lost by a 1 C charge to explain why two 6 V batteries connected together in series can give an e.m.f. of 12 V or 0 V, but connected in parallel they give an e.m.f. of 6 V.

Answer

7 Apply Kirchhoff's laws to the circuit shown in Figure 14.12 to determine the current that will be shown by the ammeters A_1, A_2 and A_3.

Hint

Answer

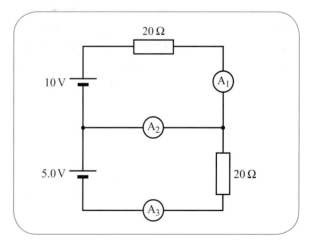

Figure 14.12 Kirchhoff's laws make it possible to deduce the ammeter readings.

Resistor combinations

You are already familiar with the formulae used to calculate the combined resistance R of two or more resistors connected in series or in parallel. To derive these formulae we have to make use of Kirchhoff's laws.

Resistors in series

Take two resistors of resistances R_1 and R_2 connected in series (Figure 14.13). According to Kirchhoff's first law, the current in each resistor is the same. The p.d. V across the combination is equal to the sum of the p.d.s across the two resistors:

$$V = V_1 + V_2$$

Since $V = IR$, $V_1 = IR_1$ and $V_2 = IR_2$, we can write:

$$IR = IR_1 + IR_2$$

Cancelling the common factor of current I gives:

$$R = R_1 + R_2$$

For three or more resistors, the equation for total resistance R becomes:

$$R = R_1 + R_2 + R_3 + \dots$$

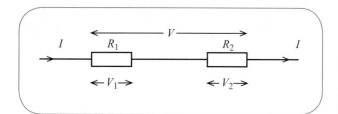

Figure 14.13 Resistors in series.

Resistors in parallel

For two resistors of resistances R_1 and R_2 connected in parallel (Figure 14.14), we have a situation where the current divides between them. Hence, using Kirchhoff's first law, we can write:

$$I = I_1 + I_2$$

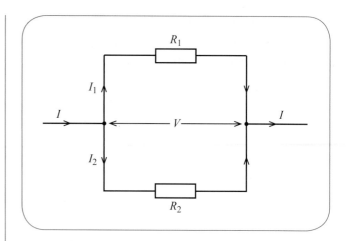

Figure 14.14 Resistors connected in parallel.

If we apply Kirchhoff's second law to the loop that contains the two resistors, we have:

$$I_1R_1 - I_2R_2 = 0\,\text{V}$$

(because there is no source of e.m.f. in the loop). This equation states that the two resistors have the same p.d. V across them. Hence we can write:

$$I = \frac{V}{R}$$

$$I_1 = \frac{V}{R_1}$$

$$I_2 = \frac{V}{R_2}$$

Substituting in $I = I_1 + I_2$ and cancelling the common factor V gives:

$$\frac{1}{R} = \frac{1}{R_1} + \frac{1}{R_2}$$

For three or more resistors, the equation for total resistance R becomes:

$$\frac{1}{R} = \frac{1}{R_1} + \frac{1}{R_2} + \frac{1}{R_3} + \dots$$

SAQ

8 There are two ways to calculate the current *I* in the ammeter in Figure 14.15. Both should give the same answer.

   a Apply Kirchhoff's laws to determine the current *I*.

   b Calculate the total resistance *R* of the two parallel resistors, and hence determine the current *I*.

Answer

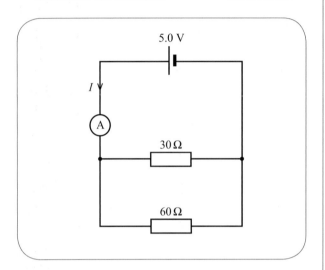

Figure 14.15 For SAQ 8.

9 Apply Kirchhoff's laws to find the current at point X in the circuit shown in Figure 14.16. What is the direction of the current?

Answer

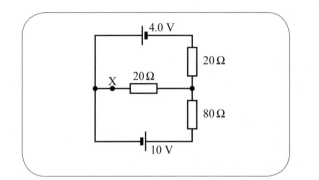

Figure 14.16 For SAQ 9.

Summary

Glossary

● Kirchhoff's first law represents the conservation of charge at a point in a circuit:

    sum of currents entering a point = sum of currents leaving that point

● Kirchhoff's second law represents the conservation of energy in an electric circuit:

    sum of all the e.m.f.s around a circuit loop = sum of all the p.d.s around that loop

Questions

1 a The statement of Kirchhoff's second law is based on which conservation law?   [1]

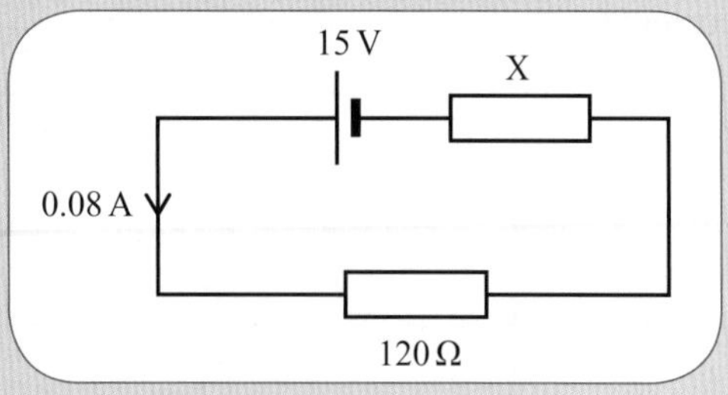

   b In the circuit above, determine:
      i   the p.d. across the resistor X in the circuit   [3]
      ii the resistance R of the resistor labelled X.   [2]   Hint

                                                                          [Total 6]

                                                                                   Answer

2 a State Kirchhoff's first law.   [2]   Hint

   b Apply Kirchhoff's laws to the circuit below to determine the current I at point A in
      milliamperes (mA).   [4]   Hint

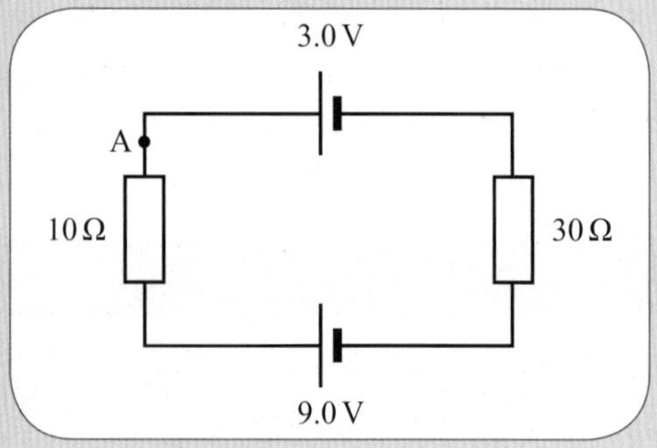

                                                                          [Total 6]

                                                                                   Answer

Chapter 15

Waves

Background

e-Learning

Objectives

Vibrations making waves

What is a vibration or oscillation? An object or particle is vibrating when it moves backwards and forwards about a fixed point. You will have met many examples of vibrations, such as:

- air moving from a loudspeaker
- a ruler being twanged over the edge of a bench
- the string on a guitar or a violin vibrating
- a car or a bike vibrating when it goes over a bumpy road
- a shock wave through the ground produced by an explosion
- vibrating quartz crystals used in watches
- water particles in a sea wave.

Wave quantities

When you pluck the string of a guitar, it vibrates. The vibrations create a wave in the air which we call sound. In fact, all vibrations produce **waves** of one type or another (Figure 15.1). Waves that move through a material (or a vacuum) are called **progressive waves**. A progressive wave transfers energy from one position to another.

Figure 15.1 Radio telescopes detect radio waves from distant stars and galaxies; a rainbow is an effect caused by the reflection and refraction of light waves by water droplets in the atmosphere.

Vibrations and time

You can see from the examples above that vibrations are repeated movements. We can use this as a basis for measuring time. There is a story that Galileo, at the age of 18, observed a lamp swinging in the cathedral at Pisa. He noticed that the swing was regular, and timed the swings using his pulse as a timer. He found that their period was the same, regardless of the size of the swing. He realised that a pendulum like this could form the basis of a clock.

Figure 15.2 shows Galileo and the lamp. This is a rather fanciful image; the lamp in the picture was not installed in the cathedral until 1587, five years after Galileo's observations. However, the image does commemorate a significant change in scientific practice, when measurements of time intervals came to be made using mechanical vibrations rather than the less reliable vibrations of the human heart.

Figure 15.2 Galileo pondering the swinging of a lamp in Pisa cathedral.

At the seaside, a wave is what we see on the surface of the sea. The water moves around and a wave travels across the surface. In Physics, we extend the idea of a wave to describe many other phenomena, including light, sound, etc. We do this by imagining an idealised wave, as shown in Figure 15.3 – you will never see such a perfect wave on the sea!

Figure 15.3 illustrates the following important definitions about waves and wave motion:

- The distance of a point on the wave from its undisturbed position or equilibrium position is called the **displacement** x.
- The maximum displacement of any point on the wave from its undisturbed position is called the **amplitude** A. Amplitude is measured in metres. The greater the amplitude of the wave, the louder the sound or the rougher the sea!
- The distance from any point on a wave to the next exactly similar point (e.g. crest to crest) is called the **wavelength** λ (the Greek letter *lambda*). Wavelength is usually measured in metres.
- The time taken for one complete oscillation of a point in a wave is called the **period** T. It is the time taken for a point to move from one particular position and return to that same position, moving in the same direction. It is measured in seconds (s).

- The number of oscillations per unit time of a point in a wave is called its **frequency** f. For sound waves, the higher the frequency of a musical note, the higher is its pitch. Frequency is measured in hertz (Hz), where 1 Hz = one oscillation per second (1 kHz = 10^3 Hz and 1 MHz = 10^6 Hz). The frequency f of a wave is the reciprocal of the period T:

$$f = \frac{1}{T}$$

Waves are called *mechanical waves* if they need a substance (medium) through which to travel. Sound is one example of such a wave. Other cases are waves on strings, seismic waves and water waves (Figure 15.4).

Some properties of these waves are given later in Table 15.1 (see page 164).

Figure 15.4 The impact of a droplet on the surface of a liquid creates a vibration, which in turn gives rise to waves on the surface.

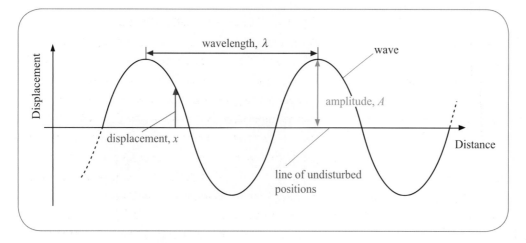

Figure 15.3 A displacement against distance graph illustrating the terms *displacement*, *amplitude* and *wavelength*.

SAQ

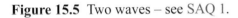

1 Determine the wavelength and amplitude of each of the two waves shown in Figure 15.5.

Hint

Answer

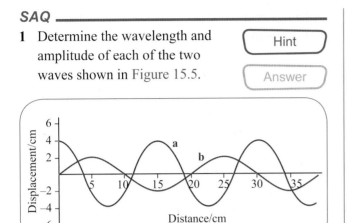

Figure 15.5 Two waves – see SAQ 1.

Longitudinal and transverse waves

There are two distinct types of wave, **longitudinal** and **transverse**. Both can be demonstrated using a slinky spring lying along a bench.

Push the end of the spring back and forth; the segments of the spring become compressed and then stretched out, along the length of the spring. Wave pulses run along the spring. These are longitudinal waves.

Waggle the end of the slinky spring from side to side. The segments of the spring move from side to side as the wave travels along the spring. These are transverse waves.

So the distinction between longitudinal and transverse waves is as follows:

● In longitudinal waves, the particles of the medium vibrate *parallel* to the direction of the wave velocity.

● In transverse waves, the particles of the medium vibrate at *right angles* to the direction of the wave velocity.

Sound waves are an example of a longitudinal wave. Light and all other electromagnetic waves are transverse waves. Waves in water are quite complex. Particles of the water may move both up and down and from side to side as a water wave travels through the water. You can investigate water waves in a ripple tank. There is more about this later in this chapter (page 165) and in Chapter 17.

Representing waves

Figure 15.6 shows how we can represent longitudinal and transverse waves. The longitudinal wave shows how the material through which it is travelling is alternately compressed and expanded. This gives rise to high and low pressure regions respectively. However, this is rather difficult to draw, so you will often see a longitudinal wave represented as if it were a sine wave. The **compressions** and expansions (or **rarefactions**) of the longitudinal wave are equivalent to the peaks and troughs of the transverse wave.

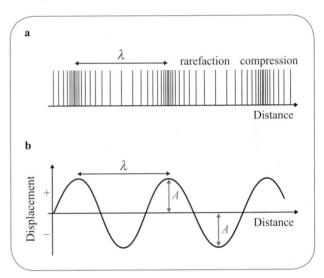

Figure 15.6 a Longitudinal waves, and **b** transverse waves; A = amplitude, λ = wavelength.

Phase and phase difference

All points along a wave have the same pattern of vibration. However, different points do not necessarily vibrate in step with one another. As one point on a stretched string vibrates up and down, the point next to it vibrates slightly out-of-step with it. We say that they vibrate out of phase with each other – there is a **phase difference** between them. This is the amount by which one oscillation leads or lags behind another. Phase difference is measured in degrees.

As you can see from Figure 15.7, two points A and B, with a separation of one whole wavelength λ, vibrate in phase with each other. The phase difference between these two points is 360°. (You can also say it is 0°.) The phase difference between any other two points between A and B can have any value between 0° and 360°. A complete cycle of the wave is thought of as 360°. In Chapter 17 we will see what it means to say that two waves are 'in phase' or 'out of phase' with one another.

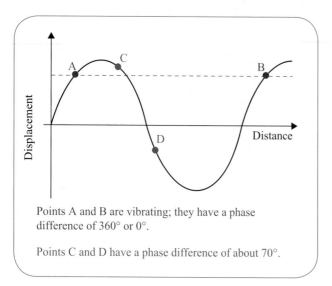

Points A and B are vibrating; they have a phase difference of 360° or 0°.

Points C and D have a phase difference of about 70°.

Figure 15.7 Different points along a wave have different phases.

2   On displacement against distance axes, sketch two waves A and B such that A has twice the wavelength and half the amplitude of B.

Answer

Wave energy

It is important to realise that, for both types of mechanical wave, the particles that make up the material through which the wave is travelling do not move along – they only oscillate about a fixed point. It is *energy* that is transmitted by the wave. Each particle vibrates; as it does so, it pushes its neighbour, transferring energy to it. Then that particle pushes its neighbour, which pushes its neighbour. In this way, energy is transmitted from one particle to the next, to the next, and so on down the line.

Intensity

The term **intensity** has a very precise meaning in Physics. The intensity of a wave is defined as the rate

of energy transmitted per unit area at right angles to the wave velocity.

$$\text{intensity} = \frac{\text{power}}{\text{cross-sectional area}}$$

Intensity is measured in watts per square metre (W m^{-2}). For example, when the Sun is directly overhead, the intensity of its radiation is about $1.0\,\text{kW m}^{-2}$ (1 kilowatt per square metre). This means that energy arrives at the rate of about $1\,\text{kW}$ ($1000\,\text{J s}^{-1}$) on each square metre of the surface of the Earth. At the top of the atmosphere, the intensity of sunlight is greater, about $1.37\,\text{kW m}^{-2}$.

3   A 100 W lamp emits electro-magnetic radiation in all directions. Assuming the lamp to be a *point source*, calculate the intensity of the radiation:

   a   at a distance of 1.0 m from the lamp

   b   at a distance of 2.0 m from the lamp.

Hint

Answer

The intensity of a wave generally decreases as it travels along. There are two reasons for this:

● The wave may 'spread out' (as in the example of light spreading out from a light bulb in SAQ 3).

● The wave may be absorbed or scattered (as when light passes through the Earth's atmosphere).

Intensity and amplitude

As a wave spreads out, its amplitude decreases. This suggests that the intensity I of a wave is related to its amplitude A. In fact, intensity is proportional to the square of the amplitude

$$\text{intensity} \propto \text{amplitude}^2$$

$$I \propto A^2$$

The relationship also implies that for a particular wave:

$$\frac{\text{intensity}}{\text{amplitude}^2} = \text{constant}$$

So, if one wave has *twice* the amplitude of another, it has *four* times the intensity. This means that it is carrying energy at four times the rate.

Shock waves

The energy carried by a wave can be considerable. For example, the shock (seismic) waves from the eruption of a volcano can cause serious structural damage over a wide area. The energy carried in such shock waves is of the order of 10^{20} J!

Similarly, earthquakes, which are a mixture of longitudinal and transverse waves, transmit great amounts of stored energy from deep underground up to the surface, often with devastating effects (Figure 15.8).

Figure 15.9 Machines like this send small shock waves through the ground. The reflected waves are detected, and the pattern of reflections shows up underground features, such as layers of rock or trapped liquid. This can help geologists to find new reserves of oil and other natural resources.

Figure 15.8 The severe earthquake which struck San Francisco in April 1906 released vast amounts of energy. Hundreds of buildings toppled, and tens of thousands of people were killed.

Scientists produce small shock waves to help them in their study of the Earth, for example in exploring for underground resources (Figure 15.9). Most of what we know about the internal structure of the Earth, other planets, the Moon, and even the Sun, has come from observations of shock waves moving through these giant bodies.

SAQ

4 Waves from a source have an amplitude of 5.0 cm and an intensity of 400 W m^{-2}.

  a The amplitude of the waves is increased to 10.0 cm. What is their intensity now?

  b The intensity of the waves is decreased to 100 W m^{-2}. What is their amplitude?

    (Answer)

(Extension)

Wave speed

The speed with which energy is transmitted by a wave is known as the wave speed v. This is measured in m s^{-1}. The wave speed for sound in air at a pressure of 10^5 Pa and a temperature of 0 °C is about 340 m s^{-1}, while for light in a vacuum it is almost 300 000 000 m s^{-1}.

The wave equation

An important equation connecting the speed v of a wave with its frequency f and wavelength λ can be determined as follows. We can find the speed of the wave using:

$$\text{speed} = \frac{\text{distance}}{\text{time}}$$

But a wave will travel a distance of one whole wavelength in a time equal to one period T. So:

$$\text{wave speed} = \frac{\text{wavelength}}{\text{period}}$$

or

$$v = \frac{\lambda}{T}$$

$$v = \left(\frac{1}{T}\right) \times \lambda$$

However, $f = \frac{1}{T}$ and so:

$$\text{wave speed} = \text{frequency} \times \text{wavelength}$$

$$v = f \times \lambda$$

A numerical example may help to make this clear. Imagine a wave of frequency 5 Hz and wavelength 3 m going past you. In 1 s, five complete wave cycles, each of length 3 m, go past. So the total length of the waves going past in 1 s is 15 m. The distance covered by the wave in one second is its speed, therefore the speed of the wave is $15\,\text{m s}^{-1}$.

Clearly, for a given speed of wave, the greater the wavelength, the smaller the frequency and vice versa. The speed of sound in air is constant (for a given temperature and pressure). The wavelength of sound can be made smaller by increasing the frequency of the source of sound.

Table 15.1 gives typical values of v, f and λ for some mechanical waves. You can check for yourself that $v = f\lambda$ is satisfied.

Worked example 1

Middle C on a piano tuned to concert pitch should have a frequency of 264 Hz (Figure 15.10). If the speed of sound is $330\,\text{m s}^{-1}$, calculate the wavelength of the sound produced when this key is played.

Step 1 We use the above equation in slightly rewritten form:

$$\text{wavelength} = \frac{\text{speed}}{\text{frequency}}$$

Step 2 Substituting the values for middle C we get:

$$\text{wavelength} = \frac{330}{264} = 1.25\,\text{m}$$

The human ear can detect sounds of frequencies between 20 Hz and 20 kHz, i.e. with wavelengths between 15 m and 15 mm.

Figure 15.10 Each string in a piano produces a different note.

	Water waves in a ripple tank	Sound waves in air	Waves on a slinky spring
Speed v/m s^{-1}	about 0.12	about 300	about 1
Frequency f/Hz	about 6	20 to 20 000 (limits of human hearing)	about 2
Wavelength λ/m	about 0.2	15 to 0.015	about 0.5

Table 15.1 Properties of some mechanical waves readily investigated in the laboratory.

SAQ

5   Sound is a mechanical wave that can be transmitted through a solid. Calculate the frequency of sound of wavelength 0.25 m that travels through steel at a speed of 5060 m s^{-1}. [Answer]

6   A cello string vibrates with a frequency of 64 Hz. Calculate the speed of the transverse waves on the string given that the wavelength is 140 cm. [Answer]

7   An oscillator is used to send waves along a stretched cord. Four complete wave cycles fit on a 20 cm length of the cord when the frequency of the oscillator is 30 Hz. For this wave, calculate: [Hint]
    a   its wavelength
    b   its frequency
    c   its speed. [Answer]

8   Copy and complete Table 15.2. (You may assume that the speed of radio waves is 3.0×10^8 m s^{-1}.) [Hint] [Answer]

Station	Wavelength λ/m	Frequency f/MHz
Radio A (FM)		97.6
Radio B (FM)		94.6
Radio B (LW)	1515	
Radio C (MW)	693	

Table 15.2 For SAQ 8.

Waves in a ripple tank

The behaviour of water waves can easily be seen in a ripple tank, and the **reflection** of these waves is shown in Figure 15.11. These diagrams represent waves as wavefronts; the waves are viewed from above, with the lines showing the positions of the

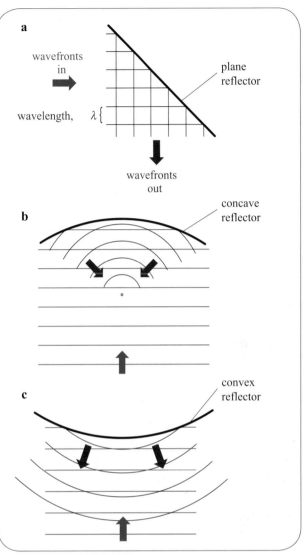

Figure 15.11 Reflection of waves in a ripple tank. **a** Waves reflected from a 45° barrier. Their wavelength λ stays the same. **b** Straight (plane) waves approach a concave barrier. The reflected waves are focused to a point. **c** Plane waves approach a convex barrier. The reflected waves

wave crests. The separation between adjacent wave fronts is equal to the wavelength λ of the waves. The initial wavefronts are shown in blue and the reflected wavefronts in red.

In reflection, waves change direction when they meet an impenetrable barrier and bounce off it.

Demonstrating refraction

Refraction can also be demonstrated using a ripple tank. Refraction occurs when waves change speed, usually when the medium through which they are travelling changes. Water waves slow down when they enter shallower water. Figure 15.12 shows that when waves approach the boundary between deep and shallow water at an angle, the effect is for the waves to change direction. Notice also that their wavelength decreases; the waves become closer together.

When the waves pass from deep water to shallow water:

- their frequency remains constant
- there is a decrease in wave speed and wavelength
- the ratio of the speed of the waves in deep water to that in shallow water is equal to that of their wavelengths (if their speed is halved, their wavelength is also halved).

Reflection and refraction are two characteristic properties of waves. Three other wave properties are discussed in later chapters (polarisation in Chapter 16, diffraction and interference in Chapter 17).

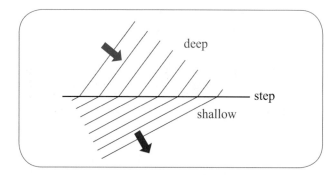

Figure 15.12 Refraction of water waves at a 'step'; they travel more slowly in shallower water, so the part of the wavefront which enters the shallow water first lags behind.

9 Estimate the ratio of the wave speeds in deep and shallow water in Figure 15.13.

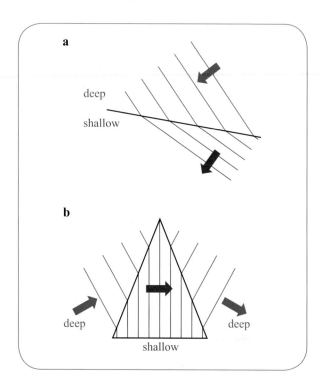

Figure 15.13 Waves travel more slowly in shallow water than in deep water (see SAQ 9).

Extension

Summary

- Mechanical waves are produced by vibrating objects.

- A progressive wave carries energy from one place to another.

- Two points on a wave separated by a distance of one wavelength have a phase difference of 0° or 360°.

- The intensity of a wave is defined as the wave power transmitted per unit area at right angles to the wave velocity. Hence intensity $= \dfrac{\text{power}}{\text{cross-sectional area}}$. Intensity has the unit W m^{-2}.

- The intensity I of a wave is proportional to the square of the amplitude A ($I \propto A^2$).

- There are two types of wave – longitudinal and transverse. Longitudinal waves have vibrations parallel to the direction in which the wave travels, whereas transverse waves have vibrations at right angles to the direction in which the wave travels. Surface water waves, waves on a string and light waves are all examples of transverse waves. Sound is a longitudinal wave.

- The frequency f of a wave is related to its period T by the equation:

$$f = \frac{1}{T}$$

- The speed of all waves is given by the wave equation:

  wave speed = frequency × wavelength

$$v = f\lambda$$

- All waves can be reflected and refracted.

Glossary

Questions

1 The diagram shows, at a given instant, the surface of the water in a ripple tank when plane water waves are travelling from left to right.

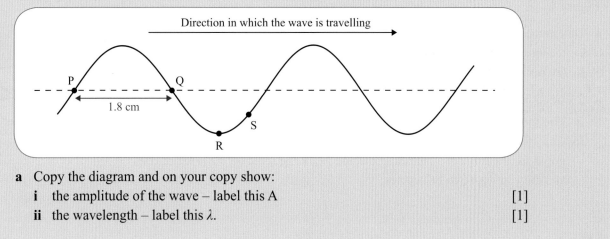

a Copy the diagram and on your copy show:
  i the amplitude of the wave – label this A [1]
  ii the wavelength – label this λ. [1]

continued

b On your copy of the diagram:
  i draw the position of the wave a short time, about one-tenth of a period, later [2]
  ii draw arrows to show the directions in which the particles at Q and S are moving
  during this short time. [2]
c State the phase difference between the movement of particles at P and Q. [1]
d The frequency of the wave is 25 Hz and the distance between P and Q is 1.8 cm.
  Calculate:
  i the period of the wave [2]
  ii the speed of the wave. [3]
e **i** Suggest how the speed of the waves in the ripple tank could be changed. [1]
  ii The frequency of the wave source is kept constant and the wave speed is halved.
  State what change occurs to the wavelength. [2]

OCR Physics AS (2823) January 2005 [Total 15]

Hint

Hint

Hint

Answer

2 Figure 1 shows the displacement against time graph for a particle in a medium as a progressive wave
passes through the medium.

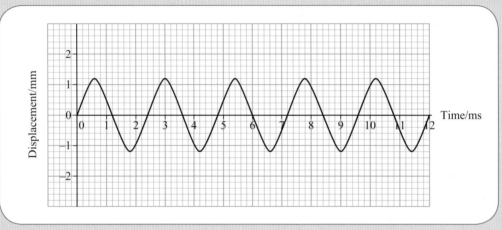

Figure 1

a Determine from the graph:
  i the amplitude of the wave [1]
  ii the period of the wave. [1]

b **i** What is the frequency of the wave? [2]
  ii The speed of the wave is 1500 m s⁻¹. Calculate its wavelength. [2]
  iii Copy the grid in Figure 2 and use it to sketch a displacement against position
  graph for the wave at a particular instant. Mark the scale on the position axis
  and draw at least two full cycles. [3]

Hint

Hint

continued

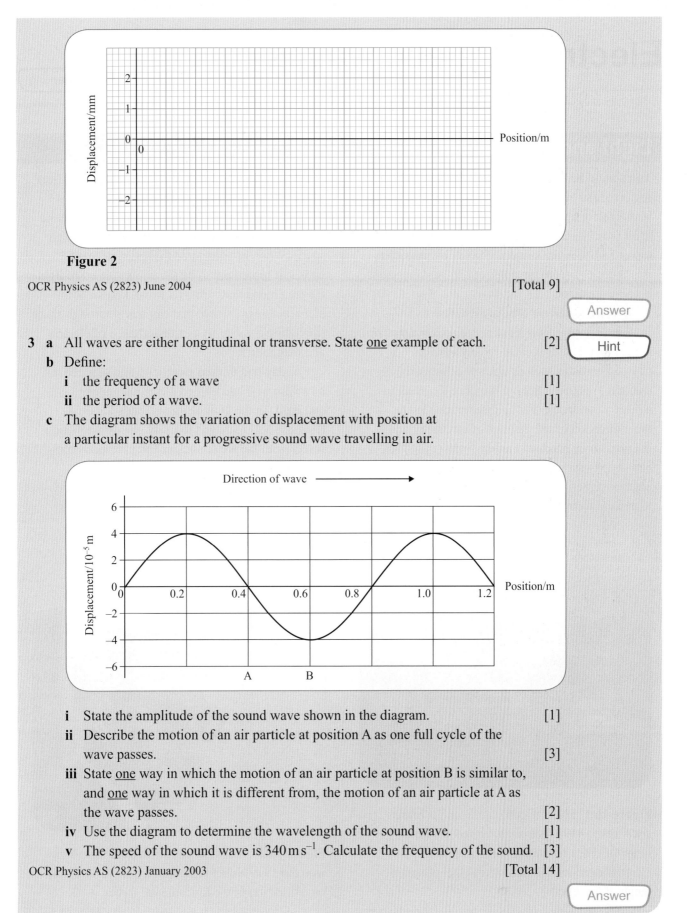

Figure 2

OCR Physics AS (2823) June 2004 [Total 9]

Answer

3 **a** All waves are either longitudinal or transverse. State <u>one</u> example of each. [2]

Hint

b Define:
   i the frequency of a wave [1]
   ii the period of a wave. [1]
c The diagram shows the variation of displacement with position at a particular instant for a progressive sound wave travelling in air.

   i State the amplitude of the sound wave shown in the diagram. [1]
   ii Describe the motion of an air particle at position A as one full cycle of the wave passes. [3]
   iii State <u>one</u> way in which the motion of an air particle at position B is similar to, and <u>one</u> way in which it is different from, the motion of an air particle at A as the wave passes. [2]
   iv Use the diagram to determine the wavelength of the sound wave. [1]
   v The speed of the sound wave is $340\,\mathrm{m\,s^{-1}}$. Calculate the frequency of the sound. [3]

OCR Physics AS (2823) January 2003 [Total 14]

Answer

Chapter 16

Electromagnetic waves

e-Learning

Objectives

Light and electromagnetism

You should be familiar with the idea that light is a region of the **electromagnetic spectrum**. It is not immediately obvious that light has any connection at all with electricity, magnetism and waves. These topics had been the subject of study by physicists for centuries before the connections between them became apparent.

An electric current always gives rise to a **magnetic field** (this is known as electromagnetism). A magnetic field is created by any *moving* charged particles such as electrons. Similarly, a changing magnetic field will induce a current in a nearby conductor. These observations led to the unification of the theories of electricity and magnetism by Michael Faraday in the mid-19th century. A vast technology based on the theories of electromagnetism developed rapidly, and continues to expand today (Figure 16.1).

Faraday's studies were extended by James Clerk Maxwell. He produced mathematical equations that predicted that a changing electric or magnetic field would give rise to waves travelling through space. When he calculated the speed of these waves, it turned out to be the known speed of light. He concluded that light is a wave, known as an *electromagnetic wave*, that can travel through space (including a vacuum) as a disturbance of electric and magnetic fields.

Faraday had unified electricity and magnetism; now Maxwell had unified electromagnetism and light. In the 20th century, Abdus Salam (Figure 16.2) managed to unify electromagnetic forces with the weak nuclear force, responsible for radioactive decay. Physicists continue to strive to unify the big ideas of physics; you may occasionally hear talk of a *theory of everything*. This would not truly explain *everything*, but it would explain all known forces, as well as the existence of the various fundamental particles of matter.

Figure 16.1 These telecommunications masts are situated 4500 metres above sea level in Ecuador. They transmit microwaves, a form of electromagnetic radiation, across the mountain range of the Andes.

Figure 16.2 Abdus Salam, the Pakistani physicist, won the 1979 Nobel Prize for Physics for his work on unification of the fundamental forces.

Electromagnetic radiation

By the end of the 19th century, several types of electromagnetic wave had been discovered:

- radio waves – these were discovered by Heinrich Hertz when he was investigating electrical sparks
- infrared and ultraviolet waves – these lie beyond either end of the visible spectrum
- X-rays – these were discovered by Wilhelm Röntgen and were produced when a beam of electrons collided with a metal target such as tungsten
- γ-rays – these were discovered by Henri Becquerel when he was investigating radioactive substances.

We now regard all of these types of radiation as parts of the same electromagnetic spectrum, and we know that they can be produced in a variety of different ways.

The speed of light

James Clerk Maxwell showed that the speed c of electromagnetic radiation in a vacuum (free space) was independent of the frequency of the waves. In other words, all types of electromagnetic wave travel at the same speed in a vacuum. In the SI system of units, c has the value:

$$c = 299\ 792\ 458\ \text{m s}^{-1}$$

The approximate value for the speed of light in a vacuum (often used in calculations) is 3.0×10^8 m s^{-1}.

The wavelength λ and frequency f of the radiation are related by the *wave equation*:

$$c = f\lambda$$

When light travels from a vacuum into a material medium such as glass, its speed *decreases* but its frequency *remains the same*, and so we conclude that its wavelength must decrease. We often think of different forms of electromagnetic radiation as being characterised by their different wavelengths, but it is better to think of their different frequencies as being their fundamental characteristic, since their wavelengths depend on the medium through which they are travelling.

SAQ

1 Red light of wavelength 700 nm in a vacuum travels into glass, where its speed decreases to 2.0×10^8 m s^{-1}. Determine:
   a the frequency of the light in a vacuum
   b its frequency and wavelength in the glass.

Hint

Answer

Orders of magnitude

Table 16.1 shows the approximate ranges of wavelengths in a vacuum of the principal bands which make up the electromagnetic spectrum. A diagram of the electromagnetic spectrum is shown in Chapter 19. Here are some points to note:

- There are no clear divisions between the different ranges or bands in the spectrum. The divisions shown here are somewhat arbitrary.
- Similarly, the naming of subdivisions is arbitrary. For example, microwaves are sometimes regarded as a subdivision of radio waves.
- The ranges of X-rays and γ-rays overlap. The distinction is that X-rays are produced when electrons decelerate rapidly or when they hit a target metal at high-speeds. γ-rays are produced by nuclear reactions such as radioactive decay. There is no difference whatsoever in the radiation between an X-ray and a γ-ray of wavelength, say, 10^{-11} m.

SAQ

2 Copy Table 16.1. Add a third column showing the range of frequencies of each type of radiation.

Answer

Radiation	Wavelength range/m
radio waves	>10^6 to 10^{-1}
microwaves	10^{-1} to 10^{-3}
infrared	10^{-3} to 7×10^{-7}
visible	7×10^{-7} (red) to 4×10^{-7} (violet)
ultraviolet	4×10^{-7} to 10^{-8}
X-rays	10^{-8} to 10^{-13}
γ-rays	10^{-10} to 10^{-16}

Table 16.1 Wavelengths (in a vacuum) of the electromagnetic spectrum.

3 Study Table 16.1 and answer the questions:
  a Which type of radiation has the narrowest range of wavelengths?
  b Which has the second narrowest range?
  c What is the range of wavelengths of microwaves, in millimetres?
  d What is the range of wavelengths of visible light, in nanometres?
  e What is the frequency range of visible light?

4 For each of the following wavelengths measured in a vacuum, state the type of electromagnetic radiation it corresponds to:
  a 1 km   **b** 3 cm   **c** 5000 nm
  d 500 nm   **e** 50 nm   **f** 10^{-12} m

  Answer

5 For each of the following frequencies, state the type of electromagnetic radiation it corresponds to:

  Hint

  a 200 kHz   **b** 100 MHz
  c 5×10^{14} Hz   **d** 10^{18} Hz.

  Answer

Radiation	Practical uses
radio waves	• broadcasting radio and TV • radio astronomy • magnetic resonance imaging (MRI)
microwaves	• radar • telecommunications (mobile phones) • cooking
infrared	• night-vision goggles and cameras • remote controls • cooking
visible	• signalling • photography
ultraviolet	• sterilisation • security marking • suntanning
X-rays and γ-rays	• sterilisation • medical imaging • medical treatment

Table 16.2 Uses of electromagnetic radiation.

Using electromagnetic radiation

We use electromagnetic waves in many different ways. The wavelength must be chosen appropriately for each application. For example, X-rays are used to investigate the structure of materials. X-rays have a wavelength comparable to the spacing between the atoms in a crystal. This means that they can be diffracted (see Chapter 17). The diffraction patterns can be used to determine the arrangement and separation of the atoms.

Table 16.2 lists a number of uses of electromagnetic waves. Figure 16.3 shows images of a tooth taken using terahertz radiation. This is electromagnetic radiation with frequencies of the order of 10^{12} Hz, sometimes described as the 'forgotten band' of the electromagnetic spectrum because it is only now beginning to find applications.

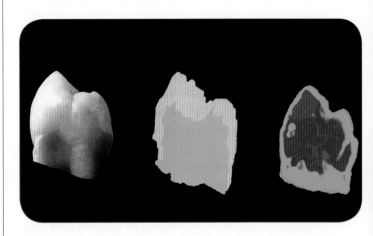

Figure 16.3 Three images of a decaying tooth; on the left, visible light allows us to see only the outer surface. Terahertz radiation penetrates to the interior (centre and right), revealing a serious cavity which appears as a purple/red colour. Terahertz radiation is much safer than X-rays.

Ultraviolet hazards

Many people seek the pleasures of a sunny beach at holiday time (Figure 16.4). People of north European stock generally have fair skin, and they hope to develop 'a healthy tan'. However, this is a naive idea; tanning is the body's response to hazardous radiation. Ultraviolet radiation damages skin and can cause cancer. The UK death rate from skin cancer is rising as people take inadequate precautions when they are exposed to strong sunlight. (Australians, who are mostly of the same stock, have learned to behave more wisely.)

The ultraviolet (UV) band of the electromagnetic spectrum is divided into three subdivisions, with different wavelength ranges:

- UV-A: 400–320 nm
- UV-B: 320–280 nm
- UV-C: < 280 nm.

The Sun produces all three types of ultraviolet radiation, but most is absorbed by the atmosphere before it reaches us on the ground. About 99% of the UV at sea level is UV-A. Almost all UV-C radiation is absorbed by the ozone layer. We all need some exposure to sunlight – perhaps half an hour a day, on average. This is because the UV-B in sunlight acts on the skin to produce vitamin D. That's the positive side. Here's the negative side:

- UV-A is very penetrating, and causes the skin to become wrinkled.
- UV-B can damage DNA in skin cells and this can trigger cancer.
- All UV can damage the eyes. Some people such as welders are exposed to high levels and have to take precautions.

Wise sunbathers make use of sunscreen on their skin (Figure 16.5). This includes substances such as titanium dioxide to absorb the UV. They also wear sunglasses to avoid suffering from cataracts later in life.

Figure 16.4 Sun-worshippers exposing themselves to hazardous radiation from the Sun.

Figure 16.5 This is how to be safe in the Sun – with plenty of sunscreen and dark glasses.

The nature of electromagnetic waves

An electromagnetic wave is a disturbance in the electric and magnetic fields in space. Figure 16.6 shows how we can represent such a wave. In this diagram, the wave is travelling from left to right.

The electric field is shown oscillating in the vertical plane. The magnetic field is shown oscillating in the horizontal plane. These are arbitrary choices; the point is that the two fields vary at right angles to each other, and also at right angles to the direction in which the wave is travelling. This shows that electromagnetic waves are transverse waves.

(Extension)

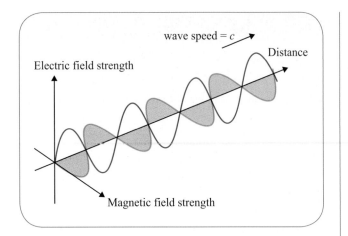

Figure 16.6 An electromagnetic wave is a periodic variation in electric and magnetic fields.

Polarisation

Polarisation is a wave property which allows us to distinguish between transverse and longitudinal waves.

Tie one end of a rubber rope to a post, get hold of the other end and pull the rope taut. If you move your wrist up and down, a wave travels along the rope. The rope itself moves up and down vertically. Repeat the experiment, but this time move your wrist from side to side. Again a transverse wave is created, with bumps which move horizontally. Repeat again, this time moving your wrist diagonally. You have observed a characteristic of transverse waves: there are many different directions in which they can vibrate, all at right angles to the direction in which the wave travels. You cannot do this for a longitudinal wave because the oscillations are always parallel to the direction in which the wave travels.

The first wave you created on the rubber rope, by moving your wrist up and down, is said to be *vertically polarised*. The second was *horizontally polarised*. So the phenomenon of polarisation is something which distinguishes transverse waves from longitudinal ones.

Polarised light

Light is a transverse wave and this can be shown by polarising it. Light consists of vibrations of electric and magnetic fields travelling through space. Light which is unpolarised (such as the light emitted by the Sun, or by a light bulb) has vibrations in all directions at right angles to the direction in which it is travelling.

When the light passes through a piece of Polaroid (a polarising filter), it becomes polarised. How does this work? Polaroid consists of long-chain molecules that absorb the energy from the oscillating electric field. If these molecules are arranged vertically, they absorb light waves which are polarised vertically, that is, light waves whose electric field is oscillating up and down. Horizontally polarised light waves (whose electric field is oscillating from side to side) pass through unaffected (Figure 16.7a). The light is now described as **plane polarised**.

Plane polarised light will be stopped by a second piece of Polaroid placed with its axis at 90° to the first, as shown in Figure 16.7b.

Polarisation can also be shown with other electromagnetic waves such as microwaves, radio and TV. The last of these can be demonstrated simply by rotating a set-top aerial and watching the effect on the picture. You can show that a microwave transmitter used in the physics laboratory emits plane polarised

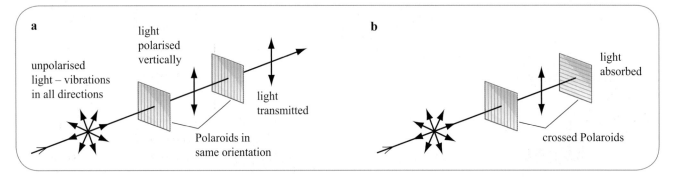

Figure 16.7 a Light, initially unpolarised, becomes vertically polarised after passing through the first Polaroid. **b** It is absorbed by a second Polaroid oriented at 90° to the first.

microwaves. This can be done by rotating a metal grille between the transmitter and the receiver (Figure 16.8). The metal rods of the grille behave very much like the long-chain molecules of a Polaroid.

The light we receive from the sky is sunlight which has been scattered by the atmosphere. This scattering polarises the light. We cannot see this, but many insects such as bees can, and perhaps some birds, too. This means that bees can tell the direction of the Sun even when it is overcast, and this helps them to navigate. A good simulation of the polarisation of scattered light in the atmosphere is to fill a transparent rectangular plastic tank with water and add a little milk to it (a few millilitres per litre should be sufficient). Shine a bright beam of light through the mixture, and observe the polarisation at different points around the tank using a piece of Polaroid and light meter.

Effects that use polarisation of light

Some examples of effects which involve the polarisation of light are given below.

Polaroid sunglasses

These reduce glare by selecting one polarisation of light waves only, so the amount of unpolarised light reaching the eyes is reduced. Light reflected from a shiny, level road or water surface is partially polarised in the horizontal plane, and the Polaroid in sunglasses is arranged to cut out this light (Figure 16.9). You can use a light meter to measure the amount of light transmitted through a pair of sunglasses. Place one lens over the other and rotate it.

Figure 16.9 A Polaroid filter can help in photography. By cutting out light reflected from the surface of the water, it allows us to see down to the seabed.

Stresses in materials

When materials are stressed (for instance, when they form part of a structure such as a bridge), some parts may become more stressed than others. This can lead to unexpected failure of the structure. Engineers make models from transparent plastic; an example is shown in Figure 16.10. If the model is viewed through a Polaroid, areas of stress concentration show up where the coloured bands are closest together.

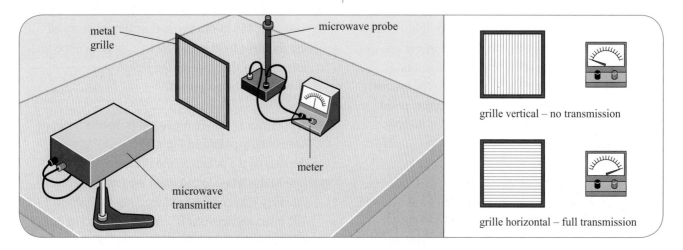

grille vertical – no transmission

grille horizontal – full transmission

Figure 16.8 In one orientation, the metal grille blocks the microwaves; at 90°, it lets them through. This shows that the source produces polarised radiation. The microwave transmitter emits vertically plane polarised waves.

Figure 16.10 A plastic hook as seen through a polarising filter. The coloured pattern shows up places where stress is concentrated in the material.

Liquid-crystal displays

The liquid-crystal displays of some calculators and laptop screens produce plane polarised light. You can investigate this effect by putting a piece of Polaroid over the display and rotating it.

Malus's law

You can find the orientation of polarisation of light as follows:

- Pass light through a single polarising filter. This will make the light plane polarised.
- Pass this plane polarised light through a second polarising filter. This second filter is called the *analyser*. Rotate the analyser until no light is transmitted. This means that the axis of the analyser is at 90° to the plane of polarisation.
- Alternatively, rotate the analyser until the intensity of transmitted light is a maximum. At this point the light is polarised in the direction of the axis of the analyser.

What happens if the plane of polarisation is at an angle (other than 0° or 90°) to the axis of the analyser? The answer is given by Malus's law (named after the French physicist Étienne-Louis Malus).

Consider plane polarised light of amplitude A_0 incident on an analyser. The angle between the axis of the analyser and the plane of polarisation of the

incident light is θ. The amplitude A of the light transmitted through the analyser *along its axis* is a *component* of the incident amplitude. Hence:

$$A = A_0 \cos \theta$$

But as we saw in Chapter 15, the intensity of light is directly proportional to the square of the amplitude. Therefore, the intensity I of the light transmitted through the analyser is given by:

$$I = I_0 \cos^2 \theta$$

where I_0 is the intensity before the light enters the analyser (see Figure 16.11). The relationship above is known as Malus's law. Note that the *fraction* of the light intensity transmitted is equal to $\cos^2 \theta$.

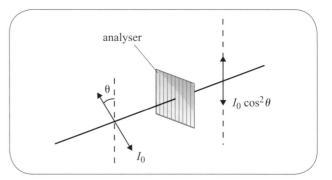

Figure 16.11 Here, the axis of the analyser is vertical; the incoming light is polarised at an angle θ to the vertical. The transmitted light is vertically polarised, but less intense than the incident light.

SAQ

6 Light which is polarised vertically is incident on a Polaroid whose axis is at 45° to the vertical. If the intensity of the incident light is 200 W m^{-2}, what will be the intensity of the transmitted light? How will it be polarised?

Hint

Answer

7 A polariser is slowly rotated in front of a beam of horizontally polarised light. The angle between the axis of the polariser and the horizontal is θ. Use Malus's law to calculate the fraction of light intensity transmitted from the filter for values of θ at 10° intervals between 0° and 180°. Sketch a graph of fraction of light intensity transmitted against angle θ.

Answer

Summary

- All electromagnetic waves travel at the same speed of 3.0×10^8 m s^{-1} in a vacuum, but have different wavelengths and frequencies.

- The regions of the electromagnetic spectrum in order of increasing wavelength are: γ-rays, X-rays, ultraviolet, visible, infrared, microwaves and radio waves.

- Polarisation is a phenomenon which is only associated with transverse waves.

- A plane polarised wave has oscillations in only one plane.

- Light is partially polarised on reflection.

- Malus's law gives the intensity I of light transmitted through a polarising filter:

$$I = I_0 \cos^2 \theta$$

Questions

1 a State <u>two</u> main properties of electromagnetic waves. [2]
  b State <u>one</u> major difference between microwaves and radio waves. [1]
  c i Estimate the wavelength in metres of X-rays. [1]
    ii Use your answer to **i** to determine the frequency of the X-rays. [2]
[Total 6]

Answer

2 The diagram shows a laboratory microwave transmitter T positioned directly opposite a microwave detector D, which is connected to a meter.

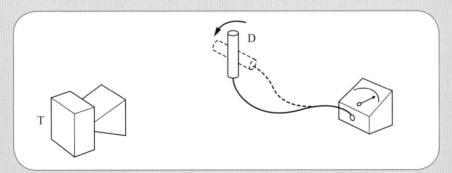

Initially the meter shows a maximum reading. When the detector is rotated through 90°, in a vertical plane as shown, the meter reading falls to zero.
  a Explain why the meter reading falls. [2]
    Hint
  b Predict what would happen to the meter reading if the detector were rotated through a further 90°. [1]
  c State what the observations tell you about the nature of microwaves. [1]
OCR Physics AS (2823) January 2003 [Total 4]

Answer

continued

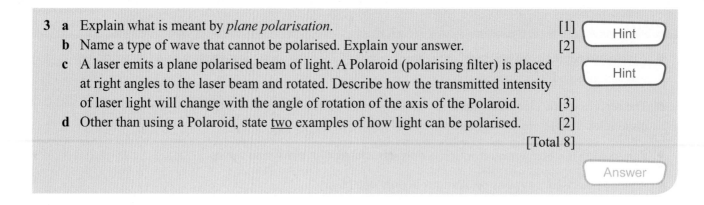

3 a Explain what is meant by *plane polarisation*. [1]

b Name a type of wave that cannot be polarised. Explain your answer. [2]

c A laser emits a plane polarised beam of light. A Polaroid (polarising filter) is placed at right angles to the laser beam and rotated. Describe how the transmitted intensity of laser light will change with the angle of rotation of the axis of the Polaroid. [3]

d Other than using a Polaroid, state <u>two</u> examples of how light can be polarised. [2]

[Total 8]

Hint

Hint

Answer

Chapter 17

Superposition of waves

e-Learning

Objectives

Combining waves

In Chapter 15 and Chapter 16, we looked at how to describe the behaviour of **waves**. We saw how they can be reflected, refracted and polarised. In this chapter we are going to consider what happens when two or more waves meet at a point in space and combine together (Figure 17.1).

Figure 17.1 Here we see ripples produced when drops of water fall into a swimming pool. The ripples overlap to produce a complex pattern of crests and troughs.

So what happens when two waves arrive together at the same place? We can answer this from our everyday experience. What happens when the beams of light waves from two torches cross over? They pass straight through one another. Similarly, sound waves pass through one another, apparently without affecting each other. This is very different from the behaviour of *particles*. Two bullets meeting in mid-air would ricochet off one another in a very un-wave-like way.

The principle of superposition of waves

Figure 17.2 shows the displacement against distance graphs for two sinusoidal waves (blue and black) of different wavelengths. It also shows the resultant wave (red), which comes from combining these two. How do we find this resultant displacement shown in red?

Consider position A. Here the displacement of both waves is zero, and so the resultant must also be zero.

At position B, both waves have positive displacement. The resultant displacement is found by adding these together.

At position C, the displacement of one wave is positive while the other is negative. The resultant displacement lies between the two displacements. In fact, the resultant displacement is the *algebraic sum* of the displacements of waves A and B; that is, their sum, taking account of their signs (positive or negative).

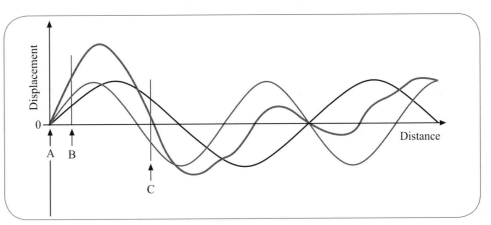

Figure 17.2 Adding two waves by the principle of superposition – the red line is the resultant wave.

We can work our way along the distance axis in this way, calculating the resultant of the two waves by algebraically adding them up at intervals. Notice that, for these two waves, the resultant wave is a rather complex wave with dips and bumps along its length.

The idea that we can find the resultant of two waves which meet at a point simply by adding up the displacements at each point is called the **principle of superposition** of waves. This principle can be applied to more than two waves and also to all types of waves A statement of the principle of superposition is shown below.

When two or more waves meet at a point, the resultant displacement is the algebraic sum of the displacements of the individual waves.

SAQ

1 On graph paper, draw two 'triangular' waves like those shown in Figure 17.3. (These are easier to work with than sinusoidal waves.) One should have wavelength 8 cm and amplitude 2 cm; the other wavelength 16 cm and amplitude 3 cm. Use the principle of superposition of waves to determine the resultant displacement at suitable points along the waves, and draw the complete resultant wave.

Answer

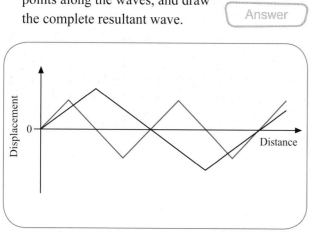

Figure 17.3 Two triangular waves – see SAQ 1.

Diffraction of waves

In Chapter 15 we saw how all waves can be reflected and refracted. Transverse waves, such as light, can also be polarised (Chapter 16). Another wave phenomenon that applies to all waves is that they can be diffracted. **Diffraction** is the spreading of a wave as it passes through a gap or around an edge. It is easier to observe and investigate diffraction effects using water waves.

Diffraction of ripples in water

A ripple tank can be used to show diffraction. Plane waves are generated using a vibrating bar, and *move towards* a gap in a barrier (Figure 17.4). Where the ripples strike the barrier, they are reflected back. Where they arrive at the gap, however, they pass through and spread out into the space beyond. It is this spreading out of waves as they travel through a gap (or past the edge of a barrier) that is called diffraction.

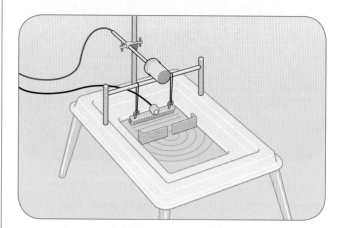

Figure 17.4 Ripples, initially straight, spread out into the space beyond the gap in the barrier.

The extent to which ripples are diffracted depends on the width of the gap. This is illustrated in Figure 17.5. The lines in this diagram show the wavefronts. It is as if we are looking down on the ripples from above, and drawing lines to represent the tops of the ripples at some instant in time. The separation between adjacent wavefronts is equal to the wavelength λ of the ripples.

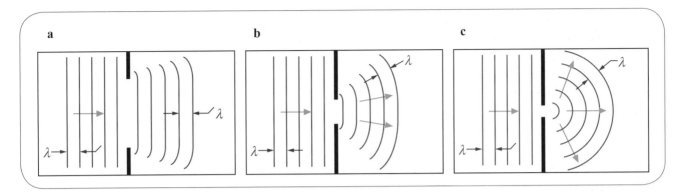

Figure 17.5 The extent to which ripples spread out depends on the relationship between their wavelength and the width of the gap. In **a**, the width of the gap is very much greater than the wavelength and there is hardly any noticeable diffraction. In **b**, the width of the gap is greater than the wavelength and there is limited diffraction. In **c**, the gap width is equal to the wavelength and the diffraction effect is greatest.

Figure 17.5 shows the effect on the ripples when they encounter a gap in a barrier. The amount of diffraction depends on the width of the gap. There is hardly any noticeable diffraction when the gap is very much larger than the wavelength. As the gap becomes narrower, the diffraction effect becomes more pronounced. It is greatest when the width of the gap is equal to the wavelength of the ripples.

Diffraction of some other waves

Sound and light

Diffraction effects are greatest when waves pass through a gap with a width equal to their wavelength. This is useful in explaining why we can observe diffraction readily for some waves, but not for others. For example, sound waves in the audible range have wavelengths from a few millimetres to a few metres. Thus we might expect to observe diffraction effects for sound in our environment. Sounds, for example, diffract as they pass through doorways. The width of a doorway is comparable to the wavelength of a sound and so a noise in one room spreads out into the next room.

Visible light has much shorter wavelengths (about 5×10^{-7} m). It is not diffracted noticeably by doorways because the width of the gap is a million times larger than the wavelength of light.

However, we can observe diffraction of light by passing it through a very narrow slit or a small hole. When laser light is directed onto a slit whose width is comparable to the wavelength of the incident light, it spreads out into the space beyond to form a smear on the screen (Figure 17.6). An adjustable slit allows you to see the effect of gradually narrowing the gap.

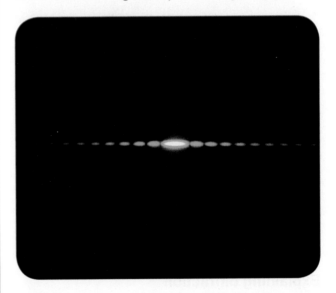

Figure 17.6 Light is diffracted as it passes through a slit.

Radio and microwaves

Radio waves can have wavelengths of the order of a kilometre. These waves are easily diffracted by the gaps in the hills and by the tall buildings around our towns and cities. Microwaves, used by the mobile phone network, have wavelengths of about 1 cm. These waves are not easily diffracted (because their wavelengths are much smaller than the dimensions of the gaps) and mostly travel through space in straight lines.

Cars need external radio aerials because radio waves have wavelengths longer than the size of the windows, so they cannot diffract into the car. If you try listening to a radio in a train without an external aerial, you will find that FM signals can be picked up weakly (their wavelength is about 3 m), but AM signals, with longer wavelengths, cannot get in at all.

SAQ

2 A microwave oven (Figure 17.7) uses microwaves whose wavelength is 12.5 cm. The front door of the oven is made of glass with a metal grid inside; the gaps in the grid are a few millimetres across. Explain how this design allows us to see the food inside the oven, while the microwaves are not allowed to escape into the kitchen (where they might cook us).

> Answer

Figure 17.7 A microwave oven has a metal grid in the door to keep microwaves in and let light out.

Explaining diffraction

Diffraction is a wave effect that can be explained by the principle of superposition. We have to think about what happens when a plane ripple reaches a gap in a barrier (Figure 17.8). Each point on the surface of the water in the gap is moving up and down. Each of these moving points acts as a source of new ripples spreading out into the space beyond the barrier. Now we have a lot of new ripples, and we can use the principle of superposition to find their resultant effect. Without trying to calculate the effect of an infinite number of ripples, we can say that in some directions the ripples add together while in other directions they cancel out.

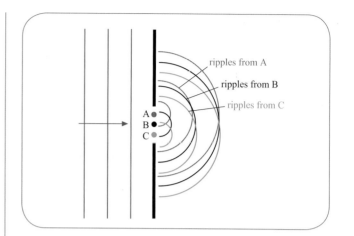

Figure 17.8 Ripples from all points across the gap contribute to the pattern in the space beyond.

Interference

Adding waves of different wavelengths and amplitudes results in complex waves. We can find some interesting effects if we consider what happens when two waves of the same wavelength overlap at a point. Again, we will use the principle of superposition to explain what we observe.

A simple experiment shows the effect we are interested in here. Two loudspeakers are connected to a single signal generator (Figure 17.9). They each produce sound waves of the same wavelength. Walk around in the space in front of the loudspeakers; you will hear the resultant effect. A naive view might be that we would hear a sound twice as loud as that from a single loudspeaker. However, this is not what we hear. At some points, the sound is *louder* than for a single speaker. At other points, the sound is much

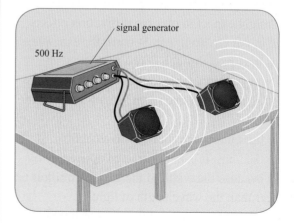

Figure 17.9 The sound waves from two loudspeakers combine to give an interference pattern.

quieter. The space around the two loudspeakers consists of a series of loud and quiet regions. We are observing the phenomenon known as **interference**.

Explaining interference

Figure 17.10 shows how interference arises. The loudspeakers are emitting waves that are in phase because both are connected to the same signal generator. At each point in front of the loudspeaker in Figure 17.9, waves are arriving from the two loudspeakers. At some points, the two waves arrive in phase (in step) with one another and with equal amplitude (Figure 17.10a). The principle of superposition predicts that the resultant wave has twice the amplitude of a single wave. We hear a louder sound.

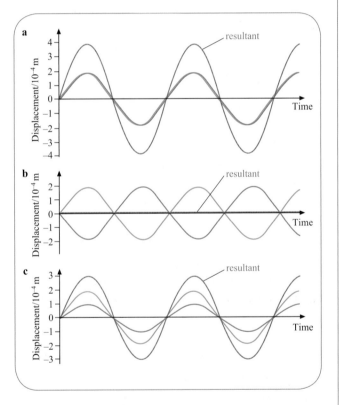

Figure 17.10 Adding waves by the principle of superposition. Blue and green waves of the same amplitude may give **a** constructive or **b** destructive interference, according to the phase difference between them. **c** Waves of different amplitudes can also interfere constructively.

At other points, something different happens. The two waves arrive completely out of phase or in antiphase (phase difference is 180°) with one another (Figure 17.10b). There is a cancelling out, and the resultant wave has zero amplitude. At this point, we would expect silence.

At other points again, the waves are neither perfectly out of step nor perfectly in step, and the resultant wave has amplitude less than that at the loudest point.

Where two waves arrive at a point in phase with one another so that they add up, we call this effect **constructive interference**. Where they cancel out, the effect is known as **destructive interference**.

Where two waves have different amplitudes (Figure 17.10c), constructive interference results in a wave whose amplitude is the sum of the two individual amplitudes.

SAQ

3 Explain why the two loudspeakers must be producing sounds of precisely the same frequency in order for us to hear the effects of interference described above.

> Answer

Observing interference

In a ripple tank

The two dippers in the ripple tank (Figure 17.11) should be positioned so that they are just touching the surface of the water. When the bar vibrates, each dipper acts as a source of circular ripples spreading outwards. Where these sets of ripples overlap, we observe an interference pattern. Another way to observe interference in a ripple tank is to use plane waves passing through two gaps in a barrier. The water waves are diffracted at the two gaps and then interfere beyond the gaps.

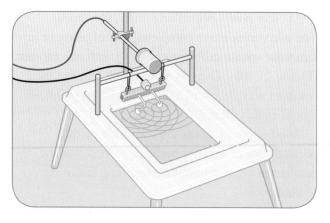

Figure 17.11 A ripple tank can be used to show how two sets of circular ripples combine.

Figure 17.12 shows the interference pattern produced by two vibrating sources in a ripple tank. How can we explain such a pattern? Look at Figure 17.13 and compare it to Figure 17.12. Figure 17.13 shows two sets of waves setting out from their sources. At a position such as A, ripples from the two sources arrive in phase with one another, and constructive interference occurs. At B, the two sets of ripples arrive out of phase, and there is destructive interference. Although waves are arriving at B, the surface of the water remains approximately flat.

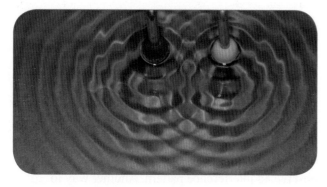

Figure 17.12 Ripples from two point sources produce an interference pattern.

Whether the waves combine constructively or destructively at a point depends on the **path**

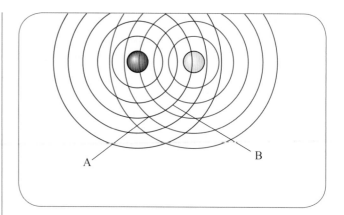

Figure 17.13 The result of interference depends on the path difference between the two waves.

difference of the waves from the two sources. The path difference is defined as the *extra* distance travelled by one of the waves compared with the other.

At point A, the waves from the red source have travelled 3 whole wavelengths. The waves from the yellow source have travelled 4 whole wavelengths. The path difference between the two sets of waves is 1 wavelength. A path difference of 1 wavelength is equivalent to a phase difference of zero. This means that they are in phase so that they interfere constructively.

Now think about destructive interference. At point B, the waves from the red source have travelled 3 wavelengths; the waves from the yellow source have travelled 2.5 wavelengths. The path difference between the two sets of waves is 0.5 wavelengths, which is equivalent to a phase difference of 180°. The waves interfere destructively because they are in antiphase.

In general, the conditions for constructive interference and destructive interference are outlined below. These conditions apply to *all* waves (water waves, light, microwaves, radio waves, sound, etc.) that show interference effects. In the equations below, n stands for any integer (any whole number – including zero).

- For *constructive interference* the path difference is a whole number of wavelengths:

    path difference = 0, λ, 2λ, 3λ, etc.

    or   path difference = $n\lambda$

- For *destructive interference* the path difference is an odd number of half wavelengths:

    path difference = $\frac{1}{2}\lambda$, $1\frac{1}{2}\lambda$, $2\frac{1}{2}\lambda$, etc.

    or   path difference = $(n + \frac{1}{2})\lambda$

Interference of light

We can also show the interference effects produced by light. A simple arrangement involves directing the light from a laser through two slits (Figure 17.14). The slits are two clear lines on a black slide, separated by a fraction of a millimetre. Where the light falls on the screen, a series of equally spaced dots of light are seen (see Figure 17.19). These bright dots are referred to as interference 'fringes', and they are regions where light waves from the two slits are arriving in phase with each other, i.e. constructive interference. The dark regions in between are the result of destructive interference.

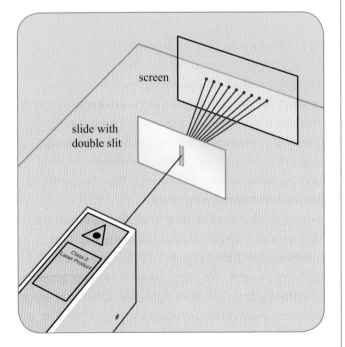

Figure 17.14 Light beams from the two slits interfere in the space beyond.

These bright and dark fringes are the equivalent of the loud and quiet regions that you detected if you investigated the interference pattern of sounds from the two loudspeakers described above. Bright fringes correspond to loud sound, dark fringes to soft sound or silence.

You can check that light is indeed reaching the screen from both slits as follows. Mark a point on the screen where there is a dark fringe. Now carefully cover up one of the slits so that light from the laser is only passing through one slit. You should find that the pattern of interference fringes disappears. Instead, a broad band of light appears across the screen. This broad band of light is the diffraction pattern produced by a single slit. The point that was dark is now light. Cover up the other slit instead, and you will see the same effect. You have now shown that light is arriving at the screen from both slits, but at some points (the dark fringes) the two beams of light cancel each other out.

You can achieve similar results with a bright light bulb rather than a laser, but a laser is much more convenient because the light is concentrated into a narrow, more intense beam. This famous experiment is called the Young double-slit experiment (see page 187), but Thomas Young had no laser available to him when he first carried it out in 1801.

Interference of microwaves

Using 2.8 cm wavelength microwave equipment (Figure 17.15), you can observe an interference pattern. The microwave transmitter is directed towards the double gap in a metal barrier. The microwaves are diffracted at the two gaps so that they spread out into the region beyond, where they can be detected using the probe receiver. By moving the probe around, it is possible to detect regions of high intensity (constructive interference) and low intensity (destructive interference). The probe may be connected to a meter, or to an audio amplifier and loudspeaker to give an audible output.

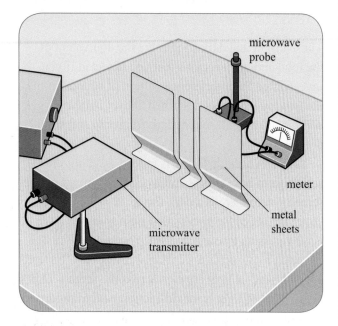

Figure 17.15 Microwaves can also be used to show interference effects.

SAQ

4 Suppose that the microwave probe is placed at a point of low intensity in the interference pattern. What do you predict will happen if one of the gaps in the barrier is now blocked?

Answer

Coherence

We are surrounded by many types of wave – light, infrared radiation, radio waves, sound, and so on. There are waves coming at us from all directions. So why do we not observe interference patterns all the time? Why do we need specialised equipment in a laboratory to observe these effects?

In fact, we can see interference of light occurring in everyday life. For example, you may have noticed haloes of light around street lamps or the Moon on a foggy night. You may have noticed light and dark bands of light if you look through fabric at a bright source of light. These are interference effects.

We usually need specially arranged conditions to observe interference effects. Think about the demonstration with two loudspeakers. If they were connected to different signal generators with slightly different frequencies, the sound waves might start off in phase with one another, but they would soon go out of phase (Figure 17.16). We would hear loud, then soft, then loud again. The interference pattern would keep shifting around the room.

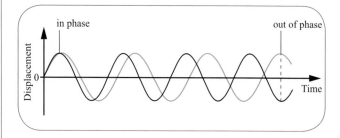

Figure 17.16 Waves of slightly different wavelengths move in and out of phase with one another.

By connecting the two loudspeakers to the *same* signal generator, we can be sure that the sound waves that they produce are constantly in phase with one another. We say that they act as two **coherent** sources of sound waves (*coherent* means *sticking together*). Coherent sources emit waves that have a *constant phase difference*. Note that the two waves can only have a constant phase difference if their frequency is the same and remains constant.

Now think about the laser experiment. Could we have used two lasers producing exactly the same wavelength of light? Figure 17.17a represents the light from a laser. We can think of it as being made up of many separate bursts of light. We cannot guarantee that these bursts from two lasers will always be in phase with one another.

This problem is overcome by using a single laser and dividing its light using the two slits (Figure 17.17b). The slits act as two coherent sources of light.

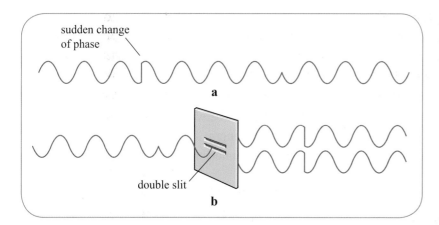

sudden change
of phase

a

double slit

b

Figure 17.17 Waves must be coherent if they are to produce a clear interference pattern.

They are constantly in phase with one another (or there is a constant phase difference between them). If they were not coherent sources, the interference pattern would be constantly changing, far too fast for our eyes to detect. We would simply see a uniform band of light, without any definite bright and dark regions. From this you should be able to see that, in order to observe interference, we need two coherent sources of waves.

SAQ

5 Draw displacement against time sketch sketches to illustrate the following:
  a two waves having the same amplitude and in phase with one another
  b two waves having the same amplitude and with a phase difference of 90°
  c two waves initially in phase but with slightly different wavelengths.
  Use your sketches to explain why two coherent sources of waves are needed to observe interference.

Answer

The Young double-slit experiment

Now we will take a close look at a famous experiment which Thomas Young performed in 1801. He used this experiment to show the wave nature of light. A beam of light is shone on a pair of parallel slits placed at right angles to the beam. Light diffracts and spreads outwards from each slit into the space beyond; the light from the two slits overlaps on a screen. An interference pattern of light and dark bands called 'fringes' is formed on the screen.

Explaining the experiment

In order to observe interference, we need two sets of waves. The sources of the waves must be coherent – the phase difference between the waves emitted at the sources must remain constant. This also means that the waves must have the same wavelength. Today, this is readily achieved by passing a single beam of laser light through the two slits. A laser produces intense coherent light. As the light passes through the slits, it is diffracted so that it spreads out into the space beyond (Figure 17.18). Now we have two overlapping sets of waves, and the pattern of fringes on the screen shows us the result of their interference (Figure 17.19).

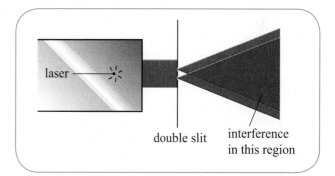

laser

double slit   interference
                     in this region

Figure 17.18 Interference occurs where diffracted beams from the two slits overlap.

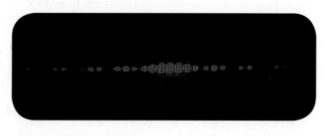

Figure 17.19 Interference fringes obtained using a laser and a double slit.

187

How does this pattern arise? We will consider three points on the screen (Figure 17.20), and work out what we would expect to observe at each.

- *Point A*

  This point is directly opposite the midpoint of the slits. Two rays of light arrive at A, one from slit 1 and the other from slit 2. Point A is equidistant from the two slits, and so the two rays of light have travelled the same distance. The path difference between the two rays of light is zero. If we assume that they were in phase (in step) with each other when they left the slits, then they will be in phase when they arrive at A. Hence they will interfere constructively, and we will observe a bright fringe at A.

- *Point B*

  This point is slightly to the side of point A, and is the midpoint of the first dark fringe. Again, two rays of light arrive at B, one from each slit. The light from slit 1 has to travel slightly further than the light from slit 2, and so the two rays are no longer in step. Since point B is at the midpoint of the dark fringe, the two rays must be in antiphase (phase difference of 180°). The path difference between the two rays of light must be half a wavelength and so the two rays interfere destructively.

- *Point C*

  This point is the midpoint of the next bright fringe with AB = BC. Again, ray 1 has travelled further than ray 2; this time, it has travelled an extra distance equal to a whole wavelength λ. The path difference between the rays of light is now a whole wavelength. The two rays are in phase at the screen. They interfere constructively and we see a bright fringe.

The complete interference pattern (Figure 17.19) can be explained entirely in this way.

SAQ

6 Consider points D and E on the screen, where BC = CD = DE. State and explain what you would expect to observe at D and E.

Hint

Answer

Determining wavelength λ

The double-slit experiment can be used to determine the wavelength λ of light. The following three quantities have to be measured.

- *Slit separation a*

  This is the distance between the centres of the slits, though it may be easier to measure between the edges of the slits. (It is difficult to judge the position of the centre of a slit. If the slits are the same width, the separation of their left-hand edges is the same as the separation of their centres.) A travelling microscope is suitable for measuring a.

- *Fringe separation x*

  This is the distance between the centres of adjacent bright (or dark) fringes. It is best to measure across several fringes (say, 10) and then to calculate later the average separation. A metre rule or travelling microscope can be used.

- *Slit-to-screen distance D*

  This is the distance from the midpoint of the slits to the central fringe on the screen. It can be measured using a metre rule or a tape measure.

Once these three quantities have been measured, the wavelength λ of the light can be found using:

$$\lambda = \frac{ax}{D}$$

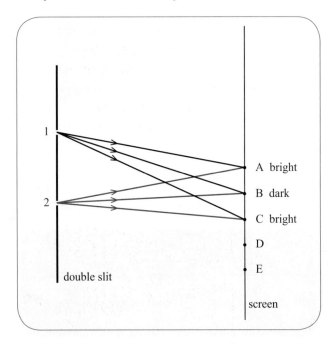

A bright

B dark

C bright

D

E

double slit

screen

Figure 17.20 Rays from the two slits travel different distances to reach the screen.

Worked example 1

In a double-slit experiment using light from a helium–neon laser, a student obtained the following results:

width of 10 fringes $10x = 1.5$ cm
separation of slits $a = 1.0$ mm
slit-to-screen distance $D = 2.40$ m

Determine the wavelength of the light.

Step 1 Work out the fringe separation:

$$\text{fringe separation } x = \frac{1.5 \times 10^{-2}}{10} = 1.5 \times 10^{-3} \text{ m}$$

Step 2 Substitute the values of a, x and D in the expression for wavelength λ:

$$\lambda = \frac{ax}{D}$$

Therefore:

$$\lambda = \frac{1.0 \times 10^{-3} \times 1.5 \times 10^{-3}}{2.40} = 6.3 \times 10^{-7} \text{ m}$$

So the wavelength is 6.3×10^{-7} m or 630 nm.

Guidance

SAQ

7   If the student in Worked example 1 moved the screen to a distance of 4.8 m from the slits, what would the fringe separation become?

Hint

Answer

Experimental details

An alternative arrangement for carrying out the double-slit experiment is shown in Figure 17.21. Here, a white light source is used, rather than a laser. A monochromatic filter allows only one wavelength of light to pass through. A single slit diffracts the light. This light arrives in phase at the double slit. This ensures that the two parts of the double slit behave as coherent sources of light. The double slit is placed a centimetre or two beyond, and the fringes are observed on a screen a metre or so away. The experiment has to be carried out in a darkened room, as the intensity of the light is low and the fringes are hard to see. There are three important factors involved in the way the equipment is set up.

● The slits are a fraction of a millimetre in width. Since the wavelength of light is less than a micrometre (10^{-6} m), this gives a small amount of diffraction in the space beyond. If the slits were narrower, the intensity of the light would be too low for visible fringes to be achieved.

● The slits are about a millimetre apart. If they were much further apart, the fringes would be too close together to be distinguishable.

● The screen is about a metre from the slits. This gives fringes which are clearly separated without being too dim.

With a laser, the light beam is more concentrated, and the first single slit is not necessary. The greater intensity of the beam means that the screen can be further from the slits, so that the fringes are further apart; this reduces the percentage error in measurements of x and D, and hence λ can be determined more accurately.

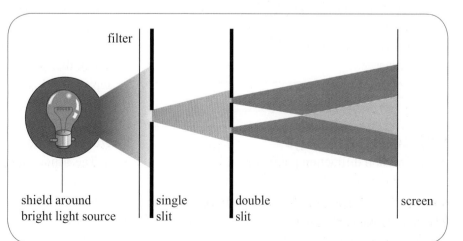

Figure 17.21 To observe interference fringes with white light, it is necessary to use a single slit before the double slit.

filter

shield around bright light source

single slit

double slit

screen

A laser has a second advantage. The light from a laser is monochromatic; that is, it consists of a single wavelength. This makes the fringes very clear, and many of them are formed across the screen. With white light and no monochromatic filter, a range of wavelengths are present. Different wavelengths form fringes at different points across the screen. The central fringe is white (because all wavelengths are in phase here), but the other fringes show coloured effects, and only a few fringes are visible in the interference pattern.

SAQ

8 Use $\lambda = \dfrac{ax}{D}$ to explain the following observations.

   a With the slits closer together, the fringes are further apart.

   b Interference fringes for blue light are closer together than for red light.

   c In an experiment to measure the wavelength of light, it is desirable to have the screen as far from the slits as possible.

9 Yellow sodium light of wavelength 589 nm is used in the Young double-slit experiment. The slit separation is 0.20 mm, and the screen is placed 1.20 m from the slits. Calculate the separation of neighbouring fringes formed on the screen.   **Hint**   **Answer**

10 In a double-slit experiment, filters were placed in front of a white light source to investigate the effect of changing the wavelength of the light. At first, a red filter was used ($\lambda = 600$ nm) and the fringe separation was found to be 2.40 mm. A blue filter was then used ($\lambda = 450$ nm). Determine the fringe separation with the blue filter.   **Answer**

   Extension

Diffraction gratings

A transmission diffraction grating is similar to the slide used in the double-slit experiment, but with many more slits than just two. It consists of a large number of equally spaced lines ruled on a glass or plastic slide. Each line is capable of diffracting the

incident light. There may be as many as 10 000 lines per centimetre. When light is shone through this grating, a pattern of interference fringes is seen.

In a reflection diffraction grating, the lines are made on a reflecting surface so that light is both reflected and diffracted by the grating. The shiny surface of a compact disc (CD) or DVD is an everyday example of a reflection diffraction grating. Hold a CD in your hand and twist it so that you are looking at the reflection of light from a lamp. You will observe coloured bands (Figure 17.22). A CD has thousands of equally spaced lines of microscopic pits on its surface; these carry the digital information. It is the diffraction from these lines that produces the coloured bands of light from the surface of the CD.

Figure 17.22 A CD acts as a reflection diffraction grating. White light is reflected and diffracted at its surface, producing a display of spectral colours.

Monochromatic light from a laser is incident normally on a transmission diffraction grating. In the space beyond, interference fringes are formed. These can be observed on a screen, as with the double slit. However, it is usual to measure the angle θ at which they are formed, rather than measuring their separation (Figure 17.23). With double slits, the fringes are equally spaced and the angles are very small. With a diffraction grating, the angles are much greater and the fringes are not equally spaced.

The fringes are also referred to as *maxima*. The central fringe is called the zeroth-order maximum, the next fringe is the first-order maximum, and so on. The pattern is symmetrical, so there are two first-order maxima, two second-order maxima, and so on.

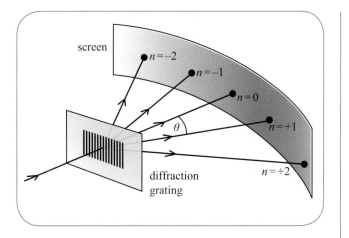

Figure 17.23 The diffracted beams form a symmetrical pattern on either side of the undiffracted central beam.

Explaining the experiment

The principle is the same as for the double-slit experiment, but here we have light passing through many slits. As it passes through each slit, it diffracts into the space beyond. So now we have many overlapping beams of light, and these interfere with one another. It is difficult to achieve constructive interference with many beams, because they all have to be in phase with one another.

There is a bright fringe, the zeroth-order maximum, in the straight-through direction ($\theta = 0$) because all of the rays here are travelling parallel to one another and in phase, so the interference is constructive (Figure 17.24a).

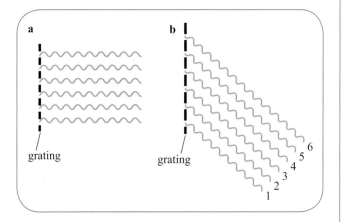

Figure 17.24 a Waves from each slit are in phase in the straight-through direction. **b** In the direction of the first-order maximum, the waves are in phase, but each one has travelled one wavelength further than the one below it.

The first-order maximum forms as follows. Rays of light emerge from all of the slits; to form a bright fringe, all the rays must be in phase. In the direction of the first-order maximum, ray 1 has travelled the least distance (Figure 17.24b). Ray 2 has travelled an extra distance equal to one whole wavelength and is therefore in phase with ray 1. The path difference between ray 1 and ray 2 is equal to one wavelength λ. Ray 3 has travelled two extra wavelengths and is in phase with rays 1 and 2. In fact, the rays from all of the slits are in step in this direction, and a bright fringe results.

SAQ

11 Explain how the second-order maximum arises. Use the term *path difference* in your explanation.

> Answer

Determining wavelength λ with a grating

By measuring the angles at which the maxima occur, we can determine the wavelength of the incident light. The wavelength λ of the monochromatic light is related to the angle θ by:

$$d \sin \theta = n\lambda$$

where d is the distance between adjacent lines of the grating and n is known as the *order* of the maximum; n can only have integer values 0, 1, 2, 3, etc. The distance d is known as the grating element or grating spacing.

This is illustrated in Worked example 2.

Worked example 2

Monochromatic light is incident normally on a diffraction grating having 3000 lines per centimetre. The angular separation of the zeroth- and first-order maxima is found to be 10°. Calculate the wavelength of the incident light.

Step 1 Calculate the slit separation (grating spacing) d. Since there are 3000 slits per centimetre, their separation must be:

$$d = \frac{1\ \text{cm}}{3000} = 3.33 \times 10^{-4}\ \text{cm} = 3.33 \times 10^{-6}\ \text{m}$$

continued

Step 2 Rearrange the equation $d \sin \theta = n\lambda$ and substitute values:

$\theta = 10.0°$, $n = 1$

$$\lambda = \frac{d \sin \theta}{n} = \frac{3.36 \times 10^{-6} \times \sin 10°}{1}$$

$\lambda = 5.8 \times 10^{-7}$ m $- 580$ nm

SAQ

12 **a** For the case described in Worked example 2, at what angle would you expect to find the second-order maximum ($n = 2$)?

    b Repeat the calculation of θ for $n = 3$, 4, etc. What is the limit to this calculation? How many maxima will there be altogether in this interference pattern?

Hint

Answer

13 Consider the equation $d \sin \theta = n\lambda$. How will the diffraction pattern change if:

    a the wavelength of the light is increased

    b the diffraction grating is changed for one with more lines per centimetre (slits that are more closely spaced)?

Answer

Extension

Many slits are better than two

It is worth comparing the use of a diffraction grating to determine wavelength with the Young two-slit experiment.

- With a diffraction grating the maxima are very *bright* and very *sharp*.
- With two slits, there may be a large inaccuracy in the measurement of the slit separation a; and the fringes are close together, so their separation may also be measured imprecisely.
- With a diffraction grating, there are many slits per centimetre, so d can be measured accurately; and because the maxima are widely separated, the angle θ can be measured to a high degree of precision.

So an experiment with a diffraction grating can be expected to give measurements of wavelength to a much higher degree of precision than a simple double-slit arrangement.

SAQ

14 A student is trying to make an accurate measurement of the wavelength of green light from a mercury lamp ($\lambda = 546$ nm). Using a double slit of separation 0.50 mm, he finds he can see 10 clear fringes on a screen at a distance of 0.80 m from the slits. The student can measure their overall width to within ±1 mm.

He then tries an alternative experiment using a diffraction grating that has 3000 lines per centimetre. The angle between the two second-order maxima can be measured to within ±0.1°.

    a What will be the width of the 10 fringes that he can measure in the first experiment?

    b What will be the angle of the second-order maximum in the second experiment?

    c Suggest which experiment you think will give the more accurate measurement of λ.

Answer

Diffracting white light

A diffraction grating can be used to split white light up into its constituent colours (wavelengths). This splitting of light is known as **dispersion**, shown in Figure 17.25. A beam of white light is shone onto the grating. A zeroth-order, white maximum is observed at $\theta = 0°$, because all waves of each wavelength are in phase in this direction.

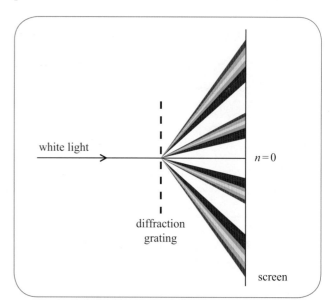

Figure 17.25 A diffraction grating is a simple way of separating white light into its constituent wavelengths.

On either side, a series of spectra appear, with violet closest to the centre, and red furthest away. We can see why different wavelengths have their maxima at different angles if we rearrange the equation

$$d \sin \theta = n\lambda$$

to give:

$$\sin \theta = \frac{n\lambda}{d}$$

From this it follows that the greater the wavelength λ, the greater the value of $\sin \theta$ and hence the greater the angle θ. Red light is at the long wavelength end of the visible spectrum, and so it appears at the greatest angle.

SAQ

15 White light is incident normally on a diffraction grating with a slit separation d of 2.00×10^{-6} m.

   a Calculate the angle *between* the red and violet ends of the first-order spectrum. The visible spectrum has wavelengths between 400 nm and 700 nm.

   b Explain why the second- and third-order spectra overlap.

Answer

Summary

Glossary

- The principle of superposition states that when two or more waves meet at a point, the resultant displacement is the algebraic sum of the displacements of the individual waves.

- When waves pass through a slit, they may be diffracted so that they spread out into the space beyond. The diffraction effect is greatest when the wavelength of the waves is similar to the width of the gap.

- Interference is the superposition of waves from two coherent sources.

- Two sources are coherent when they emit waves that have a *constant phase difference*. (This can only happen if the waves have the same frequency or wavelength.)

- For *constructive interference* the path difference is a whole number of wavelengths:

  path difference = $0, \lambda, 2\lambda, 3\lambda$, etc.   or   path difference = $n\lambda$

- For *destructive interference* the path difference is an odd number of half wavelengths:

  path difference = $\frac{1}{2}\lambda, 1\frac{1}{2}\lambda, 2\frac{1}{2}\lambda$, etc.   or   path difference = $(n + \frac{1}{2})\lambda$

- When light passes through a double slit, it is diffracted and an interference pattern of equally spaced light and dark fringes is observed. This can be used to determine the wavelength of light using the equation:

  $$\lambda = \frac{ax}{D}$$

  The equation $\lambda = \frac{ax}{D}$ can be used for all waves, including sound and microwaves.

- A diffraction grating diffracts light at its many slits or lines. The diffracted light interferes in the space beyond the grating. The equation for a diffraction grating is:

  $$d \sin \theta = n\lambda$$

Questions

1 a When waves from two coherent sources meet, they interfere. The principle of superposition of waves helps to explain this interference. State what is meant by:

    i coherent sources [2]

    ii principle of superposition of waves. [1]

b The diagram shows an arrangement to demonstrate interference effects with microwaves. A transmitter, producing microwaves of wavelength 3.0 cm, is placed behind two slits 6.0 cm apart. A receiver is placed 50 cm in front of the slits and is used to detect the intensity of the resultant wave as it moves along the line AB.

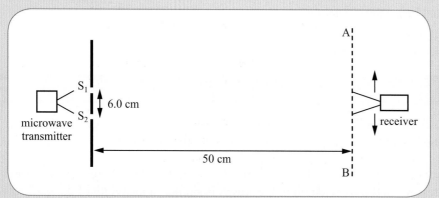

    i Explain, in terms of the path difference between the waves emerging from the slits S_1 and S_2, why a series of interference maxima and minima are produced along the line AB. [3]

    ii Assuming that the interference of the microwaves is similar to double slit interference using light, calculate the distance in centimetres between neighbouring maxima along the line AB. [3]

    iii The microwaves from the transmitter are *plane polarised*. State what this means and suggest what would happen if the receiver were slowly rotated through 90° while still facing the slits. [2]

OCR Physics AS (2823) January 2006   [Total 11]

2 a State the term used to describe two wave sources that have a constant phase difference. [1]

b Using suitable diagrams, state and explain what is meant by:

    i constructive interference

    ii destructive interference. [4]

c Describe an experiment to determine the wavelength of monochromatic light (i.e. light of one wavelength) using a double slit of known slit separation. Include in your answer:

    ● a labelled diagram showing how the apparatus is arranged

    ● a list of the measurements required to determine the wavelength λ of the light

    ● the formula, with all symbols identified, that could be used to determine λ. [6]

OCR Physics AS (2823) January 2005   [Total 11]

continued

3 The diagram shows an arrangement to demonstrate the interference of light. A double slit, consisting of two very narrow slits very close together, is placed in the path of a laser beam.

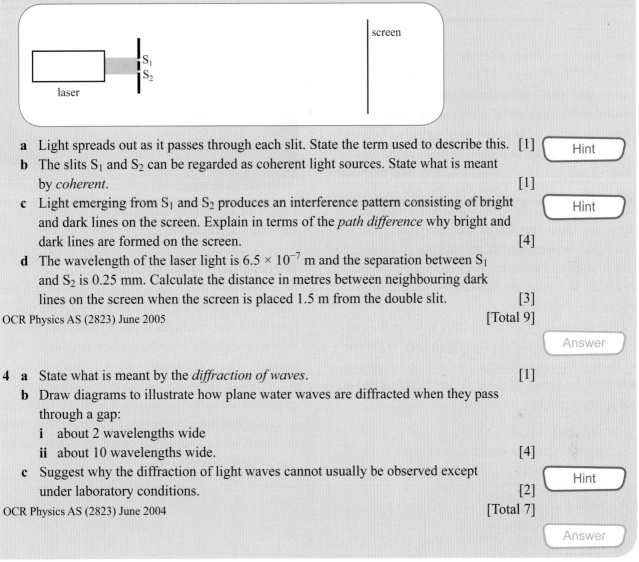

a Light spreads out as it passes through each slit. State the term used to describe this. [1]

b The slits S_1 and S_2 can be regarded as coherent light sources. State what is meant by *coherent*. [1]

c Light emerging from S_1 and S_2 produces an interference pattern consisting of bright and dark lines on the screen. Explain in terms of the *path difference* why bright and dark lines are formed on the screen. [4]

d The wavelength of the laser light is 6.5×10^{-7} m and the separation between S_1 and S_2 is 0.25 mm. Calculate the distance in metres between neighbouring dark lines on the screen when the screen is placed 1.5 m from the double slit. [3]

OCR Physics AS (2823) June 2005   [Total 9]

Hint

Hint

Answer

4 a State what is meant by the *diffraction of waves*. [1]

b Draw diagrams to illustrate how plane water waves are diffracted when they pass through a gap:
  i about 2 wavelengths wide
  ii about 10 wavelengths wide. [4]

c Suggest why the diffraction of light waves cannot usually be observed except under laboratory conditions. [2]

OCR Physics AS (2823) June 2004   [Total 7]

Hint

Answer

Chapter 18

Stationary waves

The waves we have considered so far in Chapter 15, Chapter 16 and Chapter 17 have been *progressive waves*; they start from a source and travel outwards. A second important class of waves is **stationary waves** (standing waves). These can be observed as follows.

Use a long spring or a slinky spring. A long rope or piece of rubber tubing will also do. Lay it on the floor and fix one end firmly. Move the other end from side to side so that transverse waves travel along the length of the spring and reflect off the fixed end (Figure 18.1). If you adjust the frequency of the shaking, you should be able to achieve a stable pattern like one of those shown in Figure 18.2. Alter the frequency in order to achieve one of the other patterns.

You should notice that you have to move the end of the spring with just the right frequency to get one of these interesting patterns. The pattern disappears when the frequency of the shaking of the free end of the spring is slightly increased or decreased.

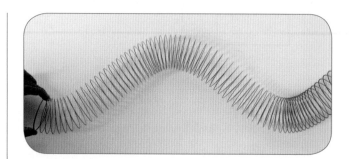

Figure 18.1 A slinky spring is used to generate a stationary wave pattern.

Nodes and antinodes

What you have observed is a stationary wave on the long spring. There are points along the spring that remain (almost) motionless while points on either side are oscillating with the greatest amplitude. The points that do not move are called the **nodes** and the points where the spring oscillates with maximum amplitude are called the **antinodes**. At the same time, it is clear that the wave profile is not travelling along the length of the spring. Hence we call it a stationary wave or a standing wave.

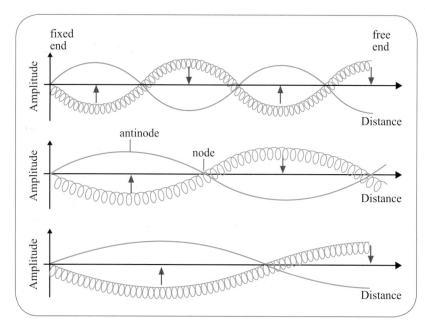

Figure 18.2 Different stationary wave patterns are possible, depending on the frequency of vibration.

We normally represent a stationary wave by drawing the shape of the spring in its two extreme positions (Figure 18.3a). The spring appears as a series of loops, separated by nodes. In this diagram, point A is moving downwards. At the same time, point B in the next loop is moving upwards. The phase difference between points A and B is 180°. Hence the sections of spring in adjacent loops are always moving in antiphase; they are half a cycle out of phase with one another.

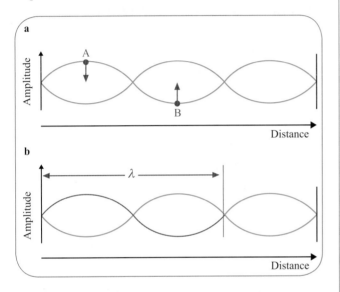

Figure 18.3 The fixed ends of a long spring must be nodes in the stationary wave pattern.

Formation of stationary waves

Imagine a string stretched between two fixed points, for example a guitar string. Pulling the middle of the string and then releasing it produces a stationary wave. There is a node at each of the fixed ends and an antinode in the middle. Releasing the string produces two progressive waves travelling in opposite directions. These are reflected at the fixed ends. The reflected waves combine to produce the stationary wave.

Figure 18.1 shows how a stationary wave can be set up using a long spring. A stationary wave is formed whenever two progressive waves of the same amplitude and wavelength, travelling in *opposite* directions, superimpose. Figure 18.4 uses a displacement s against distance x graph to illustrate the formation of a stationary wave along a long spring (or a stretched length of string).

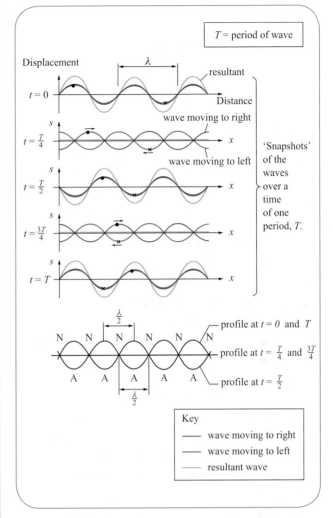

Figure 18.4 The blue-coloured wave is moving to the left and the red-coloured wave to the right. The *principle of superposition* of waves is used to determine the resultant displacement. The profile of the long spring is shown in green.

- At time $t = 0$, the progressive waves travelling to the left and right are in phase. The waves combine *constructively* giving amplitude twice that of each wave.
- After a time equal to one quarter of a period ($t = \frac{T}{4}$), each wave travels a distance of one quarter of a wavelength to the left or right. Consequently, the two waves are in antiphase (phase difference = 180°). The waves combine *destructively* giving zero displacement.

- After a time equal to one half of a period ($t = \frac{T}{2}$), the two waves are back in phase again. They once again combine *constructively*.
- After a time equal to three quarters of a period ($t = \frac{3T}{4}$), the waves are in antiphase again. They combine *destructively* with the resultant wave showing zero displacement.
- After a time equal to one whole period ($t = T$), the waves combine *constructively*. The profile of the slinky spring is as it was at $t = 0$.

This cycle repeats itself, with the long spring showing nodes and antinodes along its length. The separation between adjacent nodes or antinodes tells us about the progressive waves that produce the stationary wave.

A closer inspection of the graphs in Figure 18.4 shows that the separation between adjacent nodes or antinodes is related to the wavelength λ of the progressive wave. The important conclusions are:

separation between two adjacent nodes
$$\text{(or antinodes)} = \frac{\lambda}{2}$$

separation between adjacent node and antinode $= \frac{\lambda}{4}$

The wavelength λ of *any* progressive wave can be determined from the separation between neighbouring nodes or antinodes of the resulting standing wave pattern. (This is $= \frac{\lambda}{2}$.) This can then be used to determine either the speed v of the progressive wave or its frequency f by using the wave equation:

$$v = f\lambda$$

It is worth noting that a stationary wave does not travel and therefore has no speed. It does not transfer energy between two points like a progressive wave. Table 18.1 shows some of the key features of a progressive wave and its stationary wave.

	Progressive wave	Stationary wave
wavelength	λ	λ
frequency	f	f
speed	v	zero

Table 18.1 A summary of progressive and stationary waves.

SAQ

1 A stationary (standing) wave is set up on a vibrating spring. Adjacent nodes are separated by 25 cm. Determine:
   a the wavelength of the stationary wave   Hint
   b the distance from a node to an adjacent antinode.   Answer

Observing stationary waves

Stretched strings

A string is attached at one end to a vibration generator, driven by a signal generator (Figure 18.5). The other end hangs over a pulley and weights maintain the tension in the string. When the signal generator is switched on, the string vibrates with small amplitude. However, by adjusting the frequency, it is possible to produce stationary waves whose amplitude is much larger.

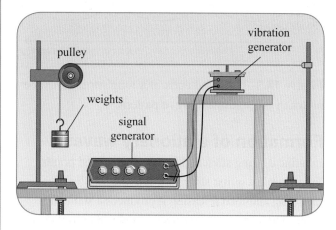

Figure 18.5 Melde's experiment for investigating stationary waves on a string.

The pulley end of the string is unable to vibrate; this is a node. Similarly, the end attached to the vibrator is only able to move a small amount, and this is also a node. As the frequency is increased, it is possible to observe one loop (one antinode), two loops, three loops and more. Figure 18.6 shows a vibrating string where the frequency of the vibrator has been set to produce two loops.

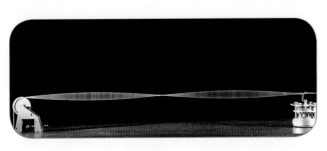

Figure 18.6 When a stationary wave is established, one half of the string moves upwards as the other half moves downwards. In this photograph, the string is moving too fast to observe the effect.

A flashing stroboscope is useful to reveal the motion of the string at these frequencies, which look blurred to the eye. The frequency of vibration is set so that there are two loops along the string; the frequency of the stroboscope is set so that it almost matches that of the vibrations. Now we can see the string moving 'in slow motion', and it is easy to see the opposite movements of the two adjacent loops.

This experiment is known as *Melde's experiment*, and it can be extended to investigate the effect of changing the length of the string, the tension in the string and the thickness of the string.

SAQ

2 Look at the stationary (standing) wave on the string in Figure 18.6. The length of the vibrating section of the string is 60 cm.

a Determine the wavelength of the stationary wave and the separation of the two neighbouring antinodes.

The frequency of vibration is increased until a stationary wave with three antinodes appears on the string.

b Sketch a stationary wave pattern to illustrate the appearance of the string.   [Hint]

c What is the wavelength of this stationary wave?   [Answer]

Microwaves

Start by directing the microwave transmitter at a metal plate, which reflects the microwaves back towards the source (Figure 18.7). Move the probe

receiver around in the space between the transmitter and the reflector and you will observe positions of high and low intensity. This is because a stationary wave is set up between the transmitter and the sheet; the positions of high and low intensity are the antinodes and nodes respectively.

If the probe is moved along the direct line from the transmitter to the plate, the wavelength of the microwaves can be determined from the distance between the nodes. Knowing that microwaves travel at the speed of light c (3.0×10^8 m s^{-1}), we can then determine their frequency f using the wave equation $c = f\lambda$.

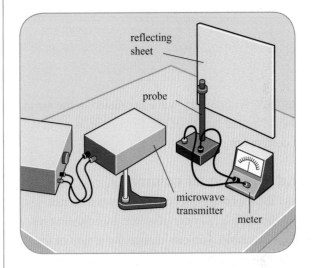

Figure 18.7 A stationary wave is created when microwaves are reflected from the metal sheet.

SAQ

3 a Draw a stationary wave pattern for the microwave experiment above. Clearly show whether there is a node or an antinode at the reflecting sheet.

b The separation of two adjacent points of high intensity is found to be 14 mm. Calculate the wavelength and frequency of the microwaves.   [Hint]   [Answer]

[Extension]

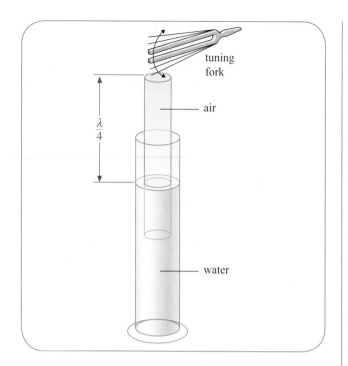

Figure 18.8 A stationary wave is created in the air in the tube when the length of the air column is adjusted to the correct length.

Sound waves in air columns

A glass tube (open at both ends) is clamped so that one end dips into a cylinder of water; by adjusting its height in the clamp, you can change the length of the column of air in the tube (Figure 18.8). When you hold a vibrating tuning fork above the open end, the air column may be forced to vibrate, and the note of the

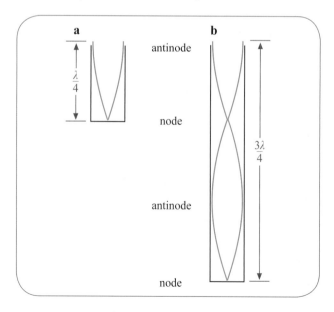

Figure 18.9 Stationary wave patterns for air in a tube with one end closed.

tuning fork sounds much louder. This is an example of a phenomenon called *resonance*. The experiment described here is known as the *resonance tube*.

For resonance to occur, the length of the air column must be just right. The air at the bottom of the tube is unable to vibrate, so this point must be a node. The air at the open end of the tube can vibrate most freely, so this is an antinode. Hence the length of the air column must be one-quarter of a wavelength (Figure 18.9a). (Alternatively, the length of the air column could be set to equal three-quarters of a wavelength – see Figure 18.9b.)

SAQ

4   Explain how two sets of identical but oppositely travelling waves are established in the microwave and air column experiments described above.

> Answer

Stationary waves and musical instruments

The production of different notes by musical instruments often depends on the creation of stationary waves (Figure 18.10). For a stringed instrument such as a guitar, the two ends of a string are fixed, so nodes must be established at these points. When the string is plucked half-way along its length, it vibrates with an antinode at its midpoint. This is known as the *fundamental mode of vibration* of the string. The **fundamental frequency** is the *minimum frequency* of a standing wave for a given system or arrangement.

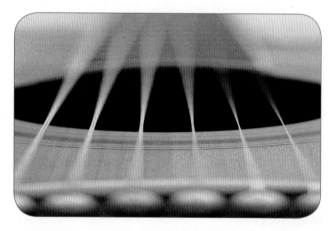

Figure 18.10 When a guitar string is plucked, the vibrations of the strings continue for some time afterwards. Here you can clearly see a node close to the end of each string.

Similarly, the air column inside a wind instrument is caused to vibrate by blowing, and the note that is heard depends on a stationary wave being established. By changing the length of the air column, as in a trombone, the note can be changed. Alternatively, holes can be uncovered so that the air can vibrate more freely, giving a different pattern of nodes and antinodes.

In practice, the sounds that are produced are made up of several different stationary waves having different patterns of nodes and antinodes. For example, a guitar string may vibrate with two antinodes along its length. This gives a note having twice the frequency of the fundamental, and is described as a *harmonic* of the fundamental. The musician's skill is in stimulating the string or air column to produce a desired mixture of frequencies.

The frequency of a harmonic is always a multiple of the fundamental frequency. The diagrams show some of the modes of vibrations for a fixed length of string (Figure 18.11) and an air column in a tube of a given length that is closed at one end (Figure 18.12).

Extension

Determining the wavelength and speed of sound

Since we know that adjacent nodes (or antinodes) of a stationary wave are separated by half a wavelength, we can use this fact to determine the wavelength λ of a progressive wave. If we also know the frequency f of the waves, we can find their speed v using the wave equation $v = f\lambda$.

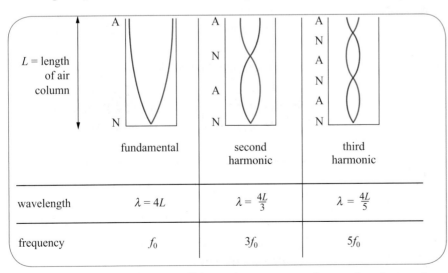

Figure 18.11 Some of the possible stationary waves for a fixed string of length L. The frequency of the harmonics is a multiple of the fundamental frequency f_0.

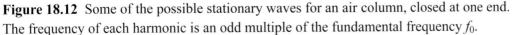

Figure 18.12 Some of the possible stationary waves for an air column, closed at one end. The frequency of each harmonic is an odd multiple of the fundamental frequency f_0.

One approach uses Kundt's dust tube (Figure 18.13). A loudspeaker sends sound waves along the inside of a tube. The sound is reflected at the closed end. When a stationary wave is established, the dust (fine powder) at the antinodes vibrates violently. It tends to accumulate at the nodes, where the movement of the air is zero. Hence the positions of the nodes and antinodes can be clearly seen.

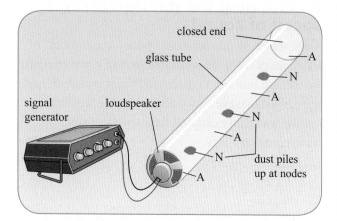

Figure 18.13 Kundt's dust tube can be used to determine the speed of sound.

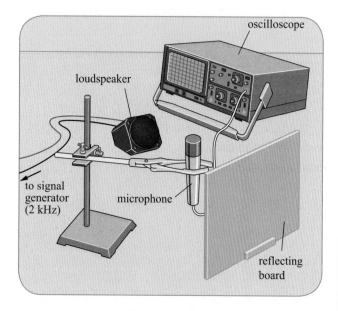

Figure 18.14 A stationary sound wave is established between the loudspeaker and the board.

An alternative method is shown in Figure 18.14; this is the same arrangement as used for microwaves. The loudspeaker produces sound waves, and these are reflected from the vertical board. The microphone detects the stationary sound wave in the space between the speaker and the board, and its output is displayed on the oscilloscope. It is simplest to turn off the time base of the oscilloscope, so that the spot no longer moves across the screen. The spot moves up and down the screen, and the height of the vertical trace gives a measure of the intensity of the sound.

By moving the microphone along the line between the speaker and the board, it is easy to detect nodes and antinodes. For maximum accuracy, we do not measure the separation of adjacent nodes; it is better to measure the distance across several nodes.

The resonance tube experiment (Figure 18.8) can also be used to determine the wavelength and speed of sound with a high degree of accuracy. However, to do this, it is necessary to take account of a systematic error in the experiment, as discussed in the 'Eliminating errors' section on page 203.

SAQ

5 a For the arrangement shown in Figure 18.14, suggest why it is easier to determine accurately the position of a node rather than an antinode.

   b Explain why it is better to measure the distance across several nodes.

   Answer

6 For sound waves of frequency 2500 Hz, it is found that two nodes are separated by 20 cm, with three antinodes between them.

   a Determine the wavelength of these sound waves.

   b Use the wave equation $v = f\lambda$ to determine the speed of sound in air.

   Answer

Eliminating errors

The resonance tube experiment illustrates an interesting way in which one type of experimental error can be reduced or even eliminated.

Look at the representation of the stationary waves in the tubes shown in Figure 18.9. In each case, the antinode at the top of the tube is shown extending slightly beyond the open end of the tube. This is because experiment shows that the air slightly beyond the end of the tube vibrates as part of the stationary wave. This is shown more clearly in Figure 18.15.

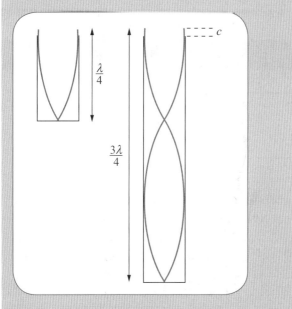

Figure 18.15 The antinode at the open end of a resonance tube is formed at a distance c beyond the open end of the tube.

The antinode is at a distance c beyond the end of the tube, where c is called the *end-correction*. Unfortunately, we do not know the value of c. It cannot be measured directly. However, we can write:

for the shorter tube, $\dfrac{\lambda}{4} = l_1 + c$

for the longer tube, $\dfrac{3\lambda}{4} = l_2 + c$

Subtracting the first equation from the second equation gives:

$$\frac{3\lambda}{4} - \frac{\lambda}{4} = (l_2 + c) - (l_1 + c)$$

Simplifying gives:

$$\frac{\lambda}{2} = l_2 - l_1$$

and hence $\lambda = 2(l_2 - l_1)$

So, although we do not know the value of c, we can make two measurements (l_1 and l_2) and obtain an accurate value of λ. (You may be able to see from Figure 18.15 that the difference in lengths of the two tubes is indeed equal to half a wavelength.)

The end-correction c is an example of a *systematic error*. When we measure the length l of the tube, we are measuring a length which is consistently less than the quantity we really need to know ($l + c$). However, by understanding how the systematic error affects the results, we have been able to remove it from our measurements.

Other examples of systematic errors in physics include:

- meters and other instruments which have been incorrectly zeroed (so that they give a reading when the correct value is zero)
- meters and other instruments which have been incorrectly calibrated (so that, for example, all readings are consistently reduced by a factor of, say, 1.0%).

SAQ

7 In a resonance tube experiment, resonance is obtained for sound waves of frequency 630 Hz when the length of the air column is 12.6 cm and again when it is 38.8 cm. Determine:

a the wavelength of the sound waves causing resonance

b the end-correction for this tube

c the speed of sound in air.

Answer

Summary

Glossary

- Stationary waves are formed when two identical waves travelling in opposite directions meet and superimpose. This usually happens when one wave is a reflection of the other.

- A stationary wave has a characteristic pattern of nodes and antinodes.

- A node is a point where the amplitude is always zero.

- An antinode is a point of maximum amplitude.

- Adjacent nodes (or antinodes) are separated by a distance equal to half a wavelength.

- We can use the wave equation $v = f\lambda$ to determine the speed v or the frequency f of a progressive wave. The wavelength λ is found using the nodes or antinodes of the stationary wave pattern.

Questions

1 The diagram shows a stretched wire held horizontally between supports 0.50 m apart. When the wire is plucked at its centre, a standing wave is formed and the wire vibrates in its fundamental mode (lowest frequency).

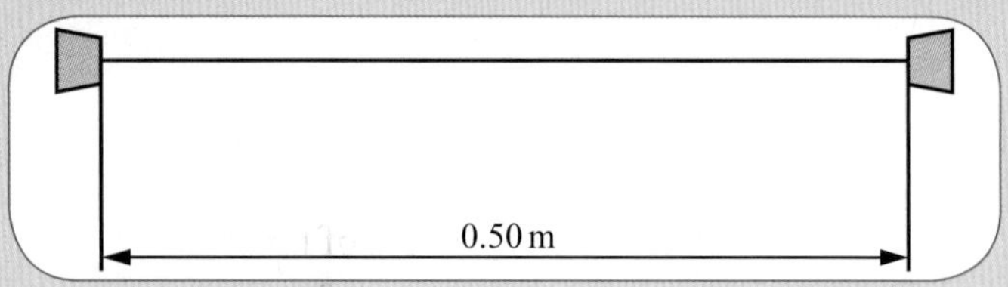

0.50 m

  a Explain how the standing wave is formed. [2]

  b Draw the fundamental mode of vibration of the wire. Label the position of any nodes with the letter N and any antinodes with the letter A. [2]

  c What is the wavelength of this standing wave? [1]

OCR Physics AS (2823) January 2006   [Total 5]

Hint

Answer

2 The diagram shows an arrangement where microwaves leave a transmitter T and move in a direction TP which is perpendicular to a metal plate P.

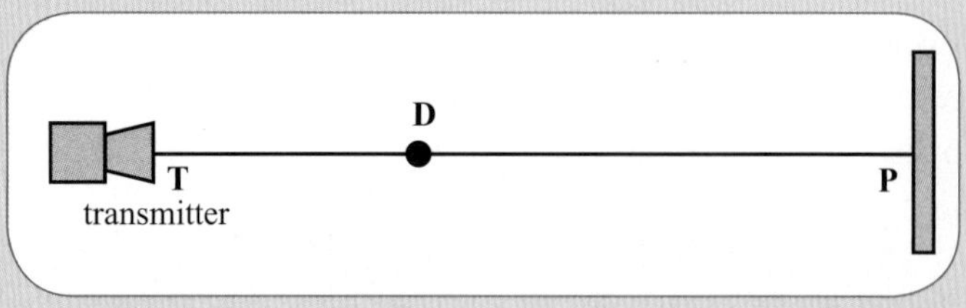

D

T
transmitter

P

  a When a microwave detector D is slowly moved from T towards P the pattern of the signal strength received by D is high, low, high, low … etc.

     Explain:

- why these maxima and minima of intensity occur
- how you would measure the wavelength of the microwaves
- how you would determine their frequency. [6]

  b Describe how you could test whether the microwaves leaving the transmitter are plane polarised. [2]

OCR Physics AS (2823) June 2004   [Total 8]

Hint

Answer

continued

3 a In standing waves, there are *nodes* and *antinodes*. Explain what is meant by:
   i a *node*   [1]
   ii an *antinode*.   [1]

> Hint

   b The diagram shows a long glass tube within
      which standing waves can be set up.
      A vibrating tuning fork is placed above the
      glass tube and the length of the air column is
      adjusted, by raising or lowering the tube in
      the water, until a sound is heard.

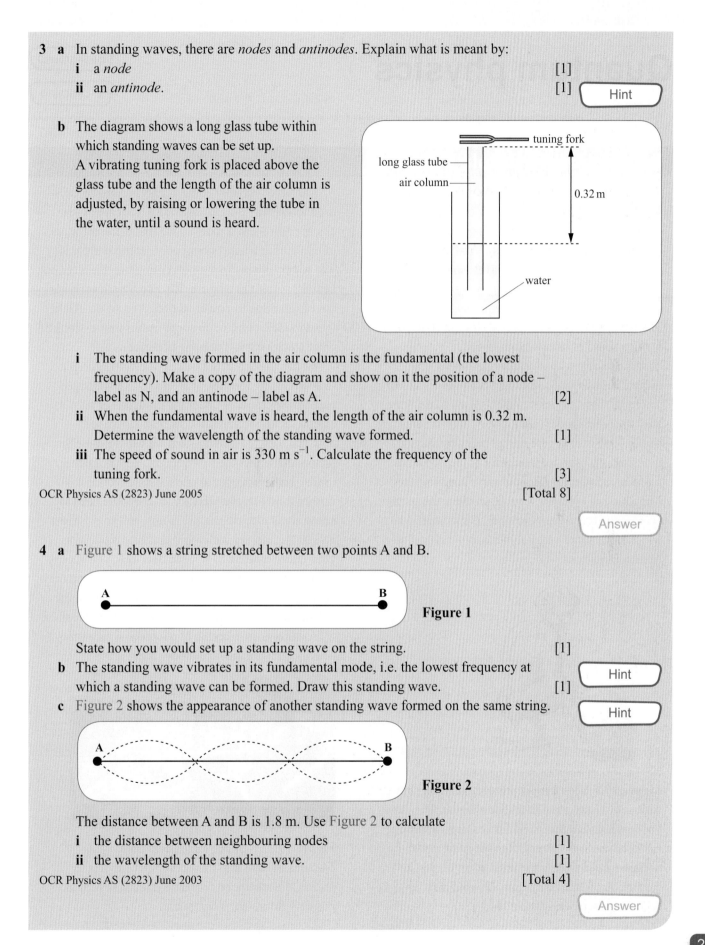

   i The standing wave formed in the air column is the fundamental (the lowest
      frequency). Make a copy of the diagram and show on it the position of a node –
      label as N, and an antinode – label as A.   [2]
   ii When the fundamental wave is heard, the length of the air column is 0.32 m.
       Determine the wavelength of the standing wave formed.   [1]
   iii The speed of sound in air is 330 m s^{-1}. Calculate the frequency of the
        tuning fork.   [3]

OCR Physics AS (2823) June 2005   [Total 8]

> Answer

4 a Figure 1 shows a string stretched between two points A and B.

      A ●————————————————————————————● B   **Figure 1**

      State how you would set up a standing wave on the string.   [1]
   b The standing wave vibrates in its fundamental mode, i.e. the lowest frequency at
      which a standing wave can be formed. Draw this standing wave.   [1]

> Hint

   c Figure 2 shows the appearance of another standing wave formed on the same string.

> Hint

      A ●〜〜〜● B   **Figure 2**

      The distance between A and B is 1.8 m. Use Figure 2 to calculate
   i the distance between neighbouring nodes   [1]
   ii the wavelength of the standing wave.   [1]

OCR Physics AS (2823) June 2003   [Total 4]

> Answer

Chapter 19

Quantum physics

Background

e-Learning

Objectives

Making macroscopic models

Science tries to explain a very complicated world. We are surrounded by very many objects, moving around, reacting together, breaking up, joining together, growing and shrinking. And there are many invisible things, too – radio waves, sounds, ionising radiation. If we are to make any sense of all this, we need to simplify it. We use models, in everyday life and in science, as a method of simplifying and making sense of what we observe.

A model is a way of explaining something difficult in terms of something more familiar. For example, there are many models used to describe how the brain works (see Figure 19.1). It's like a telephone exchange – nerves carry messages in to and out from various parts of the body. It's like a computer. It's like a library. The brain has something in common with all of these things, and yet it is different from them all. These are models, which have some use; but inevitably a model also has its limitations.

Figure 19.1 This 17th-century illustration shows a model of how a reflex reaction works. The man's toe gets hot, and this pulls a tiny thread attached to his brain. Spirit pours from the brain down the hollow tube, inflating the muscles in the leg and causing the foot to withdraw. (From *Traité de l'Homme*, René Descartes, 1664.)

You have probably come across various models used to explain current electricity. We cannot see electric current in a wire, so we find different ways of explaining what is going on. Electric current is like water flowing in a pipe. A circuit is like a central heating system in a house. It's like a train carrying coal from mine to power station. And so on. All of these models conjure up some useful impressions of what electricity is, but none is perfect.

We can make a better model of electric current in a wire using the idea of electrons. Tiny charged particles are moving under the influence of an electric field. We can say how many there are, how fast they are moving, and we can describe the factors that affect their movement. This is a better model, but it is harder to understand because it is further from our everyday experience. We need to know about electric charge, atoms, and so on. Most people are happier with more concrete models; as your understanding of science develops, you accept more and more abstract models. Ultimately, you may have to accept a model that is purely mathematical – some equations that give the right answer. Weather forecasting is an example of a science which relies heavily on mathematical modelling (Figure 19.2).

Figure 19.2 Weather forecasters input vast amounts of data into their computer models to predict the weather a few days ahead, as well as possible future climate change.

Modelling with particles and waves

In this chapter, we will look at two very powerful models – particles and waves. Remember that all models have their limitations. We are going to see what happens in situations where the ideas of particle and wave models start to overlap.

Particle models

In order to explain the properties of matter, we often think about the particles of which it is made and the ways in which they behave. We imagine particles as being objects that are hard, have mass, and move about according to the laws of Newtonian mechanics (Figure 19.3). When two particles collide, we can predict how they will move after the collision, based on knowledge of their masses and velocities before the collision. If you have played snooker or pool, you will have a pretty good idea of how particles behave.

Particles are a macroscopic model. Our ideas of particles come from what we observe on a macroscopic scale – when we are walking down the street, or observing the motion of stars and planets, or working with trolleys and balls in the laboratory. But what else can we use a particle model to explain?

The importance of particle models is that we can apply them to the microscopic world, and explain more phenomena.

Figure 19.3 Snooker balls provide a good model for the behaviour of particles on a much smaller scale.

We can picture gas molecules as small, hard particles, rushing around and bouncing haphazardly off one another and the walls of their container. This is called the kinetic model of a gas. We can explain the macroscopic (larger scale) phenomena of pressure and temperature in terms of the masses and speeds of the microscopic particles. This is a very powerful model, which has been refined to explain many other aspects of the behaviour of gases.

Table 19.1 shows how, in particular areas of science, we can use a particle model to interpret and make predictions about macroscopic phenomena.

Area	Model	Macroscopic phenomena
electricity	flow of electrons	current
gases	kinetic theory	pressure, temperature and volume of a gas
solids	crystalline materials	mechanical properties
radioactivity	nuclear model of atom	radioactive decay, fission and fusion reactions
chemistry	atomic structure	chemical reactions

Table 19.1 Particle models in science.

Wave models

Waves are something that we see on the sea. There are tidal waves, and little ripples. Some waves have foamy tops, others are breaking on the beach.

Physicists have an idealised picture of a wave – it is shaped like a sine graph. You will not see any waves quite this shape on the sea. However, it is a useful picture, because it can be used to represent some simple phenomena. More complicated waves can be made up of several simple waves, and physicists can cope with the mathematics of sine waves. (This is the principle of superposition, which we looked at in detail in Chapter 17.)

Waves are a way in which energy is transferred from one place to another. In any wave, something is changing in a regular way, while energy is travelling along. In water waves, the surface of the water moves up and down periodically, and energy is transferred horizontally.

Table 19.2 shows some other phenomena that we explain in terms of waves.

The characteristic properties of waves are that they all show reflection, refraction, diffraction and interference. Waves also do not have mass or charge. Since particle models can also explain reflection and refraction, it is diffraction and interference that we regard as the defining characteristics of waves. If we can show diffraction and interference, we know that we are dealing with waves (Figure 19.4).

Phenomenon	Varying quantity
sound	pressure (or density)
light (and other electromagnetic waves)	electric and magnetic field strengths
waves on strings	displacement

Table 19.2 Wave models in science.

Waves or particles?

Wave models and particle models are both very useful. They can explain a great many different observations. But which should we use in a particular situation? And what if both models seem to work when we are trying to explain something?

This is just the problem that physicists struggled with for over a century, in connection with light. Does light travel as a wave or as particles?

For a long time, Newton's view prevailed – light travels as particles. This was set out in 1704 in his famous book *Opticks*. He could use this model to explain both reflection and refraction. His model suggested that light travels faster in glass than in air. In 1801 Thomas Young, an English physicist, demonstrated that light showed diffraction and interference effects. Physicists were still very reluctant to abandon Newton's particle model of light. The ultimate blow to Newton's model came from the work carried out by the French physicist Léon Foucault in

Figure 19.4 A diffraction grating splits up light into its component colours and can produce dramatic effects in photographs.

1853. His experiments on the speed of light showed that light travelled more slowly in water than in air. Newton's model was in direct contradiction with experimental results. Most scientists were convinced that light travelled through space as a wave.

Particulate nature of light

We expect light to behave as waves, but can light also behave as particles? The answer is yes, and you are probably already familiar with some of the evidence.

If you place a Geiger counter next to a source of gamma radiation you will hear an irregular series of clicks. The counter is detecting γ-rays (gamma rays). But γ-rays are part of the electromagnetic spectrum (Chapter 16). They belong to the same family of waves as visible light, radio waves, X-rays, etc.

So, here are waves giving individual or discrete clicks, which are indistinguishable from the clicks given by α-particles (alpha particles) and β-particles (beta particles). We can conclude that γ-rays behave like particles when they interact with a Geiger counter.

This effect is most obvious with γ-rays, because they are at the most energetic end of the electromagnetic spectrum. It is harder to show the same effect for visible light.

Photons

The photoelectric effect, and Einstein's explanation of it, convinced physicists that light could behave as a stream of particles. Before we go on to look at this in detail (page 212), we need to see how to calculate the energy of photons.

Newton used the word *corpuscle* for the particles which he thought made up light. Nowadays, we call them **photons** and we believe that all electromagnetic radiation consists of photons. A photon is a 'packet of energy' or a quantum of electromagnetic energy. Gamma photons (γ-photons) are the most energetic. According to Albert Einstein, who based his ideas on the work of another German physicist Max Planck, the energy E of a photon in joules (J) is related to the frequency f in hertz (Hz) of the electromagnetic radiation of which it is part, by the equation:

$$E = hf$$

The constant h has an experimental value equal to 6.63×10^{-34} J s.

This constant h is called the *Planck constant*. It has the unit joule seconds (J s), but you may prefer to think of this as 'joules per hertz'. The energy of a photon is directly proportional to the frequency of the electromagnetic waves, that is:

$$E \propto f$$

Hence, high-frequency radiation means high-energy photons.

Notice that this equation tells us the relationship between a particle property (the photon energy E) and a wave property (the frequency f). It is called the **Einstein relation** and applies to all electromagnetic waves.

The frequency f and wavelength λ of an electromagnetic wave are related to the wave speed c by the wave equation $c = f\lambda$, so we can also write this equation as:

$$E = \frac{hc}{\lambda}$$

It is worth noting that the energy of the photon is inversely proportional to the wavelength. Hence the short-wavelength X-ray photon is far more energetic than the long-wavelength photon of light.

Now we can work out the energy of a γ-photon. Gamma rays typically have frequencies greater than 10^{20} Hz. The energy of a γ-photon is therefore greater than

$$(6.63 \times 10^{-34} \times 10^{20}) \approx 10^{-13} \text{ J}$$

This is a very small amount of energy on the human scale, so we don't notice the effects of individual γ-photons. However, some astronauts have reported seeing flashes of light as individual cosmic rays, high-energy γ-photons, have passed through their eyeballs.

To answer SAQs 1–7 you will need these values:

speed of light in a vacuum $c - 3.0 \times 10^8$ m s^{-1}

Planck constant $h = 6.63 \times 10^{-34}$ J s

SAQ

1   Calculate the energy of a high-energy γ-photon, frequency 10^{26} Hz.   [Answer]

2   Visible light has wavelengths in the range 400 nm (violet) to 700 nm (red). Calculate the energy of a photon of red light and a photon of violet light.   [Hint]   [Answer]

3   Determine the wavelength of the electromagnetic waves for each photon below and hence use Figure 19.5 (page 210) to identify the region of the electromagnetic spectrum to which each belongs. The photon energy is:
    a 10^{-12} J
    b 10^{-15} J
    c 10^{-18} J
    d 10^{-20} J
    e 10^{-25} J   [Answer]

4   A 1.0 mW laser produces red light of wavelength 6.48×10^{-7} m. Calculate how many photons the laser produces per second.   [Hint]   [Answer]

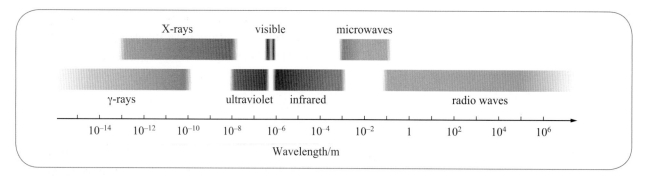

Figure 19.5 Wavelengths of the electromagnetic spectrum. The boundaries between some regions are fuzzy.

The electronvolt (eV)

The energy of a photon is extremely small and far less than a joule. Hence the joule is not a very convenient unit for measuring photon energies. In Chapter 11, we saw how the kilowatt-hour was defined as a unit for large amounts of energy. Now we will define another energy unit, the **electronvolt**, which is useful for amounts of energy much smaller than a joule.

When an electron travels through a potential difference, energy is transferred. If an electron, which has a charge of magnitude 1.6×10^{-19} C, travels through a potential difference of 1 V, its energy change W is given by:

$$W = QV = 1.6 \times 10^{-19} \times 1 = 1.6 \times 10^{-19} \text{ J}$$

We can use this as the basis of the definition of the electronvolt:

> One electronvolt (1 eV) is the energy transferred when an electron travels through a potential difference of one volt.

Therefore:

$$1 \text{ eV} = 1.6 \times 10^{-19} \text{ J}$$

So when an electron moves through 1 V, 1 eV of energy is transferred. When one electron moves through 2 V, 2 eV of energy are transferred. When five electrons move through 10 V, a total of 50 eV are transferred, and so on.

- To convert from eV to J, multiply by 1.6×10^{-19}.
- To convert from J to eV, divide by 1.6×10^{-19}.

SAQ

5 An electron travels through a cell of e.m.f. 1.2 V. How much energy is transferred to the electron? Give your answer in eV and in J.

[Answer]

6 Calculate the energy in eV of an X-ray photon of frequency 3.0×10^{18} Hz.

[Answer]

7 To which region of the electromagnetic spectrum (Figure 19.5) does a photon of energy 10 eV belong?

[Hint]

[Answer]

When a charged particle is accelerated through a potential difference V, its kinetic energy increases. For an electron (charge e), accelerated from rest, we can write:

$$eV = \tfrac{1}{2} mv^2$$

We need to be careful when using this equation. It does not apply when a charged particle is accelerated through a large voltage to speeds approaching the speed of light c. For this, we would have to take account of relativistic effects. (The mass of a particle increases as its speed gets closer to 3.0×10^8 m s^{-1}.)

Rearranging the equation gives the electron's speed:

$$v = \sqrt{\frac{2eV}{m}}$$

This equation applies to any type of charged particle, including protons (charge $+e$) and ions.

SAQ

8 A proton (charge = $+1.6 \times 10^{-19}$ C, mass = 1.7×10^{-27} kg) is accelerated through a potential difference of 1500 V. Determine:

a its final kinetic energy in joules (J)

b its final speed.

Answer

Extension

Estimating the Planck constant

You can obtain an estimate of the value of the Planck constant h by means of a simple experiment. It makes use of light-emitting diodes (LEDs) of different colours (Figure 19.6). You may recall from Chapter 10 that an LED conducts in one direction only (the forward direction), and that it requires a minimum voltage, the **threshold voltage**, to be applied in this direction before it allows a current. This experiment makes use of the fact that LEDs of different colours require different threshold voltages before they conduct and emit light.

- A red LED emits photons that are of low energy. It requires a low threshold voltage to make it conduct.
- A blue LED emits higher-energy photons, and requires a higher threshold voltage to make it conduct.

Figure 19.6 Light-emitting diodes (LEDs) come in different colours. Blue (on the right) proved the trickiest to develop.

What is happening to produce photons of light when an LED conducts? The simplest way to think of this is to say that the electrical energy lost by a single electron passing through the diode reappears as the energy of a single photon.

Hence we can write:

energy lost by electron = energy of photon

$$eV = \frac{hc}{\lambda}$$

where V is the threshold voltage for the LED. The values of e and c are known. Measurements of V and λ will allow you to calculate h. So the measurements required are:

- V – the voltage across the LED when it begins to conduct – its threshold voltage. It is found using a circuit as shown in Figure 19.7a;
- λ – the wavelength of the light emitted by the LED. This is found by measurements using a diffraction grating or from the wavelength quoted by the manufacturer of the LED.

If several LEDs of different colours are available, V and λ can be determined for each and a graph of V against $\frac{1}{\lambda}$ drawn (see Figure 19.7b) The gradient of this graph will be $\frac{hc}{e}$ and hence h can be estimated.

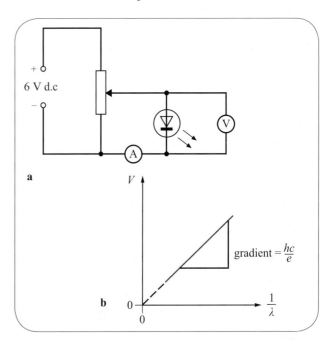

Figure 19.7 a A circuit to determine the threshold voltage required to make an LED conduct. An ammeter helps to show when this occurs.

b The graph used to determine h from this experiment.

SAQ

9 In an experiment to determine the Planck constant h, LEDs of different colours were used. The p.d. required to make each conduct was determined, and the wavelength of their light was taken from the manufacturer's catalogue. The results are shown in Table 19.3. For each LED, calculate the experimental value for h and hence determine an average value for the Planck constant.

Answer

Colour of LED	Wavelength/ 10^{-9} m	Threshold voltage/V
infrared	910	1.35
red	670	1.70
amber	610	2.00
green	560	2.30

Table 19.3 Results from an experiment to determine h.

The photoelectric effect

You can observe the photoelectric effect yourself by fixing a clean zinc plate to the top of a gold-leaf electroscope (Figure 19.8). Give the electroscope a negative charge and the leaf deflects. Now shine

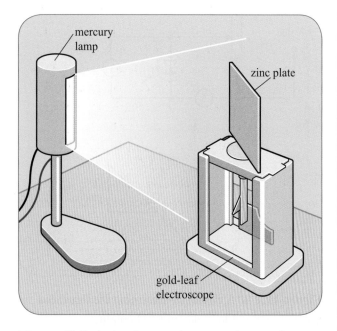

mercury lamp

zinc plate

gold-leaf electroscope

Figure 19.8 A simple experiment to observe the photoelectric effect.

electromagnetic radiation from a mercury discharge lamp on the zinc and the leaf gradually falls. (A mercury lamp strongly emits ultraviolet radiation.) Charging the electroscope gives it an excess of electrons. Somehow, the electromagnetic radiation from the mercury lamp helps the electrons to escape from the surface of the metal. The radiation causes electrons to be removed. The Greek word for light is *photo*, hence the word 'photoelectric'. The electrons removed from the metal plate in this manner are often known as photoelectrons.

Placing the mercury lamp closer causes the leaf to fall more rapidly. This is not very surprising. However, if you insert a sheet of glass between the lamp and the zinc, the radiation from the lamp is no longer effective. The gold leaf does not fall. Glass absorbs ultraviolet radiation and it is this component of the radiation from the lamp that is effective.

If you try the experiment with a bright filament lamp, you will find it has no effect. It does not produce ultraviolet radiation. There is a minimum frequency that the incident radiation must have in order to release electrons from the metal. This is called the **threshold frequency**. The threshold frequency is a property of the metal plate being exposed to electromagnetic radiation.

> The threshold frequency is defined as the minimum frequency required to release electrons from the surface of a metal.

Physicists found it hard to explain why weak ultraviolet radiation could have an immediate effect on the electrons in the metal, but very bright light of lower frequency had no effect. They imagined light waves arriving at the metal, spread out over its surface, and they could not see how weak ultraviolet waves could be more effective than the intense visible waves. In 1905, Albert Einstein came up with an explanation based on the idea of photons.

Metals (such as zinc) have electrons that are not very tightly held within the metal. These are the conduction electrons and they are free to move about within the metal. When photons of electromagnetic radiation strike the metal, some electrons break free from the surface of the metal (Figure 19.9). They

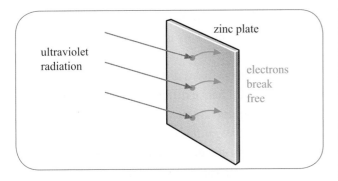

Figure 19.9 The photoelectric effect. When a photon of ultraviolet radiation strikes the metal plate, its energy may be sufficient to release an electron.

only need a small amount of energy (about 10^{-19} J) to escape from the metal surface.

We can picture the electrons as being trapped in an energy 'well' (Figure 19.10). A single electron requires a minimum energy ϕ (Greek letter phi) to escape the surface of the metal. The *work function energy*, or simply **work function**, of a metal is the minimum amount of energy required by an electron to escape its surface. (Energy is needed to release the surface electrons because they are attracted by the electrostatic forces due to the positive metal ions.)

Einstein did not picture electromagnetic *waves* interacting with all of the electrons in the metal. Instead, he suggested that a single photon could provide the energy needed by an individual electron to escape. The photon energy would need to be at least as great as ϕ. By this means, Einstein could explain the threshold frequency. A photon of visible light has energy less than ϕ, so it cannot release an electron from the surface of zinc.

When a photon arrives at the metal plate, it may be captured by an electron. The electron gains all of the photon's energy and the photon no longer exists. Some of the energy is needed for the electron to escape from the energy well; the rest is the electron's kinetic energy.

Now we can see that the photon model works because it models electromagnetic waves as concentrated 'packets' of energy, each one able to release an electron from the metal.

Here are some rules for the photoelectric effect:
- Electrons from the surface of the metal are removed.
- A single photon can only interact, and hence exchange its energy, with a single electron (one-to-one interaction).

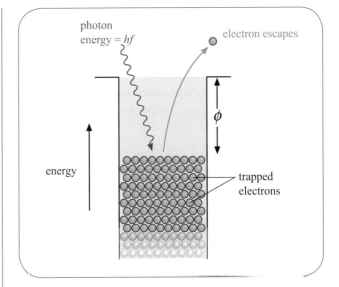

Figure 19.10 A single photon may interact with a single electron to release it.

- A surface electron is removed *instantaneously* from the metal surface when the energy of the incident photon is greater than, or equal to, the work function ϕ of the metal. (The frequency of the incident radiation is greater than, or equal to, the threshold frequency of the metal.)
- Energy must be conserved when a photon interacts with an electron.
- Increasing the intensity of the incident radiation does not release a single electron when its frequency is less than the threshold frequency. The intensity of the incident radiation is proportional to the rate at which photons arrive at the plate. Each photon still has energy less than the work function.

Photoelectric experiments showed that the electrons released had a range of kinetic energies up to some maximum value, KE_{max}. These fastest-moving electrons are the ones which were least tightly held in the metal.

Imagine a single photon interacting with a single surface electron and freeing it. According to Einstein:

energy of photon = work function +
$\qquad$ maximum kinetic energy of electron

$$hf = \phi + KE_{max}$$

or

$$hf = \phi + \tfrac{1}{2}mv^2_{max}$$

This equation, known as Einstein's photoelectric equation, can be understood as follows:

● We start with a photon of energy hf.
● It is absorbed by an electron.
● Some of the energy (ϕ) is used in escaping from the metal. The rest remains as kinetic energy of the electron.
● If the photon is absorbed by an electron that is lower in the energy well, the electron will have less kinetic energy than KE_{max} (Figure 19.11).

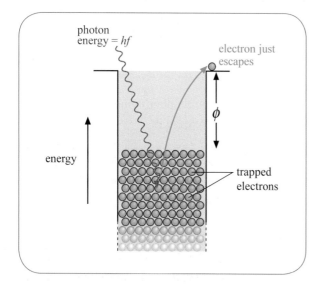

Figure 19.11 A more tightly bound electron needs more energy to release it from the metal.

What happens when the incident radiation has a frequency equal to the threshold frequency f_0 of the metal?

The kinetic energy of the electrons is zero. Hence, according to Einstein's photoelectric equation:

$$hf_0 = \phi$$

Hence, the threshold frequency f_0 is given by the expression:

$$f_0 = \frac{\phi}{h}$$

What happens when the incident radiation has frequency less than the threshold frequency? A single photon can still give up its energy to a single electron, but this electron cannot escape from the attractive forces of the positive metal ions. The energy absorbed from the photons appears as kinetic energy of the electrons. These electrons lose their kinetic energy

to the metal ions when they collide with them. This warms up the metal. This is why a metal plate placed in the vicinity of a table lamp gets hot.

Different metals have different threshold frequencies, and hence different work functions. For example, alkali metals such as sodium, potassium and rubidium have threshold frequencies in the visible region of the electromagnetic spectrum. The conduction electrons in zinc are more tightly bound within the metal and so its threshold frequency is in the ultraviolet region of the spectrum.

Table 19.4 summarises the observations of the photoelectric effect, the problems a wave model of light has in explaining them, and how a photon model is more successful.

You will need these values to answer SAQs 10–15:

speed of light in a vacuum $c = 3.0 \times 10^8$ m s^{-1}

Planck constant $h = 6.63 \times 10^{-34}$ J s

mass of electron $m_e = 9.1 \times 10^{-31}$ kg.

elementary charge $e = 1.6 \times 10^{-19}$ C

SAQ

10 Photons of energies 1.0 eV, 2.0 eV and 3.0 eV strike a metal surface whose work function is 1.8 eV.
  a State which of these photons could cause the release of an electron from the metal.
  b Calculate the maximum kinetic energies of the electrons released in each case. Give your answers in eV and in J.

  Answer

11 Table 19.5 shows the work functions of several different metals.
  a Which metal requires the highest frequency of electromagnetic waves to release electrons?
  b Which metal will release electrons when the lowest frequency of electromagnetic waves is incident on it?
  c Calculate the threshold frequency for zinc.
  d What is the longest wavelength of electromagnetic waves that will release electrons from potassium?

  Answer

Observation	Wave model	Photon model
Emission of electrons happens as soon as light shines on metal	Very intense light should be needed to have immediate effect	A single photon is enough to release one electron
Even weak (low-intensity) light is effective	Weak light waves should have no effect	Low-intensity light means fewer photons, not lower-energy photons
Increasing intensity of light increases rate at which electrons leave metal	Greater intensity means more energy, so more electrons released	Greater intensity means more photons per second, so more electrons released per second
Increasing intensity has no effect on energies of electrons	Greater intensity should mean electrons have more energy	Greater intensity does not mean more energetic photons, so electrons cannot have more energy
A minimum threshold frequency of light is needed	Low-frequency light should work; electrons would be released more slowly	A photon in a low-frequency light beam has energy that is too small to release an electron
Increasing frequency of light increases maximum kinetic energy of electrons	It should be increasing intensity, not frequency, that increases energy of electrons	Higher frequency means more energetic photons; so electrons gain more energy and can move faster

Table 19.4 The success of the photon model in explaining the photoelectric effect.

Metal	Work function ϕ/J	Work function ϕ/eV
caesium	3.0×10^{-19}	1.9
calcium	4.3×10^{-19}	2.7
gold	7.8×10^{-19}	4.9
potassium	3.2×10^{-19}	2.0
zinc	6.9×10^{-19}	4.3

Table 19.5 Work functions of several different metals.

12 Electromagnetic waves of wavelength 2.4×10^{-7} m are incident on the surface of a metal whose work function is 2.8×10^{-19} J.
a Calculate the energy of a single photon.
b Calculate the maximum kinetic energy of electrons released from the metal.
c Determine the maximum speed of the emitted photoelectrons.

[Answer]

13 When electromagnetic radiation of wavelength 2000 nm is incident on a metal surface, the maximum kinetic energy of the electrons released is found to be 4.0×10^{-20} J. Determine the work function of the metal in joules (J).

[Hint]

[Answer]

The nature of light – waves or particles?

It is clear that, in order to explain the photoelectric effect, we must use the idea of light (and all electromagnetic waves) as particles. Similarly, photons explain the appearance of line spectra (see Chapter 20). However, to explain diffraction, interference and polarisation of light, we must use the wave model. How can we sort out this dilemma?

We have to conclude that sometimes light shows wave-like behaviour; at other times it behaves as particles (photons). In particular, when light is absorbed by a metal surface, it behaves as particles. Individual photons are absorbed by individual electrons in the metal. In a similar way, when a Geiger counter detects γ-radiation, we hear individual γ-photons being absorbed in the tube.

So what is light? Is it a wave or a particle? Physicists have come to terms with the dual nature of light. This duality is referred to as the *wave–particle duality* of light. In simple terms:

- Light interacts with matter (e.g. electrons) as a particle – the photon. The evidence for this is provided by the photoelectric effect.
- Light travels through space as a wave. The evidence for this comes from the diffraction and interference of light using slits.

Electron waves

Light has a dual nature. Is it possible that particles such as electrons also have a dual nature? This interesting question was first contemplated by Louis de Broglie (pronounced 'de Broy') in 1924 (Figure 19.12).

De Broglie imagined that electrons would travel through space as a wave. He proposed that the wave-like property of a particle like the electron can be represented by its wavelength λ, which is related to its momentum p by the equation:

$$\lambda = \frac{h}{p}$$

where h is the Planck constant. The wavelength λ is often referred to as the de Broglie wavelength. The waves associated with the electron are referred to as matter waves.

The momentum p of a particle is the product of its mass m and its velocity v. Therefore, the de Broglie equation may be written as:

$$\lambda = \frac{h}{mv}$$

The Planck constant h is the same constant that appears in the equation $E = hf$ for the energy of a photon. It is fascinating how the Planck constant h is entwined with the behaviour of both matter as waves (e.g. electrons) and electromagnetic waves as 'particles' (photons).

The wave property of the electron was eventually confirmed in 1927 by researchers in America and in England. The Americans Clinton Davisson and Edmund Germer showed experimentally that electrons were diffracted by single crystals of nickel. The diffraction of electrons confirmed their wave-like property. In England, George Thomson fired electrons into thin sheets of metal in a vacuum tube. He too provided evidence that electrons were diffracted by the metal atoms.

Louis de Broglie received the 1929 Nobel Prize for Physics. Clinton Davisson and George Thomson shared the Nobel Prize for Physics in 1937.

Electron diffraction

We can reproduce the same diffraction results in the laboratory using an electron diffraction tube, see Figure 19.13.

Figure 19.12 Louis de Broglie provided an alternative view of how particles behave.

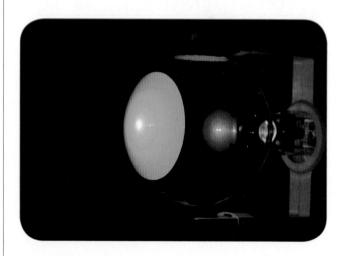

Figure 19.13 When a beam of electrons passes through a graphite film, as in this vacuum tube, a diffraction pattern is produced on the phosphor screen.

In an electron diffraction tube, the electrons from the heated filament are accelerated to high speeds by the large potential difference between the negative heater (cathode) and the positive electrode (anode). A beam of electrons passes through a thin sample of polycrystalline graphite. It is made up of many tiny crystals, each of which consists of large numbers of carbon atoms arranged in uniform atomic layers. The electrons emerge from the graphite film and produce diffraction rings on the phosphor screen. The diffraction rings are similar to those produced by light (a wave) passing through a small circular hole. The rings cannot be explained if electrons behaved as particles. Diffraction is a property of waves. Hence the rings can only be explained if the electrons pass through the graphite film as a wave. The electrons are diffracted by the carbon atoms and the spacing between the layers of carbon atoms. The atomic layers of carbon behave like a diffraction grating with many slits. The electrons show diffraction effects because their de Broglie wavelength λ is similar to the spacing between the atomic layers.

This experiment shows that electrons appear to travel as waves. If we look a little more closely at the results of the experiment, we find something else even more surprising. The phosphor screen gives a flash of light for each electron that hits it. These flashes build up to give the diffraction pattern (Figure 19.14). But if we see flashes at particular points on the screen, are

we not seeing individual electrons – in other words, are we not observing particles?

Worked example 1

Calculate the de Broglie wavelength of an electron travelling through space at a speed of 10^7 m s^{-1}. State whether or not these electrons can be diffracted by solid materials (atomic spacing in solid materials $\sim 10^{-10}$ m).

Step 1   According to the de Broglie equation, we have:

$$\lambda = \frac{h}{mv}$$

Step 2   The mass of an electron is 9.1×10^{-31} kg. Hence:

$$\lambda = \frac{6.63 \times 10^{-34}}{9.1 \times 10^{-31} \times 10^7} = 7.3 \times 10^{-11} \text{ m}$$

The electrons travelling at 10^7 m s^{-1} have a de Broglie wavelength of order of magnitude 10^{-10} m. Hence they can be diffracted by matter.

Guidance

Investigating electron diffraction

If you have access to an electron diffraction tube (Figure 19.15), you can see for yourself how a beam of electrons is diffracted. The electron gun at one end of the tube produces a beam of electrons. By changing the voltage between the anode and the cathode, you can change the energy of the electrons, and hence their speed. The beam strikes a graphite target, and a diffraction pattern appears on the screen at the other end of the tube.

You can use an electron diffraction tube to investigate how the wavelength of the electrons depends on their speed. Qualitatively, you should find that increasing the anode–cathode voltage makes the pattern of diffraction rings shrink. The electrons have more kinetic energy (they are faster); the shrinking pattern shows that their wavelength has decreased. You can find the wavelength λ of the electrons by measuring the angle θ at which they are diffracted:

$$\lambda = 2d \sin \theta$$

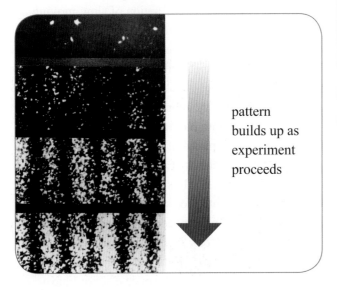

pattern builds up as experiment proceeds

Figure 19.14 The speckled diffraction pattern shows that it arises from many individual electrons striking the screen.

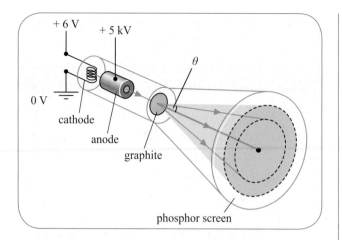

Figure 19.15 Electrons are accelerated from the cathode to the anode; they form a beam which is diffracted as it passes through the graphite film.

In the previous equation d is the spacing of the atomic layers of graphite.

You can find the speed of the electrons from the anode–cathode voltage V:

$$\tfrac{1}{2}mv^2 = eV$$

SAQ

14 X-rays are used to find out about the spacings of atomic planes in crystalline materials.

   a Describe how beams of electrons could be used for the same purpose.

   b How might electron diffraction be used to identify a sample of a metal?

   [Answer]

People waves

The de Broglie equation applies to all matter; anything that has mass. It can also be applied to objects like golf balls and people!

Imagine a 65 kg person running at a speed of 3.0 m s^{-1} through an opening of width 0.80 m. According to the de Broglie equation, the wavelength of this person is:

$$\lambda = \frac{h}{mv}$$

$$\lambda = \frac{6.63 \times 10^{-34}}{65 \times 3.0}$$

$$\lambda = 3.4 \times 10^{-36} \text{ m}$$

This wavelength is very small indeed compared with the size of the gap, hence no diffraction effects would be observed. People cannot be diffracted through everyday gaps. The de Broglie wavelength of this person is much smaller than any gap the person is likely to try to squeeze through! For this reason, we do not use the wave model to describe the behaviour of people; we get much better results by regarding people as large particles.

SAQ

15 A beam of electrons is accelerated from rest through a p.d. of 1.0 kV.

   a What is the energy (in eV) of each electron in the beam?

   b Calculate the speed, and hence the momentum (mv), of each electron.

   c Calculate the de Broglie wavelength of each electron.

   d Would you expect the beam to be significantly diffracted by a metal film in which the atoms are separated by a spacing of 0.25×10^{-9} m?

   [Hint]

   [Answer]

Probing matter

All moving particles have a de Broglie wavelength. The structure of matter can be investigated using the diffraction of particles. Diffraction of slow-moving neutrons (known as thermal neutrons) from nuclear reactors is used to study the arrangements of atoms in metals and other materials. The wavelength of these neutrons is about 10^{-10} m, which is roughly the separation between the atoms.

Diffraction of slow-moving electrons is used to explore the arrangements of atoms in metals (Figure 19.16) and the structures of complex molecules such as DNA (Figure 19.17). It is possible to accelerate electrons to the right speed so that their wavelength is similar to the spacing between atoms, around 10^{-10} m.

High-speed electrons from particle accelerators have been used to determine the diameter of atomic nuclei. This is possible because high-speed electrons have shorter wavelengths of order of magnitude 10^{-15} m. This wavelength is similar to the size of atomic nuclei. Electrons travelling close to the speed

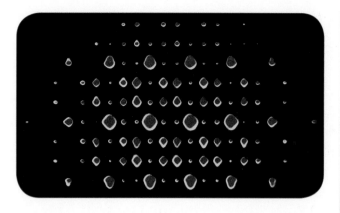

Figure 19.16 Electron diffraction pattern for an alloy of titanium and nickel. From this pattern, we can deduce the arrangement of the atoms and their separations.

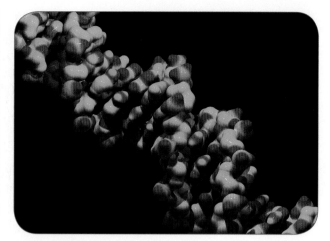

Figure 19.17 The structure of the giant molecule DNA, deduced from electron diffraction studies.

of light are being used to investigate the internal structure of the nucleus. These electrons have to be accelerated by voltages up to 10^9 V.

The nature of the electron – wave or particle?

The electron has a dual nature, just like electromagnetic waves. This duality is referred to as the *wave–particle* *duality* of the electron. In simple terms:

- An electron interacts with matter as a particle. The evidence for this is provided by Newtonian mechanics.
- An electron travels through space as a wave. The evidence for this comes from the diffraction of electrons.

Summary

Glossary

- For electromagnetic waves of frequency f and wavelength λ, each photon has energy E given by: $E = hf$ or $E = \frac{hc}{\lambda}$, where h is the Planck constant.

- One electronvolt is the energy transferred when an electron travels through a potential difference of 1 V.

  $1 \text{ eV} = 1.6 \times 10^{-19} \text{ J}$

- A particle of charge e accelerated through a voltage V has kinetic energy given by:

  $eV = \frac{1}{2}mv^2$

- The photoelectric effect is an example of a phenomenon explained in terms of the particle-like (photon) behaviour of electromagnetic radiation.

- Einstein's photoelectric equation is:

  $hf = \phi + \text{KE}_{max}$

  where ϕ = work function = minimum energy required to release an electron from the metal surface.

- The threshold frequency is the minimum frequency of the incident electromagnetic radiation that will release an electron from the metal surface.

continued

219

- Electron diffraction is an example of a phenomenon explained in terms of the wave-like behaviour of matter.

- The de Broglie wavelength λ of a particle is related to its momentum (mv) by the de Broglie equation:

$$\lambda = \frac{h}{mv}$$

- Both electromagnetic radiation (light) and matter (electrons) exhibit wave–particle duality; that is, they show both wave-like and particle-like behaviours, depending on the circumstances. In wave–particle duality:

  - interaction is explained in terms of particles

  - travel through space is explained in terms of waves.

Questions

1 The diagram shows an electrical circuit including a photocell.

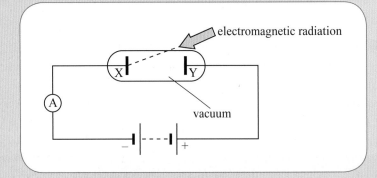

The photocell contains a metal plate X that is exposed to electromagnetic radiation. Photoelectrons emitted from the surface of the metal are accelerated towards the positive electrode Y. A sensitive ammeter measures the current in the circuit due to the photoelectrons emitted by the metal plate X. The metal of plate X has work function of 2.2 eV. The maximum kinetic energy of an emitted photoelectron from this plate is 0.3 eV.

a Calculate the energy of a single photon in:
  i electronvolts, eV [1]
  ii joules. [2]
b Calculate the frequency of the incident electromagnetic radiation. [2]
c Deduce the effect on the current if the radiation has the same intensity but the frequency of the electromagnetic radiation is greater than in b. [2]

OCR Physics AS (2822) June 2004 [Total 7]

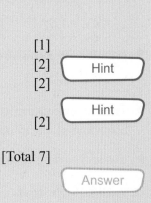

continued

2 A negatively charged metal plate is exposed to electromagnetic radiation of frequency f. The diagram shows the variation with f of the maximum kinetic energy KE_{max} of the photoelectrons emitted from the surface of the metal.

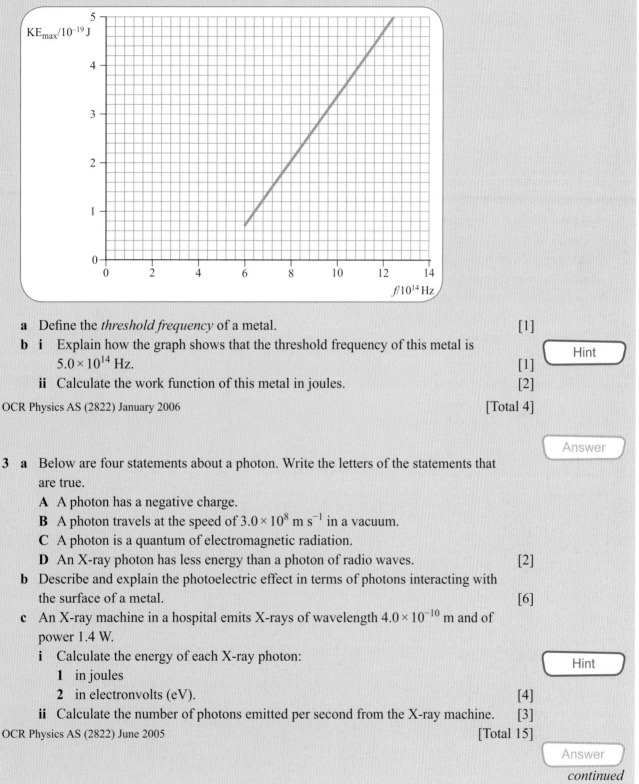

    a Define the *threshold frequency* of a metal. [1]

    b **i** Explain how the graph shows that the threshold frequency of this metal is 5.0 × 10^{14} Hz. [1]

       ii Calculate the work function of this metal in joules. [2]

OCR Physics AS (2822) January 2006   [Total 4]

Hint

Answer

3 **a** Below are four statements about a photon. Write the letters of the statements that are true.

      A A photon has a negative charge.

      B A photon travels at the speed of 3.0×10^8 m s^{-1} in a vacuum.

      C A photon is a quantum of electromagnetic radiation.

      D An X-ray photon has less energy than a photon of radio waves. [2]

    b Describe and explain the photoelectric effect in terms of photons interacting with the surface of a metal. [6]

    c An X-ray machine in a hospital emits X-rays of wavelength 4.0×10^{-10} m and of power 1.4 W.

      i Calculate the energy of each X-ray photon:

         1 in joules

         2 in electronvolts (eV). [4]

      ii Calculate the number of photons emitted per second from the X-ray machine. [3]

OCR Physics AS (2822) June 2005   [Total 15]

Hint

Answer

continued

4 Wave–particle duality suggests that an electron can exhibit both particle-like and wave-like properties. The diagram shows the key features of an experiment to demonstrate the wave-like behaviour of electrons.

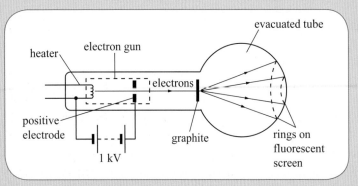

The electrons are accelerated to high speeds by the electron gun. These high-speed electrons pass through a thin layer of graphite (carbon atoms) and emerge to produce rings on the fluorescent screen.

a Use the ideas developed by de Broglie to explain how this experiment demonstrates the wave-like nature of electrons. Suggest what happens to the appearance of the rings when the speed of the electrons is increased. [5]

b Suggest how, within the electron gun, this experiment provides evidence for the particle-like property of the electrons. [1]

OCR Physics AS (2822) January 2005 [Total 6]

Answer

Chapter 20

Spectra

e-Learning

Objectives

Light and atoms

In the mid-19th century, scientists debated whether there were any limits to the questions that science could answer. It was suggested that scientists would never be able to discover what the stars were made of – they were too far away, and too hot. For example, in 1835 the French philosopher Auguste Comte wrote:

On the subject of stars, all investigations which are not ultimately reducible to simple visual observations are ... necessarily denied to us. While we can conceive of the possibility of determining their shapes, their sizes, and their motions, we shall never be able by any means to study their chemical composition ... Our knowledge concerning their gaseous envelopes is necessarily limited to their existence, size ... and refractive power, we shall not at all be able to determine their chemical composition or even their density ... I regard any notion concerning the true mean temperature of the various stars as forever denied to us.

Today, it seems rather surprising that Comte should have thought this. Earlier in the 19th century, Fraunhofer had examined the spectrum of sunlight and identified wavelengths characteristic of many familiar elements – iron, sodium, calcium, etc. As telescopes and optical spectrometers (devices for determining wavelengths of visible light) improved, it became possible to analyse the light from stars (Figure 20.1). These techniques were developed by Kirchhoff and Bunsen (two familiar names) in the 1850s, and this attracted the attention of the British astronomer William Huggins (Figure 20.2). He described how he became inspired by their work:

I soon became a little dissatisfied with the routine character of ordinary astronomical work, and in a vague way sought about in my mind for the possibility of research upon the heavens in a new direction or by new methods. It was just at this time ... that the news reached me of Kirchhoff's great discovery of the true nature and the chemical constitution of the sun from his interpretation of the Fraunhofer lines.

This news was to me like the coming upon a spring of water in a dry and thirsty land. Here at last presented itself the very order of work for which in an indefinite way I was looking – namely, to extend his novel methods of research upon the sun to the other heavenly bodies. A feeling as of inspiration seized me: I felt as if I had it now in my power to lift a veil which had never before been lifted; as if a key had been put into my hands which would unlock a door which had been regarded as for ever closed to man – the veil and the door behind which lay the unknown mystery of the true nature of the heavenly bodies.

Huggins, working with his neighbour William Miller, a professor of chemistry, attached a high-precision spectrometer to a large telescope in order to analyse starlight. From the spectra of starlight, he showed that stars consist of the same elements as all the familiar matter we know from the Earth. He was even able to show that gas clouds in space, known as nebulae, have different spectra from galaxies of stars.

continued

Figure 20.1 One of the earliest attempts to record the spectrum of sunlight. This image was recorded by John Draper in 1842 – an early use of colour photography, applied to astronomy. You can see the names of the spectral colours down the left hand side.

Figure 20.2 William Huggins, the British astronomer who first deduced the composition of stars from their starlight.

This story illustrates the way in which developments in scientific techniques (better telescopes and spectrometers), allied with theoretical developments (the understanding of spectra), led to new discoveries and an extension of our scientific understanding of the Universe.

Line spectra

We rely a great deal on light to inform us about our surroundings. Using our eyes we can identify many different colours. Scientists take this further by analysing light, by breaking or splitting it up into a spectrum. (The technical term for the splitting of light into its components is *dispersion*.) You will be familiar with the ways in which this can be done, using a prism or a diffraction grating (Figure 20.3). The spectrum of white light shows that it consists of a range of wavelengths, from about 4×10^{-7} m (violet) to about 7×10^{-7} m (red), as in Figure 20.4a. This is a continuous spectrum.

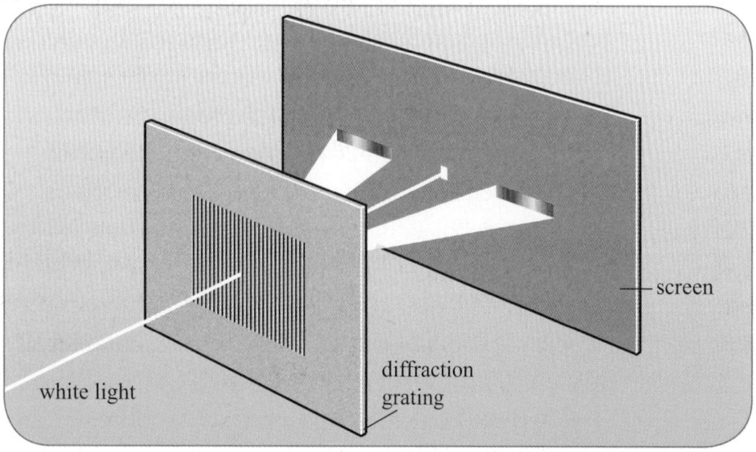

Figure 20.3 White light is split up into a continuous spectrum when it passes through a diffraction grating.

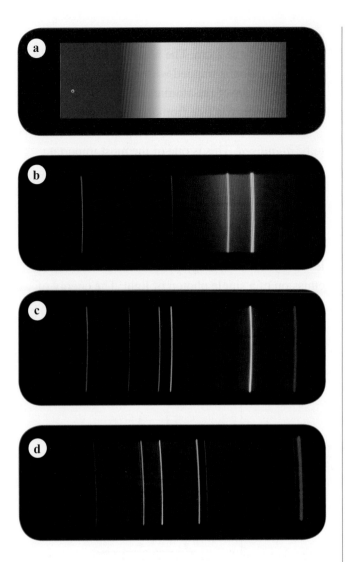

Figure 20.4 Spectra of **a** white light, and light from **b** mercury, **c** helium and **d** cadmium vapours.

It is more interesting to look at the spectrum from a hot gas. If you look at a lamp that contains a gas such as neon or sodium, you will see that only certain colours are present. Each colour has a unique wavelength. If the source is narrow and it is viewed through a diffraction grating, a *line spectrum* is seen.

Figures 20.4b and 20.4c show the line spectra of hot gases of the elements mercury and helium. Each element has a spectrum with a unique collection of wavelengths. Therefore line spectra can be used to identify elements. This is exactly what the British astronomer William Huggins did when he deduced which elements are the most common in the stars.

These line spectra, which show the composition of light emitted by hot gases, are called **emission line spectra**.

There is another kind of spectrum, called **absorption line spectra**, which are observed when white light is passed through cool gases. After the light has passed through a diffraction grating (Figure 20.5), the continuous white light spectrum is found to have black lines across it. Certain wavelengths have been absorbed as the white light passed through the cool gas.

Figure 20.5 An absorption line spectrum formed when white light is passed through cool mercury vapour.

Absorption line spectra are found when the light from stars is analysed. The interior of the star is very hot and emits white light of all wavelengths in the visible range. However, this light has to pass through the *cooler* outer layers of the star. As a result, certain wavelengths are absorbed. Figure 20.6 shows the spectrum for the Sun. (Compare this modern spectrum with the one made in 1842, shown in Figure 20.1.)

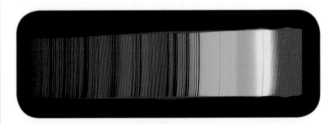

Figure 20.6 The Sun's spectrum shows dark lines. These dark lines arise when light of specific wavelengths is absorbed by the cooler atmosphere of the Sun.

Explaining the origin of line spectra

From the description above, we can see that the atoms of a given element (e.g. helium) can only emit or absorb light of certain wavelengths.

Different elements emit and absorb different wavelengths. How can this be? To understand this, we need to establish two points:

- First, as with the photoelectric effect, we are dealing with light (an electromagnetic wave) interacting with matter. Hence we need to consider light as consisting of photons. For light of a single wavelength λ and frequency f, the energy E of each photon is given by the equation:

$$E = hf \quad \text{or} \quad E = \frac{hc}{\lambda}$$

- Secondly, when light interacts with matter, it is the electrons that absorb the energy from the incoming photons. When the electrons lose energy, light is emitted by matter in the form of photons.

What does the appearance of the line spectra tell us about electrons in atoms? They can only absorb or emit photons of certain energies. From this we deduce that electrons in atoms can themselves only have certain fixed values of energy. This idea seemed very odd to scientists a hundred years ago. Figure 20.7 shows diagrammatically the permitted **energy levels** (or *energy states*) of the electron of a hydrogen atom. An electron in a hydrogen atom can have only one of these values of energy. It cannot have an energy that is between these energy levels. The energy levels of the electron are analogous to the rungs of a ladder. The energy levels have *negative* values because

external energy has to be supplied to remove an electron from the atom. The negative energy shows that the electron is trapped within the atom by the attractive forces of the atomic nucleus. An electron with zero energy is free from the atom.

The energy of the electron in the atom is said to be *quantised*. This is one of the most important statements of quantum physics.

Now we can explain what happens when an atom emits light. One of its electrons falls from a high energy level to a lower one (Figure 20.8a). The electron makes a **transition** to a lower energy level. The loss of energy of the electron leads to the emission of a single photon of light. The energy of this photon is exactly equal to the energy difference

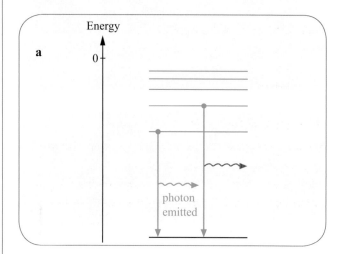

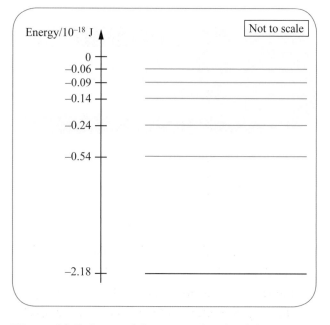

Figure 20.7 Some of the energy levels of the hydrogen atom.

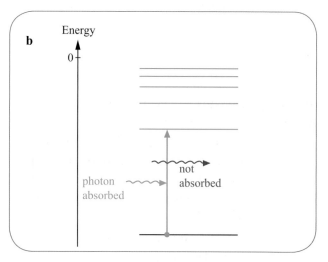

Figure 20.8 a When an electron drops to a lower energy level, it emits a single photon. **b** A photon must have just the right energy if it is to be absorbed by an electron.

between the two energy levels. If the electron makes a transition from a higher energy level, the energy loss of the electron is larger and this leads to the emission of a more energetic photon. The distinctive energy levels of an atom mean that the energy of the photons emitted, and hence the wavelengths emitted, will be unique to that atom. This explains why only certain wavelengths are present in the emission line spectrum of a hot gas.

Atoms of different elements have different line spectra because they have different spacings between their energy levels. It is not within the scope of this book to discuss why this is.

Similarly, we can explain the origin of absorption line spectra. White light consists of photons of many different energies. For a photon to be absorbed, it must have exactly the right energy to lift an electron from one energy level to another (Figure 20.8b). If its energy is too little or too great, it will *not* be absorbed.

Photon energies

When an electron changes its energy from one level E_1 to another E_2, it either emits or absorbs a *single* photon. The energy of the photon hf is simply equal to the *difference* in energies between the two levels:

photon energy $= \Delta E$

$$hf = E_1 - E_2$$

or

$$\frac{hc}{\lambda} = E_1 - E_2$$

Referring back to the energy level diagram for hydrogen (Figure 20.7), you can see that, if an electron falls from the second level to the lowest energy level (known as the **ground state**), it will emit a photon of energy:

photon energy $= \Delta E$

$$hf = [(-0.54) - (-2.18)] \times 10^{-18} \text{ J}$$

$$hf = 1.64 \times 10^{-18} \text{ J}$$

We can calculate the frequency f and wavelength λ of the emitted electromagnetic radiation.

The frequency is:

$$f = \frac{E}{h} = \frac{1.64 \times 10^{-18}}{6.63 \times 10^{-34}}$$

$$f = 2.47 \times 10^{15} \text{ Hz}$$

The wavelength is:

$$\lambda = \frac{c}{f} = \frac{3.0 \times 10^8}{2.47 \times 10^{15}}$$

$$\lambda = 1.21 \times 10^{-7} \text{ m} = 121 \text{ nm}$$

This is a wavelength in the ultraviolet region of the electromagnetic spectrum.

SAQ

1 Figure 20.9 shows part of the energy level diagram of an imaginary atom. The arrows represent three transitions between the energy levels. For each of these transitions:
- calculate the energy of the photon
- calculate the frequency and wavelength of the electromagnetic radiation (emitted or absorbed)
- state whether the transition contributes to an emission or an absorption spectrum.

Hint

Answer

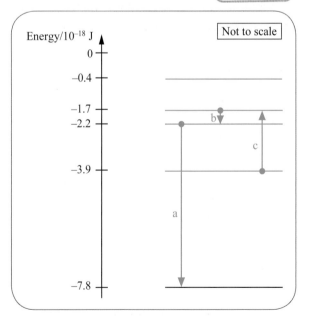

Figure 20.9 An atomic energy level diagram, showing three electron transitions between levels – see SAQ 1.

2 Figure 20.10 shows another energy level diagram. In this case, energies are given in electronvolts (eV). From the list below, state which photon energies could be absorbed by such an atom:

[Hint]

  6.0 eV   9.0 eV   11 eV
  20 eV   25 eV   34 eV   45 eV

[Answer]

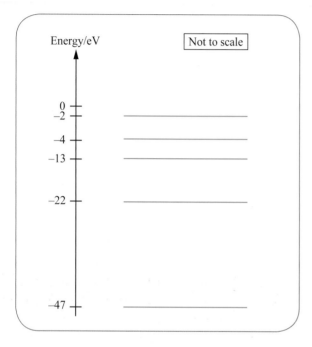

Figure 20.10 An energy level diagram – see SAQ 2.

3 The line spectrum for a particular type of atom is found to include the following wavelengths:
  83 nm   50 nm   25 nm
a Calculate the corresponding photon energies in eV.
b Sketch the energy levels which could give rise to these photons. On the diagram indicate the corresponding electron transitions responsible for these three spectral lines.

[Answer]

Isolated atoms

So far, we have only discussed the spectra of light from hot gases. In a gas, the atoms are relatively far apart, so they do not interact with one another very much. Gas atoms that exert negligible electrical forces on each other are known as *isolated atoms*. As a consequence, they give relatively simple line spectra. Similar spectra can be obtained from some gemstones and coloured glass. In these, the basic material is clear and colourless, but it gains its colour from impurity atoms, which are well separated from one another within the material.

In a solid or liquid, however, the atoms are close together. The electrons from one atom interact with those of neighbouring atoms. This has the effect of altering the energy level diagram, which becomes much more complicated, with a greater number of closely spaced energy levels. The corresponding spectra have many, many different wavelengths present; further discussion of this is beyond the scope of this book. In general, hot liquids and solids tend to produce continuous spectra.

[Extension]

Summary

- Line spectra arise for isolated atoms (the electrical forces between such atoms is negligible).

- The energy of an electron in an isolated atom is quantised. The electron is allowed to exist in specific energy states known as energy levels.

- An electron loses energy when it makes a transition from a higher energy level to a lower energy level. A photon of electromagnetic radiation is emitted because of this energy loss. The result is an emission line spectrum.

- Absorption line spectra arise when electromagnetic radiation is absorbed by isolated atoms. An electron absorbs a photon of the correct energy to allow it to make a transition to a higher energy level.

- The frequency f and the wavelength λ of the emitted or absorbed radiation are related to the energy levels E_1 and E_2 by the equations:

$$hf = \Delta E = E_1 - E_2$$

and

$$\frac{hc}{\lambda} = \Delta E = E_1 - E_2$$

Questions

1 The spectrum of sunlight has dark lines. These dark lines are due to the absorption of certain wavelengths by the cooler gases in the atmosphere of the Sun.
   a One particular dark spectral line has a wavelength of 590 nm. Calculate the energy of a photon with this wavelength. [3]
   b The diagram below shows some of the energy levels of an isolated atom of helium.

   i Explain the significance of the energy levels having negative values. [1]   Hint
   ii Explain, with reference to the energy level diagram above, how a dark line in the spectrum may be due to the presence of helium in the atmosphere of the Sun. [2]
   iii All the light absorbed by the atoms in the Sun's atmosphere is *re-emitted*. Suggest why a dark spectral line of wavelength of 590 nm is still observed from the Earth. [1]

[Total 7]   Answer

continued

2 The diagram below shows the energy levels of an isolated hydrogen atom.

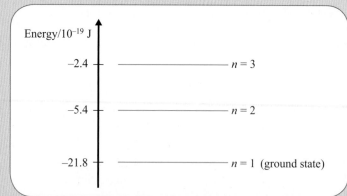

The lowest energy level of the atom is known as its *ground state*. Each energy level is assigned an integer number n, known as the principal quantum number. The ground state has $n = 1$.

a Explain what happens to an electron in the ground state when it absorbs the energy from a photon of energy 21.8×10^{-19} J. [1]

b i Explain why a photon is emitted when an electron makes a transition between energy levels of $n = 3$ and $n = 2$. [2]

ii Calculate the wavelength of electromagnetic radiation emitted when an electron makes a jump between energy levels of $n = 3$ and $n = 2$. [3]

iii Use the energy level diagram above to show that the energy E of an energy level is inversely proportional to n^2. [2]

[Total 8]

Hint

Answer

Experimental errors and uncertainties

Background

e-Learning

Millikan and the electron

If you look in a Physics data book, you will find some very long numbers. Here are two examples:

charge of electron $e = 1.602\ 177\ 335 \times 10^{-19}$ C

mass of electron $m_e = 9.109\ 389\ 754 \times 10^{-31}$ kg

Each of these values is given to ten *significant figures*. This shows us that these quantities have been measured to a high degree of precision. The experimental methods used to measure them have been gradually refined over the years, so that the physicists who make these measurements can be sure that their results are accurate.

The charge of the electron was first determined in 1912, by the American Robert Millikan (Figure A1). His result was:

magnitude of charge of electron
(the elementary charge) $e = 1.67 \times 10^{-19}$ C

(This has been converted to modern units.)

His result can only be quoted to three significant figures because his experimental method did not give such precise results as today's methods. Millikan's result was a triumph in its time, and he won the Nobel Prize for determining the elementary charge, e. Today, Physics students working in university laboratories can obtain a better result using similar equipment in the course of a couple of hours.

Millikan could not look in a data book to find the value of the charge of an electron. He had to measure it. His experimental equipment was the best he could contrive, but it was not perfect – equipment never is. So he could not hope to arrive at a perfect result. Instead, he had to aim for the best possible result using the equipment and techniques available to him. This is what all scientists and science students must endeavour to do.

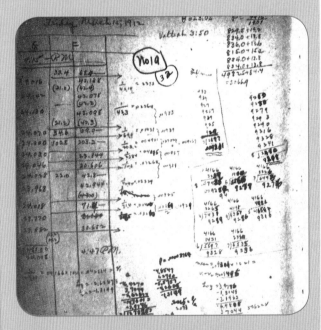

Figure A1 A page from Robert Millikan's notebook for Friday 15 March, 1912. It may look untidy, but it is still possible to understand what his scribbles mean and to deduce from them a value for the electron charge.

Estimating errors

Making an experimental measurement often involves making a judgement. For example, suppose that you are trying to determine the resistivity of a metal (see page 234). You take a length of the wire and determine its resistance. Then you measure its length and diameter. How sure can you be of the accuracy of these measurements?

Think about measuring the length of the wire. You would probably use a metre rule (Figure A2). You have to make a judgement of the reading. Is it 374 mm or 375 mm? You decide that 374 mm is the closest mark on the rule. Since this can only be judged to the nearest millimetre, we write:

length of wire = (374 ± 1) mm

The resolution in the measurement of the length of ±1 mm is known as the *absolute error* (or absolute uncertainty) in the measurement of the length when using a metre rule. The percentage error in the measurement of length is:

$$\text{percentage error} = \frac{\text{absolute error}}{\text{value of quantity}} \times 100\%$$

$$\%\ \text{error in length} = \frac{\pm 1}{374} \times 100\% \approx \pm 0.27\%$$

To reduce the percentage error or uncertainty, you would need to use a different measuring device, such as a travelling microscope. The absolute error when using this instrument is ±0.1 mm. Alternatively, you

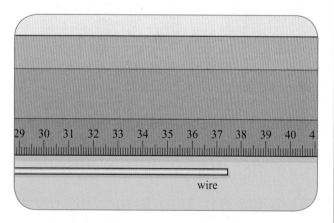

Figure A2 Measuring the length of a piece of wire involves making a judgement of the position of its end against the scale.

could use a much longer piece of wire, so that the ±1 mm would be a smaller fraction of the total length.

Going on to measure the diameter of the wire, you would reject the metre rule and travelling microscope in favour of something with an even higher degree of precision, such as a micrometer. This can measure to within one-hundredth of a millimetre. The result might then be:

diameter of wire = (1.04 ± 0.01) mm

Anyone reading your results would then be aware that the length and diameter of the wire had been measured to different degrees of precision, as indicated by the ± figures.

Experimental error

In practice, virtually all experimental measurements have some degree of error associated with them. The error is shown by the number of significant figures quoted, and by the ± figures attached to the results. The term 'error' does not indicate that the experimenter has made a mistake; it simply indicates that the experimenter is aware that there is an uncertainty in the values presented which reflects the experimental method.

It is not just measurements of length which have an error associated with them. All measuring instruments introduce some degree of error. For example, for analogue ammeters and voltmeters (in which a needle moves across a scale), it is necessary to judge the position of the needle against the scale. The reading can be made to the nearest whole division on the scale, or the nearest half division.

Digital meters may seem more reliable, because they give an unambiguous reading – you just have to write it down. However, we usually assume that the meter is only accurate to ±1 in the final digit of the display. So, if the reading is, say, 1.25 V, we write this as:

voltage = (1.25 ± 0.01) V

This implies that the voltage lies somewhere between 1.24 V and 1.26 V. The ± sign indicates that we do not know whether the true value lies above or below the central value.

Reducing error

In order to get closer to a true result, we have to minimise the errors in an experiment. This can involve improving the equipment, or improving the technique which is being used. As you go through your Physics course, you will learn some standard ways of reducing error. You should also learn to look critically at your own techniques, to see whether you can improve them in any way. The aim is to generate results which are reproducible; that is, you (or someone else) could repeat your experiment and obtain the same end result, within experimental error. Then you can be confident that you have done your best to achieve an answer close to the true result.

It helps to have an understanding of the different sorts of error which may arise in experiments. There are two main types of errors – random and systematic.

If you repeat an experiment, you will not achieve precisely the same results as the first time. The experimental conditions will vary slightly, one ammeter may be slightly different from another, the wire may have a slightly different composition, and so on. This means that a repeat result will be slightly higher or lower than a first result. (If you have estimated errors accurately, the repeat result should lie within the error of the original result.) Variabilities of this sort introduce *random error* into the final result.

The errors associated with reading from scales on meters or rules are examples of random errors. Sometimes the actual length will be above the nearest scale division, sometimes below it. This means that we would expect about half of measurements to be too high and half too low. They are scattered randomly around the true value, rather like darts scattered around the bull's-eye on a dart board. Reducing random errors results in a more *precise* result.

The second type of error is the *systematic error*. An example of this is shown in Figure A3. The student is measuring the volume of a liquid, but his eye is not correctly aligned with the meniscus of the liquid – this is known as *parallax error*. The result is that he records a value which is too high. This can be corrected by looking horizontally at the meniscus.

Two other examples of systematic errors can be illustrated by considering an electronic balance for measuring mass (Figure A4). Firstly, it may be incorrectly zeroed. With no object to be weighed, it

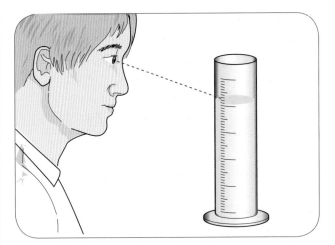

Figure A3 A systematic error (also known as parallax error) is introduced to the measurement of volume when the student does not look horizontally at the meniscus.

does not indicate zero. Secondly, even when correctly zeroed, it may show an incorrect reading because it has not been correctly calibrated. Shopkeepers have their balances regularly checked by trading standards officers to ensure that they do not suffer from either of these faults. Reducing systematic errors results in a more *accurate* result.

From this discussion, you should see that there is an important difference between random and systematic errors.

- Random errors can be reduced, by improving techniques, making multiple measurements or using instruments with a higher degree of precision. However, they can never be eliminated completely. This increases the *precision* of the final result.
- Systematic errors can be reduced or totally eliminated by the use of better techniques and instruments. This increases the *accuracy* of the final result.

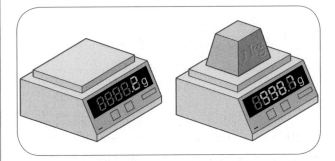

Figure A4 The first balance is incorrectly zeroed; the second is incorrectly calibrated, so that it underestimates the mass of the standard kilogram mass.

Figure A5 illustrates the difference between the terms *precision* and *accuracy*.

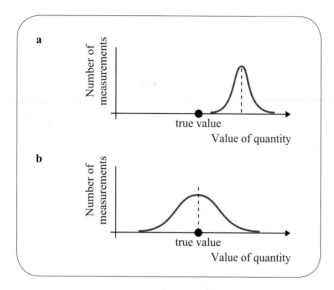

Figure A5 In **a**, the result is precise but not accurate. In **b**, the result is accurate but not precise.

Combining errors

Most final results are found by combining several individual measurements, each with its own degree of error. This also means that the final result has a degree of uncertainty. How can we determine this uncertainty?

The first step is to express each error as a percentage, rather than as an absolute amount. For example, we might have a value of voltage $V = (2.54 \pm 0.01)$ V. The *absolute error* in V is ± 0.01 V.

To calculate the *percentage error*, we calculate this as a percentage of V:

$$\text{percentage error} = \frac{\text{absolute error}}{\text{value of quantity}} \times 100\%$$

$$\% \text{ error in } V = \frac{\pm 0.01 \text{ V}}{2.54 \text{ V}} \times 100\% = \pm 4.0\%$$

So we could write $V = 2.54$ V $\pm 4.0\%$.

Note that errors are usually given to two significant figures, or occasionally one.

Now, suppose this result was part of a measurement of resistance. The current in the circuit is found to be

$$I = (0.96 \pm 0.01) \text{ A}$$

or

$$I = 0.96 \text{ A} \pm 1.0\%$$

What is the error in the final value for resistance? Obviously, both V and I contribute to the error in the value of the resistance R. V is more uncertain ($\pm 4.0\%$), so its contribution is greater.

In this case, the combined error is simply the sum of the two individual percentage errors, i.e. $\pm 5.0\%$.

$$R = \frac{V}{I} = \frac{2.54}{0.96} = 2.65 \ \Omega$$

Hence

$$R = 2.65 \ \Omega \pm 5\%$$

> When two quantities are multiplied or divided, their percentage errors are added to find the percentage error in the result.

If a quantity is squared, we can think of this as the quantity multiplied by itself, and so its error contributes twice to the error in the result.

A numerical example

It is possible to find a rough value for the resistivity of a metal by making four measurements using a short piece of wire. Table A1 shows some results.

Examining the data shows that the errors are dominated by the error ($\pm 8.0\%$) in the measurement of the diameter of the wire. All other errors are less

Quantity	Measured by ...	Value ± absolute error	Percentage error
current I	ammeter	(7.40 ± 0.01) A	$\pm 0.14\%$
voltage V	voltmeter	(1.44 ± 0.01) V	$\pm 0.70\%$
length l	metre rule	(125 ± 1) mm	$\pm 0.80\%$
diameter d	vernier callipers	(1.2 ± 0.1) mm	$\pm 8.0\%$

Table A1 Sample results of measurements to determine the resistivity of a metal.

than 1%. This immediately suggests that, to improve the overall accuracy of the measurement, a better method is needed for measuring the diameter of the wire. A micrometer would reduce this error to $\pm 0.80\%$. It would be possible to use digital meters which read to three decimal places to measure I and V, and this would reduce the errors in these quantities. However, there would be little benefit from this since the biggest source of error is in the measurement of the diameter.

Since resistivity ρ is given by:

$$\rho = \frac{\text{resistance} \times \text{cross-sectional area}}{\text{length}}$$

$$\rho = \frac{RA}{L}$$

with:

$$\text{resistance } R = \frac{\text{voltage}}{\text{current}} = \frac{V}{I}$$

and

$$\text{cross-sectional area } A = \frac{\pi d^2}{4}$$

we have:

$$\rho = \frac{V \times \pi d^2}{4IL} = \frac{1.44 \times \pi \times (1.2 \times 10^{-3})^2}{4 \times 7.40 \times 0.125}$$

$$= 1.76 \times 10^{-6} \; \Omega \, \text{m}$$

The percentage error in ρ will be given by:

$$\% \text{ error in } \rho = \% \text{ error in } V + (2 \times \% \text{ error in } d) + \% \text{ error in } I + \% \text{ error in } L$$

(Note that the error in d is doubled because the equation involves d^2.) So:

$$\% \text{ error in } \rho = \pm (0.70\% + 2 \times 8.0\% + 0.14\% + 0.80\%)$$

$$\% \text{ error in } \rho = \pm 17.64\% \approx \pm 18\%$$

Using a micrometer would reduce the % error in d to $\pm 0.80\%$ and the % error in ρ would become $\pm 3.24\%$, or about 3%.

Summary

- An analysis of the errors in experimental results indicates how reliable they are. It can also suggest which aspects of the experimental method could be altered to reduce the error in the final result.

- Random errors are associated with most measurements. They can never be eliminated entirely, but reducing them increases the precision of the final result.

- Systematic errors result in readings which are all too high, or all too low. They can be reduced or eliminated entirely, and this increases the accuracy of the final result.

Physical quantities and units

Physical quantities have a numerical value and a unit. In Physics, it is essential to give the units of physical quantities. For example, mass is measured in kilograms. Hence you might write the mass of the trolley as:

mass of trolley = 0.76 kg

It would be a serious error to omit the unit kg at the end of the numerical value.

The scientific system of units is called the Système Internationale d'Unités (or SI system). Five of the seven *base units* of this system are listed in Table B1. Each of the units is carefully defined, but the definitions need not concern us here.

Physical quantity	Unit
mass	kilogram, kg
length	metre, m
time	second, s
temperature	kelvin, K
electric current	ampere, A

Table B1 Five base units of the SI system.

All other units can be derived from the seven base units. For example:
- volume is measured in cubic metres (m^3)
- velocity is measured in metres per second ($m\,s^{-1}$)
- density is measured in kilograms per cubic metre ($kg\,m^{-3}$).

Prefixes

In Physics, you will have to cope with very small and very large numbers. Numbers are written using powers of ten to make them less awkward. This is known as *scientific notation*. Prefixes are used as an abbreviation for some of the powers of ten. For example, the height of a 5400 m high mountain may be written as either 5.4×10^3 m or 5.4 km. The prefixes needed for the OCR Physics A specification are shown in Table B2.

Estimation

When you carry out an experiment or a calculation, it is sensible to look at the answer that you get (and the results of intermediate calculations) to see if they seem reasonable. The only way you can know if an answer is absurd is if you have an awareness of some benchmarks. Some suggestions are given below. Try to add to this list as you go through your Physics course.

mass of a person	70 kg
height of a person	1.5 m
walking speed	$1\,m\,s^{-1}$
speed of a car on the motorway	$30\,m\,s^{-1}$
volume of a can of drink	$300\,cm^3$
density of water	$1000\,kg\,m^{-3}$
weight of an apple	1 N
typical current in domestic appliance	13 A
e.m.f. of a car battery	12 V

Prefix	pico	nano	micro	milli	centi	kilo	mega	giga	tera
Symbol	p	n	µ	m	c	k	M	G	T
Value	10^{-12}	10^{-9}	10^{-6}	10^{-3}	10^{-2}	10^3	10^6	10^9	10^{12}

Table B2 Some of the prefixes used in the SI system.

Appendix C

Data, formulae and relationships

Data

Values are given to three significant figures, except where more significant figures are useful.

speed of light in a vacuum	c	$3.00 \times 10^8 \, \text{m s}^{-1}$
permittivity of free space	ε_0	$8.85 \times 10^{-12} \, \text{C}^2 \, \text{N}^{-1} \, \text{m}^{-2} \, (\text{F m}^{-1})$
elementary charge	e	$1.60 \times 10^{-19} \, \text{C}$
Planck constant	h	$6.63 \times 10^{-34} \, \text{J s}$
gravitational constant	G	$6.67 \times 10^{-11} \, \text{N m}^2 \, \text{kg}^{-2}$
Avogadro constant	N_A	$6.02 \times 10^{23} \, \text{mol}^{-1}$
molar gas constant	R	$8.31 \, \text{J mol}^{-1} \, \text{K}^{-1}$
Boltzmann constant	k	$1.38 \times 10^{-23} \, \text{J K}^{-1}$
electron rest mass	m_e	$9.11 \times 10^{-31} \, \text{kg}$
proton rest mass	m_p	$1.673 \times 10^{-27} \, \text{kg}$
neutron rest mass	m_n	$1.675 \times 10^{-27} \, \text{kg}$
alpha particle rest mass	m_α	$6.646 \times 10^{-27} \, \text{kg}$
acceleration of free fall	g	$9.81 \, \text{m s}^{-2}$

Conversion factors

unified atomic mass unit $\quad 1 \, \text{u} = 1.661 \times 10^{-27} \, \text{kg}$

electronvolt $\quad 1 \, \text{eV} = 1.60 \times 10^{-19} \, \text{J}$

$\quad 1 \, \text{day} = 8.64 \times 10^4 \, \text{s}$

$\quad 1 \, \text{year} \approx 3.16 \times 10^7 \, \text{s}$

$\quad 1 \, \text{light year} \approx 9.5 \times 10^{15} \, \text{m}$

Mathematical equations

arc length $= r\theta$

circumference of circle $= 2\pi r$

area of circle $= \pi r^2$

curved surface area of cylinder $= 2\pi r h$

volume of cylinder $= \pi r^2 h$

surface area of a sphere $= 4\pi r^2$

volume of sphere $= \frac{4}{3}\pi r^3$

Pythagoras' theorem: $a^2 = b^2 + c^2$

For small angle θ: $\sin\theta \approx \tan\theta \approx \theta$ and $\cos\theta \approx 1$

$\lg(AB) = \lg(A) + \lg(B)$

$\lg(\frac{A}{B}) = \lg(A) - \lg(B)$

$\ln(x^n) = n \ln(x)$

$\ln(e^{kx}) = kx$

Formulae and relationships

Unit G481 Mechanics

$F_x = F\cos\theta$

$F_y = F\sin\theta$

$a = \dfrac{\Delta v}{\Delta t}$

$v = u + at$

$s = \frac{1}{2}(u + v)t$

$s = ut + \frac{1}{2}at^2$

$v^2 = u^2 + 2as$

$F = ma$

$W = mg$

moment $= Fx$

torque $= Fd$

$\rho = \dfrac{m}{V}$

$p = \dfrac{F}{A}$

$W = Fx\cos\theta$

$E_k = \frac{1}{2}mv^2$

$E_p = mgh$

efficiency $= \dfrac{\text{useful energy output}}{\text{total energy output}} \times 100\%$

$F = kx$

$E = \frac{1}{2}Fx$

$E = \frac{1}{2}kx^2$

stress $= \dfrac{F}{A}$

strain $= \dfrac{x}{L}$

Young modulus $= \dfrac{\text{stress}}{\text{strain}}$

Unit G482 Electrons, waves and photons

$\Delta Q = I\Delta t$

$I = Anev$

$W = VQ$

$V = IR$

$R = \dfrac{\rho L}{A}$

$P = VI$

$P = I^2 R$

$P = \dfrac{V^2}{R}$

$W = VIt$

e.m.f $= V + Ir$

$V_{out} = \dfrac{R_2}{R_1 + R_2} \times V_{in}$

$v = f\lambda$

$\lambda = \dfrac{ax}{D}$

$d\sin\theta = n\lambda$

$E = hf$

$E = \dfrac{hc}{\lambda}$

$hf = \phi + KE_{max}$

$\lambda = \dfrac{h}{mv}$

$R = R_1 + R_2 + \ldots$

$\dfrac{1}{R} = \dfrac{1}{R_1} + \dfrac{1}{R_2} + \ldots$

Answers to SAQs

Chapter 1

1 $\dfrac{1600}{174.29} = 9.18\,\mathrm{m\,s^{-1}}$

2 **a** $\mathrm{mm\,s^{-1}}$
   b mph
   c $\mathrm{km\,s^{-1}}$
   d $\mathrm{m\,s^{-1}}$
   e $\mathrm{km\,h^{-1}}$

3 $2.0\,\mathrm{mm\,s^{-1}}$

4 $0.125\,\mathrm{m\,s^{-1}} \approx 0.13\,\mathrm{m\,s^{-1}}$

5 **a** Constant speed.
   b Increasing speed (accelerating).

6 For example, attach a card to a weight and drop it through a light gate. Alternatively, attach ticker-tape to the falling mass.

7 **a** Displacement.
   b Speed.
   c Velocity.
   d Distance.

8 $300\,\mathrm{m}$

9 The Earth's speed is $29.9\,\mathrm{km\,s^{-1}} \approx 30\,\mathrm{km\,s^{-1}}$. As the Earth orbits the Sun, its direction of motion keeps changing. Hence its velocity keeps changing. In the course of one year, its displacement is zero so its average velocity is zero.

10 Sloping sections: bus moving; horizontal sections: bus stationary (e.g. at bus stops).

11

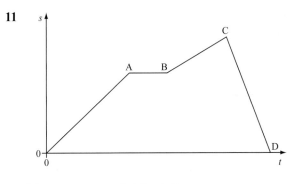

OA: constant speed; AB: stationary;
BC: reduced constant speed;
CD: running back to gate.

12 a $85\,\mathrm{m\,s^{-1}}$
   b Graph is a straight line through the origin, with gradient $= 85\,\mathrm{m\,s^{-1}}$.

13 a Graph is a straight line for the first 3 h; then less steep for the last hour.
   b $23\,\mathrm{km\,h^{-1}}$
   c $21\,\mathrm{km\,h^{-1}}$

Chapter 2

1 $3.0\,\mathrm{m\,s^{-2}}$

2 $a = -0.60\,\mathrm{m\,s^{-2}}$
   The magnitude of the deceleration is $0.60\,\mathrm{m\,s^{-2}}$.

3 **a** $9.8\,\mathrm{m\,s^{-1}}$
   b $29.4\,\mathrm{m\,s^{-1}} \approx 29\,\mathrm{m\,s^{-1}}$

4

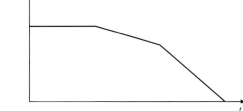

5 **a** Graph line at centre.
   b Near centre.
   c Constant distance from centre.
   d Getting closer to centre.

6 **a** See figure.
   b, c $3.0\,\mathrm{m\,s^{-2}}$
   d $-1.0\,\mathrm{m\,s^{-2}}$
   e From area under graph: $525\,\mathrm{m}$

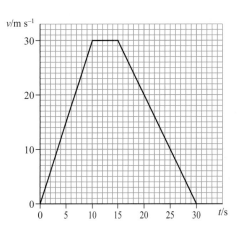

7 $u = 0.25\,\text{m}\,\text{s}^{-1}$; $v = 1.0\,\text{m}\,\text{s}^{-1}$;
   $\Delta t = 0.30\,\text{s}$; $a = 2.5\,\text{m}\,\text{s}^{-2}$

8 Dots evenly spaced, then getting steadily closer together.

9 $u = 1.0\,\text{m}\,\text{s}^{-1}$; $v = 1.6\,\text{m}\,\text{s}^{-1}$;
   $\Delta t = 0.10\,\text{s}$; $a = 6.0\,\text{m}\,\text{s}^{-2}$

10 a $20\,\text{m}\,\text{s}^{-1}$
   b $100\,\text{m}$
   c $12\,\text{s}$

11 a $0.16\,\text{m}\,\text{s}^{-2}$
   b $12\,\text{m}\,\text{s}^{-1}$
   c $1200\,\text{m}$

12 $10\,\text{m}\,\text{s}^{-1}$

13 $64.3\,\text{m} \approx 64\,\text{m}$

14 Speed $25.5\,\text{m}\,\text{s}^{-1}$; only just over the speed limit.

15 a $t = 7.5\,\text{s}$; $v = 220\,\text{m}\,\text{s}^{-1}$
   b Approximately $20\,\text{m}\,\text{s}^{-2}$

16 a The car is slowing down with constant (uniform) deceleration.
   b $20\,\text{m}\,\text{s}^{-1}$; $8\,\text{m}\,\text{s}^{-1}$
   c $-0.40\,\text{m}\,\text{s}^{-2}$
   d $420\,\text{m}$
   e $420\,\text{m}$

17 a Change in displacement in each second.
   b $10.2\,\text{m}\,\text{s}^{-1}$
   c $4.1\,\text{m}\,\text{s}^{-2}$; $0.1\,\text{m}\,\text{s}^{-2}$
   d Sketch graph – there is no need for a detailed graph.

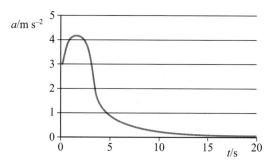

   e The area under the velocity against time graph is distance.
      distance = area under graph = $200\,\text{m}$
      (the length of the race)

18 $100\,\text{m}$

19 The train comes to a halt at the end of the $100\,\text{s}$; distance travelled = $2500\,\text{m}$.

20 a $800\,\text{m}$
   b $1.25\,\text{m}\,\text{s}^{-2} \approx 1.3\,\text{m}\,\text{s}^{-2}$; $750\,\text{m}$
   c $5.0\,\text{s}$
   d $1000\,\text{m}$

Chapter 3

1 $1600\,\text{N}$

2 $40\,\text{m}\,\text{s}^{-2}$

3 $10\,\text{m}\,\text{s}^{-1}$

4 Apples vary in mass; gravity varies from place to place.

5 Estimated masses are shown in brackets:
   a $(1.0\,\text{kg})$ $10\,\text{N}$
   b $(1.0\,\text{kg})$ $10\,\text{N}$
   c $(60\,\text{kg})$ $600\,\text{N}$
   d $(0.025\,\text{kg})$ $0.25\,\text{N}$
   e $400\,000\,\text{N}$

6 a See table.
   b Graph is a parabola through the origin.
   c $30.6\,\text{m} \approx 31\,\text{m}$
   d $2.86\,\text{s} \approx 2.9\,\text{s}$ (Check using $s = ut + \frac{1}{2}at^2$.)

Time t/s	0	1.0	2.0	3.0	4.0
Displacement s/m	0	4.9	19.6	44.1	78.4

7 a $0.40\,\text{s}$
   b $3.9\,\text{m}\,\text{s}^{-1}$

8 a $9.36\,\text{m}\,\text{s}^{-2} \approx 9.4\,\text{m}\,\text{s}^{-2}$
   b Air resistance; delay in release of ball.

9 a See table and figure.
   b $1.6\,\text{m}\,\text{s}^{-2}$ (approx.)
   c This object is not falling on the Earth; perhaps on the Moon.

Height h/m	0.70	1.03	1.25	1.60	1.99
Time t/s	0.99	1.13	1.28	1.42	1.60
Time^2 t^2/s^2	0.98	1.28	1.64	2.02	2.56

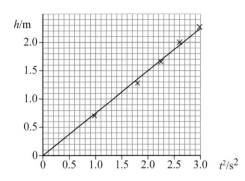

10 Drop an object towards the sensor, but take care not to break it. A better method is to use a sloping ramp with a trolley; gradually increase the angle of slope. Deduce value of acceleration when ramp is vertical.

11 The greater the mass of the car, the greater the force needed to slow it down with a given deceleration. For large cars, it is less demanding on the driver if the engine supplies some of the force.

12 Inertia: the driver continues forward although the car stops. A seat belt provides the force needed to overcome this inertia.

13 The large one; its weight is greater, so it reaches a greater speed before air resistance is sufficient to equal its weight.

14 a Lubricate skis.
   b Wear tight-fitting, smooth clothing to reduce air resistance.
   c Develop powerful muscles to provide a large forward force.
   d The steeper the slope, the better.

15 a The lighter one; lower terminal velocity.
   b Turn head-first, and pull in arms and legs to produce streamlined shape.

Chapter 4

1 a 7.0 km
   b, c 5.0 km; 53° E of N (or 37° N of E)

2 $2.154\,\mathrm{m\,s^{-1}} \approx 2.2\,\mathrm{m\,s^{-1}}$ at 68° to the river bank

3 a See figure.
   b 1000 N upwards
   c She will accelerate upwards (i.e. decelerate).

4 a Yes, constant velocity (not accelerating).
   b 1000 kN
   c 50 kN

5 a 2.5 N at 37° to vertical
   b No.

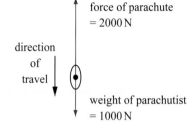

6 a $F_x = 17.3\,\mathrm{N} \approx 17\,\mathrm{N}$; $F_y = 10\,\mathrm{N}$
   b $v_x = 1.7\,\mathrm{m\,s^{-1}}$; $v_y = -4.7\,\mathrm{m\,s^{-1}}$
   c $a_x = -5.2\,\mathrm{m\,s^{-2}}$; $a_y = -3.0\,\mathrm{m\,s^{-2}}$
   d $F_x = 77.3\,\mathrm{N} \approx 77\,\mathrm{N}$; $F_y = 20.7\,\mathrm{N} \approx 21\,\mathrm{N}$

7 With rope horizontal, the force pulling the box is F. With the rope at an angle θ to the horizontal, the horizontal component ($= F\cos\theta$) is less, since $\cos\theta$ is less than 1.

8 a See figure.
   b 250 N
   c It's at 90°.
   d Friction; up the slope.

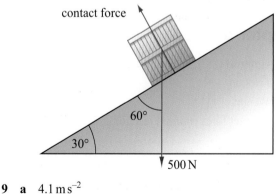

9 a $4.1\,\mathrm{m\,s^{-2}}$
   b $2.1\,\mathrm{m\,s^{-2}}$

10 5 s (i.e. 1 s more)

In solving the quadratic equation, you will have found a second solution, $t = -1$ s. Obviously, the stone could not take a negative time to reach the foot of the cliff. However, this solution does have a meaning: it tells us that, if the stone had been thrown upwards from the foot of the cliff at the correct speed, it would have been travelling upwards at $20\,\mathrm{m\,s^{-1}}$ as it passed the top of the cliff at $t = 0$ s.

11 a See table.

   b See figure.

   c, d 3.1 s

Velocity/m s^{-1}	30	20.19	10.38	0.57	−9.24	−19.05
Time/s	0	1.0	2.0	3.0	4.0	5.0

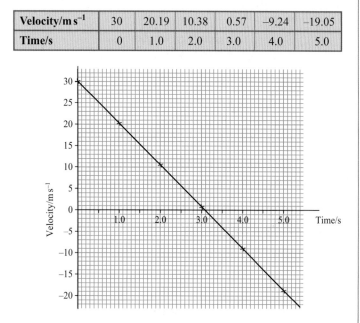

12 163 m ≈ 160 m

Chapter 5

1 a Upthrust.

   b Friction.

   c Weight.

   d Contact force (normal reaction).

   e Tension.

   f Drag.

2

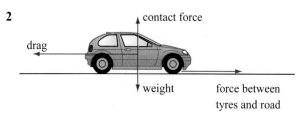

3 a Going up   **b** Going down

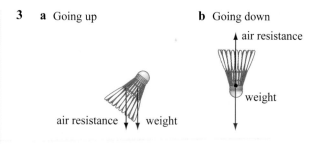

4 a 67 N

   b 160 N

5 a 173 g.

   b By this method, weighing could be carried out with a limited selection of relatively small masses.

6 a, b F_1, 0 N m; F_2, 2.5 N m clockwise; F_3, 2.5 N m clockwise; F_4, 5 N m anticlockwise.

   c Yes, the moments are balanced.

7 28.3 N ≈ 28 N

8 9.83 N ≈ 9.8 N

9 381 N ≈ 380 N

10 20 kPa

11 Taking weight = 600 N, area of feet = 500 cm^2 = 0.05 m^2, pressure = 12 kPa.

Chapter 6

1 Thinking time = 0.67 s.

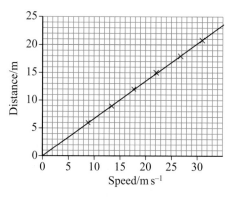

2 a See table.

b See figure.

c $-6.4\,\mathrm{m\,s^{-2}}$

Speed/$\mathrm{m\,s^{-1}}$	Speed^2/$\mathrm{m^2\,s^{-2}}$	Braking distance/m
8.9	79	6
13.3	177	14
17.8	317	24
22.2	493	38
26.7	713	55
31.1	967	75

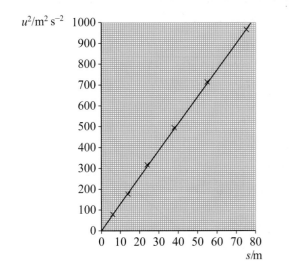

3 Thinking distance = 18 m

Braking distance = 150 m

Therefore stopping distance = 18 + 150 = 168 m; the car will not stop before the incident.

4 The driver in front may have faster reactions (so that their thinking distance is less); they may also have better brakes, allowing them to stop in a shorter distance. If the driver behind cannot stop in the same distance or less, there will be a collision.

5 A wide belt gives reduced pressure (for a given force) and so is less likely to damage the wearer.

6 $4.47 \times 10^{-8}\%$

Chapter 7

1 a Yes, work done against friction.

b Yes, gravity does work in making you go faster.

c No, because the conker remains at constant distance from the centre of the circle.

d No, because the force does not move.

2 1700 J

3 a 2500 J

b 2500 J (ignoring work done against air resistance)

4 20 kJ

5 Work done by force up slope = 50 J; work done by contact force = 0 J; work done by force down slope = −15 J; work done by gravity = 35 J.

6 $1274\,\mathrm{J} \approx 1300\,\mathrm{J}$

7 5400 kJ or 5.4 MJ

8 The motorcycle has more KE.

9 10 J

10 The result is unchanged for any value of mass.

11 $7.1 \times 10^9\,\mathrm{J}$. This energy becomes increased energy of the air – its temperature rises.

12 $14\,\mathrm{m\,s^{-1}}$

13 a 0.92 (92%)

b Heat (because work is done against air resistance).

14 $3.0 \times 10^6\,\mathrm{J}$ (or 3.0 MJ)

15 70 kW

16 a 28 000 J (28 kJ)   **b** 28 kW

17 560 W

Chapter 8

1 a D

b A

c C

2 Metals from most stiff to least stiff:

	Metal	Young modulus/GPa
Most stiff	steel	210
	iron (wrought)	200
	copper	130
	brass	90–110
	aluminium	70
	tin	50
Least stiff	lead	18

3 Stiffest non-metal is glass (Young modulus = 70–80 GPa).

4 A, 15 GPa; B, 5.0 GPa

5 1.0×10^8 Pa, 5.0×10^{-4} (0.05%), 2.0×10^{11} Pa

6 9.79×10^{-5} m $\approx 9.8 \times 10^{-5}$ m

7 Stress = 8.0×10^6 Pa; strain = 1.25×10^{-3} (at most); Young modulus = 6.4×10^9 Pa (but could be more, because extension may be less than 1 mm).

8 **a** Small loads, iron bath is elastic. Large loads, the cast iron is brittle and breaks.
  b At high pressure (load) the aluminium undergoes plastic deformation: it is ductile.
  c Small loads and slowly, plastic deformation. Large loads and rapidly, brittle.

9 **a** 50 GPa, 150 MPa
  b 100 GPa, 125 MPa
  c 25 GPa, 100 MPa

10 1.08 J ≈ 1.1 J
The rubber band is assumed to obey Hooke's law; hence the answer is an estimate.

11 9.6×10^3 J

12 **a** A has greater stiffness (less extension per unit force).
  b A requires greater force to break (line continues to higher force value).
  c B requires greater amount of work done to break (larger area under graph).

Chapter 9

1 Towards the right – look at the movement of the positive ions.

2 **a** Current to left.
  b Current towards A, away from B (clockwise).
  c Positive terminal of cell at B.

3 6.0 C

4 5.0 A

5 2.5 A

6 **a** 0.25 h (or 15 minutes)
  b 1.8×10^5 C

7 6.25×10^{18} protons

8 4.5 A

9 1.5 A, towards P

10 1.89 A ≈ 1.9 A

11 4.68×10^{-4} m s^{-1} $\approx 4.7 \times 10^{-4}$ m s^{-1}

12 The electrons will speed up because there are fewer of them in the silver wire than in the copper. (Their mean drift velocity will increase in the inverse ratio of the number densities, i.e. by a factor of 8.5/5.9.)

Chapter 10

1 0.33 A

2 60 watt

3 **a** 50 V
  b 100 V

4 575 Ω

5 **a** See figure.
  b All except point at 7.9 V – ignore this one.
  c 48 Ω
  d Yes.

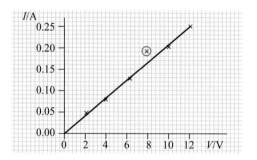

6 At 2.0 V, $R = 200 \,\Omega$; at 8.0 V, $R = 133 \,\Omega \approx 130 \,\Omega$; it does not obey Ohm's law.

7 **a** θ_1: 12.5 Ω, θ_2: 10 Ω
  b θ_1

8 **a** A = lamp, B = steel wire
  b 8.0 V
  c $2.35 \,\Omega \approx 2.4 \,\Omega$

9 **a** **i** 3.1 kΩ
    ii 1.5 kΩ
  b **i** 5 °C
    ii 36 °C
  c **i** about -0.09 kΩ °C^{-1}
    ii about -0.04 kΩ °C^{-1}
    iii about -0.01 kΩ °C^{-1} (almost zero)

10 Total resistance in circuit decreases; current increases; lamp becomes brighter.

11 Advantage of a thermistor: its resistance changes by a large amount over a small temperature range, and this is easy to detect. Advantage of a metal: its resistance changes over a wide temperature range; a thermistor is only useful within a narrow range of temperatures.

12 a 0.45 m
 b 2.2 m
 c 4.5 m

13 $0.106\,\Omega \approx 0.11\,\Omega$

14 a 2.5 Ω
 b 2.0 Ω

15 40 Ω

Chapter 11

1 a 6.0 J
 b 5.0×10^3 J (5.0 kJ)

2 a 120 C
 b 1440 J
 c 1440 J

3 In 1 s, 3.0 C flows round circuit. 18 J of energy is transferred to charge in 1 s; 18 J of energy is transferred by charge to resistor.

4 0.26 A

5 1.0×10^9 W (1000 MW or 1 GW)

6 a $43.48\,A \approx 43\,A$
 b 50 A (for example)

7 4.5×10^{-4} W

8 a 0.65 A
 b $353\,\Omega \approx 350\,\Omega$

9 $541\,\Omega \approx 540\,\Omega$

10 2.16 MJ

11 a 200 C
 b $2.0\,J\,C^{-1}$
 c 2.0 V

12 100 kWh

Chapter 12

1 20 Ω

2 0.80 V

3 a All five cells connected in series.
 b Three facing one way, two the other.
 c Four facing one way, one the other.

4 2.5 Ω

5 a 300 Ω
 b $66.7\,\Omega \approx 67\,\Omega$
 c 120 Ω

6 a 0.024 A (= 24 mA)
 b 0.008 A (= 8.0 mA)
 c 0.036 A (= 36 mA)

7 Total resistances possible are (in Ω): 40, 50, 67, 75, 100 (two ways), 167, 200, 250, 300 and 400.

8 10 Ω

9 0.50 A

10 0.95 A

11 20 Ω

12 Two in series, connected in series with two in parallel.

13 **A**, **B** and **E**: 6.0 A; **C**: 1.0 A; **D**: 5.0 A

14 a 0.10 A
 b 0.095 A

Chapter 13

1 Current = 0.5 A

$E = 5.0$ V, $r = 2.0$ Ω

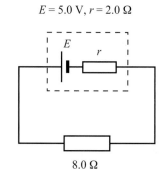

8.0 Ω

2 a 0.125 A, 0.5 V, 2.5 V
 b 0.33 A, 1.33 V, 1.67 V

3 2.5 A

4 $0.71\,\Omega$

5 $1.5\,\text{V}$, $0.5\,\Omega$ (approx.)

6 **a** $8.0\,\text{V}$

    b $4.0\,\Omega$

    c $16\,\text{W}$

7 $0\,\text{V}$ to $8.0\,\text{V}$

8 $20\,°\text{C}$: $9.5\,\text{V}$; $60\,°\text{C}$: $0.91\,\text{V}$

9 Resistance of LDR decreases so V_out decreases.

10 Full sunlight: $6\,\text{V}$; darkness: $11.996\,\text{V} \approx 12\,\text{V}$

11 Show the usual potential divider circuit with resistor and thermistor connected in series to a battery. The voltmeter must be placed across the resistor to give the desired output.

Chapter 14

1 $\Sigma I_\text{in} = \Sigma I_\text{out} = 6.5\,\text{A}$;
Kirchhoff's first law is satisfied.

2 $I_x = -2.0\,\text{A}$ (i.e. $2.0\,\text{A}$ towards P)

3 $8.0\,\text{V}$; $80\,\Omega$

4 **a** The loop containing the $5.0\,\text{V}$ cell at the top, the $10\,\Omega$ resistor with current I, and the central $5.0\,\text{V}$ cell (because the only current involved is I).

    b $1.0\,\text{A}$

5 $18\,\Omega$

6 In series, the $1\,\text{C}$ charge passes through both batteries and gains or loses $6\,\text{J}$ in each. If they are connected back-to-front, it gains energy in one cell but loses it in the next. In parallel, half the charge flows through each cell, so total energy gained is $6\,\text{J}$.

7 A_1: $0.50\,\text{A}$, A_2: $0.25\,\text{A}$, A_3: $0.25\,\text{A}$

8 **a** $0.25\,\text{A}$

    b $20\,\Omega$, $0.25\,\text{A}$

9 $0.033\,\text{A}$ to the right

Chapter 15

1 **a** $15\,\text{cm}$, $4.0\,\text{cm}$

    b $20\,\text{cm}$, $2.0\,\text{cm}$

2

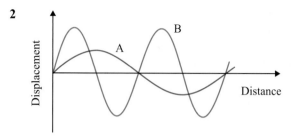

3 **a** $7.96\,\text{W m}^{-2} \approx 8.0\,\text{W m}^{-2}$

    b $1.99\,\text{W m}^{-2} \approx 2.0\,\text{W m}^{-2}$

4 **a** $1600\,\text{W m}^{-2}$

    b $2.5\,\text{cm}$

5 $20\,240\,\text{Hz} \approx 20\,\text{kHz}$

6 $89.6\,\text{m s}^{-1} \approx 90\,\text{m s}^{-1}$

7 **a** $5.0\,\text{cm}$

    b $30\,\text{Hz}$

    c $1.5\,\text{m s}^{-1}$

8

Station	Wavelength λ/m	Frequency f/MHz
Radio A (FM)	3.07	
Radio B (FM)	3.17	
Radio B (LW)		0.198
Radio C (MW)		0.433

9 **a** $1.7:1$

    b $2.3:1$

Chapter 16

1 **a** $4.3 \times 10^{14}\,\text{Hz}$

    b $4.3 \times 10^{14}\,\text{Hz}$; $470\,\text{nm}$

2

Radiation	Wavelength range/m	Frequency/Hz
radio waves	$>10^6$ to 10^{-1}	300 to 3×10^9
microwaves	10^{-1} to 10^{-3}	3×10^9 to 3×10^{11}
infrared	10^{-3} to 7×10^{-7}	3×10^{11} to 4.3×10^{14}
visible	7×10^{-7} (red) to 4×10^{-7} (ultraviolet)	4.3×10^{14} to 7.5×10^{14}
ultraviolet	4×10^{-7} to 10^{-8}	7.5×10^{14} to 3×10^{16}
X-rays	10^{-8} to 10^{-13}	3×10^{16} to 3×10^{21}
γ-rays	10^{-10} to 10^{-16}	3×10^{18} to 3×10^{24}

3 a Visible.

b Ultraviolet.

c 1–100 mm

d 400–700 nm

e 4.3×10^{14} Hz to 7.5×10^{14} Hz

4 a Radio waves, **b** microwaves, **c** infrared,
d visible light, **e** ultraviolet, **f** X-rays or γ-rays.

5 a Radio waves, **b** radio waves, **c** visible light,
d X-rays or γ-rays.

6 100 W m^{-2}; polarised at 45° to the vertical.

7

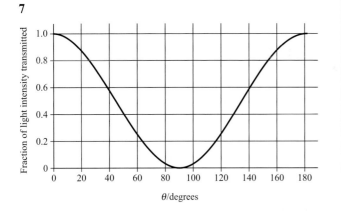

θ/degrees

Chapter 17

1

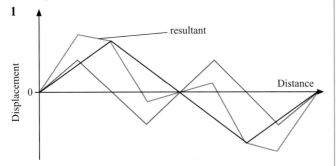

2 The grid spacing is much smaller than the wavelength
of the microwaves, so the waves do not pass through.
However, the wavelength of light is much smaller, so it
can pass through unaffected.

3 Two loudspeakers with slightly different frequencies
might start off in step, but they would soon go out of
step. The interference at a particular point might be
constructive at first, but would become destructive.

4 The intensity would increase.

5

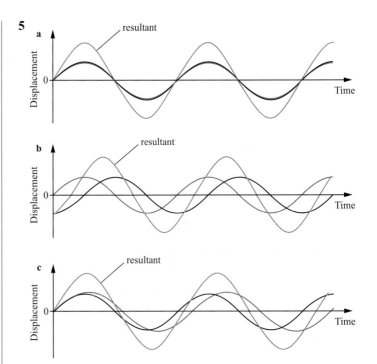

6 D: dark fringe, because rays from slits 1 and 2 differ in
path length by one-and-a-half wavelengths ($1\frac{1}{2}\lambda$).
E: bright fringe, because the path difference is 2λ.

7 3.0 mm

8 a $x = \dfrac{\lambda D}{a}$. Therefore $x \propto \dfrac{1}{a}$, so decreasing a gives
increased x.

b Blue light has shorter wavelength, so x is less ($x \propto \lambda$).

c For larger D, x is greater, so there is greater
precision in x ($x \propto D$).

9 3.5 mm

10 D and a are fixed. So:

$$\frac{\lambda_1}{x_1} = \frac{\lambda_2}{x_2}$$

and so:

$$x_2 = \frac{4.5 \times 10^{-7} \times 2.4 \times 10^{-3}}{6.0 \times 10^{-7}}$$

$$= 1.8 \times 10^{-3} \text{ m} = 1.8 \text{ mm}$$

(Or, wavelength is $\frac{3}{4}$ of previous value, so spacing of
fringes is $\frac{3}{4}$ of previous value.)

11 For the second-order maximum, rays from adjacent
slits have a path difference of 2λ, so
they are in phase.

12 a 20.4°

  b Maxima at 31.5°, 44.2°, 60.6°. You cannot have $\sin\theta > 1$. There are 11 maxima.

13 a θ increases, so the maxima are more spread out and there may be fewer of them. (Note: $\sin\theta \propto \lambda$)

  b d decreases, so again θ increases. (Note: $\sin\theta \propto \frac{1}{d}$)

14 a *Calculation* gives a total width of 8.7 mm, but with a ruler the student will *measure* 9 mm.

  b *Calculation* gives an angle of 19.12°, but the student will *measure* 19.1°.

  c For the double-slit experiment, a measured width of 9 mm for 10 fringes will give an answer for the wavelength of 562 nm. For the diffraction grating experiment, the measured second-order angle of 19.1° will give an answer of 545 nm. Hence the diffraction grating method is more accurate. In practice, it is also much more precise because the fringes are bright and sharp (well-defined).

15 a $\theta_{red} = 20.5°$; $\theta_{violet} = 11.5°$; angular separation = 9.0°.

  b The third-order maximum for violet light is deflected through a smaller angle than the second-order maximum for red light.

Chapter 18

1 a 50 cm

  b 12.5 cm

2 a 60 cm; 30 cm

  b

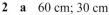

  c 40 cm

3 a

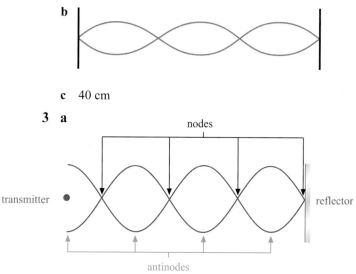

  b 28 mm, 1.07×10^{10} Hz ≈ 11 GHz

4 In both cases, waves are reflected (by the metal sheet or by the water). The outgoing and reflected waves combine to produce a stationary wave pattern.

5 a Much easier to detect where sound falls to zero than where sound is a maximum.

  b Increased accuracy – if the wavelength is short it is difficult to measure just one wavelength.

6 a 13.3 cm $\approx$ 13 cm

  b 330 m s^{-1}

7 a 52.4 cm $\approx$ 52 cm

  b 0.50 cm

  c 330 m s^{-1}

Chapter 19

1 6.63×10^{-8} J $\approx 6.6 \times 10^{-8}$ J

2 2.8×10^{-19} J, 5.0×10^{-19} J

3 a γ-ray.

  b X-ray.

  c Ultraviolet.

  d Infrared.

  e Radio wave.

4 3.26×10^{15} s^{-1} $\approx 3.3 \times 10^{15}$ s^{-1}

5 1.2 eV, 1.92×10^{-19} J $\approx 1.9 \times 10^{-19}$ J

6 12 400 eV $\approx$ 12 keV

7 Ultraviolet (wavelength $\approx 1.24 \times 10^{-7}$ m).

8 a 2.4×10^{-16} J

  b 5.31×10^5 m s^{-1} $\approx 5.3 \times 10^5$ m s^{-1}

9 $\sim 6.5 \times 10^{-34}$ J s

10 a 2.0 eV, 3.0 eV

  b 0.2 eV and 1.2 eV; 3.2×10^{-20} J and 1.9×10^{-19} J

11 a Gold.

  b Caesium.

  c 1.04×10^{15} Hz

  d 620 nm

12 a 8.3×10^{-19} J

  b 5.5×10^{-19} J

  c 1.1×10^6 m s^{-1}

13 5.9×10^{-20} J

14 a Electrons can behave as waves so they can be diffracted by spaces between atoms.

b Each metal has a different lattice structure, so each will produce a different diffraction pattern.

15 a 1.0 keV

b 1.9×10^7 m s^{-1}; 1.7×10^{-23} kg m s^{-1}

c 3.9×10^{-11} m

d The wavelength is much smaller than the spacing, so there will only be a small amount of diffraction.

Chapter 20

1 a 5.6×10^{-18} J, 8.4×10^{15} Hz, 3.6×10^{-8} m (emission)

b 5.0×10^{-19} J, 7.5×10^{14} Hz, 4.0×10^{-7} m (emission)

c 2.2×10^{-18} J, 3.3×10^{15} Hz, 9.0×10^{-8} m (absorption)

2 9.0 eV, 11 eV, 25 eV, 34 eV and 45 eV correspond to differences between energy levels, so they can all be absorbed. 6.0 eV and 20 eV do not correspond to differences between energy levels and so cannot be absorbed.

3 a 15.0 eV, 24.9 eV, 49.7 eV

b See figure for one possible solution.

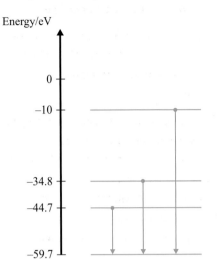

Glossary

absorption line spectrum A dark line of a unique wavelength seen in a continuous spectrum.

acceleration The rate of change of an object's velocity: $a = \dfrac{\Delta v}{\Delta t}$. Unit: $\mathrm{m\,s^{-2}}$.

ampere The SI unit of electric current.

amplitude The maximum displacement of a particle from its equilibrium position.

antinode A point on a stationary wave with maximum amplitude.

average speed The total distance travelled by an object divided by the total time taken.

braking distance The distance travelled by a vehicle from the moment when the brakes are applied until the vehicle comes to a stop.

brittle Describes a material that shows no plastic deformation and breaks just beyond its elastic limit.

centre of gravity The point where the entire weight of an object appears to act.

charge carrier Any charged particles, such as electrons, responsible for a current.

coherent Two sources are coherent when they emit waves with a constant phase difference.

components (of a vector) The magnitudes of a vector quantity in two perpendicular directions.

compression A region in a sound wave where the air pressure is greater than its mean value.

compressive A force that squeezes an object.

constructive interference When two waves reinforce to give increased amplitude.

coulomb The SI unit of electrical charge. A charge of 1 C passes a point when a current of 1 A flows for 1 s. $1\,\mathrm{C} = 1\,\mathrm{A\,s}$.

density The mass per unit volume of a material: $\rho = \dfrac{m}{V}$. Unit: $\mathrm{kg\,m^{-3}}$.

destructive interference When two waves cancel to give reduced amplitude.

diffraction The spreading of a wave when it passes through a gap or past the edge of an object.

dispersion The splitting of light into its different wavelengths.

displacement The distance moved by an object in a particular direction (measured from a fixed starting point).

ductile Describes a material that can easily be drawn into wires (e.g. copper).

dynamics A study of motion involving force and mass.

efficiency The ratio of useful output energy to the total input energy for a device, expressed as a percentage:
$$\text{efficiency} = \frac{\text{useful output energy}}{\text{total input energy}} \times 100\%$$

Einstein relation This refers to the equation for the energy of a photon – that is: $E = hf$ or $E = \dfrac{hc}{\lambda}$.

elastic Describes a material which will return to its original shape when the forces are removed.

elastic limit The value of stress beyond which an object will not return to its original dimensions.

elastic potential energy Energy stored in an extended or compressed material.

electrical resistance The ratio of potential difference to current. Unit: ohms (Ω).

electrolyte An electrically conducting solution. The conduction is due to positive and negative ions in the solution.

electromagnetic spectrum A family of waves that travel through a vacuum at a speed of $3.0 \times 10^8\,\mathrm{m\,s^{-1}}$.

electromotive force (e.m.f.) The energy gained per unit charge by charges passing through a supply. Unit: $\mathrm{J\,C^{-1}}$ or volt (V).

electronvolt The energy gained by an electron travelling through a p.d. of 1 volt. $1\,\mathrm{eV} = 1.6 \times 10^{-19}\,\mathrm{J}$.

elementary charge The smallest unit of charge that a particle or an object can have. It has a magnitude of $1.6 \times 10^{-19}\,\mathrm{C}$.

emission line spectrum A sharp and bright line of a unique wavelength seen in a spectrum.

energy level The quantised energy states of an electron in an atom.

equations of motion Four equations that can be used to determine quantities such as displacement, initial velocity, final velocity and acceleration.

equilibrium An object in equilibrium is either at rest or travelling with a constant velocity because the net force on it is zero.

extension The change in the length of a material from its original length.

force constant The ratio of force to extension for a spring or a wire. Unit: $\mathrm{N\,m^{-1}}$.

frequency The number of oscillations of a particle per unit time. Unit: hertz (Hz).

fundamental frequency The lowest frequency stationary wave for a particular system.

gravitational potential energy Energy stored by an object by virtue of its position in the Earth's gravitational field.

ground state The lowest energy state that can be occupied by an electron in an atom.

Hooke's law The extension produced in an object is proportional to the force producing it, provided the elastic limit is not exceeded.

inertia A measure of the mass of an object. A massive object has a large inertia.

instantaneous speed The speed of an object measured over a very short period of time.

intensity The power transmitted normally through a surface per unit area:

$$\text{intensity} = \frac{\text{power}}{\text{cross-sectional area}}$$

Unit: $W\,m^{-2}$.

interference The formation of points of cancellation and reinforcement where two coherent waves pass through each other.

internal resistance The resistance of an e.m.f. source. The internal resistance of a battery is due to its chemicals.

I–V characteristic A graph of current against voltage for a particular component. You can identify a component from its I–V graph.

kilowatt-hour The energy transferred by a 1 kW device in a time of 1 hour. $1\,kW\,h = 3.6\,MJ$.

kinematics A study of motion using quantities such as time, distance, displacement, speed, velocity and acceleration.

kinetic energy Energy of an object due to its motion.

Kirchhoff's first law The sum of the currents entering any point (or junction) in a circuit is equal to the sum of the currents leaving that same point. This law conveys the conservation of charge.

Kirchhoff's second law The sum of the e.m.f.s round a loop in a circuit is equal to the sum of p.d.s in that same loop.

light-emitting diode (LED) A semiconductor component that emits light when it conducts.

longitudinal wave A wave in which particles oscillate along the direction in which the wave travels.

lost volts The difference between the e.m.f. and the terminal p.d. It is also equal to the voltage across the internal resistance.

magnetic field A force field created by magnets and moving charges.

mass A measure of the amount of matter within an object. Unit: kilograms (kg).

mean drift velocity The average speed of charged particles along the length of a conductor.

moment The moment of a force about a point is the magnitude of the force, multiplied by the perpendicular distance of the point from the line of the force. Unit: N m.

newton The force that will give a 1 kg mass an acceleration of $1\,m\,s^{-2}$ in the direction of the force. $1\,N = 1\,kg\,m\,s^{-2}$.

node A point on a stationary wave with zero amplitude.

number density The number of charged particles per unit volume. Unit: m^{-3}.

Ohm's law The current in a metallic conductor is directly proportional to the potential difference across its ends, provided its temperature remains constant.

parallel A term used when components are connected across each other in a circuit.

path difference The difference in the distances travelled by two waves from coherent sources at a particular point.

period The time taken for one complete oscillation of a particle. Unit: seconds (s).

phase difference The fraction of a cycle between the oscillations of two particles, expressed in degrees.

photon A quantum of electromagnetic energy.

plane polarised Describes transverse waves that oscillate in only one plane.

plastic deformation The deformation of a material beyond the elastic limit.

potential difference (p.d.) The energy lost per unit charge by charges passing through a component. Unit: $J\,C^{-1}$ or volt (V).

potential divider A circuit in which two or more components are connected in series to a supply. The output voltage from the circuit is taken across one of the components.

power The rate at which energy is transferred or the rate at which work is done. Unit: watt (W).

pressure The force acting normally per unit area of a surface: $p = \dfrac{F}{A}$. Unit: $N\,m^{-2}$ or Pa.

principle of moments The sum of clockwise moments about a point is equal to the sum of anticlockwise moments about the same point.

principle of superposition When two or more waves meet at a point, the resultant displacement is the sum of the displacements of the individual waves.

progressive wave A wave that carries energy from one place to another.

projectile Any object thrown in the Earth's gravitational field.

range The horizontal distance covered by an object.

rarefaction A region in a sound wave where the air pressure is less than its mean value.

reflection The bouncing back of a wave from a surface.

refraction The change in direction of a wave as it crosses an interface between two materials where its speed changes.

resistivity The property of a material defined by:

$$\text{resistivity} = \frac{\text{resistance} \times \text{cross-sectional area}}{\text{length}}$$

$$\rho = \frac{RA}{L}$$

Unit: $\Omega\,\text{m}$.

resistor An electrical component whose resistance in a circuit remains constant. Its resistance is independent of current or potential difference.

resultant Total or net.

resultant force The net force acting on an object.

scalar quantity A scalar quantity has magnitude but no direction.

semiconductor diode An electrical component made from a semiconductor material (e.g. silicon) that only conducts in one direction. A diode in 'reverse bias' has an infinite resistance.

series A term used when components are connected end-to-end in a circuit.

speed The rate of change of the distance moved by an object:

$$\text{speed} = \frac{\text{distance}}{\text{time}}$$

Unit: $\text{m}\,\text{s}^{-1}$.

stationary wave A wave pattern produced when two progressive waves of the same frequency travelling in opposite directions combine. It is characterised by nodes and antinodes. Also known as a standing wave.

stopping distance The sum of the braking distance and the thinking distance.

strain The extension per unit length produced by tensile or compressive forces:

$$\text{strain} = \frac{\text{extension}}{\text{original length}}.$$

stress The force acting per unit cross-sectional area:

$$\text{stress} = \frac{\text{force}}{\text{cross-sectional area}}$$

tensile A term used to denote tension or pull.

terminal p.d. The potential difference across the external resistor connected to an e.m.f. source.

terminal velocity The constant velocity of an object travelling through a fluid. The net force on the object is zero.

thinking distance The distance travelled by a vehicle in a time equal to the reaction time of the driver.

threshold frequency The minimum frequency of the electromagnetic radiation that will eject electrons from the surface of a metal.

threshold voltage The minimum forward bias voltage across a light-emitting diode (LED) when it starts to conduct and emit light.

torque The product of one of the forces of a couple and the perpendicular distance between them. Unit: N m.

transition When an electron makes a 'jump' between two energy levels.

transverse wave A wave in which the oscillation is at right angles to the direction in which the wave travels.

triangle of forces A closed triangle drawn for an object in equilibrium. The sides of the triangle represent the forces in both magnitude and direction.

ultimate tensile strength (UTS) The breaking stress of a material:

$$\text{UTS} = \frac{\text{breaking force}}{\text{cross-sectional area}}$$

uniform acceleration Acceleration that remains constant.

uniform motion Motion of an object travelling with a constant acceleration.

vector addition Using a drawing, often to scale, to find the resultant vector.

vector quantity A vector quantity has both magnitude and direction.

vector triangle A triangle drawn to determine the resultant of two vectors.

velocity The rate of change of the displacement of an object:

$$\text{velocity} = \frac{\text{change in displacement}}{\text{time}}$$

Unit: $m\,s^{-1}$.

wave A periodic disturbance travelling through space, characterised by vibrating particles.

wavelength The distance between two adjacent peaks or troughs.

weight The force on an object caused by a gravitational field acting on its mass:

weight = mass × acceleration of free fall

Unit: newtons (N).

work done The product of the force and the distance moved by the force in the direction of travel.

work function The minimum energy required by a single electron to escape the metal surface.

Young modulus The ratio of stress to strain for a given material, resulting from tensile forces, provided Hooke's law is obeyed:

$$\text{Young modulus} = \frac{\text{stress}}{\text{strain}}$$

Unit: Pa (or MPa, GPa).

Index